THE
SEARCHERS

THE
SEARCHERS

The Making of an American Legend

GLENN FRANKEL

B L O O M S B U R Y

NEW YORK LONDON NEW DELHI SYDNEY

Published by Bloomsbury USA, New York

All papers used by Bloomsbury USA are natural, recyclable products made from wood grown in well-managed forests. The manufacturing processes conform to the environmental regulations of the country of origin.

LIBRARY OF CONGRESS CATALOGING-IN-PUBLICATION DATA

Frankel, Glenn.
The searchers : the making of an American legend / Glenn Frankel.
p. cm.
Includes bibliographical references and index.
ISBN 978-1-60819-105-5 (alk. paper)
1. Searchers (Motion picture) 2. Historical films—United States—History and criticism. 3. Motion pictures and history. 4. Comanche Indians—Texas—History—19th century. 5. Massacres—Texas—History—19th century. 6. Indian captivities—Texas.
I. Title.
PN1997.S3197F83 2013
791.43'72—dc23
2012029453

First U.S. Edition 2013

7 9 10 8 6

Typeset by Westchester Book Group
Printed and bound in U.S.A. by Thomson-Shore Inc., Dexter, Michigan

For Betsyellen Yeager
Everyday

Myths are neither true nor untrue, but the product and process of man's yearning. As such, they're the most primal thing bonding us to other people. Yet the phenomenon is much more than a snake feeding on its own tail. Myths gather momentum because they provide hope.

—CYNTHIA BUCHANAN, "COME HOME,
JOHN WAYNE, AND SPEAK FOR US"

CONTENTS

INTRODUCTION

Pappy (Hollywood, 1954)

The most disastrous moment of John Ford's illustrious Hollywood career took place at the U.S. Navy base on Midway Island in the Pacific Ocean in September 1954. The legendary film director was starting work on *Mister Roberts*, the movie version of the fabulously successful Broadway play, starring his old friend Henry Fonda. It should have been a great project: directing a comedy about Ford's beloved Navy with one of his favorite stars, surrounded by his informal stock company of familiar supporting actors and film crew members, with a script by his trusted screenwriter, Frank S. Nugent. What could go wrong?

Almost everything, as it turned out. The biggest problem, surprisingly, was Fonda. Ford had gone to bat for him against the studio executives at Warner Brothers. They had wanted a younger, sexier, and more potent box office attraction like Marlon Brando or William Holden for the title role of Doug Roberts, a young Navy officer consigned to a backwater cargo ship during World War Two and desperate to see combat before the war ends. But Ford had insisted that Fonda, despite being forty-nine, owned the part after playing it to great acclaim for four years on Broadway, and even Jack Warner felt compelled to agree. Fonda was grateful; in a "Dear Pappy" letter he expressed his appreciation that he was working again with the complicated genius who had directed him in *Young Mr. Lincoln*, *Drums Along the Mohawk*, *The Grapes of Wrath*, *My Darling Clementine*, *The Fugitive*, and *Fort Apache*. "It's so absolutely right that you are going to do the picture," Fonda gushed.

Nonetheless, from the moment they got to the location, the two men clashed. Fonda didn't like Nugent's script, felt it was neither as funny nor as nuanced as the original play, and didn't care for the excessive physical comedy and coarse broad strokes of Ford's direction. The Navy opened its gates to the film company: no one in uniform dared to say no to retired admiral John Ford, a decorated World War Two veteran. But on the first day of shooting at Midway, Fonda was disturbed by the way Ford rushed through the scenes and discomfited costar William Powell, who had trouble adjusting to Ford's swift, one-take-and-let's-move-on pace. Ford, who dominated his film sets the way Louis XIV presided over the court at Versailles, could not help but notice Fonda's worried expression.

At the end of the day, producer Leland Hayward arranged for a clear-the-air meeting in Ford's room in the bachelor officers' quarters. Ford was sprawled on a chaise longue with a tall drink in his hand. The conversation was short.

"I understand you're not happy with the work," said Ford.

Fonda tried to be diplomatic. "Pappy, you know I love you," Fonda began, and then went on to explain that the play had special meaning for him and Hayward. "It has a purity that we don't like to see lost. And I'm confessing that I'm not happy with that first scene with Powell."

Ford had heard enough. Without warning, he sprang from the lounge chair, reared back, and punched Fonda in the face. The actor fell backwards, knocking over a pitcher of water, got up, and fled the room in stunned silence. Fifteen minutes later, Ford knocked on Fonda's door and stumbled through a tearful, abject apology. Fonda says he accepted on the spot, but things after that were never the same. Ford was a lifelong alcoholic who prided himself on staying sober during a film shoot, but now he started grimly working his way through a case of chilled beer each day on the set. Sometimes, when Ford was too wasted to go on, either Fonda or Ward Bond, another old Ford crony who had a minor role in the picture, finished up the day's filming.

A few weeks later, soon after the film company returned to Hollywood, Ford was rushed to St. Vincent's Hospital for emergency gall bladder surgery. Mervyn LeRoy took over and finished the picture. *Mister Roberts* was a box office hit, and won three Academy Awards, including Jack Lemmon's first, for best supporting actor. But Ford and Fonda were both bitterly disappointed with the film and with each other. They never worked together again.

John Ford emerged from the *Roberts* debacle weakened physically and emotionally. He was sixty, a smoker and a drinker, and in poor health. He had had cataract surgery on both eyes a year before, feared he was going blind, and now wore a black patch over his blurred left eye. His beloved older brother Francis was dying of cancer, and the modest but comfortable house on Odin Street where Ford and his wife, Mary, had lived for thirty years and raised their two children was about to be demolished under a city order to help create a parking lot for the new Hollywood Bowl. Even before *Mister Roberts*, his most recent films had proven to be unsatisfying ventures for him. Even *Mogambo* (1953), a box-office hit starring Clark Gable, Ava Gardner, and Grace Kelly, left him worn-out and frustrated with the studio, the actors, and his own flagging health. Ford's world—which he had carefully organized to serve his immense personal needs and protect him from those outside forces he could not control—seemed to be caving in. "It was clear," wrote Maureen O'Hara, another of the recurring cast of actors who both worshipped and feared him, "that John Ford was going through changes and that they were terrible ones."

Still, Ford wasn't finished. As he tried to put back together the pieces of his damaged career following the humiliation of *Mister Roberts*, he turned to what he knew and loved best.

The Western had been John Ford's favorite movie genre ever since he first arrived in Hollywood forty years earlier in the formative days of moving pictures, and he had made nearly fifty Westerns during the course of his career. There was something about a man riding a horse through the rugged landscape, Ford liked to say, that made it the most natural subject for a movie camera. He loved telling stories of cowboys

John Ford at Monument Valley, June 1955, during *The Searchers* film shoot.

and Indians and cavalrymen, and he loved taking his company of actors, cameramen, wranglers, and stuntmen on location to Monument Valley along the Utah-Arizona border, famous for its scenic beauty and its utter remoteness, far from the reach of the studio money men and their regiments of sycophantic retainers. There he would harangue and abuse his loyal crew, bend them to his will, and inspire them to do their finest work. And he loved working with John Wayne, his favorite actor and occasional whipping boy. Under Ford's demanding and meticulous direction, Wayne had become America's most iconic Western star: the solitary, taciturn man on horseback, true to his own code and adept with his fists and his guns. They were like father and son, wise old mentor and humble pupil, with Wayne in the subordinate role even after he became the country's top box-office attraction.

No surprise, then, that Ford once introduced himself to a roomful of fellow directors by declaring, "My name is John Ford and I make Westerns." The genre was at the core of his identity.

And now, at the moment of Ford's greatest need, his longtime friend and business partner, Merian C. Cooper, came up with the idea for a Western he thought John Ford would find irresistible.

THE SEARCHERS, a new novel by the author and screenwriter Alan Le-May, was a captivity narrative set in Texas during pioneer days, and it was rich with strong characters, dramatic scenes, and an undercurrent of sexual obsession. It was based in part on a true story: the abduction of a nine-year-old girl in eastern Texas in 1836 by Comanche raiders who slaughtered her father, grandfather, and uncle, and kidnapped her and four other young people. Cynthia Ann Parker had been raised by her captors and became the wife of a Comanche warrior and mother of three. James Parker, her uncle, a backwoodsman and devout Baptist who possessed a dubious set of morals and an abiding hatred for Indians, searched eight years for her and her fellow captives—one of them his own daughter Rachel—and helped recover four of the missing.

But not Cynthia Ann. She lived with the Comanches for twenty-four years, until she was recaptured in 1860 by the U.S. Cavalry and Texas Rangers in another murderous raid and restored to her white relatives. Kept apart from her Comanche family, she died in misery and obscurity. But her surviving son, Quanah, became one of the last great warriors and later on an apostle of reconciliation, helping preserve the remnants of the Comanche nation and invoking the spirit of his dead mother to preach peace and understanding between whites and Native Americans. The two sides of the Parker family—one of them Texan, the other Comanche—still honored the legacy of their distant ancestors at family reunions and had even begun sending emissaries to each other's events.

The story of Cynthia Ann Parker had been told and retold, altered and reimagined, by each generation to fit its own needs and sensibility, until fact and fiction had blended together to form a foundational American myth about the winning of the West. Cynthia Ann, in the version published and passed down by Texas historians, became a romantic and tragic figure, rescued from savages but doomed to unhappiness because the barbarians had corrupted her soul by subjecting her to a fate worse than death: sexual relations with Indians. Her half-white son was the Noble Savage who led his childlike people down the path to civilization. There were other accounts, compiled mostly by female relatives, that paint a sadder and more complex portrait of mother and son. But those accounts were never published and remain scattered and unannotated in the American History archives at the University of Texas at Austin.

The legend gave rise to a prairie opera, one-act plays, fanciful narratives, and fables—and in 1954 to Alan LeMay's powerful novel, one of the best Westerns of its era. LeMay moved the original story forward some thirty years to the late 1860s, when Comanche power was waning, added elements from other captivity narratives he had compiled, and turned the focus from the female captive to two relatives—her uncle and her adopted brother—who spend seven years searching for her.

Ford, a voracious reader who was steeped in the history of the American West, had once commissioned a screenplay about Quanah for a film that never got made. Now he read LeMay's novel and saw its cinematic possibilities. Ford had Cooper quickly arrange for Cornelius Vanderbilt Whitney, a scion of two massive family fortunes who was looking to get into the movie business, to acquire the screen rights on his behalf. Leveraging Whitney's money, Cooper made a deal with Warner Brothers for additional financing and distribution rights, and Ford and his crew set out for Monument Valley.

The movie Ford sought to make had all the elements of the classic Western—a harsh and stunningly beautiful setting, hardy settlers, stoic pioneer women, brutal and rapacious Indians, and a hard, relentless protagonist who stalks the frontier like an angry lion on a mission of vengeance. It was, as the publicity posters proclaimed, "THE BIGGEST,

ROUGHEST, TOUGHEST . . . AND MOST BEAUTIFUL PIC-TURE EVER MADE!" But Ford also celebrated the frontier community and its rituals—its weddings, family meals, square dances, and funerals—the coming together of hardworking people to share their triumphs and humor and mourn their losses. *The Searchers* was not just an adventure story but a parable about the conquest of the American frontier.

But while *The Searchers* pays homage to the familiar themes of the classic Western, it also undermines them. Its central character possesses all of the manly virtues and dark charisma of the Western hero yet is tainted by racism and crazed by revenge, his quest fueled by hatred. His goal is not to restore his lost niece to the remnants of their broken family but to kill her, because she has grown into a young woman and has become a Comanche bride and, willingly or not, has had sex with Indians. He is bent on enforcing sexual and racial purity by performing an honor killing as twisted and remorseless as any carried out in the medieval recesses of the Middle East.

Ford was a storyteller who loved to create and manipulate myths, and as he grew older and more complex, he loved to challenge them as well, reaffirming the audience's deepest conventional wisdom and then gently shattering it. Despite all of his personal setbacks, he rose to the height of his creative powers in *The Searchers*. He is responsible for the film's visual poetry—its skill in moving from the intimacy of domestic interiors and family life to the terrible beauty of the gothic sandstone cathedrals and vast, obliterating plains of Monument Valley—as well as its deep and passionate emotions.

At the heart of *The Searchers* is John Wayne's towering performance as Ethan Edwards. Despite his reputation for knowing how to play only the righteous hero, Wayne had portrayed morally ambiguous men before, most notably the autocratic trail boss in *Red River* (1948) and the brutish Marine sergeant in *Sands of Iwo Jima* (1949). But in *The Searchers* he is darker, angrier, and more troubled than ever. This dark knight is determined to exterminate the damsel and anyone who stands in his way. He shoots the eyes out of a Comanche Indian corpse, scalps another dead Indian, disrupts a funeral service, fires at warriors collecting their dead and wounded from the battlefield, and slaughters a buffalo herd to deprive Comanche families of food for the winter. Still, because he is played by John Wayne, we identify with Ethan's quest even as we recoil from his purpose. His charisma draws us in, making us complicit in his terrible vendetta.

"Wayne is plainly Ahab," writes the cultural critic Greil Marcus. "He is the good American hero driving himself past all known limits and into madness, his commitment to honor and decency burned down to a core of vengeance."

Largely overlooked in its time—it was not nominated for a single Academy Award—*The Searchers* has become recognized as one of the greatest of Hollywood movies. It was extraordinarily influential on a generation of modern American filmmakers—from Steven Spielberg to George Lucas to Martin Scorsese—imprinting itself on their psyches and their ambitions during their formative years. "It was a sacred feeling," recalled Scorsese, who first saw the film at age thirteen, "seeing that movie on that big screen." The film was also the forerunner of the postmodern wave of introspective Westerns—from Ford's own *The Man Who Shot Liberty Valance* (1962) to Sam Peckinpah's *The Wild Bunch* (1969) to Clint Eastwood's *Unforgiven* (1992)—that dissect the values and assumptions of the genre even while honoring them. Just as Ernest Hemingway noted that "all modern American literature comes from one book by Mark Twain called *Huckleberry Finn*," film critic Stuart Byron once declared, "in the same broad sense it can be said that all recent American cinema derives from John Ford's *The Searchers*."

Like Spielberg, Lucas, and Scorsese, I, too, was entranced by *The Searchers* as a boy coming of age in the 1960s. Everything about it thrilled and frightened me. Wayne's command of the screen, his terrifying anger, and his unpredictable blend of affection and derision toward his young nephew and fellow Searcher, played by Jeffrey Hunter, at times reminded me of my own father. There was dust and grit in every scene, and even the gunshot sounds seemed sharper and more real than in other Westerns. And the climactic moment when the uncle chases down his niece and must decide whether to wreak his terrible revenge made me weep with fear and pleasure.

But what entranced me most were the Comanches. They make only a few appearances in the film, yet they are the psychological terror in the night that haunts the white settlers, and they haunted me as well. Ford's portrait of them is mostly one-dimensional: Indians in *The Searchers* are for the most part murderers and rapists, and some critics have accused the film of practicing the same racism it purports to condemn. Yet Ford also grants Indians their humanity: the evil war chief Scar justifies his campaign of murder and abduction as revenge for the killing of his own two sons by whites. The aftermaths of two massacres are depicted in the film, with the burning farmhouse where a pioneer family has been slaughtered in the first act of the story balanced later by a burning Indian village strewn with the corpses of men, women, and children mowed down by soldiers. And even as a boy I could see that when Ethan Edwards finally confronts Scar, the two warriors share a mutual hatred that binds them in a fatal embrace.

I grew up to become a journalist, and my travels as foreign correspondent for the *Washington Post* took me to the Middle East and the Israeli-Palestinian conflict. Like the Plains Indian wars, this, too, was an intimate war of populations in which women and children were both victims and participants. Each side saw the struggle, in Kipling's imperial phrase, as a "Savage War of Peace" in which only one could triumph and the loser must be exterminated physically or culturally or both.

When I came home in 2006, I came back to *The Searchers*. It was the fiftieth anniversary of the film's release and a time of critical acclaim and retrospection. Yet while critics celebrated Ford's cinematic mastery, what struck me as an even greater achievement was his ability to weave myth and truth into a seamless fabric.

As the movie ends, Ford pivots back to the young woman at the heart of the legend, played by the luminous sixteen-year-old Natalie Wood. We first see her as a silent servant in the teepee of the war chief who abducted her and butchered her family. Then she appears as a dark speck at the top of a golden sand dune, slowly moving toward us and her would-be rescuers as she plunges down the hill. At first she insists she wants to stay with the Comanches who have raised her and who she says are now her people. Later, however, she passively accepts her rescue and the embrace first of her adopted brother and then of white civilization, even while her expression remains wary and uncertain.

In *The Searchers* she is the idealized passive damsel, dressed like a Hollywood Pocahontas in buckskins, beads and feathers. But the real Cynthia Ann Parker, abducted by Indians as a child on a sunny spring morning and recaptured by soldiers on a cold December morning twenty-four years later, was a frightened and bewildered victim of war who watched in horror as friends and relatives were slaughtered by both sides. The making of an American legend begins with her, on a small, fortified farm in East Texas, where her pioneer family and an Indian raiding party meet in a primitive clash of civilizations.

I

CYNTHIA ANN

1.

The Girl (Parker's Fort, 1836)

For three months they had trekked south from Illinois—some two hundred men, women, and children and twenty-five ox-drawn wagons, crossing the vast, alarming Mississippi near what is now the town of Chester, Missouri, tethered to long rafts like papooses strapped tightly to their mothers' backs, then navigating the tenuous Southwest Trail through Missouri, Arkansas, and Louisiana, a virgin landscape of rolling hills, deep valleys, and thick marshes. Because the wagons had no suspension to quell the jarring of deep furrows in the rough-cut dirt pathway, few of the pilgrims rode inside; instead they plodded on foot alongside the wagons with a steady, determined pace. The teamsters walked alongside as well, cajoling the oxen teams with a rhythmic monologue punctuated by the periodic crack of the whip, the entire wagon train a noisy, hesitant organism pulling itself toward an unseen destination, a colony with a name both blunt and mysterious: *Texas*.

The trek had a dual purpose: a fresh start on fertile soil for yeomen who relied upon the earth for sustenance and survival; but also a way and means to reconsecrate their covenant with God. Each Saturday evening as the autumn sun retreated, the pilgrims stopped to pitch tents and prepare for a Sabbath of worship and rest under the vigilant instruction of the Reverend Daniel Parker, farmer, politician, Indian fighter, and raw-boned Baptist preacher. "Thus was the wilderness—the home of the Savage and the wild beasts of the forest—made vocal with hymns of praise to the most high God, by this pilgrim brand of christians," wrote James W. Parker, Daniel's devoted younger brother.

In mid-November they reached the brown, placid Sabine River, bordered by pine trees as tall and erect as sentinels, and crossed over into

Texas. They camped that first evening, November 12, 1833, near San Augustine, twenty miles deep inside their new promised land, just in time for one of the most awesome celestial events in human history.

On the Night the Stars Fell, the heavens blazed with shooting stars as large as moons trailing clouds of bluish light like divine afterthoughts. Although well past midnight, the bright burning sky illuminated the wide, awestruck faces of the pilgrims as if it were high noon. For some of them, already predisposed to millennial visions, it was impossible not to detect the hand of God. "The old women seemed to think the Day of Judgment had come like a thief in the night," recalled Garrison Greenwood, Daniel Parker's first cousin.

Daniel was equally stunned. Was God blessing their journey, or was He warning of dangers ahead? Daniel, within whom zealotry and common sense waged a ceaseless struggle, could not say for sure. But after the celestial light show he and his followers could not sleep. "The remainder of the night was spent in prayer," Greenwood recalled.

It was a fitting moment in the long spiritual and geographical journey of the preacher, his family, and his flock. The Parkers, after all, believed in omens, sought miracles, and created narratives out of the sky, the wind, and the weather.

As they traveled deeper and deeper into the American wilderness, they fashioned their own myth to fit their religious beliefs and their patriotic fervor, a myth in which the Lord and the Land were seamlessly interwoven. Although they seldom wrote it down, they were storytellers whose most compelling characters were themselves. According to the broad brushstrokes of their self-portrait, they were God's righteous pilgrims, preaching His gospel and living their lives according to His commandments. They were children of the Second Great Awakening, a burst of passionate, postmillennial fervor that inflamed the hearts, minds, and imaginations of Americans who believed they had a special mission and that their own good deeds and the rise of a great new nation would somehow hasten the day when Christ would return to rule the earth. And they were pioneers—rough-hewn, self-sufficient, beholden to no one but God—spreading their brand of civilization to a richly abundant but untamed territory. They were the living reality of George Caleb Bingham's painting of Daniel Boone, like a frontier Moses, escorting settlers through the Cumberland Gap to the promised land.

The Parkers had come to the American colonies a century earlier, refugees from the hierarchical but unstable world of seventeenth-century England. They were a restless, unschooled, and unruly clan, one of many that drove inland from the Atlantic seaboard in the years after the Revolutionary War shattered British colonial rule and kicked open the gates to western settlement.

The patriarch, Elder John Parker, was born in Baltimore County, Maryland, in 1758, moved to Culpeper County in the Virginia piedmont in the 1770s, and served two militia hitches with his younger brother in the War of Independence. Elder John moved to Georgia in 1785 in search of richer farmland and more pious brethren. There he unsuccessfully sought to start a cotton farm, then headed west, first to Tennessee in 1803 and then to Illinois in 1824—"the Bible in one hand and the reins of the future in the other," as a family history proclaims. Along the way he acquired a wife, eight sons, four daughters, and a primitive brand of Calvinism. He also acquired the nickname "Squealing Johnny" for his emphatic sermonizing. But his reputation for piety was mixed. The minutes of Turnbull Church in Dickson County, Tennessee, record that on April 7, 1809, John Parker came before the elders to acknowledge the sin of drunkenness. "The Church agreed to wait with him awhile," they noted. Another entry suggests that he was excommunicated after accusations of betting on a horse race.

By the time he got to Coles County in southeastern Illinois, John Parker called himself a "Two-Seed Baptist Traveling Preacher." He held the first church service in the history of the county in his own log cabin with eleven people in attendance—the entire adult white population. He once closed a sermon with the announcement that he would be back again "to preach at that place, that day in four weeks if it was not a good day for bee hunting."

The Parkers were the thin edge of a rough-hewn frontier movement— not so much the paragons of civilization but, as Texas historian T. R. Fehrenbach put it, "civilization's heroic and necessary vanguard." A less forgiving observer might say they failed their way west. In each place they settled, they eventually wore out their soil and their welcome, then moved on to what looked like a better opportunity. They had little formal schooling. Daniel, the eldest child, born in Virginia in 1781 but raised in Georgia, said he grew up "without an education, except to read in the New Testament, but very imperfect." He added, "To this day I have never examined the English Grammar five minutes, neither do I understand even one rule in the Arithmetic." In his youth, he later wrote, he "ranged the woods as a hunter, nearly as much in company with Indians as with the whites." James Parker, the ninth child and sixth son, born in

Georgia in 1797, said he was "raised a back woodsman . . . the advantages for obtaining an education being very limited, I was not enabled to do more than learn to read." His own great pleasures, he reported, lay elsewhere: "hunting, fishing, and trapping."

Daniel and James emerged as the natural leaders of the new generation of Parkers. They left no photographs and few physical descriptions, but the impression they made on others was often enduring. Ordained in Tennessee in 1806, Daniel preached the gospel even though it was largely unpaid work. He farmed at night so that he would be free to sermonize during the day, and he rode a suffering, unshod horse for two years because he could not afford horseshoes. "Farming was my only way to make a support," he wrote. "I avoided everything like trade or traffic, lest I should bring reproach on the tender cause of God."

Some found him enchanting. James Ross, a church elder, was unmoved by Daniel's physical appearance—"a small, dry-looking man, of the gipsy [sic] type, with black eyes and hair and dark complexion"—nor by the ritual he performed before sermonizing: pulling off his coat and vest and laying them carefully on the pulpit, and unbuttoning his short collar as if preparing for fisticuffs. "After this preparation it is almost incredible with what ease and fluency he spoke," Ross wrote. "He seemed full of his subject, and went through it in a way that was truly wonderful."

Others were appalled. John Mason Peck, a rival Baptist minister in Illinois, depicted Daniel as "without education, uncouth in manners, slovenly in dress, diminutive in person, unprepossessing in appearance, with shriveled features and a small piercing eye . . . with a zeal and enthusiasm bordering on insanity."

Daniel was devout, passionate, and demanding—an evangelical preacher in constant search of a new pulpit; James entrepreneurial, opportunistic, and impetuous—a land speculator, horse trader, and perhaps much worse. And as James idolized Daniel, so did Silas Parker, born in Tennessee in 1804, seem to worship his older brother James, following him faithfully down dangerous paths.

They were tribesmen and warriors, just one tenuous step removed from barbarism. Not so different, in truth, from the native peoples they fought along the way. In the story the Parkers and their fellow frontiersmen were creating about the conquest of the West, Indians were the Other—inhuman, barbaric, and easily manipulated. Even in the Declaration of Independence, among some of history's most ringing celebrations of the human spirit, Thomas Jefferson evoked the evil specter of Indians, accusing George III of having "endeavored to bring on the inhabitants of our frontiers, the merciless Indian Savages, whose known rule of warfare is an undistinguished destruction of all ages, sexes, and conditions."

John Parker, one of the brothers, was killed by Delaware Indians near Cape Girardeau, Missouri, in 1811. James wrote that his brother's death "awakened in me feelings of the most bitter hostility towards the Indians, and I firmly resolved upon and impatiently awaited for an opportunity to avenge his death."

Daniel and his younger brother Isaac served in the Tennessee volunteer militia of General Andrew Jackson under a young commander named Sam Houston, vanquishing Creek Indians allied with the British during the War of 1812. Indians and settlers traded massacres and retribution in an escalating spiral of bloody deeds. The Creeks carried out a brutal massacre at Fort Mims in Alabama in August 1813, slaughtering more than 250 volunteers and their families, mutilating women, and smashing small children's heads against the stockade walls. At Tallushatchee and Talladega, Jackson and his men took their revenge. "We now shot them down like dogs," boasted one of the volunteers, the soon-to-be legendary David Crockett. The myth of Indian fighters Jackson, Houston, and Crockett was born.

Daniel, the most impassioned preacher among the Parkers, was the most successful politician as well. He served as a state assemblyman for two terms in Illinois. Church and state were separate in practice as well as principle in the early days of the American republic, and Daniel's published appeal for votes made no mention of his religious beliefs. His neighbors described him "as a man of truth and as a man of talents and of liberal and Republican principles." In 1823 he and fourteen other Illinois lawmakers banded together to block an attempt to legalize slavery in the state.

Still, his Calvinism was anything but liberal, embracing a fierce, unyielding vision of mankind as pathetic and weak, devoid of free will, and incapable of virtue. It was a hard faith that mistrusted human nature as sinful and easily corrupted. "We believe that God created man good and upright," his church constitution proclaimed, "but that man by his sins and transgressions has become dead in trespasses and sins and is utterly unable to change his own heart, or to deliver himself from the fallen depraved state which he has fallen into under the influence of the Power of Darkness."

*　*　*

TEXAS SEEMED VAST ENOUGH to hold the Parker clan and their visions. American settlers had been trickling in since the early 1800s, but in 1824 the Mexican government officially opened the province to foreign immigration. Every able-bodied white man could claim 4,428 acres for just thirty dollars in one of the privately owned colonies that the Mexican authorities had sanctioned in hopes of creating a buffer between their small communities and hostile Indian tribes to the north. Stephen F. Austin, a young Virginia-born lawyer living in New Orleans who became an authorized *empresario* for the first colony, sang the praises of the gently rolling land between the burgeoning new town of Nacogdoches and the Sabine River: "The grass is more abundant and of a ranker and more luxuriant growth than I have ever seen before in any country and is indicative of a strong rich soil."

Like the Parkers, many of the newcomers were farmers who hauled their families and livestock to the new frontier seeking a fresh start on free land. The new American peasantry was hardworking, self-sufficient, and resolutely egalitarian: they shook hands rather than bowed. Many were refugees from the Panic of 1819, when the fledgling American banking system had collapsed and thousands of smallholders lost their farms. "Gone to Texas" became a familiar sign hung on the doors of log cabins across the South. Alongside the pioneers were men of greater ambitions and lesser repute, gamblers and adventurers like James Bowie, a Kentucky-born slave trader, Indian fighter, smuggler, and land speculator; William Barret Travis, an Alabama lawyer fleeing serious debts and an unfaithful wife; and Crockett himself, seeking new fortune and redemption after losing his seat in the U.S. House of Representatives. And some were far worse. "A great number of the foreigners who have entered the frontier are vicious and wild men with evil ways," reported Mexican general Manuel de Mier y Terán, who led a fact-finding mission to the colony in 1827. "Some of them are fugitive criminals from the neighboring republic; within our borders they create disturbances and even criminal acts."

James W. Parker was restless in Illinois—"that country being very sickly," he reported after three of his nine children died of fever—and always looking for new pastures. He was the first Parker to visit Texas; in 1831 he explored the forested eastern half, riding through areas teeming with wild game and fertile soil, and lived for a season along the Colorado River, which began in the High Plains of what is now the Texas Panhandle and flowed southeast to Matagorda Bay and the Gulf of Mexico. Hostile Indians, as always, were a problem: James noted that several of his neighbors were killed during his stay; one of them, a Mr. Wilbarger, "was literally shot to pieces, scalped and left as dead." Still, James traveled back to Illinois with a positive report for his brothers. He returned to Texas two years later with his wife and six children and three of his brothers: Daniel, Benjamin, and Joseph. Younger brother Silas came separately.

Doctrinal battles with Methodists and his fellow Baptists in Illinois had taken their toll on Daniel, and he was ready for a new spiritual home. The laws of Catholic-dominated Mexico forbade the organization of a new Protestant church within its borders, but they did not prohibit Protestants from bringing in a preexisting church from outside. He founded the Pilgrim Predestinarian Regular Baptist Church on August 11, 1833, in his house in Crawford County, with himself as moderator and six other members, then set out the next day for Texas with all six and their families, along with his father and brothers. Before he left for Texas, Elder John applied for and received a government pension of $80 per month for his Revolutionary War service.

Thirteen of Daniel's constituents in Illinois signed a character certificate that he carried with him to the new colony; Daniel Parker, they averred, was "an honest man and a good citizen" who had "discharged his duty faithfully to the satisfaction of a majority of his constituents." Others were less sorry to see him go. "Mr. Parker, you are an Enemy to truth and your doctrine came from hell and will go back there again," wrote one anonymous letter writer.

Many of the new colonists chose land close to the small towns and villages rising up in southeast Texas for their own safety and sense of community. But James and Silas Parker were more daring. They picked out a promising patch of farmland near the banks of the Navasota River, a narrow branch of the Brazos. With crude handmade tools and farming implements, no fertilizer or irrigation, and little cash, the Parkers needed to choose their new property wisely. The Navasota coursed along a seam of dark, rich bottomland where the woodlands of the southeast slowly gave way to the high plains of the north.

James liked what he saw. This was, he believed, his promised land. "The country on the Navasott is the most fertile, most healthy, and subject to fewer objections than any other part of Texas," he wrote. "There are springs in this section that afford water enough to run a mill. The timber is very large, and of an excellent quality. The rock found along these creeks . . . is well adapted for building purposes. The range for stock is not surpassed in any country."

But the garden was not empty. Several thousand Indians—mostly Caddos, Wichitas, and Kichais—lived in villages along the river banks. They were farmers, hunters, and gatherers, and many of their settlements dated back hundreds of years. Farther to the north and west were thousands more native peoples—Comanches, Lipan Apaches, and Kiowas—who lived a more nomadic and aggressive existence on horseback in the high, arid limestone plains where white men seldom ventured.

Between these two dramatically distinct regions was a thick belt of forest land known as the Cross Timbers that stretched from southeastern Kansas through the heart of the Indian territories—what is now Oklahoma—and into northern Texas. Washington Irving, who traveled the area in 1832, described a rough terrain of open rolling hills and deep ravines. The land was pleasant during the spring rains when the vegetation grew green and damp, but by the time Irving and his party arrived in the fall, "the herbage was parched; the foliage of the scrubby forests was withered; the whole woodland prospect, as far as the eye could reach, had a brown and arid hue." Frequent fires scorched and calcified the vegetation, "leaving them black and hard, so as to tear the flesh of man and horse that had to scramble through them . . . It was like struggling through forests of cast iron."

To James Parker, the Cross Timbers seemed like a natural boundary line between the northernmost reaches of white settlement and the southern fringe of Indian territory. But the Comanches, masters of horsemanship and mobility, treated the Timbers like an open door. For decades they swooped down every spring to hunt game and raid other tribes for horses and food. James didn't seem to grasp—or chose to ignore—that he was putting himself and his extended family in jeopardy. His younger brother Silas went along.

Daniel Parker chose not to. When he and his caravan arrived in Texas in December 1833, he broke away from James and Silas and settled farther to the south and east, in what is now the town of Elkhart. Daniel feared the new colony that James had in mind was too close to the hostile native peoples and too isolated from the rest of the settler community. He also did not care to preach to an empty choir. He quickly became a prominent member of the fledgling community and served, as in Illinois, as a legislator. Meanwhile, James, Silas, and their older brother Benjamin, a recent widower at age forty-eight, continued along with Elder John and their families to the banks of the Navasota, where they set up camp and began to farm.

The Parkers were a distinctly American breed—both settlers and warriors. They always traveled with their families, and their homes formed their front line, exposing their wives and children to whatever dangers existed. James Parker and his wife, Martha, brought six children with them to the new settlement. Their red-haired, eighteen-year-old daughter Rachel, married to a prosperous young farmer named Luther Plummer, was the first to give birth in the new colony in January 1835. Rachel and Luther named their son James Pratt, after her father. Sarah, another of James's and Martha's daughters, married Lorenzo Nixon on March 26, 1836, with Elder John, her grandfather, presiding. Silas and his wife, Lucy, who was Martha's sister, had four children. The oldest, Cynthia Ann, born in Illinois in 1827, was a blonde, blue-eyed princess who prowled the new farmland as if it were her private preserve and licked fresh warm milk from the cows.

The local Indians felt hemmed in and besieged by the interlopers. Hostilities began with the theft of horses and cattle, each side raiding the other. James Parker helped establish treaties with a dozen local chiefs, but not all Indians, nor all whites, honored these arrangements. In July 1835, a band of white settlers seeking stolen horses attacked a Kichai village that had signed a peace accord. The Indian villagers greatly outnumbered the white attackers, who were forced to flee to the Parker settlement. On another occasion, a party of white settlers led by a Colonel Burleson discovered stolen American horses in the possession of two Caddo chiefs, whom they seized and tied to a tree. The chiefs claimed they had recovered the horses on behalf of the colonists but the men refused to believe them. They shot the two chiefs in cold blood. The wife of one of the Indians reported to her fellow tribesmen what had happened.

James Parker styled himself as a Man Who Knows Indians—their customs, their way of thinking, and their purported talent for treachery. But when it came to Comanches, the most warlike of the native peoples, James knew little. To him these Indians were just another potential obstacle on the road to prosperity and redemption, to be outmaneuvered or eliminated depending upon their level of resistance. "If this region was not infested by hostile Indians, it would be very soon settled," James would write, as if the natives were a particularly noxious species of disease, "and when once settled and cultivated by civilized man, it will approximate to an earthly paradise."

At first the colonists and Comanches circled each other warily, trading horses, food, and firearms. Comanches expected gifts and tribute. It took time for them to discover that the Texans were more aggressive and less pliable than their Mexican neighbors, just as it took time for Texans to realize the Comanches were impossible to intimidate and harder to kill than most Indians. Still, the gap was wide and blood-stained. Each group told stories about the other, and they were inevitably tales of bloodshed and destruction.

JAMES W. PARKER had extravagantly promised Stephen Austin that he could attract dozens of Americans to his new settlement, but very few actually came. Still, he was a man to seize opportunities. Early on, there were allegations that James was engaged in dealings with local Indians, paying them in counterfeit money for stolen horses. These claims were never proven but they were a calumny that long haunted James's good name—after all, in Texas the only thing worse than a horse thief was a man who colluded with savages. James solemnly denied the allegations, saying his accusers were seeking "to destroy my reputation, degrade my family, and make my life a burden to me."

His new settlement, being far removed from the rest of the pioneer community, was increasingly vulnerable as hostilities between native peoples and newcomers intensified. To protect their families and their livestock, the Parkers in 1835 built a stockade of a half dozen cabins and two blockhouses enclosed by a twelve-foot-tall fence of split cedar timbers. It was home to about forty men, women and children—Parkers, Faulkenberrys, Anglins, and Frosts, all of them related by blood or marriage—and was crammed with farm tools, implements, and supplies, barefoot youngsters with dirty necks, and barnyard animals. The

Old Fort Parker Cabin, July 2008, Groesbeck, Texas. The replica fort was built in 1936 for the centennial of Texas independence and the raid in which Indians abducted Cynthia Ann Parker and four relatives.

settlers had no nails, screws, or bolts; instead, they split and notched their logs so that the pieces fit snugly together like the fingers of a pair of folded hands. They did their cooking inside the cabins and slept in makeshift lofts that served both as beds and storage areas. Privacy was minimal, clothing was harsh burlap, bathing with strong homemade soap was an occasion rather than an everyday occurrence. The block-houses were placed at diagonal ends of the fort; the second stories pro-jected beyond the stockade walls and there were gun slots in the floor and on all four walls. At night the livestock were brought inside the walls for protection.

James and Silas formed one of the original three Texas Ranger com-panies, which began using Parker's Fort as a base of operations. The Texas General Council authorized Silas to contract and employ twenty-five men, at a salary of $1.25 per day, "to secure the inhabitants residing on the frontiers from the invasions of the hostile Indians." The Indians increasingly viewed the fort as a military installation, not a settlement. In any case, it didn't really matter: settlements, after all, were fair game in the intimate warfare both sides engaged in.

The winter of 1836 was a desperate time for local Indians, with many deaths due to hunger and disease. They blamed the white settlers for both. According to Comanche oral tradition, a young warrior named Peta Nocona stepped forward to challenge others to join him in a raid on the Texans. Nocona styled himself a wanderer—a man of no fixed ties or kinship in a community in which kinship was essential for sur-vival. But his warrior skills and his single-minded determination won him respect. He was feared, not loved, neither a chief nor a foot soldier.

The settlers had other reasons to be fearful. Relations between the colonists and the central government in Mexico City were disintegrat-ing due to conflicts over land, money, and control. Daniel Parker was aligned at first with the peace camp that sought reconciliation with the Mexican regime. But the lines quickly shifted and moderates hardened into hawks. Daniel participated in the popular Consultation Assembly that met on November 3, 1835, and approved a "Declaration of the Peo-ple of Texas," forming a provisional government even while pledging loyalty to the 1824 constitution under which many of the colonists had entered Texas. They pledged to resist General Antonio López de Santa Anna, the military leader who had seized control of the government in Mexico City. Daniel signed his name just below that of his old militia commander, Sam Houston, by now a registered resident of the *munici-palidad* of Nacogdoches.

As hostilities spiraled, Daniel became one of the original signers of the Texas Declaration of Independence and joined the Council of the Provisional Government. Santa Anna mustered a force of 5,000 soldiers and invaded Texas, laid siege to and conquered the Alamo, the fortified mission in San Antonio, killing all of its 189 defenders—including Bowie, Travis, and Crockett—on March 6, 1836, then slowly pushed north. Although their fort was more than 200 miles northeast of San Antonio, the Parkers and their neighbors abandoned the stockade and fled east toward the Trinity River for fear that the Mexicans and the Indians would forge an unholy alliance and overrun their small settlement. Houston, appointed as commander of the ragtag Texas army, sent out dispatches urging settlers to flee. But rain fell steadily and the Trinity was too swollen for them to safely cross. "To our minds this was a far more trying time than when Moses led the children of Israel across the Red Sea, for unlike them, we had no inspired leader to call on the Lord to part the waters for us," recalled J. H. Greenwood, son of Garrison, one of the settler leaders. Instead the Parkers and their neighbors huddled on the western bank along with hundreds of other colonists, hungry, wet, desperate, and fearful they would be trapped. The exodus was known as the Runaway Scrape.

Then the Lord seemed to intervene. On April 21, Houston's volunteer army vanquished Santa Anna's forces at San Jacinto, some 120 miles to the south. Like Israelites miraculously delivered from a vengeful Pharaoh, the Parkers and their neighbors rejoiced, then rushed home and set about hurriedly planting their summer corn crop. There were steady reports and rumors that Indians were preparing to attack. Daniel Parker claimed that an Indian named Jinie Jim warned him that some five hundred warriors, Caddos and other tribes, were gathering on the Trinity River near the Cross Timbers and planning to destroy Parker's Fort and then move on to other settlements "for the purpose of Killing the white people." Sam Houston himself expressed misgivings about the vulnerable location of the Parker stockade. But the planting season could not wait: corn had to be sown now or else the Parkers risked a disastrous winter ahead. In any event the danger seemed to have passed, and James Parker disbanded his small Ranger company. The Parkers and their neighbors still carried their aging single-shot rifles when they went to work the fields, but the main gate of the stockade was left open so that the settlers could move in and out easily while catching up on their farmwork. There was, they believed, nothing to fear.

And so it was a shock on the morning of May 19, while James Parker,

his son-in-law Luther Plummer, and most of the other men were out
working fields a mile or more away, that a large band of Indians on
horseback appeared before the fort waving a soiled white flag. There
were dozens, perhaps hundreds, of young warriors—some of the settlers' accounts would later claim as many as eight hundred. Benjamin
Parker approached the group unarmed and asked what they wanted. He
came back to tell his brother Silas that the Indians were demanding a
steer for meat and directions to a waterhole. Benjamin feared these requests were just a pretext, but he insisted on going back out again in
hope of preventing an attack or at least buying time. Silas pleaded with
him not to go, but Benjamin felt he had no choice. Silas ran inside to get
his ammunition pouch while Benjamin slowly strode back to the Indians. It was a noble but fatal gesture. The warriors surrounded him,
clubbed him senseless, and stuck his lifeless body repeatedly with lances.
Then they let out a piercing cry, with "voices that seemed to reach the
very skies," and rushed the fort.

Everything after that was panic and noise and blood and pandemo-
nium. The Indians sprinted for the open gate, while the settlers, mostly
women and children, fled wildly. Silas Parker got off one shot before the
Indians engulfed him, pounded his head to a wet crimson pulp, and
ripped off his scalp with a butcher knife. They killed Samuel Frost and his
teenage son Robert inside the fort, then seized Elder John in front of his
wife, Sally, shattered his skull with hatchets, and hacked off his scalp and
his genitals, then pinned Sally to the ground with a lance through her
chest, stripped off her clothes, and left her writhing. Rachel Plummer,
bundling eighteen-month-old James Pratt in her arms, tried to flee, but
she was cut off by the raiders, knocked down by an Indian wielding one
of the farm's hoes, and beaten over the head until she stopped screaming
and let go of the boy. She was forced to remain on the ground, silent,
dazed, swollen, and bleeding, burning with fear, certain that the attackers
were killing her little boy, until she saw him on a horse, held tight in the
blunt arms of a warrior, crying out, "Mother, oh Mother!"

Some of the hysterical women and children made it to the fields.
Sarah Parker Nixon, the other of James's married daughters, reached her
father first, followed by James's wife, Martha, and their four younger
children. James shepherded them across the river; at first he planned to
hide them there and set out for the fort, but they pleaded with him not
to leave them. Luther Plummer went looking for the other farmers to
organize a rescue mission, while Sarah's husband Lorenzo started immediately for the fort.

The Indians commenced to plunder the stockade. They slashed open mattresses and scattered the feathers. They tore open James's books and smashed his medicine bottles. Lucy Parker, Silas's wife, tried to flee with her four small children. She ran into Lorenzo Nixon, but before he could lead her and the children to safety, Indians surrounded all of them and marched them back to the fort. The Indians forced Lucy to help load her two oldest children behind mounted warriors, and they were in the process of taking the younger two, Silas junior and Orlena, when David Faulkenberry, a lone farmer armed with a single-shot rifle, emerged from the woods and trained his weapon on the attackers. Faulkenberry gathered Lucy, her two young ones, and Nixon behind him and forced the Indians to retreat. But no one could help the other captives.

Rachel Plummer, covered in blood and bruises, was dragged by her long red hair to the back of an Indian pony and forced to climb on. She saw the Indians shove her young aunt, Elizabeth Kellogg, onto another pony and watched as a warrior triumphantly waved a handful of bloody scalps; the only one she recognized was the long gray hair of her beloved grandfather, Elder John.

The raiders mounted up and rode away with a flourish, lancing any cattle they came across in a final gesture of vandalism and contempt. They had killed five people and taken five more captive without a single casualty of their own, and now they rode deep into the night, weaving their way through the heavy forested bottomlands with their prisoners: two young women—Rachel Plummer and Elizabeth Kellogg—Rachel's toddler son, James Pratt, and her eight-year-old nephew, John. And on another mount, alone and terrified after watching her father, her uncle, and her grandfather all killed before her eyes, and held tight by her Indian captor, the late Silas Parker's oldest child and the late Elder John Parker's forty-ninth grandchild: nine-year-old Cynthia Ann.

2.

The Captives (Comancheria, 1836)

A lmost from the moment of her abduction, Cynthia Ann Parker's family began telling and retelling the story, and shaping the facts to fit their own needs and understanding. The first narrators were her uncle James and the other men at Parker's Fort who had failed to rescue her and the other captives. Their excuse was simple: they had been caught by surprise, and the vast numbers and brutality of the assailants had left them no time nor means to respond. Were there, in reality, eight Indians or, as some of the witnesses claimed, eight hundred? We will never know.

James Parker claimed he had grabbed his long gun and started immediately for the stockade, only to be intercepted by his fleeing wife, Martha, and their children. Fellow farmer George Dwight, who had also fled the fort, told him that everyone there had either been killed or taken prisoner. At that point, James said, he abandoned his rescue plans and gathered the terrified survivors; he led them up the Navasota River, retracing their steps by walking backwards so that the Indians couldn't track them along the sandy riverbank. Six adults—including Martha, who was eight months pregnant—and twelve children set off under cover of darkness for the safety of Tinnin's settlement some forty miles to the east. They had no horses, food, blankets, or spare clothing. Most had no shoes. The grown-ups carried the smaller children on their backs. "We were in the howling wilderness, barefooted and bare-headed," James would write, "a savage and relentless foe on the one hand; on the other, a traceless and uninhabited country literally covered with venomous reptiles and ravenous beasts."

Terrified that the Indians would return, the little band traveled only at night, concealing themselves during daylight like moles hiding from the sun. On the second night, with the children crying out for food, James caught a skunk and held it under water until it drowned. "We soon had it cooked," he wrote. It was all they had to eat for three days.

On the fourth night they caught another skunk and two small turtles, a veritable feast. It took two more days to reach the settlement. The next day, Rachel's husband, Luther Plummer, arrived on foot. The other survivors also straggled in, with their own harrowing tale to tell. Abram Anglin, Silas Bates, and David and Evans Faulkenberry said that as soon as they heard the alarm they had grabbed their rifles but got to the fort too late to save the victims or rescue the captives. Seeing that they were badly outnumbered, they hid in the forest until sunset, long after the invaders had ridden off. Anglin was exploring the ruined grounds when he saw what looked like an apparition wandering dazed and senseless, "dressed in white with long, white hair streaming down its back." It was Sally Duty Parker, Elder John's wife. Stabbed, perhaps raped, and left for dead by the warriors, she had somehow managed to yank the Comanche lance out of her shoulder.

Anglin threw a blanket around her bare shoulders and gave her water. She led him to a hole where she had buried $125 in cash. They dug up the money, grabbed the five remaining horses, saddles, bacon, and honey from the stockade, and fled. Terrified by the prospect that at any moment the Indians might return, the four men and Mrs. Parker left behind the livestock and dogs howling for food and five corpses lying exposed. They found Lucy Parker and her two remaining children hidden nearby and began the trek to safety. Traveling only at night, they reached Fort Houston in three days.

James was desperate to get back to Parker's Fort as quickly as possible to pick up the trail of the captives. Officials authorized several hundred volunteers to accompany him but withdrew them almost immediately after a false report that Santa Anna's troops were regrouping on the western frontier of the new Texas republic. "To go alone was useless, and to raise a company was impossible, as every person capable of service was already in the Texas army," James would recall.

With everyone focused on the Mexican threat, it took James more than a month to organize a group of fourteen men to return to the fort—far too late to pursue the raiding party. "We found the houses still standing, but the crops were entirely destroyed, the horses stolen, nearly all the cattle killed," James would write. He gathered the bare bones of his father and two brothers and Samuel and Robert Frost: all of the

Monument to the victims of the massacre at Fort Parker Memorial Cemetery, Groesbeck, Texas.

flesh had already been devoured by animals. There was, of course, no sign of the captives.

The dead were gone; the living, too, seemed to have vanished.

THE INDIANS HAD RIDDEN until midnight, keen to put distance between themselves and any possible pursuers. They finally stopped in a clearing, hog-tied Rachel Plummer and Elizabeth Kellogg facedown on the ground with plaited leather straps, punching and kicking them for amusement and increasing the intensity of the blows whenever the two young women cried out. Rachel's head wound opened up again and she struggled to keep from smothering in her own blood. When Elizabeth called out to her and she sought to respond, their captors stomped on both of them. The three children—Cynthia Ann, her brother John, and Rachel's young son James Pratt—were tied down nearby. If they called out or cried, they, too, were punched and kicked.

The warriors danced throughout the night, young men high on adrenaline, reenacting scenes from their glorious victory, working themselves into a frenzy and tormenting and humiliating their captives. Rape was often part of these rituals. Although Rachel was not explicit, she later wrote that her captors treated her with such barbarity she could not bear to describe the details: "It is with feelings of the deepest mortification that I think of it."

The next morning they were off again, passing out of the rich, forested bottomlands and threading their way through the dense wooded fabric of the Cross Timbers, then pouring out onto the flat, open countryside. They trampled swift, yielding buffalo grass and skirted the rocky outcroppings and ravines that punctuated the vast, blunt landscape.

The raiding party rode for five days, until they finally reached the High Plains, where they stopped to divide their captives. A group of Kichais took Elizabeth, while separate bands of Comanches claimed Cynthia Ann and John. Rachel had one last tender moment with her son James Pratt. The raiders untied her and brought her the child for breast-feeding. James Pratt's swollen body was covered in bruises and she hugged him tightly. But when the Indians saw that he had already been weaned, they pulled him out of her arms and sent him off with another small band.

Rachel never saw him again.

JAMES PARKER'S NEXT OBJECTIVE was to put together a company of men to journey directly to Indian Territory, north of the Red River in what is now Oklahoma, in pursuit of Rachel, Elizabeth Kellogg, and the three children. To accomplish that, he needed the blessing of the commander who was widely celebrated for defeating Santa Anna, a man whom from the beginning James mistrusted and antagonized.

Sam Houston's mythic life was ax-cut from the same rough block of pioneer timber as the Parkers. Born in Virginia in 1793, he had migrated at age thirteen with his widowed mother and eight siblings to the mountains of Tennessee after the death of his father. Farm life in Tennessee did not agree with young Houston; he soon ran away from home and spent three years on and off living with Cherokee Indians, who adopted him and gave him the name Colonneh—"the Raven." Houston called Cherokee chief Oolooteka his "Indian Father," treated the Cherokees as a surrogate family, and later helped them resettle west of the Mississippi in Indian Territory after the federal government expelled them from their tribal homeland. Along with two of Elder John Parker's sons, he fought under Andrew Jackson's command against the Creek Indians during the War of 1812. Jackson treated him like a protégé, and under Old Hickory's guidance Houston completed law school, served in the U.S. House of Representatives, and was elected governor of Tennessee.

Tall, dashing, moody, and intensely ambitious, Houston carved his own flamboyant legend as a two-fisted backwoodsman, soldier, and Indian fighter. He was a hard drinker and a brawler: he caned a fellow congressman on the streets of Georgetown after the man publicly questioned his honesty. Still, Houston looked like Old Hickory's political heir and a surefire presidential candidate until his marriage to nineteen-year-old Eliza Allen mysteriously collapsed after only eleven weeks, and he resigned the governorship and fled Tennessee for Indian Territory. He lived there with the Cherokees in self-imposed exile for nearly three years—choosing, he wrote, to "abandon once more the habitations of civilized men, with their coldness, their treachery, and their vices, and pass years among the children of the Great Spirit." Houston added to his own myth when he visited Washington to lobby on the behalf of the Cherokees clad in native garb: turban, leggings, breechclout, and blanket. He became that classic American frontier figure: the Man Who Knows Indians.

Like the Parkers, Houston eventually made his way to Texas, the land of fresh beginnings, where as an experienced military man he quickly became commander of the newly declared republic's makeshift army. After his troops vanquished Santa Anna's forces at San Jacinto, Houston's popularity skyrocketed and he easily defeated Stephen F. Austin to become the first president of the new nation. Not all were enamored of their charismatic new leader. "He's eloquent, patriotic, and talented," wrote Texas newspaper editor John Henry Brown, a contemporary, but also "jealous, envious, dissipated, wicked, artful, and overbearing."

Houston's backwoods upbringing and experiences as an Indian fighter were similar to that of James Parker, but he and James had little else in common. While James was a teetotaling, sanctimonious Baptist, Houston was a proud and profane man whose bouts with alcohol were legendary. While James learned to hate Indians indiscriminately, Houston sympathized with many of them and celebrated his adoptive Cherokee heritage. He concluded early on that Indians, like whites, came in many varieties, some trustworthy and some not, and that it was important to be able to discern between them. In effect, the two men represented the American empire's conflicting approaches to native peoples: the carrot versus the stick.

During the independence war, Houston worked hard to tamp down hostilities between Texans and Indians and prevent native peoples from allying with Santa Anna and launching a second front. He showered friendly Indians with gifts and promises that Texans would not impinge on their territory. "Your enemies and ours are the same," he wrote to a group of Comanche chiefs in December 1836. If so, it was at best a temporary state of affairs.

Houston expressed his condolences to the Parker family for the attack on Parker's Fort and the abduction of the five captives, but he was reluctant to help James pursue a scorched-earth campaign to get them back. He saw James as an irrational Indian hater and a one-man wrecking crew who could single-handedly demolish the good-neighbor policy Houston was working so hard to establish with native peoples.

After tending to his sick wife and children, James went in early July to see Houston, who was himself recovering from a severe leg wound he had received at the battle of San Jacinto. Houston rejected James's demand for a large company of soldiers to hunt down the Indians and rescue the captives, telling James a peace treaty would be a more effective means of securing their release. James argued that the Indians would never agree "until they were whipped, and well whipped," but Houston was unmoved. "All argument failed," wrote James, who felt that "Gen. Houston betrayed too great an indifference to the matter."

James was still lobbying Houston in mid-August when Elizabeth Kellogg suddenly appeared in Nacogdoches. She had been purchased for $150 by a band of friendly Delaware Indians, who proceeded to ransom her to the Texans for a similar amount—paid by Houston, according to James, who says he himself was penniless. James returned her to her family. But first there was an ugly scene when he and Elizabeth came across a wounded Indian who had been shot while allegedly trying to steal a horse. By James's account, Elizabeth recognized the man as one of the raiders who had killed Elder John: she claimed to remember the distinctive scars on each of the man's arms. James reacted "with mingled feelings of joy, sorrow and revenge." He gave no details of what he did to the Indian, but afterward, "suffice it to say . . . it was the unanimous opinion of the company that he would never kill and scalp another white man."

Uncle James had killed his first Indian.

ALL THREE OF THE PARKER CHILDREN—Cynthia Ann, John, and James Pratt—disappeared into the heart of the Comanche world and left no written account of their experiences. Rachel Plummer, by contrast, would leave a compact, detailed, and brutally frank written narrative that depicts the stunning violence of her abduction and captivity.

After they separated her from her young son and the other captives,

Rachel's abductors headed north. Each day the vegetation receded further and the landscape grew more stark and naked, until they entered what seemed like a vast, arid sea of brown rock, dry dirt, and scrub. The imperious sun beat down, and even in May a hot breeze clawed at the ground. Washington Irving, who had passed through the same area four years earlier accompanying a government surveying mission, found "something inexpressibly lonely . . . [H]ere we have an immense extent of landscape without a sign of human existence. We have the consciousness of being far, far beyond the bounds of human habitation; we feel as if moving in the midst of a desert world."

This was the heart of Comancheria, homeland and sanctuary of the Comanche nation, an empire without borders, signposts, fences, or walls. It was a roughly egg-shaped territory stretching some six hundred miles north to south from Kansas and the headwaters of the Arkansas River to the Rio Grande, and four hundred miles east to west from modern-day Oklahoma to New Mexico. The Comanches were supreme nomads: they built nothing they could not tear down overnight, load onto a travois strapped to the backs of horses or dogs, and drag to a new location. They left no monuments, temples, or enduring architecture. Even the term "Comanche" was created by others. It was derived from the Ute Indians, who described their foes as *Koh-mahts*, "Those Who Are Always Against Us." The Comanches called themselves *Nemernuh*—"the People"—a name that suggested that non-Comanches were less than human.

There was in fact not one overarching Comanche nation but rather a collection of bands that spoke the same language and recognized each other as distantly related even while living in separate geographic areas. There may have been a dozen or more of these bands: among the larger and more noteworthy were the Penateka ("Honey-Eaters"), who dominated southern and central Texas; the Nokoni ("Those Who Turn Back") in the northeast region; the Quahadi ("Antelope Eaters") in the northwest and New Mexico, and the Yamparika ("Root Eaters") in western Kansas and southeastern Colorado. There was no central authority, no chief whose word was law or could be considered binding on the others, no rulers and no subjects.

Still, by the mid-eighteenth century the Comanches had become the most relentless and feared war machine in the Southwest. They butchered their prisoners—torturing, amputating, eviscerating, mutilating, decapitating, and scalping—for entertainment, for prestige as warriors, and for the belief that to destroy the body of an enemy was to doom his soul to eternal limbo. Comanche warriors practiced a ritualized form of warfare: counting coup by striking an enemy and escaping untouched was as prestigious as killing him. The battlefield was a place to make a fashion statement. A Spanish priest who watched hundreds of Comanches form outside the Franciscan mission of San Saba in central Texas in 1758 noted the Indians' "most horrible attire." They painted their faces red and black and dressed in animal skins, horns, tails, and feather headdresses. But the fashion show was a prelude to a brutal slaughter: eight men at the mission were butchered, scalped, and decapitated.

The intense brutality reflected the harsh conditions Comanches faced. Food and other resources were scarce. These were meant to be shared with kinsmen, not with others, and violence reinforced this code. The modern image of Indians—nurtured by the Native American rights movement, revisionist historians, and the film *Dances With Wolves*—has been one of profoundly spiritual and environmentally friendly genocide victims seeking harmony with the land and humankind. But the Comanches were nobody's victims and no one's friends. They were magnificent, brutal, and relentless.

"The Comanche constitute the largest and most terrible nomadic nation anywhere in the territory of the Mexican republic," wrote Jean-Louis Berlandier, a French-born naturalist who traveled throughout the region in the late 1820s and was captivated by the native peoples he observed. "These constantly wandering savages are incredible in their agility. The extremes of the weather and the privations of a life of constant turmoil combine to give them a physical hardiness peculiarly their own."

Raiding and trading were their way of life—for goods, horses, food, and captives. Imported to the new world by the Spanish conquistadores, horses proved to be a technological breakthrough that transformed Comanche life. Once they mastered the horse, the newly mobile Comanches expanded their field of operations. They quickly turned New Mexico into what the historian Pekka Hämäläinen calls "a vast hinterland of extractive raiding," rampaged through Texas and crossed the Rio Grande into the vast, unprotected underbelly of northern Mexico. Under the decaying colonial rule of Spain, the Mexican authorities responded with wildly shifting policies, mixing retribution with appeasement, gift giving, and rewards that amounted to paying extortion. "The peace lasted only as long as the gift distributions did," writes Hämäläinen. With the outbreak of a revolt against Spain in 1810, the gift giving dried up—and the raiding resumed.

Rachel Plummer never said which band of Comanches she was held by—perhaps she never knew—but she and her captors were constantly on the move, never stopping for more than three or four days at a time except when the weather grew too raw for travel. They roamed from the stark alkaline flats of the Llano Estacado—the "Staked Plains"—in West Texas and New Mexico, north to the southeastern slopes of the Rocky Mountains, covered in snow even in July. Rachel, barefoot and lightly clothed, suffered terribly from the cold. She was enslaved to a small family consisting of a man, woman, and daughter, and her duties were to mind the horses, dress the buffalo skins, and perform other menial tasks. The two women beat her frequently.

She became an involuntary traveler through a world of primitive wonder. In her narrative she describes endless miles of salt plains, mirages of vast lakes, stunning mountains, and a wide range of animals, from elk, antelope, bears, wild mustangs, and wolves, to rumors of a man-tiger who looked like a human being, only taller, with huge paws and long claws instead of hands. The riverbanks were populated with turtles, deer, coyote, cattle ducks, geese, and slender gray cranes. The stars were as intense as candles, the moon so large it stretched across the night sky. "Its light turned the evening mist to a color like pearl," Texas native son Larry McMurtry would later write.

Rachel was four months pregnant when she was captured, and in October she gave birth to a baby boy. She pleaded with her older mistress to help her care for and protect the infant, but to no avail. At first the warriors left mother and baby alone. But as the child demanded more and more of her time, Rachel's work suffered. One cold morning when he was around six weeks old, a half dozen men surrounded her as she was breast-feeding him. While several of the men held her down, one took the baby by the throat and held tight until the infant turned blue and lost consciousness. Then the others took turns throwing him in the air and letting him fall on the hard ground. They handed the lifeless body back to Rachel, but when the baby began to breathe again they grabbed him one more time, tied a rope around his neck, and dragged the corpse for several hundred yards. "My little innocent was not only dead, but literally torn in pieces," Rachel would write in her narrative.

She took comfort in believing the child had gone to heaven. And she noticed a curious thing: even as she watched her son being murdered before her eyes, her tears ceased to flow; all she could manage were deep, dry sighs.

Rachel Plummer decided she was ready to die; indeed, so far as she was concerned, she was dead already.

ALTHOUGH SHE COULD NOT KNOW it at the time, Rachel's written account of her ordeal would become part of a long-standing American tradition. The captivity narrative was the country's first indigenous literary genre.

The first published account, Mary Rowlandson's 1682 narrative of the abduction of herself and her three children by Narragansett Indians from the Massachusetts village of Lancaster, became America's first homegrown bestseller. Rowlandson set the pattern. The early stories were both harrowing and redemptive. White women and their children were seized as spoils of war by dark-skinned savages who slaughtered their menfolk and pillaged their homes. The captives were spirited off to the untamed wilderness, where they faced a series of ordeals that tested their Christian faith. Usually they resisted barbaric depravity and eventually won their freedom and safe return to their families and communities. The Indians in these sagas served, in the words of cultural historian Richard Slotkin, as "the special demonic personification of the American wilderness."

The narratives reflected the intimate nature of the struggle between settlers and native peoples on the shores of the new world. Women and children were not merely collateral damage but primary targets, not prisoners of war but the spoils. Hundreds of white settlers were taken during captive by Indians during the colonial wars. Their stories of life among the natives fascinated, frightened, and repelled their fellow settlers.

There was an undercurrent of anxiety and ambiguity in the captivity narratives that was all about sex. Indian men were portrayed as the most hideous of creatures—dark, unclean, untamed, and rapacious—and to be raped by an Indian was a Fate Worse than Death. Faced with this horrific possibility, Mary Rowlandson writes that she had promised to kill herself rather than be abducted. When the time came, however, she could not go through with it. "Their glittering weapons so daunted my spirit that I chose rather to go along with those ravenous bears than that moment to end my days," she writes.

Rowlandson claims she was lucky: no one tried to rape her during her months of captivity. But few captives returned from their time with Indians unscathed either physically or emotionally. Fewer still were reabsorbed into white society without trauma—many died within the first year or two of their return to white civilization—and some of the children resisted returning at all. Mary Rowlandson's daughter married one of her captors and chose to remain with the Indians.

From Mary Rowlandson through the next century, true tales of Indian captivity dominated American bookshelves. But it was the novels of James Fenimore Cooper in the early nineteenth century that most openly focused upon the sexual obsession underlying the captivity narrative. In *The Last of the Mohicans* (1826), two beauteous sisters, Cora and Alice, are abducted by Huron Indians led by the treacherous chief Magua. He offers to release Alice, provided that Cora, the older sister, agrees to become his wife. Cora is a ravishing beauty—"the tresses of this lady were shining and black, like the plumage of the raven. Her complexion . . . appeared charged with the color of the rich blood that seemed ready to burst its bounds." She is deeply revolted by the horrifying prospect of having sex with Magua, no more so than when he stares at her with a lust so fierce "that her eyes sank with shame, under an impression that for the first time they had encountered an expression that no chaste female might endure." But Cora does not surrender. She tells Magua that she would rather die than become his wife.

At the time of the massacre at Parker's Fort, three of the nation's four biggest sellers were novels by Cooper—*The Last of the Mohicans*, *The Pathfinder*, and *The Deerslayer*, all of which featured captivity as an important plot element. The fourth was Everett Seaver's *A Narrative of the Life of Mrs. Mary Jemison*, the story of a young woman who was captured and absorbed into the Seneca Indian tribe in western New York. When her first Indian husband died, Jemison married another, had seven children and stayed with her adoptive tribe rather than return to white civilization. These books offered a more nuanced version than their literary forerunners of life with native peoples, who were no longer depicted as purely evil. But anxiety about the spiritual and physical pollution of sex with Indians remained a constant, if unspoken, theme in the conquest of the West.

WALLOWING IN SELF-JUSTIFICATION and hungry for vindication, James Parker left his own narrative of his search for the captives, fittingly titled *Perilous Adventures, Miraculous Escapes and Sufferings of the Rev. James W. Parker*. It is a ninety-page report of his trials and tribulations, packed with braggadocio and self-pity. But his account of his many failed expeditions to Indian Territory in search of the captive Parker children sounds authentic, if only because each episode inevitably ends in failure. Like so many storytellers, the real story James was telling was about himself.

After failing to raise a company of men for his rescue mission, James set out on his own for his first foray into Indian Territory. The eastern part of this semicharted zone had been designated by the federal government for the dispossessed tribes of Cherokees, Creeks, Choctaws, Chickasaws, and Seminoles who had been expelled from their homelands in the eastern United States; the western part was no-man's-land—wild, rugged, and lawless—where Comanches, Kiowas, and other hostile tribes roamed freely. The only whites who ventured there were traders, outlaws, and hunters prepared to risk their scalps for profit.

Boastful of his backwoods acumen, James undertook a solitary three-hundred-mile journey to Coffee's Trading Post on the Red River to see what he could find out about the captives. When he got there he heard that a white woman had been brought to another trading post sixty miles to the north. He constructed a raft with the help of a friend and crossed the Red River, leaving his horse behind. Traveling on foot inside Indian Territory in October with a hard rain pounding daily, James proceeded without food or sleep for three days. He reached his destination only to discover that the white woman wasn't Rachel. But the traders told him they had seen her at a Comanche camp yet another sixty miles away. They also told him they had heard that the Indians had killed her baby. "This intelligence kindled anew the flame that was raging in my breast," writes James, who makes clear his journey was as much about vengeance as it was about rescue.

For four days James followed the Comanche tracks, only to find that the Indians had already broken camp and recrossed the Red River into Texas. He was feverish, hungry, and parched, and he lived in constant fear of ambush. His clothes were drenched by a rainstorm, then frozen in a late-autumn blizzard. He writes that he barely avoided starvation by killing and roasting a skunk.

Frail, ill, and hungry, James finally abandoned the search. His travels on foot through Indian country had taken a total of two months. "The thought that I was so near my child drove sleep from my eyes," he wrote. ". . . I pursued my journey with little hope of being alive at night, or ever again beholding the face of a human being."

By mid-November James was back home, his fruitless journey ended. It was the first of many.

AMONG RACHEL PLUMMER's many labors as a captive, none was more important to her survival than the monthly quota of buffalo skins that she was required to tan. She would soak the hides to soften and clean them, stretch them out on a wooden frame, scrape them with a sharp tool, and massage them with a mixture of brains, bone marrow, and animal fat. The job kept her busy all day, every day, and into the night; she would take the skins with her in the evening when she took up her other duty: guarding the horses. "I dared not complain," she recalled.

Two to three million buffalo roamed Comancheria, floating across the High Plains like vast schools of giant, rumbling fish. "I have often seen the ground covered with them as far as the eye can see," Rachel would recall. Comanches hunted and killed the buffalo with far more reverence than they showed for most humans, honoring and giving thanks to the animal's spirit even while dismembering its body.

The dead bison provided food, hardware, clothing, and shelter. Each corpse belonged to the man who had killed it. One of the women in his household would make a quick slit under the belly to allow the steaming insides to cool and to minimize bloating, then pull out the stomach and intestines, which would be cleaned, stuffed with meat, and roasted. The hot, still-quivering raw liver was usually shared among wives and children, who wolfed it down immediately. The tongue was another delicacy; it would be boiled and saved for later. The front shoulders were removed at the joint, cut into thin slices, and spread along the grass or hung on poles to dry into jerky. The stomach lining was washed and used to carry water or as a cooking container. The bladder was inflated like a balloon and dried for use as a water canteen or to store food. The foot bone was separated from the foreleg and the metacarpal was used as a sharp fleshing tool. The sinew was stretched for string, thread, and straps. The hide was staked out, dried, and tanned for use as a teepee cover, clothing, robes, and blankets. The horn sheaths from the dried skull became drinking cups. The mashed brains were stirred into a paste to soften and waterproof the buffalo skin.

For T. A. "Dot" Babb, who was abducted by Comanches at age thirteen along with his nine-year-old sister, the taste of a dead bison calf's freshly ingested milk was so intense he could recall it fifty years later. A squaw split open the calf, scooped the milk from its stomach, and distributed it among her children. "It was the sweetest stuff I ever tasted, and was thick like our gelatin," he said.

The labor involved in rendering the dead beasts into useful products underscored a basic fact of Comanche life: men were dominant and women at all times subservient. Squaws would lace their babies tightly to cradle boards that they would strap to their backs each morning and set to work. The fresh buffalo skins could weigh up to one hundred pounds; women would carry or drag them to the campsite. "The squaws did all the manual labor and camp work generally, such as setting up or taking down and moving the teepees, carrying the wood and water, doing the cooking," wrote Babb. "They skinned and dried the buffalo meat, dressed the hides, and prepared all of the food, supplied the drinking water, moved the teepees, and in fact were the servants and menials of their lords in every manner of domestic work and service."

Rachel Plummer was treated in effect as the slave of slaves, at the service and mercy of her female masters. But after the murder of her baby boy, Rachel crossed a psychological boundary. Because she no longer wanted to live, she did not fear her captors. She became more brazen and more demanding.

One day in the Rockies she convinced her younger mistress to accompany her on an exploration of a nearby cave. After seeing the length and depth of the cavern, the girl became alarmed and insisted on going back, and when Rachel refused to leave the girl clubbed her with a piece of wood, Rather than submit, Rachel grabbed another piece of wood and knocked her mistress to the ground. Rachel ignored the girl's cries, warning her "that if she attempted again to force me to return until I was ready, I would kill her."

On another occasion Rachel and the girl were scavenging for edible roots when her mistress ordered Rachel back to camp for a digging tool. Rachel refused to go. When the girl attacked her, Rachel grabbed hold of a large buffalo bone and savagely beat the girl over the head. "I was determined, if they killed me, to make a cripple of her," she wrote. A group of Indians formed around them as they fought, and Rachel fully expected to be killed on the spot. No one touched her. She finally let go of the girl, who was bleeding profusely from the head. "A new adventure this . . ." Rachel would recall. To her surprise, "all the Indians seemed as unconcerned as if nothing had taken place. I washed her face and gave her water. She appeared remarkably friendly."

A chief took Rachel aside. "You are brave to fight," he told her. "She began with you, and you had a right to kill her. Your noble spirit forbid you."

The girl's mother was furious. She ordered Rachel to gather straw and it soon became clear she planned to use it to burn Rachel at the stake. But when the woman tried to tie Rachel's hands, Rachel knocked her down and pushed her into the fire. "As she raised, I knocked her down into the fire again, and kept her there until she was as badly burned as I was," Rachel wrote. She and the woman fought desperately, breaking through the side of the teepee and spilling outside where other Indians could see them. Once again, no one intervened.

The next day, twelve chiefs convened a tribunal and ordered Rachel and her two mistresses to appear before them to testify. Afterward, the chiefs ruled that Rachel needed to replace the broken teepee pole. She consented, provided the younger woman agreed to help. "This was made a part of the decree, and all was peace again."

BESIDES CLEANING AND TANNING buffalo hides, Rachel's other duty, just as essential to her Comanche owner's stature and prosperity, was to look after the horses each night.

Horses gave Comanches the mobility and the means to conquer their enemies and to kill vast numbers of buffalo, but they also created a huge labor problem: Comanches needed more and more workers, not only to tend to the vast new herds of horses, ponies, and mules, but also to render the buffalo into its various products. And the easiest way to get more workers was the same way Comanches obtained many of life's other necessities: they stole them.

Most of the captives were abducted from small defenseless villages in northern Mexico. One rough estimate suggested there were at least two thousand captives by the early 1800s. Besides their need for labor, the Comanches had another economic motive for abduction. Ever since the first exchanges between native peoples and Spanish authorities, trade in human beings had been part of the equation. Prisoners were taken as slaves but also held for ransom or to exchange for prisoners held by the other side. Humans became just one more commodity, and commodities were negotiable.

There were other, more sentimental reasons for abducting young people. Smallpox, cholera, and other diseases imported from the white world eventually wiped out entire Comanche villages and extended families. From a height of twenty thousand to thirty thousand in the late

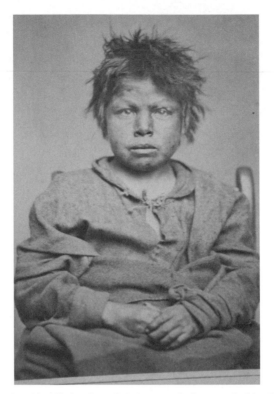

A Comanche captive, identified only as "Mexican Boy," photographed by Will Soule at Fort Sill, Oklahoma, in the early 1870s.

1700s, the Comanche population fell to below ten thousand by the 1830s. Comanche women were said to be prone to miscarriage. Child captives were one way to replenish the population and bring comfort to bereaved families.

While each captive's fate was different, certain patterns emerged. Comanche raiders kept those who were young and strong enough to be effective workers, and killed most of the others. Babies and small children who couldn't keep pace with the raiders who had carried them off, or who cried or caused any inconvenience to their captors, were casually dispatched in the same manner as Rachel Plummer's baby son.

The cruelty shown to Rachel by Comanche women was also not unusual. Dolly Webster and her two children were beaten and starved in their first days in captivity, and lacerated periodically by women who had painted themselves in black to mourn fifteen dead warriors. Another young girl taken from Grayson County, Texas, was forced to scrape and clean her own dead mother's scalp.

Sarah Ann Horn, an Englishwoman who was abducted by Comanches near the Rio Grande just weeks before Rachel Plummer, wrote her own harrowing account of life as a captive. She and her two young sons were taken in a raid in which her husband was clubbed to death in front of them. Sarah Ann described how the Indians continually dunked the boys, ages three and five, in a stream for their amusement. When Joseph, the younger of the two, slipped off a mule into the water and struggled to regain the shore, a warrior stabbed him in the face with a lance, sending him back into the foaming stream. Her captors, she concluded, were "trained, from infancy to age, to deeds of cruelty and bloodshed . . . They literally live by slaying and murdering all of man and beast that come in their way."

Yet at the same time, she noted, Comanches were exceedingly tender with each other. There was playfulness, humor, and a willingness to sacrifice all for a fellow tribesman. They loved their own children and indulged them endlessly, and never used corporal punishment.

Sarah Ann Horn had stumbled upon a fundamental paradox that would long puzzle outsiders who got a glimpse of Comanche life: How could a people be so solicitous of each other yet so cruel and brutal to others? "The strength of their attachment to each other, and the demonstration they give of the same, even to the dividing of the last morsel with each other upon the point of starvation, might put many professed Christians to the blush!" she wrote. "But they are just the reverse of all this to all the world outside."

Rape was a fact of life for many captives, although it was seldom discussed by those women who escaped or were ransomed back to the white world. Rachel Plummer's language in her written account leaves little doubt that she and Elizabeth Kellogg were gang-raped on their first night in captivity. "I would venture to assert [that] . . . no woman has, in the last thirty years, been taken prisoner by any wild Indians who did not, as soon after as practicable, become a victim to the brutality of every one of the party of her captors," wrote Colonel Richard Irving Dodge, who served throughout the Great Plains. T. R. Fehrenbach, the most widely read of modern Texas historians, echoed Dodge's words: "To the Plains tribes all females were chattels, and despite a great deal of studied delicacy on the subject, there was never to be a known case of white women captives who were not subjected to abuse and rape."

Recent historians have disagreed. Joaquin Rivaya-Martínez, a Texas State University scholar, collected and studied archival documents, ethnographic field studies, and other data on 350 kidnapped women, both Anglos and Mexicans, and found clear indications of sexual abuse in only nine cases. He conceded the evidence is spotty: those who recorded the contemporary accounts of these women may have omitted sexual episodes to protect the reputations of the victims, and many of the younger women may well have become the wives or concubines of their captors. The line between rape and coerced marriage was fuzzy, Rivaya-Martínez concluded. Still, he did not uncover any evidence suggesting that Comanches seized women for the explicit purpose of sexual gratification. Indeed, on the warpath, men would have shunned sex so as not to dilute their *puha*, or medicine.

Once removed from the battlefield, however, the men had no such fear. A captive woman could be considered the common property of an entire war party or of the man who captured her. Those like Rachel who were destined to be kept as slaves might be treated well enough to survive. Others were sexually violated and left to die. Geoffrey and Susan Michno, who compiled accounts of captives throughout the Great Plains, reported that of eighty-three women ages thirteen or older whose stories they studied, forty-eight were almost certainly raped and another twenty-nine probably were. "The sweeping generalizations by Dodge and Fehrenbach are overstatements—but only slightly," they write.

No matter what the numbers, it only took a few incidents of rape to terrorize Texas settlers and feed the legend of Indian rapacity and the notion that to be captured by Comanches was the classic Fate Worse than Death. Those women who returned to the white world were often closely scrutinized to see if their purity and moral standing had been compromised. Those who admitted they had submitted to the sexual demands of their captors in order to remain alive could find themselves shunned by husbands, friends, and relatives.

The more benign experience seemed to be that of abducted boys and girls between the ages of six and twelve. A team of modern psychologists could not have drawn up a more thorough method for absorbing a young person into the tribe. After being brutalized by his or her immediate captors and spirited north on a harrowing journey, the captive would be turned over to a family that oftentimes had lost a child of its own and treated the new addition with kindness and affection. Within a matter of months the young person would lose the ability to speak English, and memories of parents and families faded or were crowded out altogether by many kindnesses and new adventures.

* * *

COMANCHE ORAL TRADITION—handed down, buffed, and embellished over five generations—claims that nine-year-old Cynthia Ann Parker was taken to a village somewhere across the Red River, where she was adopted by a childless couple, bathed in a creek to wash off the blood, dirt, and fear, and taken into their home. Peta Nocona, the young warrior who was part of the raiding party at Parker's Fort, made a claim on her life and her labor; within a few years he would make her one of his wives. But Cynthia Ann herself left no oral or written account of her life as a Comanche. It's possible to draw conclusions from her actions, but not from her words.

There was another young girl, Dot Babb's sister Bianca, who was ten when she was abducted during the raid on her family farm, and her experience most likely closely paralleled that of Cynthia Ann. Bianca produced an unpublished memoir that is the only first-person Comanche captivity narrative by a young girl. Just as Cynthia Ann watched Indians kill her father, uncle, and grandfather, Bianca watched Indians shoot her mother in the back with an arrow, plunge a lance through her throat, and scalp her as she lay dying. After the raiders dragged a terrified Bianca from the farmhouse, she grabbed hold of a tree trunk and refused to let go even after an Indian pulled a long knife from his belt and threatened to cut her hands off. After several feints with the knife, he laughed and put it away, then "jerked me so hard that the rough bark on the post tore the flesh from the inside of my hands." Still, she pledged to herself not to cry—and the warrior who grabbed her told her later that if she had cried, he would have killed her on the spot. He threw her on the back of his horse and rode off with a band of raiders and two other captives: her older brother Dot, then fourteen, and Sarah Luster, a visitor to the house.

Mrs. Luster escaped one evening with Dot's help, after which the warriors struck him in the chest with a pistol. Dot refused to cry or beg for mercy. Next, they tied him to a tree and placed a ring of dead grass, leaves, and limbs around him and set them on fire. Still, he did not flinch. A terrified Bianca began to laugh hysterically, causing Dot to laugh as well. The warriors then aimed their bows and arrows at him. But their leader told them to put down their weapons. "They thought he was brave enough to make a good warrior, and decided not to kill him," Bianca recalled.

After a harrowing ten-day ride to the heart of Comancheria, Bianca was taken to a Comanche village. She was immediately surrounded by curious men, women, and children, most of whom had never seen a white girl before. With her fists and feet she fought off the friendly mob that pulled at her. The children stroked her long blonde hair. Even the camp's vast population of dogs "seemed to be as anxious to make my acquaintance." Her captor turned her over to his sister, Tekwashana, a childless young widow whose husband had been killed by whites. Tekwashana made Bianca a bed of dry grass, blankets, and buffalo robes on the floor of her teepee. On cold nights Tekwashana would stand Bianca in front of the fire and turn her around slowly until she was warm, then wrap her in a buffalo robe. Tekwashana dressed her in bracelets, earrings, and a headdress and taught her how to ride a horse, but also assigned her to fetch water, gather wood, and help move camp. "She was always very thoughtful of me and seemed to care as much for me as if I was her very own child," Bianca would recall.

That first night the Indians held a feast in her honor. They had a rare meal of bread and coffee with sugar. From the start, "I was made to know that my life was to be a regular Indian life," she wrote. ". . . Children came to play with me and tried to make me welcome into their kind of life." They named her Tijana—"Texas" in Comanche—although her nickname was "Smell Bad When You Walk" because she had soiled her clothing when she was first captured.

Tekwashana taught Bianca how to swim by letting go of her in the deepest part of the river. She made her adopted daughter a calico dress from a large piece of cloth without using a stitch; she pierced Bianca's ears with a red-hot needle, then adorned her in silver earrings with long silver chains that hung down to her shoulders. Mother and daughter would jump into the river, take off their dresses and rub them together, wring them out, and spread them on the bushes to dry while playing in the water.

Bianca's Comanches were not the grim warriors and harsh taskmasters of Rachel Plummer's harrowing narrative but simple people "of a jovial, happy disposition, always friendly and playing some kind of joke on the other fellow." Their children must have been exceptionally good, she wrote, because "in all the time I was with them I do not remember of seeing them correct or punish one."

"Every day," according to Bianca Babb, "seemed to be a holiday."

Seven months after Bianca was taken, a white scout named J. J. Sturm came to her village seeking to ransom her. Bianca, who could still recall her old life in Texas, told a stunned Tekwashana that she wanted to go back home with Sturm. Her adoptive mother "hung her head and would not talk to me."

That night Bianca slept outside the teepee on the side she knew Te-kwashana slept near. After Bianca fell asleep, however, Tekwashana carried her inside. Tekwashana gathered a pile of dried meat and water jugs and hatched a plan to flee with Bianca and stay away until Sturm gave up and left. An exhausted Bianca acquiesced. She quickly grew so tired that Tekwashana carried her on her back, but Sturm tracked them down the next day, put Bianca on the back of his horse, and rode off, leaving a brokenhearted Tekwashana to trail behind on foot.

Bianca Babb, who lived to be ninety-three, never saw her Comanche mother again.

3.

The Uncle (Texas, 1837–1852)

James Parker returned home from his fruitless search for the captives to a young Texas republic mired in chaos and bankruptcy. Steeped in debt, struggling for foreign recognition, facing ongoing tensions and intermittent eruptions with Mexico, uncertain borders and periodic outbreaks of violence with hostile native peoples, Sam Houston was struggling to keep his sprawling, improbable new country afloat. He had no inclination to supply James with men and money to launch a punitive rescue mission, despite steady pressure from the Reverend Daniel Parker, who used his political influence in the new capital on behalf of his younger brother. "No man can regret more sincerely than I do the misfortune which has taken place," Houston wrote to Daniel on February 13, 1837, referring to the massacre at Parker's Fort. But sympathy was one thing, money and men were another. Neither was forthcoming.

Still, James persisted. Later that month he journeyed back to Indian territory, posting a reward of $300 for the return of any white captive. After another false hope—the appearance of yet another freed white female captive who turned out not to be Rachel—James set out with a rifle, four pistols, a Bowie knife, pen and paper, and a small sum collected on a debt. He hatched a new scheme to stalk the Comanche camps and strew about written notes near watering places in the hope that Rachel would find one of them and meet him at a designated spot.

James and an unnamed companion rode for three days to Comancheria, then ran into trouble on their first night in hostile territory. Indians tried to steal their horses, and James fired his rifle and chased off the assailants. He and his sidekick didn't linger—they broke camp and rode all night to put distance between themselves and their attackers—but the next morning they rode into another ambush. A bullet grazed James's ear and cheek. He wheeled and shot one Indian with his rifle, then another, while his partner shot a third. The two men galloped away. There was no time, James would write with his trademark sarcasm, "to wish our three friends in ambush a comfortable rest and pleasant dreams."

His shaken partner headed home, but James kept going and finally managed to locate a Comanche camp. He spent weeks trying to make contact with Rachel. Sometimes he went for days without food, and his powers of reason seemed to fail him. He got nowhere—based upon Rachel's own narrative, it's not clear she was ever in the area—and after a month he gave up. He'd been gone from home this time for five months. The search was hardening into an obsession.

James journeyed to Houston City, the new capital. The young republic of Texas was like a traveling road show: it would set up shop, run up bills, wear out its welcome, then abscond to the next friendly town. Following this dubious pattern, it occupied five different capitals over the nine years of its existence. Houston was no city but rather a raw, mud-caked collection of cabins, tents, saloons, and a two-story, peach-colored, wood-framed capitol building. By one resident's reckoning, more than half the population of six hundred were gamblers and drunkards. President Houston received visitors in a log cabin of two rooms divided by an open passageway with a dirt floor—the kind of house known to settlers as a "dog trot." This was the executive mansion.

Sam Houston had long concluded that James Parker was not to be trusted, based not only on Houston's own experience but on the claims of others who had seen James in action. James himself referred to these claims in a June 1837 letter to Houston, bristling with misspellings and antagonism, that was both a heartfelt plea for aid and not-so-veiled bill of indictment. James in effect accused Houston of countenancing the murder of his daughter Rachel and the other captives by refusing to support his rescue efforts. "Calling me a fool and a mad man was entirely an unnecessary waste of time and paper, but the denying of any means to facilitate the release of the prisoners [my family] I really thought hard of," James wrote. He goaded the great man: "Will the nerve of the conquering hero of San Jacinto be still and let our bleeding fathers, mothers, brothers, sisters, and children cry in vain and offer no cheering or promising prospects of release or revenge[?]"

Somehow the letter worked. Houston authorized James to raise a company of 120 men and commanded him to go out and "flog those Indians." Even so, Houston cautioned James to discriminate between friend and foe. "The friendly Indians I hope will unite with us for the sake of spoils, and the pay which they are to receive for their services," he wrote.

But the truce did not last long. James and his company of volunteers, including his younger brothers Nathaniel and Joseph, spent more than a month combing the territory along the Red River for signs of the captives and terrorizing Indian villagers. Word of James's activities trickled back to Houston, who angrily ordered the unit disbanded. James insisted he was being falsely accused, but Houston ignored his protests.

Back on his own again, James made two more unsuccessful forays into Indian Territory in 1837 and bagged one more unsuspecting Native American. At a trading post near the Sabine River, he came across an Indian wearing an old yellow buckskin vest with buttons made out of gourds. James was certain it was one of his own garments from the cabin at Parker's Fort. When the Indian gave a vague account of how he had come by it, James grew more and more furious: "Every nerve of my system involuntarily trembled," he writes, as he thought of his slain father and brothers and the kidnapped children. He saw the Indian as "one of the authors of all my woe."

James instructed the men he was with to ride ahead. "As soon as the opportunity presented itself," he writes, "I mounted my horse, and taking a 'last fond look' at my vest—with one eye through the sight of my trusty rifle—I turned and left the spot, with the assurance that my vest *had got a new button hole*." After the shooting, other Indians attempted to grab his horse's bridle, but James fought his way through the mob, swinging his sword, and rode off after his companions.

This trip, James's fifth in eighteen months, ended like all of its predecessors. Sick, tired, and broke, he returned home empty-handed in late October. Then a few weeks later came a breakthrough. James saw a report in a Houston City newspaper: Rachel, it said, had turned up alive in Independence, Missouri.

MEXICAN TRADERS DOING BUSINESS with a band of Comanches somewhere in the foothills of the Rocky Mountains spotted a white woman with long red hair and offered to buy her, knowing they could redeem her for a good price from her relatives. After months of despair eating away at her spirit and her health like a relentless predator, Rachel suddenly came to life. One of the traders proposed a sum that her Comanche owner rejected as too low. The trader offered more, but the master again said no. The trader indicated he had reached his limit. Rachel's heart sank. "Had I the treasures of the universe, how freely I would have given it," she would recall. Then the man made a third offer and her owner consented. "My whole feeble frame was convulsed in an ecstasy of joy."

Her rescuers took her to Santa Fe—a rugged seventeen-day journey—and brought her to the home of William and Mary Donoho, American settlers in the territory, which was still ruled by Mexico. The Donohos paid off the traders and took in Rachel, who was suffering from exposure and malnutrition. They treated her with great kindness—in Mary Donoho, Rachel writes, she found "a mother to direct me in that strange land [and] a sister to condole with me in my misfortune." Santa Fe was a wild frontier town—four men had been gunned down in the streets in recent weeks—and William Donoho decided it was no longer safe for him and his family to remain. He and Mary packed up their three children, along with Rachel and Caroline Harris, another recently liberated captive whose baby, like Rachel's, had been killed before her eyes by Comanches. They organized a small caravan for the eight-hundred-mile trek east along the Santa Fe Trail to Missouri. Weakened and scarred from sixteen months in captivity, Rachel had to endure yet another grueling overland journey. She had no idea whether her husband or father or any of her relatives had survived the massacre at Fort Parker, nor whether her son James Pratt had been recovered. Once she got to Independence,

Comanche brave, photographed by Will Soule.

she was so starved for information that she immediately tried to start out on foot for Texas, and had to be restrained. She ached for a way to get home.

It was early January 1838 when Lorenzo Nixon, Rachel's brother-in-law, arrived in Independence. Overcome with emotion, Rachel was too weak to stand and embrace him. Still, she insisted they leave for Texas at once. "Every moment was an hour, and it was now very cold weather, but I thought I could stand anything if I could only get started towards my own country," she writes.

A few days later, they set out on the thousand-mile journey. Rachel arrived at her father's home in Huntsville on February 19, 1838, exactly twenty-one months after the massacre at Parker's Fort. In her narrative, she describes "the exquisite pleasure that my soul has long panted for" in embracing her family. But James Parker's spirited and robust daughter had been reduced to a fragile, uncertain creature. Her appearance was "most pitiable," he would write. "Her emaciated body was covered with the scars, the evidence of the savage barbarity to which she had been subject . . . She was in very bad health."

RACHEL'S HEALTH WAS ONLY ONE of James's pressing problems that winter. He was facing a whispering campaign of attacks on his character and his shady business dealings. Texas was an untamed and wide-open frontier society where swindles and gunplay were as much a part of the landscape as tumbleweed. But even by those rugged standards, James was a man apart. His anonymous accusers claimed he had secret dealings with Indians to steal horses from whites and had paid off the Indians with counterfeit money, angering the warriors and triggering the reprisal raid on Parker's Fort. Even worse, James was accused of killing a woman and her daughter during a botched robbery in 1837. Counterfeiting, horse theft, and murder were the kinds of accusations that could earn a man a perfunctory trial and the hangman's noose.

The accusers were not all anonymous. Late in 1838 James was accosted on the street in neighboring Montgomery by a local man named William W. Shepperd, who publicly repeated the accusations. James sued Shepperd for $10,000 for slander; Shepperd denied he had made the specific allegations. James applied to the court for a change of venue because "the prejudice existing at this time in the . . . said county . . . would prevent him from obtaining justice." The case never went to trial, but vigilantes came looking for James at his ranch house. He was away at the time, but the men warned his wife that "they would whip him and destroy the property," James wrote in a letter to Texas officials. He went into hiding and ordered his family to flee to his brother Joseph's home in Houston City, seventy miles away.

While many ransomed female captives found themselves the object of abuse and suspicion once they were returned to white society, there is no indication that Rachel's family treated her with anything but love and concern. She became pregnant soon after reuniting with her husband, Luther, and the unexpected journey to Houston City in midwinter was yet another physical ordeal for her. James joined his family there, and in January 1839 he published a five-page pamphlet denying the three main charges against him and proclaiming his innocence. "My success engendered malice in the hearts of some," he writes, "who, if they could not elevate themselves to my level, were determined to drag me down to theirs."

Although crammed into her uncle Joseph's house in Houston City, Rachel managed to complete a crisp, harrowing twenty-seven page account of her captivity. She outlined several goals in the preface, including the hope that readers would gain sympathy for captives and help campaign for their release. And she concluded with a premonition of her own fate, saying she was offering the following pages to the public "feeling assured that before they are published, the hand that penned them will be cold in death." The small book, which quickly sold out, confirmed Texans' worst fears about Comanche barbarism.

Rachel gave birth that same month to a boy, whom she and Luther named Wilson. But Rachel and her frail newborn were dying. She was still obsessed with the fate of her missing son James Pratt, who by now would have been four years old. "This life had no charms for her," her father writes. "Her only wish was that she might live to see her son restored to his friends." Crushed physically and emotionally by her long ordeal and haunted by her lost son, Rachel Plummer died on March 19, 1839. Wilson died two days later.

Spurred on by his dying daughter's last request, James continued the fruitless search for his grandson, nephew, and niece—James Pratt Plummer and John and Cynthia Ann Parker, now nearly three years in captivity. He formally applied for guardianship of all four of Silas and Lucy's children in 1840, including "John Parker and Sinthy Ann Parker supposed to be among the Comanche Indians." But he had other ambitions as well. That same year he traveled to the new Texas capital in Austin with a wild scheme to raise an army of four thousand men to invade New Mexico, which was still under Mexican control, capture Santa Fe, forge a treaty with local Indians, and take control of the Santa Fe Trail. The legislators, who were focused on more pressing concerns, paid no attention.

WHILE JAMES PARKER WAS WAGING his personal crusade against Indians, the Republic of Texas was locked in an increasingly savage war with Comanches and other tribes. Sam Houston's good-neighbor policy had produced at best a fragile peace that was constantly shattered by raiding parties and retaliation. West Texas was a lawless battleground where Comanches and Rangers regularly ambushed each other and settlers lived in constant fear of Indian attack. Houston left office in December 1838, replaced by Mirabeau Lamar, a popular hard-liner who advocated expulsion of the Cherokees and other purportedly peaceful tribes in eastern Texas and a war of extermination against the Comanches and Kiowas in the west. "If the wild cannibals of the woods will not desist from their massacres, if they continue to war upon us with the ferocity of tigers and hyenas, it is time that we should retaliate their warfare," Lamar proclaimed in his opening address to the Texas Congress in December 1838. He was not a man for half measures when it came to Indians. The goal, he said, was "their total extinction or total expulsion."

What had started as a tit-for-tat struggle over horse thievery and hunting rights was quickly evolving into the most protracted conflict ever waged on American soil, a forty-year blood feud between two alien civilizations. Neither side believed the other was fully human. Comanches saw the Texans as invaders without conscience who occupied their lands, destroyed their hunting grounds, and broke every promise. Texans saw Comanches as human vermin, brutal, merciless, and sadistic.

Still, despite the huge gap in their experiences and consciousness, Indians and settlers were intimate enemies. When they waged war against each other, they killed with rifles, pistols, tomahawks, and bows and arrows—at close range, often while looking into the faces of their victims. There were no boundaries or rules and no noncombatants. It was truly a war of populations: destroying a man's family was as important as killing the man himself. Part of any victory was to inflict the maximum amount of suffering and humiliation on the other side.

"The savage wars of peace"—Rudyard Kipling's phrase from his jingoistic poem "The White Man's Burden," the literary battle cry of racial imperialism—could only end in the extermination of one race or the other. Hence the centrality of attacks on women and children: the object was to destroy the enemy through the murder of his family or to corrupt his seed through captivity and rape.

Texans used the term "depredations" to describe Comanche atrocities. In the Texan view, this was not warfare as practiced by civilized men but rather a form of depraved, predatory attack by wild beasts. The only possible solution was to cage or kill the perpetrators.

Comanches were not the only targets. Lamar and the hard-liners saw the more peaceful, domesticated tribes of East Texas as equally culpable. When the Cherokees resisted the government's order that they "voluntarily" remove themselves from their farms and villages, Lamar's troops conducted a two-day campaign of slaughter and pillage in the summer of 1839, driving out the Indians and torching their homes and fields. The Cherokee defenders, outnumbered three to one, put up tough resistance, but the Texans killed eighteen and wounded one hundred. The elderly Cherokee leader, Chief Bowles, an old friend of Sam Houston's, greeted the invaders dressed in a brightly colored coat and hat and special cane that Houston had given him. The chief refused to abandon his village, was wounded by the Texans in the attack, and sat down in front of a cooking fire. A Texan put a pistol up against the old man's ear and blew out his brains. The Texans left the body to rot in the open, where twenty years later the bones were still bleaching in the sun.

The troops proceeded to blaze a trail of destruction throughout the region, burning out villages of Cherokees, Delawares, Shawnees, Caddos, Kickapoos, Creeks, and Seminoles. The Indians fled north across the Red River into what is now Oklahoma; white settlers quickly took their place. Revisionist historians have characterized these campaigns as exercises in ethnic cleansing. Despite the emotionally charged context, it's a hard label to refute.

IN THE VICIOUS STRUGGLE between Texans and Comanches, abductions became the abiding fault line. There was no chance for peaceful coexistence so long as Comanches held white captives, and they never grasped the deep cultural, religious, sexual, and racial hatred that kidnapping Texan women and children aroused. Texans quickly came to see Indians as subhuman in large part because of the seemingly casual cruelty with which they treated captives.

Still, the ransoms that the Texans paid out for the return of their loved ones served to encourage more abductions. And the Comanches couldn't help but notice that the more abused the victims looked, the more willing the Texans seemed to be to buy them back.

By 1840 both sides were exhausted from the conflict and even Governor Lamar entertained the possibility of accommodation. But the return of all white captives was a nonnegotiable precondition for a truce. With this in mind, Texan officials invited Comanche leaders to a peace conference in San Antonio in mid-February and told them they could have a treaty provided they returned all of their white prisoners. As an insurance policy, the Texans quietly arranged to have three companies of infantrymen waiting in the wings.

This was the moment when two alien civilizations collided. It was if the laws of physics had overcome whatever good intentions might have existed and pushed both sides into disaster.

Decked out in an exotic array of buckskin breechclouts, red jackets, blue trousers, and great eagle-feather bonnets—the Comanche equivalent of formal wear—a dozen chiefs paraded to the main plaza in San Antonio with fifty of their warriors, women, and children on March 19, 1840. The chiefs sat themselves on the floor of the small Council House in the heart of the plaza, not far from the ruins of the Alamo. They brought with them only one white captive, fifteen-year-old Matilda Lockhart. She had been taken in a raid two years earlier, along with her younger sister. Matilda, in keeping with the Comanche sense of what kind of captive made the most effective impression on white people, was thoroughly disfigured.

"Her head, arms, and face were full of bruises and sores, and her nose actually burnt off to the bone—all the fleshy end gone, and a great scab formed on the end of the bone," recalled Mary A. Maverick, one of San Antonio's first ladies. "She told a piteous tale of how dreadfully the Indians had beaten her, and how they would wake her from sleep by sticking a chunk of fire to her flesh, especially to her nose, and how they would shout and laugh like fiends when she cried. Her body had many scars from before, many of which she showed us. Ah, it was sickening to behold, and made one's blood boil."

Matilda told the Texans that the Indians were holding some fifteen other captives outside of town, hoping to bargain for each one individually. When the angry Texans demanded the return of the other captives, Chief Muguara, leader of the Penateka band, responded that they were safe but that he himself only had custody of Matilda. He said the other captors were expecting blankets, firearms, and booty in exchange for their human prizes. This made perfect sense to him, and he concluded his oration with a simple, innocent question: "How do you like that answer?"

All of which further enraged the Texans. In a pre-rehearsed maneuver, they summoned the waiting soldiers. One company of troops surrounded the building while another marched inside the room. The Texans decided to hold Muguara and his fellow chiefs until the Comanches produced the other captives. The Texans' interpreter, himself a former captive, was too terrified at first to convey the threat. When the officials insisted, he delivered their message in Comanche and immediately fled the room. The chiefs, stunned at such a flagrant violation of the sanctity of the peace council, rose to their feet. When a sentinel blocked his path, Muguara pulled a knife and stabbed the guard, after which the eleven other warriors surged forward and tried to fight their way out of the chamber. Soldiers stationed along the walls and at the windows cut loose with a thundering volley of rifle fire, transforming the tight little room into an acrid slaughterhouse reeking of flesh, blood, smoke, and gunpowder. All of the chiefs were killed. Soldiers in the courtyard opened fire on the Comanches outside, killing at least a dozen more, mostly women and children. Seven whites died as well, including a visiting judge who was shot in the heart by an arrow fired by one of the Comanche children.

The surviving warriors careened down the streets of San Antonio in terror past equally terrified residents. Soldiers followed in hot pursuit. *"Here are Indians! Here are Indians!"* Mary Maverick screamed to her brother-in-law, who pulled out a gun and shot two of the Comanches. Another Indian tried to grab the reins of Army captain Lysander Wells's horse. The two men grappled for a grim moment, swaying from side to side, until Wells managed to draw his pistol and shoot the Indian dead at point-blank range.

All of the sixty-five or so Indians who had ridden into San Antonio, including women and children, were either killed or captured. The Texans released the wife of one of the slain chiefs and sent her to the Comanche encampment with the message that the Texans would free the other prisoners when the Indians returned their remaining white captives. But when the woman reached the camp and described what had happened, the Comanches went into frenzied mourning, weeping and cutting themselves with knives. Then they turned their attention to their captives. With remorseless precision, they staked out and slowly butchered thirteen people, sparing only two young children who had been adopted into the tribe.

Stunned by the killing of their most cherished elders, the Comanches fled north. But after a period of mourning, they plotted their revenge. Under the leadership of Buffalo Hump, the last surviving Penateka chief, an invading army of some four hundred warriors and their families managed to slip undetected into the region in August. They struck first at Victoria, a small farming town at the bottom of the Guadalupe valley, killing a half dozen farmers and field hands and laying siege to the village. The settlers held them off overnight and the next day the raiders swerved east. In each town along the way they surprised inhabitants who had never anticipated such a brazen attack. In one, they seized a woman named Nancy Crosby, said to be the granddaughter of the great frontiersman Daniel Boone, killed her baby, and hauled her off on horseback. Eventually they reached the port town of Linnville. Most of the residents managed to reach the village dock and fled on boats into the Gulf of Mexico. They watched from offshore as the raiders sacked the town, pillaged shops and warehouses, and set them ablaze. The Indians rounded up cattle and slaughtered them, tied feather beds and bolts of fabric to horses, and dragged them around the streets. John J. Linn, a merchant and town father, recorded in a memoir how the warriors pulled from his warehouse several cases of hats and umbrellas belonging to James Robinson, a San Antonio merchant. "These the Indians made free with, and went dashing about the blazing village, amid their screeching squaws and 'little Injuns,' like demons in a drunken saturnalia, with Robinson's hats on their heads and Robinson's umbrellas bobbing about on every side like tipsy young balloons," he wrote.

Finally, the Comanches pulled out of the town, hauling their plunder on pack mules. Swathed in stolen clothing, men's and women's, the raiders herded some three thousand horses and perhaps a dozen captives. Twenty-three settlers had been killed, including eight black slaves and servants. Among the dead was Mrs. Crosby, speared through the heart. But the vast array of booty slowed down the retreating raiding party, as did the women and children who trailed behind. A combined force of citizen volunteers and Texas Rangers caught up to the Indians at Plum Creek, in the vicinity of the present-day Lockhart, and dealt them a major defeat. At least fifty warriors were killed and the surviving Indians abandoned most of their plunder and ran.

After Plum Creek, Lamar dispatched Colonel John Moore and a column of men to Comancheria to wreak their own special vengeance. They rode up the Colorado River toward the edge of the Staked Plains until they came across a Comanche camp of some sixty lodges. Moore had his men stampede the Indians' horses so that they had no escape. Then he positioned a group of riflemen overlooking the river's edge. When he finally attacked the camp, the warriors fled into the water and the riflemen opened fire. They shot at everything that moved and kept shooting until nothing did—resulting in a death toll of perhaps 130 Comanches. "The bodies of men, women, and children were to be seen on every hand, wounded, dying and dead," Moore reported back to Austin, betraying no hint of shame.

The Council House Massacre, the subsequent Comanche invasion of white settlements, and the aftermath marked the last time Comanches and Texans fought as armies on somewhat even terms. What's important to note is that the flashpoint here, as in so many of the spasms of violence that followed, was captives.

FOLLOWING THE LINNVILLE RAID, most Comanches retreated into the forbidding upper reaches of Comancheria. But other non-Comanche tribes saw advantages in cutting deals with the Texans. In May 1842, General Zachary Taylor, the new commander of Fort Gibson in the eastern sector of Indian Territory, held a peace conference with various tribes and urged them to bring in their captives. Three months later a party of Kickapoo Indians returned with James Pratt Plummer, now seven years old, whom they said they had purchased from the Comanches for $400. About a month later a Delaware Indian brought in thirteen-year-old John Parker. The two cousins, both of whom spoke only Comanche, exulted in each other's company.

James Parker first heard rumors of the boys' release, and then saw a newspaper report. He started out for Fort Gibson three days before Christmas, arriving three weeks later. After seven years with the Comanches, both boys had been thoroughly Indianized, although James claimed that the backs of both of them were covered with scars, "evidence . . . of the free exercise of savage barbarity." James was stunned by his red-haired grandson's resemblance to his late daughter Rachel. James Pratt, "learning that I had come after him, ran off, and went to the Dragoon encampment, about one mile from the garrison," James wrote. "Poor child, how my heart bled, when he thus avoided me . . . [H]e was incapable of appreciating my kind intentions toward him."

It took two hours of painful conversation through an interpreter for

James to explain to his grandson how they were related. James Pratt asked if he had a mother. "I told him he had not, as she had died," James recalled. "He then asked if he had a father. I told him he had . . ."

James Pratt Plummer agreed to accompany his grandfather back to Texas.

But James Parker, showing again his trademark egotism, turned what should have been a joyous reunion into a vituperative family feud. He refused to turn over James Pratt to the boy's father, Luther Plummer, claiming Plummer owed him repayment of ransom money and a share of his expenses for his many journeys to Indian Territory. When Plummer wrote to Sam Houston to complain, the Texas president replied with a stinging condemnation. For all his own problems with James, Houston wrote, he never suspected James would behave in such an ugly fashion. "It evinces a degree of heartlessness totally incompatible with the common feelings of humanity," Houston told Plummer in an April 1843 letter. Houston committed the government of Texas to cover the entire cost of the ransom. "You will, therefore, take your child home," Houston wrote. "Mr. Parker has not the shadow of right to detain him, and by so doing is not only laying himself under the imputation of extreme brutality, but is subjecting himself to the penalties of law."

James's career as a Baptist clergyman was no less turbulent. In 1841 he was excommunicated from his local church after congregants accused him of dishonesty, and three followers split off with him to form a new church. Two years later, one of his supporters, Susan Tinsley, accused him of lying about the amounts of ransom he had paid out for his relatives and other captives, of slander, fraud and of "holding correspondence with suspicious characters." James was excluded from the new church.

While James played the role of searcher, avenger, and angry paterfamilias, his older brother Daniel stuck to preaching. Under the Texas constitution, ministers were not allowed to serve in the legislature; still, Daniel wielded political influence throughout the early days of the republic. He founded at least nine Baptist churches in Texas under the "Union Association of the Regular Baptists," and prided himself on his stamina, regularly preaching four-hour marathon sermons into his sixties. In August 1844, at the relatively advanced age of sixty-three, he undertook a grueling trip to visit some of the churches, but had to cut it short when he fell ill. "My time is at hand and I must be offered up," he said. "I do not the least dread it. My Master calls. I long to obey."

Even on his deathbed, his son John wrote, Daniel was still focused on the weaknesses of mankind. He "lamented that thear was many of the deer Lambs of Jesus who was blinded by the cunning craftiness of wicked men that lie in wait to deceive." Daniel died on December 3 and was buried the next day "amid . . . cryes and tears from his numerous friends."

JAMES PARKER CONTINUED TO SEARCH for Cynthia Ann. When he heard of a young white woman who had been freed from Indian captivity in Missouri, he journeyed north again in vain. Afterward, he wrote a letter to the *Texas National Register*, describing the girl so that her relatives might recover her. "I wish to make this public, because I know from experience the anxiety of the bereaved, and wish as far as lies in my power, to alleviate distress," he declared. For all his braggadocio, James had a heart.

Still hungry for vindication, he published his ninety-page narrative that same year. He appended at the end of it a new edition of Rachel's tale as well, with the clear aim of garnering more admiration and readers for his own dubious story by connecting it with that of his more sympathetic daughter. It's clear that James edited Rachel's text to suit his own needs. The second edition makes no mention of Rachel's husband Luther, who by 1844 held a prominent place on James's long list of enemies.

After Daniel's death, James became involved in the workings of his older brother's Pilgrim Regular Predestinarian Baptist Church, formally joining the congregation in May 1845 and seeking ordination to preach at an affiliated congregation. It is clear from church records that he hoped to take Daniel's place as leader, but equally clear that the congregation was wary of this obsessed and ambitious man. A January 1846 note records a private letter from a congregant urging the church to delay James's ordination and stating, "Brother JW Parker informd the church that he had got angry and had even come very near shooting a man."

By October, the elders appeared even more concerned, although reluctant to totally part ways with the brother of their late revered leader. While the church's ruling body proclaimed James's virtues, it added "that we believe the church has bin and continues to be unjustly implecated on his account as well we believe that Bro Parker['s] reputation has as unjustly bin assailed by those calling themselves Baptists and we believe Bro Parkers usefulness has greatly bin destroid by this unlawful course."

James never did achieve ordination. In February 1851 he was accused of "using intoxicating spirits to too great an excess." One month later he was excommunicated. It was the last time his name was mentioned in the minutes of Pilgrim Church—or in any other public document. James Parker's recorded life was over, and so apparently was his search for Cynthia Ann. Perhaps his health did not allow him to continue. Or perhaps the fact that by now his niece was a woman in her twenties and surely the wife or concubine, voluntary or not, of a Comanche warrior caused James to lose interest in finding her. Unlike his fictional counterpart a century later, James Parker would search no more.

4.

The Rescue (Pease River, 1860)

A key moment in many melodramatic captivity narratives was the sighting of the innocent abductee by her would-be rescuers. In an all-too-brief encounter, the rescuers discover that the victim is a lost soul beyond the reach of civilization, condemned to remain in the clutches of depraved savagery.

So it was with Cynthia Ann Parker over the years as she grew from a little girl into a young woman. While James Parker never succeeded in finding his abducted niece, others did. Their accounts of who she had become and why they failed to secure her release do not get us very far in establishing the truth of her life and times as an Indian woman. But the stories do reveal a lot about white attitudes toward female captives and Comanches.

A retired army colonel and Indian agent named Leonard Williams first reported seeing her among Comanches camped along the Canadian River in 1846. Williams sought to purchase her release but was told the Comanches would fight rather than surrender her. He was allowed to speak to her, but she refused to answer questions, even when he pleaded with her to send a message through him to her family. He claimed that her lips quivered and she fought to control her emotions, and he speculated that she had been warned not to talk to him and was afraid of "future bad treatment" by her captors if she did. A report in the *Clarksville Northern Standard* says "she continued to weep incessantly" during his visit. Williams finally fled the encampment after being warned by a tribal elder that the younger warriors were planning to kill him.

Cynthia Ann was nineteen at the time—of marriageable age. By custom Peta Nocona, her supposed abductor, owned the right to wed her.

We do not know when nor why, but according to Comanche oral tradition he chose to make her one of his wives. Even this claim—one of the crucial parts of the legend of Cynthia Ann—is not beyond challenge, as we'll see.

Pierce M. Butler and M. G. Lewis, two federal Indian commissioners who forged a series of peace treaties with Native American bands in North Texas, reported to Congress their version of Williams's visit, which was likely closer to the truth but far less comforting for those seeking to redeem the fair damsel from savagery. They concluded that she had no wish to be rescued. Their scouts had seen her "on the head of the Washita [River]." By now she was married, and it was clear to the commissioners that "from the influence of her alleged husband, or from her own inclination, she is unwilling to leave the people with whom she associates." Although a large amount in cash and goods was offered for her release, they reported, "she would run off and hide herself to avoid those who went to ransom her."

Cynthia Ann's Comanche name was Naudah—"Keeps Warm with Us." She spoke Comanche as well as a bastardized form of Spanish, but had shed her English like a layer of dead skin. Her light-colored face and blond hair had grown dark from dirt, grease, and paint. Her body had become heavy and callused from a steady diet of buffalo meat and a life of demanding physical labor.

While Williams and the Indian commissioners make no mention of children, sometime between the mid-1840s and the early 1850s Naudah must have given birth to her first child. The birth process was a communal event for Comanches, overseen by the women elders while the men stayed far away. The women set up the pregnant woman in her own lodge, with a floor of soft earth. They dug two pits, one for heating water and the other for the afterbirth, and they drove four-foot-long stakes into the ground that the mother-to-be could grip during childbirth. A medicine woman baked rocks and sage, creating an aromatic steam. After the baby was born, the women launched into a joyful chant. Even childbirth was an occasion for storytelling and omens. The medicine woman cut the umbilical cord and hung it in a hackberry tree. If the cord was left undisturbed until it rotted, the child would enjoy a long, happy life. The medicine woman would fling the afterbirth into a running stream, while the newborn would be wrapped in soft rabbit skins and placed in a cradle board.

Cynthia Ann's firstborn was a boy. Just as his birthdate is uncertain, so is his birth name. It may have been Tseetah, meaning "Eagle," or it may have been Quanah, meaning "Sweet Smell"—one Comanche legend claims he was born in a bed of wildflowers. Soon there would be a second boy named Pecos, and several years later a girl they would name Topsannah or Totsiya, meaning "Prairie Flower."

There were other, more fanciful sightings of the white Comanche. Victor M. Rose, a Texas newspaperman, and entrepreneur, would report that a party of white hunters, including friends of the Parkers, had seen her at a Comanche encampment on the upper Canadian River curling into modern-day New Mexico around 1851. By then, Rose claimed, she had two sons. When the hunters asked her to leave with them, he wrote, "She shook her head in a sorrowful negative, and pointed to her little, naked barbarians sporting at her feet, and to the great, greasy, lazy buck sleeping in the shade near at hand, the locks of a score of scalps dangling at his belt, and whose first utterance upon arousing would be a stern command to his meek, pale-faced wife." She told the hunters, "I am happily wedded. I love my husband, who is good and kind, and my little ones who, too, are his, and I cannot forsake them!"

It's a fine but unlikely quote, impossible to verify. Rose offered this account in the 1880s, many years after the fact, never naming his sources. He himself was eleven years old when the encounter purportedly took place. None of which has prevented subsequent historians from citing it as truth. It snugly fit white sensibilities, if not the facts.

Even Cynthia Ann's brother John reputedly failed to persuade her to return to her white family. U.S. Army colonel Randolph B. Marcy reported meeting John while conducting an expedition up the Red River in 1852. John told Marcy that his mother had sent him back to the Comanches to make contact with Cynthia Ann and bring her home. "She refused to listen to the proposition," Marcy reported, "saying that her husband, children, and all that she held most dear, were with the Indians and there she should remain."

After his encounter with Marcy, John Parker's own trail grows cold. Like many former captives, John had trouble readjusting to white civilization, and according to legend he eventually rejoined a Comanche band. The story goes that he was wounded in a raid and left behind, but another Comanche captive, a young Mexican woman, nursed him back to health and fell in love with him. The couple crossed the Rio Grande and settled on a ranch in Mexico, where they lived a long and happy life. It is a romantic and optimistic fable. Cynthia Ann, by contrast, later told relatives she had heard that John had died of smallpox just a few years after their abduction.

In truth, the white world, despite tantalizing glimpses of Cynthia Ann, did not know where she was and could not reach her. "She seemed to be separated from her own people as effectively as if she had been transported to another continent," wrote the Texas historian Rupert N. Richardson.

Still, in all the witness accounts, reliable or fanciful, one thing was clear: Cynthia Ann Parker had become a Comanche.

BY THE END OF 1852 the army had established seven new outposts in strategic locations around North and West Texas. The forts—most of them so makeshift they barely deserved the name—were designed to form a protective ring around white settlements, but each attracted even more settlers, who felt safer under its flimsy shadow. The pioneers inevitably homesteaded well beyond the zone of protection, making tempting targets for Comanche raiders. The cavalry, stretched thin, poorly supplied, underpaid, and caught between hostile entities, proved incapable of preventing each side from slaughtering or abducting the women and children of the other. Into the security vacuum, the state legislature reconstituted and injected the Texas Rangers and volunteer companies who functioned as vigilantes and saw it as their mission to either drive the Indians from the frontier or wipe them out.

The savage war of peace between Texans and Comanches was now in full destructive bloom, a violent adolescent tearing at its own flesh.

In January 1858 the legislature authorized Governor H. G. Runnels to expand the Texas Rangers by an additional one hundred men. The man he chose to lead the new unit was John Salmon "Rip" Ford, a veteran politician, newspaper editor, and Indian fighter. Ford joined forces with Shapley Prince Ross, an Indian agent from Waco. They mounted a force of 102 Rangers and 113 Indian allies and set out north in April. A few weeks later they caught up to a large camp of Comanches on the Canadian River at the edge of Indian Territory. Iron Jacket, a medicine man of renown, came forward to greet them waving a white flag and wearing his trademark breastplate of Spanish armor. A Texan rifleman took aim and shot him in the head. Then the Rangers charged the camp. Many women and children were killed, as Ford himself laconically conceded. "It was not an easy matter to distinguish Indian warriors from squaws," he offered by way of justification.

The next targets were the two Indian reservations established in northern Texas under federal protection. Settlers and their leaders claimed that hostile Indians were using both as launching pads for raids and depredations. Led by John S. Baylor, a former Indian agent who championed the extermination of any Indian who dared step foot in Texas, settlers organized guerrilla bands that attacked Indian villages at night with the same vicious brutality of Comanche raiders. Six white men were arrested for killing seven Indians while they slept, but were released after the authorities concluded that no court in Texas would convict them. Baylor threatened to attack any soldiers who stood in his way. His former boss and nemesis, Robert Neighbors, who infuriated the settlers because he sought to protect the reservation Indians, was finally compelled to organize the expulsion of all the tribesmen to Indian Territory north of the Red River in September 1859. Upon his return, Neighbors was shot in the back at close range on a street in Fort Belknap by a settler. Few Texans mourned his demise.

The expulsions did nothing to quell the violence or the state of panic that gripped settlers by the fall of 1860. The pioneers may have had history and progress on their side, but neither provided any protection when Comanche raiders showed up at their doorstep. Their fear, anger, and sense of desperation were captured in the pages of the *White Man* newspaper, published in Weatherford by Baylor, who railed against both the Army and the Rangers. A typical article in September 1860 reported that the roads of northern Texas were choked with settlers fleeing the region. "The federal government has displayed a cold indifference to our condition that would do credit to the Czar of Russia," opined the newspaper.

The Rangers always seemed one day late and one step behind. B. F. Gholson, a ranch hand who served for a time as a Ranger, recalled trailing a band of Indians through the Nones Valley. The Rangers came across a man's body, pierced like a pincushion with dozens of arrows, and five hundred yards away a small wagon with the body of a seven-year-old boy, the dead man's son, "with both eyes shot out and his throat cut, lying on his back." A short distance farther was his mother's mangled corpse. "The throat had been cut and the head scalped . . . and two large wounds were made with a knife in her left side, near her heart. Her body was horribly mutilated and she had been raped."

Perhaps the worst moment came that November when a raiding party of some fifty Kiowas and Comanches rampaged through the rolling limestone plains of four counties in Northeast Texas, killing at least six settlers, five of them women. The Indians attacked the Sherman homestead in Parker County, raping, torturing, and scalping Martha Sherman, a pregnant mother of two, who lingered for three days before dying. Then they killed a woman and her husband at the Lynn homestead along the Upper Keechi River. When Charles Goodnight, a young Ranger scout, got to the Lynn house, he walked in on the dead woman's father. The man was hunched over "a large log fire in the old-fashioned fireplace with a long forked dogwood stick on which was an Indian scalp thoroughly salted. The hair was tucked inside. As he turned it carefully over the fire, the grease oozed out of it, and it had drawn up until it looked as thick as a buffalo bull's scalp. As I entered he looked back over his shoulder and bid me good morning, and then turned to his work of roasting the scalp. I don't think I ever looked at so sad a face."

Goodnight and a local posse attempted to track down the raiders. They came back reporting they had located a large encampment of Comanches along the Pease River to the north.

The task of pursuing them fell to Lawrence Sullivan Ross, Shapley's son, a fresh-faced, energetic, and supremely ambitious twenty-two-year-old rancher from Waco. He had been commissioned as a captain in the Texas Rangers by Sam Houston, who had recently returned to the governor's mansion after thirteen years in the U.S. Senate. Sul Ross was described by fellow Ranger James Thomas Pollard as "a fine horseman and a good shot and was not afraid of anything except a rattlesnake." But Ross was not well loved by local settlers, who viewed him as too sympathetic to the reservation Indians.

Ross, mindful that his own reputation and that of the Rangers as Indian fighters were none too high, declared his intention "to curb the insolence of these implacable hereditary enemies of Texas" and to "carry the war into their own homes." His unit of twenty Rangers joined forces with some seventy volunteer militiamen under Captain Jack Cureton and twenty troopers of the Second Cavalry under First Sergeant John W. Spangler. Together, they set out for the Pease River.

It was bitter cold and raining hard when Ross got word at sunset on December 18 that Comanches were camped a few miles up the river, along a small freshwater stream called Mule Creek, just south of what is now the Texas-Oklahoma border. Ross and Spangler drove their men all night. Cureton's volunteers had to stop when their horses became exhausted; Ross and Spangler pressed on. At daybreak on the nineteenth the Rangers and the troopers reached a ridge above the encamp-

L. S. ROSS.

Lawrence Sullivan "Sul" Ross: Indian fighter, Confederate general, governor of Texas, and self-proclaimed rescuer of Cynthia Ann Parker at the Pease River massacre of December 1860.

ment. The Comanches appeared to be dismantling teepees and packing up to leave.

Ross and Spangler knew their cold, bone-weary men and their spent horses would not be able to keep pace with the Indians. They couldn't wait for the volunteers to catch up. If they were going to attack, they needed to do it now.

Spangler, using cover from a chain of sand hills, took his men around the far side of the camp to cut off a retreat. Ross's men advanced over the ridge. He promised a pistol and holster to the first man to present him with an Indian scalp. Then he gave the order to charge.

THE BATTLE OF PEASE RIVER is one of those violent episodes in Texas history where fact and legend collide uneasily, leaving later generations to grope for the truth amid contradictory claims and shifting sensibilities. Sul Ross and his admirers—most notably James T. DeShields, an amateur historian whose book recounting the battle twenty years later became the definitive account—portrayed the battle as a glorious triumph for a small, intrepid band of Rangers who used the element of surprise and their own innate courage to overcome a much larger force. As Ross set out a decade later to build a political career, he and his supporters inflated his exploits at the Pease River in size and character.

The detailed but highly embroidered memories of B. F. Gholson, who was likely not even at the battle, supported the DeShields-Ross version. Meanwhile, Ross's critics, who emerged more gradually over the years, characterized the battle as a massacre of old men, women, and children.

One enduring dispute was over the size of the Comanche encampment that morning. DeShields claimed there were between 150 and 200 warriors at the site. But many of the witnesses said the camp consisted of a small band of Comanche women, servants, and old men busily preparing buffalo meat and hides for the harsh winter ahead. A hunting party was out killing buffalo, and the camp followers trailing behind had set about butchering the dead animals, drying meat, and curing skins along the riverbank. Ross himself in his original report said the camp consisted of nine grass huts. It was in effect an on-site work crew engaged in the kind of drudgery that most Comanche warriors studiously avoided.

No matter. The Rangers came rolling across the plain, guns blazing, while the troopers moved in from the right to cut off any retreat. The Indians panicked. The women in charge of moving the camp tried to flee by crossing Mule Creek on horses weighed down with hundreds of pounds of buffalo meat, tent poles, and skins. There they collided with Spangler and his troops coming at them from the opposite direction. Charles Goodnight, who arrived on the scene soon after the battle, said "the Sergeant and his men fell in behind on the squaws . . . and killed every one of them, almost in a pile." Goodnight added that the sergeant "probably did not know them from bucks and probably did not care."

Other Comanches fled in panic. One old man tried to escape on horseback with a young girl holding on behind him, according to Ross's written report to Sam Houston. Alongside them was another horse ridden by a middle-aged woman in a heavy buffalo robe. Ross said he and his top lieutenant, Tom Kelliher, gave chase and opened fire. His first shot killed the girl, who tumbled off the horse, dragging the old man after her. The man got up and let loose an arrow that struck Ross's horse. Ross, trying to steady the animal, fired wildly several times before he finally hit the old Indian in the right arm. Then he dismounted and shot the man two more times. The Indian did not fall but staggered toward a small mesquite tree and began chanting a death song. Then Antonio Martínez, Ross's Mexican servant, finished him off with a shot to the head.

"Sul ran up to him and he was lying on his back, and he looked up at him and breathed about three times, and between breaths gritted his teeth like a wild hog and died," said Gholson. Two soldiers hacked off the old man's scalp, which they then carved in half and divided between themselves.

Meanwhile, Kelliher chased down the woman in the buffalo robe. As he leveled his gun at her face, she cried out, *"Americano!"* The Ranger hesitated.

Ross rode up and ordered him not to fire. "As soon as I looked at her face," he later recalled, "I said: 'Why, Tom, this is a white woman. Indians do not have blue eyes.'"

Nestled inside the woman's robe was a baby girl.

AT FIRST THE WOMAN STRUGGLED with her captors and Martínez, who spoke Comanche, warned her to stop. "They had to force her away from there, took hold of her and just put her on her horse," Gholson recalled. "The Mexican was telling her that she would make them kill her if she didn't come on." The woman quieted down.

This was the account that James DeShields compiled from Ross, Gholson, and their supporters, and its problems are multifold. For one thing, it was Spangler's troopers, not Ross's Rangers, who captured the woman and the baby. One sign of this was the fact that it was Spangler and his men who had custody of the prisoners from the moment the fighting ended, not Ross.

The troopers escorted her back to the ruins of the encampment. She was, Ross later recalled, "very dirty and far from attractive in her scanty garments, as well as her person." Gholson was even more brutal in his description: "She was sullen, was a hard looker, was as dirty as she could be and looked to me more like an Indian than a white woman." H. B. Rogers, one of Ross's Rangers, said the woman "was so dirty you could hardly tell what she looked like, but she was red-headed and freckle-faced."

She lingered over the bodies of her dead companions, including the old man and the young woman. "She uttered some words of moaning for every one that was killed," said Gholson, "but seemed to be especially grieved over the body of one young warrior." The Rangers thought the dead boy showed "signs of white blood" and figured he might be her son. They "scalped all the others but left him unscalped through respect for her," Gholson reported.

The woman was terrified of the troopers and the Rangers, and Ross said he tried to ease her distress. "I had the Mexican tell her in the

Comanche language that we recognized her as one of our own people and would not harm her," he recalled—a direct contradiction of Gholson's account.

Even after the Rangers sought to reassure her, however, she still seemed agitated. Eventually she told Martínez that she feared for the lives of her two sons, who had been in the camp earlier. "I'm greatly distressed about my boys," she told him. "I fear they are killed." Only after Ross and his men assured her that no other young boys had been killed did she seem to calm down somewhat.

Charles Goodnight had a different explanation for her distress. She had been forced to watch as the Rangers and soldiers mutilated the corpses of the Indian dead for grisly souvenirs, looted the teepees, and set them ablaze. "We rode right over her dead companions," Goodnight recalled. "I thought then and still think how exceedingly cruel it was."

Then there was the question of how many warriors were at the scene of the battle. "I was in the Pease River fight, but I am not very proud of it," H. B. Rogers, a ranch hand, told an oral historian some sixty years later. "That was not a battle at all, but just a killing of squaws. One or two bucks and sixteen squaws were killed. The Indians were getting ready to leave when we came upon them."

James H. Baker, a young schoolteacher who was among the volunteers, put the number of dead even lower. After the battle, the volunteers caught up to Ross and his men, who were boisterously celebrating their victory with great yelling and whooping. The Rangers said they had killed twelve Indians and taken three captives. Baker reported that he and the volunteers found only four dead bodies, all of them women. Other accounts put the likely number of dead Comanches at seven.

Ross and Spangler, the cavalry commander, questioned the woman. She seemed in a daze, but they took her vague answers as confirmation of their belief that the Indians at the camp were related to the band that had conducted the bloody November raids. She indicated that most of the warriors had left for the main Comanche winter encampment, some two hundred miles west in the heart of Comancheria.

The woman claimed not to know her name in English nor the name of her white family nor where she came from originally, and she could only vaguely recall the details of her capture by Comanches many years earlier. But upon further conversation, using Martínez as his interpreter, Ross believed it was likely that she was the legendary Cynthia Ann Parker. He decided to notify her white relatives at once. He sent a quick dispatch to the *Dallas Herald*, which published his account a few weeks later, puffing up his own role and downgrading that of the caval-rymen. The article reported triumphantly that Ross and his men had caught and killed the Indians responsible for the Parker County raids. Ross also claimed to have found Martha Sherman's Bible at the camp-site. "The evidence is conclusive—clothes, papers, &c., being recovered from, which proves beyond doubt that they are the guilty wretches," the article reported.

The unnamed correspondent went on to describe the captured white female prisoner: "This woman does not know her name, nor where she was taken from . . . She says there are four tribes banded together for the purpose of depredating on the frontier this winter and spring, and that they are camping upon the head waters of the Canadian and Red Rivers in a starving condition because of lack of buffalo."

Ross dispatched another letter—this one to Isaac Parker of Birdville, Texas, just outside Fort Worth—to inform him that the captured woman might well be his long-lost niece.

As the years passed, and Sul Ross's public career migrated from Texas Ranger to Confederate general to state senator to candidate for gover-nor, his accounts of his actions at the Pease River expanded in their bravery and importance, aided and abetted by friendly historians such as DeShields, the journalist Victor Rose, who served as Ross's chief po-litical adviser, and fellow Rangers such as Gholson. For example, Ross's first two accounts, written within days of the battle, make no mention of killing an Indian chief and put the number of horses captured at a mere forty. In a letter published in the *Galveston News* and *Dallas Herald* in 1875—at the time he first began considering running for public office—Ross for the first time tells the story of running down and kill-ing a chief named Mohee. But by 1886, the year he was elected governor, Ross is claiming that the dead chief was Peta Nocona, the feared Co-manche raider and Cynthia Ann's husband. The size and composition of the Indian encampment also grew dramatically. Gholson would claim there were between 500 and 600 Indians and the number of captured Indian ponies jumped to 350.

Gholson, who gave his account in interviews in 1928 and 1931—some seventy years after the battle—seems the least reliable of sources. His name is not on any of the duty lists for the units involved, and his stories at best seem to have come from his discussions with actual participants. "They represent far more fantasy, myth, and folklore than history," wrote Paul H. Carlson and Tom Crum, two historians who have thor-oughly dissected the facts and circumstances of the battle.

Historians even got the date wrong: the granite historical marker erected by the state of Texas in 1936 near the site of the battle records the date as December 18, one day before the attack actually took place.

Nonetheless, the battle won Sul Ross enduring fame as an Indian fighter. Sam Houston sang his praises. "Your success in protecting the frontier gives me great satisfaction," the governor wrote to him.

Ross went on to distinguished service as a two-term governor and president of the forerunner of today's Texas A&M University. One contemporary observer said it was "this Pease River fight and the capture of Cynthia Ann Parker that made Sul Ross governor of Texas."

Ross himself was happy to feed the myth. "The fruits of this important victory can never be computed in dollars and cents," he wrote in a letter after he became governor that sounds ghostwritten by the bombastic Victor Rose. "The great Comanche Confederacy was forever broken, the blow was decisive; their illustrious chief slept with his fathers and with him were most of his doughty warriors."

All of which was pure fantasy. The Comanche nation was as yet far from broken. The war between Texans and Comanches would continue for another fifteen years.

The Pease River massacre, although celebrated as a great Ranger triumph over a superior force of Comanche warriors, was in truth just another revenge raid. The Comanches had killed five white women in northeastern Texas; in return, the troopers and Rangers killed at least four Comanche women. And, like the Comanches, the Rangers took scalps to verify the body count. In the merciless logic of the conflict, they had evened the score. As for Cynthia Ann Parker, a woman who twenty-four years earlier had been the victim of a massacre by one side had now been victimized again, only this time by the side that considered her one of their own.

5.

The Prisoner (Texas, 1861–1871)

S lowed by the bitter cold and their human cargo, Sergeant John Spangler and his troops, accompanied by Sul Ross and his Rangers, took ten days to deliver the captured white woman and her baby girl to Camp Cooper, one of the chain of frontier forts that formed the uneasy perimeter between the settlers and the Indians of North Texas. Despite their efforts to put her at ease, Cynthia Ann said little and ate nothing but the dried buffalo meat she carried with her. Coming to a half-frozen creek one day, Cynthia Ann's pony broke the ice with his front hoof. As she leaned over to drink some of the cold water with her hand, she lost hold of the little girl, who plunged into the stream. Cynthia Ann caught the child instantly, swooping her up and wrapping her in a shawl, then tucking her inside the vast smelly buffalo robe. Ross noted the speed and efficiency of a determined mother. He also noted that the child never cried.

Spangler had formal custody of the prisoners. When they arrived at Camp Cooper, he turned them over to his commander, Captain N. G. Evans.

Situated on the Clear Fork of the Brazos, Camp Cooper was a forlorn collection of thirteen small cabins and huts, most of them in an advanced state of disrepair. The damp cold penetrated the walls, floors, and ceilings of the six stone buildings, two mud huts, three picket-style sheds—wooden posts hammered directly into the ground with no frame or foundation—and two tarpaulins stretched over frames. Any attempt at repairs, an inspector had written the previous year, "would be a waste of the materials out of which they would be made."

Spangler and his men arrived soon after Christmas. The captives were taken to the stone guardhouse. Evans sought to question Cynthia Ann through an interpreter named Horace Jones. She told Jones she had lived among the Comanches for many years and said she had two sons who were still with them. It was unclear to Evans whether the woman was to be treated as a liberated captive or as a prisoner. "I have now the woman in the guard house and will await instructions from the department Commander as to her disposition," he wrote to his immediate superior at U.S. Army headquarters in San Antonio.

Evans turned the woman over to a fellow officer, Captain Innis Palmer, whose wife took charge of her. To the wives at the fort she looked and smelled like a savage, and so, despite her spirited objections, they stripped her of her Comanche garments, which they burned. Then they bathed and scrubbed her and dressed her in a secondhand pioneer outfit. It was the first time she had worn clothing with buttons in twenty-five years.

"They found enough clothes to clothe her, had an old Negro mammy prepare some hot water and wash her thoroughly, combed her hair and let her look at herself in a mirror," recalled Gholson. At first she seemed satisfied, but suddenly she dashed out the door. "It was a race such as I have never seen before or since," claimed Gholson. "In the lead was the squaw, jerking off clothes as she ran until she soon had on almost nothing; behind came the Negro mammy frantically waving a cloth or something, two or three bewildered white women . . . and the squaw's little child, big enough to toddle around, following after."

Palmer asked Horace Jones to take the woman to his family quarters and look after her with his wife until she was identified and restored to her relatives. Jones refused. He told Palmer that as far as he was concerned, she was a wild Indian and would be constantly attempting to escape "and in all probability succeeding by stealing my horses."

Isaac Parker, older brother of Cynthia Ann's late father, Silas, received Ross's letter and read newspaper accounts suggesting the white woman captive might be his long-lost niece. Isaac was sixty-seven years old that winter, a gray-haired man with the thick white beard and stern countenance of a biblical elder. He had served in the Texas National Congress during most of its nine years of independence, and then as a senator in the state legislature for seven more. Over the years he had honored the memory of his murdered father and brothers by pushing through bills calling for greater protection for the frontier settlements, establishing payment and equipment for Ranger and volunteer groups, and demanding the return of all white captives. He was also a loyal supporter of Sam Houston, whom he had known for more than forty years. Like his older brother Daniel, Isaac had served as a middleman and conciliator between their hotheaded brother James and Houston, helping sponsor both James's aggressive forays into Indian Territory and Houston's peace policy. Isaac raised four children of his own with his wife, Lucy, on a farm near Birdville, a village some ten miles northeast of Fort Worth. He was known for his generosity and his keen commitment to his family. When state lawmakers created a new county west of Fort Worth in 1855, they named it in his honor.

By 1860 Isaac was the only Parker of his generation still capable of undertaking the journey to determine whether the captive woman at Camp Cooper was Cynthia Ann. Lucy Duty Parker, Cynthia Ann's mother, had died in 1852 without knowing her oldest child's fate. Uncle James, who had devoted most of a decade to an obsessive search for the abducted children, was sixty-three years old and in ill health, remarried after the death of his first wife, Martha, and living three hundred miles

Isaac Parker, Cynthia Ann's uncle, who traveled to Fort Cooper in January 1861 to claim her and her daughter and return them to her Texas family.

Isaac Parker's cabin near Birdville, Texas, outside Fort Worth, where Cynthia Ann and her daughter, Prairie Flower, lived in 1861 after she was returned to her Texas family. The photo was taken in 1925 before the cabin was dismantled and relocated to the Amon Carter Ranch. It has since been moved again to the Log Cabin Village in Fort Worth.

to the southeast in Houston County. And so Isaac Parker set off by himself in a two-horse buggy for Camp Cooper. He rode forty-five miles west to the frontier town of Weatherford, where he obtained a letter of introduction from John Baylor, the former Indian agent who was editor of the *White Man*, and some clothing for Cynthia Ann, from his niece Nancy Parker. "Make them plenty big, Nancy," he told her. "The Parker people are big people." Then he and a neighbor of Nancy's rode another ninety miles to Camp Cooper, arriving in mid-January. Isaac met first with Evans and Jones and then was taken to see the prisoner.

She was stout and powerfully built. Her hair was dark and stringy, her skin callused. Her expression was edgy, like a deer caught in the harsh glare of a soldier's torch. Isaac asked a series of questions designed to test her memories of her childhood.

"She sat for a time immovable, lost in profound meditation, oblivious to every thing by which she was surrounded, ever and anon convulsed as it were by some powerful emotion which she struggled to suppress," stated one newspaper report of the meeting. "After the lapse of a few moments, she was enabled in her beautiful language of intelligible signs and Comanche tongue, with a peculiarly sweet English accent, to give the following narrative." She claimed to remember the fence around Old Fort Parker, drinking milk fresh from the stockade's cows, the Indians raiders carrying the white flag, and the ensuing slaughter.

"When Col. Parker requested the interpreter to ask her if she recollected her name," wrote one reporter, "she arose before the question could be asked by him, and striking herself on the breast exclaimed, 'Me Cynthia Ann.'"

THE WITNESS ACCOUNTS of her first meeting with Uncle Isaac portray Cynthia Ann as an indoctrinated savage desperately trying to break through the psychic chains of her long captivity to return to her natural civilized state. In the eyes of white observers it was as if the Comanches had stolen her soul, which she now struggled to reclaim. The ties that bound her emotionally and culturally to her Comanche family and to the wider Comanche world were invisible to them and made no sense. They knew neither psychology nor anthropology and possessed no intellectual or scientific tools to help them understand who she was, what she had become, or what she wanted. Most of all, they could not see that—despite her baptism and her early Christian upbringing—she was for all intents and purposes a Comanche, violently thrust, like a kidnapped time traveler, from one world into another.

Isaac sought to embrace her, but she began to weep. She said she did not wish to go home with him; she wanted either to stay at Fort Cooper until she got some word about her two sons, Quanah and Pecos, or else to return to her people—meaning, of course, the Comanches. But Isaac gave her no choice. First, however, she pleaded with Horace Jones to keep watch for her boys. If they were captured, she begged him, please protect them from harm and send them to her.

All the goods captured by individual Rangers and cavalrymen at the Pease River had been sold off, and Isaac had to buy back Cynthia Ann's pony and saddle for the long ride to Birdville. It took them several days to make the gray winter journey. Each night, when they would camp, the toddler would gather sticks and anything else she could find to put on the fire. "She was the smartest child of her age I ever saw," recalled Isaac's son, I. D. Parker. They finally arrived in Birdville on January 26.

The modest log ranch house built by Isaac in the late 1840s consisted of two separate cabins connected by a breezeway. For Cynthia Ann, who was used to sleeping under the stars or in a teepee, the crowded little room in which she was confined at night must have felt like a prison cell. The unfamiliar white women's clothing, the strange food, and the stares of outsiders could only have added to the sense that she had fallen into enemy hands. To her relatives, she seemed like an exotic wild animal, and they viewed her with pity, fascination, and revulsion.

She had grown up among the heathens, had become one herself, had even had intercourse with one, and had given birth to three little savages. She had brazenly crossed a forbidden boundary.

Rather than concede the reality that she preferred her Indian family to her white relatives, newspaper stories claimed she had been whipped and tortured into compliance by the Comanches. Her arms and body "bear the marks of having been cruelly treated," reported the *Clarksville Northern Standard*. Her supposed torments were given sexual context. Her "long night of suffering and woe could furnish the material for a tale more interesting than those found in the Arabian Nights Entertainment," opined the *Dallas Herald*.

She quickly became a local attraction. "When they got here and the news spread, the people came from near and far for a week or more," recalled I. D. Parker. "When she would see a crowd coming she would run to my wife and cling to her and sometimes crawl under the bed as she believed she would be killed."

One interpreter whom the Parkers engaged to communicate with her carefully explained to her that Isaac was her uncle. "After this interview she was more cheerful but said that the Comanches would come down here and kill all the people the next Sunday morning," wrote I. D. Parker.

Medora Robinson Turner, a Fort Worth schoolgirl, recalled being let out of class one day and taken to a retail store, where a crowd had gathered to gawk at the celebrity captive. "She looked like a squaw," Turner recalled. "She stood on a large wooden box surrounded by the curious spectators. She was bound with rope. She wore a torn calico dress. She made a pathetic figure. Tears were streaming down her face, and she was muttering in the Indian language."

Isaac's wife, Lucy, the matron of the house, oversaw all the domestic work of the farm—tending the hens, milking, butter making, weaving, and sewing—and had little time for Cynthia Ann. Instead, Lucy turned her niece over to an elderly African-American house servant. "I was told of the many futile efforts to teach her, and how she would wander away every chance she got and stay till hunted and brought back," wrote Susan Parker St. John, a cousin who later interviewed relatives about Cynthia Ann.

The Parkers were torn by conflicting impulses. On the one hand, they wanted to be as helpful as possible to a relative who had undergone a horrific trauma. "As savage-like and dark of complexion as she was, Cynthia Ann was still dear to her overjoyed uncle, and was welcomed home by relatives with all the joyous transports with which the prodigal son was hailed upon his miserable return to the parental roof," wrote Joseph and Araminta Taulman, two other cousins. But her relatives were bewildered by her own bewilderment and uncertain as to why their long-lost cousin was so fearful and expressed no gratitude for being rescued from heathens and restored to the bosom of good Baptists.

In the original captivity narratives, the white woman captive stood for the values of Christianity and civilization by resisting the threats and depredations of her godless savage captors. In doing so she demonstrated not only her own moral character but also the enduring strength of her Christian faith. Indeed she often sacrificed herself for those values. But the meaning of Cynthia Ann's story was far different. Her identification with the Comanches and their way of life and her desperate longing to return to them were a rebuke to civilization and to her own family. She had effectively reversed the narrative and subverted its meaning: instead of being abducted by Comanches, Cynthia Ann felt abducted by her white family. She was, in the deepest sense, a prisoner of war. The Parkers, as good Baptists, believed in the power of redemption. But what about someone who refused to be redeemed?

There was a sizable amount of fear, resentment, and suspicion attached to the newly liberated cousin. What deeds of cruelty had she seen? For that matter, what crimes had she herself participated in? The Parkers were well aware of the stories of Indian women who had joined with their menfolk in torturing and dismembering white captives. "Theirs must have been a hard and unsatisfactory life," Joseph and Araminta Taulman would write of Cynthia Ann and her captive brother, John. "The Comanches are veritable Ishmaelites, their hands being raised against all men, and every man's hand against them . . . Did they flaunt the blood-dabbled scalps of helpless whites in fiendish glee—and assist at the cruel torture of the unfortunate prisoners that fell into their hands? Alas! Forgetful of their race and tongue, they were thorough savages and acted in all particulars just as their Indian comrades did."

Captivity was a fate "worse than death," the Taulmans concluded, unaware of the irony of their words.

One Sunday morning, I. D. Parker recalled, Cynthia Ann went out in the yard with Prairie Flower, gathered wood chips, and kindled a fire. "When the fire was started she kneeled down by it, held up her hands and then bring them down saying some sort of ceremony then rise up and lean over the fire and cut her breast and let the blood drop in the fire muttering something all the time . . . She looked as solemn as death."

I. D. Parker made one more curious observation. "Somebody is mistaken about Nocona being her husband," he would write in a letter many years later. "We asked her husband's name and she gave a name I don't remember what it was, but it was not Nocona . . . We asked her if he was a chief, she said he was a little chief."

The suggestion here is intriguing. One of the key elements in the Cynthia Ann Parker legend is the claim that she married her abductor, a powerful war chief who fathered her three children. Her surviving son, Quanah, certainly thought so. But I. D. Parker was suggesting it was not true.

Seeking restitution for Cynthia Ann and the child, Uncle Isaac took her in March 1861 to the secessionist convention of the Texas legislature in Austin, where lawmakers were debating whether to leave the Union and join the newly formed Confederacy. During a break in the deliberations, the legislators voted to grant Cynthia Ann a league of land and a $100 annual stipend for Prairie Flower's education. Some of the ladies of Austin "dressed her neatly" and escorted her to the gallery. But as she sat overlooking the legislators with her uncle and aunt, she became convinced she was watching her own trial and that the curious white men staring up at her from the floor of the chamber below were sitting in judgment. Terrified, she bolted for the door, clutching Prairie Flower in her arms, and had to be coaxed back to the gallery by her uncle.

SOON AFTER HER RELATIVES ESCORTED her back to Birdville, Cynthia Ann Parker vanished from newspapers and other reports. Her celebrity status rapidly faded as it became clear that she was an ungrateful and unrepentant Comanche. The mythmakers disguised as historians for the most part took over—James DeShields being the first and foremost. They offered up for public consumption what became the official account of her captivity and rescue, and they insisted that she had been damaged and her soul destroyed by the Comanches.

But some of Cynthia Ann's relatives, curious to find out what actually had happened to her, did their own, less formal but more reliable research, producing a more nuanced version of her life and her fate. It is no accident that most of these researchers were women. Few of their accounts were ever published: their versions did not seem to fit the prevailing bombastic standards of Texas history. Their unannotated, mostly handwritten notes are scattered throughout boxes of archives at the

Dolph Briscoe Center for American History at the University of Texas at Austin. Some of these appear here for the first time.

Araminta Taulman, working in the 1920s, documented through interviews the circumstances behind the iconic photo of Cynthia Ann and Prairie Flower taken at A. F. Corning's photographic studio in Fort Worth a few weeks after their return from Austin. A customer named Mollie Allen was at the studio that day: her family in Kentucky had been begging her for a likeness, fearful that they would never get to see her once civil war broke out. Sixty years later, Mollie, long-married and known as Mrs. R. H. King, would recall to Araminta that the strange-looking woman had seemed deeply afraid that morning, had held her small daughter tightly, and would not let her go. Cynthia Ann, she recalled, was of "medium height and heavy build, and seemed very strong physically."

"Her hands were large and muscular apparently from the hard life she had led for nearly a quarter of a century with the Indians . . . Her skin was rough and her features coarse from hardships," but she "looked as though she had been a pretty girl in her youth." Mollie King added that Cynthia Ann had a "look of sadness in her large expressive soft-blue eyes, and despite her obvious fear, seemed to present a kindly appearance. The child, perhaps sensing her mother's anxiety, seemed wild and frightened."

Mollie and a companion, Virginia Turnbill, tried to allay Cynthia Ann's fears. But when Corning "pointed the camera at her she threw her hands before her face and moaned a deep oo-oo-oo." It was clear she feared that she would be killed or her spirit would be harmed by the cold glass eye of the camera. "She was very much afraid in the studio as she did not know what was about to happen to her."

When Corning showed her some of the pictures of Mollie and Virginia, Cynthia Ann seemed to relax. She took a seat before the camera but refused to let go of Prairie Flower. Corning had to take the shot with the little girl in her arms. To calm the child, Cynthia Ann opened her plain calico dress and began to nurse her. Cynthia Ann's skin was as "white as snow," Mollie said.

The small studio filled with "curious people who had come to see the white captive, and the photographer had a difficult time making a successful picture on account of the crowd and the excitement they caused Cynthia Ann," recalled Virginia Turnbill.

In the photograph that has survived from that day, Cynthia Ann's

This portrait is based on the famous photograph of Cynthia Ann Parker and daughter Prairie Flower taken in February 1861 at the A. F. Corning Studio in Fort Worth.

expression is hard and raw as granite. Her face is flat, weathered, and heavyset. Her lips are sealed shut. Her dark hair has been hacked short in the manner of a Comanche in mourning. She is wearing a thin bandanna around her neck and a borrowed muslin dress unbuttoned where her raven-haired little girl suckles at her right breast. There is no comprehension; at best, there is resignation, and lurking behind it a palpable sense of fear.

CYNTHIA ANN'S WELL-MEANING but puzzled relatives insisted upon instructing her with Bible lessons and homilies and praying with her. All of these rituals were disturbing to her. Even food was a source of tension. Cynthia Ann and her daughter could not adjust to the standard Texan fare of pork, bread, potatoes, and vegetables. Then one day their relatives slaughtered a cow, and the two raced to the carcass with squeals of delight. "As soon as the beef was opened she took out the kidneys and liver and they commenced eating and dancing and yelling in real savage style, the blood running down their faces and the smoke from the warm liver rising as they ate," I. D. Parker recalled. "It seemed to be the first meal they had relished."

Uncle Isaac never came to terms with his untamed niece. It was reported that he locked her and Prairie Flower inside their room each night to prevent them from escaping. The Parkers denied these reports. "All the bosh advertised in the papers and histories about her trying to escape was without foundation," wrote I. D. Parker. "She was never confined, said she did not want to be with her husband as he whipped too much, but wanted her boys."

Still, it was clear that Isaac and his wife were too old to cope with a Comanche woman and her wild young daughter. At Isaac's behest, his son William and William's wife, Mattie, agreed to take Cynthia Ann into their home two miles down the road. Mattie had a nine-month-old boy and helped induce Cynthia Ann to hop into their two-seat spring wagon for the trip home by handing her the baby and taking Prairie Flower in Mattie's own arms.

Susan Parker St. John, wife of a onetime governor of Kansas and a first cousin of Cynthia Ann, traveled to Texas in the 1880s and interviewed surviving members of the Parker family about their Comanche cousin, with an eye toward writing a family history. She interviewed William and Mattie, among others, and took handwritten notes that offer our most reliable and poignant account of Cynthia Ann's life with her Texas family after her recapture.

That first night, Mattie took Cynthia Ann into a room with two beds, washed her baby, and put on his nightie, and then did the same with Prairie Flower. Mattie then undressed herself and put on a dressing gown, and after much coaxing induced Cynthia Ann to put on a similar gown and lie down with her toddler. "Mattie smoothed back the tangled hair from her forehead and breathing a prayer kissed her," wrote Susan Parker St. John. "This was surely the first kiss she had ever known of a white woman. Cynthia Ann looked astonished but not displeased." In the morning, Mattie awoke to find Cynthia Ann and Prairie Flower sleeping inside their dirty old buffalo robe on the floor behind the door. It was the robe they had been captured in. "It took many trials before she would undress and sleep on the bed."

Prairie Flower "was dark with black bright eyes and thick black straight hair. In movement [she] was quick as a flash, would run like a quail, catch the little chickens, and loving it, squeeze it to death, every time she got a chance. She did not care for the screeching old hen flying at and scratching her. She never cried."

The girl gradually learned to speak English, and Cynthia Ann started to speak some as well. Still, "many times the 'call of the wild' came to her, especially in the fall of the year, when she had days of melancholy and would sit for hours and look up at the sky. She would go a little way from the house, make a circle about six feet across, put bark and grass in it, set it on fire, and sit looking through the smoke to the sun."

She was, Susan Parker St. John surmised, looking for the spirits of the dead.

Coho Smith was a former Indian scout who spoke fluent Comanche after spending several months as a Comanche captive in 1848. He was summoned to Birdville by William Parker and arrived one evening near dinnertime. At first Cynthia Ann treated him as if he was just one more curious gawker. But all that changed at the dinner table after Smith said the first Comanche words that occurred to him. When Cynthia Ann discovered he could speak her language, Smith later recalled, "she sprang up with a scream and knocked about half the dishes off the table . . . She was so excited I really thought she would go into a fit."

The Parkers placed Smith in a chair next to their frantic cousin and she held him by one arm all through dinner while jabbering constantly in Comanche and Spanish. She begged him to take her back to Comancheria. "My heart is crying all the time for my two sons," she told him.

He told her he had just gotten married and couldn't leave his young wife behind. Cynthia Ann said her people would give him beautiful women to replace his wife, along with horses and anything else he wanted. "My people will be so glad if you bring me to them they will give you anything I would ask of them."

She kept Smith up much of the night, pleading with him to agree to help her escape. Part of her frenzy must have stemmed from the opportunity at last to speak in her native Comanche tongue to someone who could understand her. And part was a desperate attempt to find a way back to the place she called home and to the children she considered her one true family. Smith reiterated that he couldn't help her: there were two wars raging, the war between the Union and the Confederacy as well as the conflict between Comanches and Texans. Smith said he was sure that if he attempted to take her north he'd be killed either by Comanches or by his fellow Texans once they learned what he had done. He left the next day without saying good-bye, and he did not visit again.

IN THE SPRING OF 1862, Cynthia Ann's brother Silas and her brother-in-law J. R. O'Quinn came to Birdville to take her to live at Silas's home some 115 miles away in Van Zandt County in East Texas. It took several days to persuade her to go: she seemed especially reluctant to leave Mattie and her baby boy and agreed only after Mattie promised to come visit soon. She never did.

The Civil War was draining the Texas economy at the same time it was extracting tens of thousands of young men to serve as soldiers. After Silas was drafted into the Confederate army in late 1862, Cynthia Ann was forced to move again, this time to the home of her sister Orlena, who was married to J. R. O'Quinn, at nearby Slater's Creek. T. J. Cates, a neighbor who visited with her, remembered Cynthia Ann as stout and hardworking. "She had a wild expression and would look down when people looked at her," he recalled. "She was an expert in tanning hides with the hair on them, or plaiting or knitting either ropes or whips." But despite her expertise, Cynthia Ann remained a restless, troubled soul—a mother of missing children. "She thought her two boys were lost on the prairie . . . This dissatisfied her very much."

Van Zandt County was a sparsely settled farm area far removed from the state's major population centers. After smallpox all but wiped out its Caddo Indian inhabitants, the eastern portion of the county was occupied by Cherokees, who signed peace treaties first with Mexico and later with Texas starting in 1836. But the treaty proved no protection from hard-line governor Mirabeau B. Lamar's expulsion campaign a few years later when his troops burned out and expelled thousands of Indians from East Texas. Their forced departure opened the area for white settlement. When Silas and J. R. returned from the war, Silas moved away with his family, seeking better economic opportunities. Cynthia Ann refused to go with them, and remained at Orlena's with Prairie Flower, her cow, chickens, and a sow with six piglets. Cynthia Ann's tanning skills—honed on the prairie—helped provide a decent income. Prairie Flower attended school and learned to read and write in English. "She was a happy, care free child, her mother's pride and blessing," wrote Susan St. John.

By now, the famous white Comanche was no longer news; no crowds journeyed to far-off Van Zandt County to jostle for a glimpse. Cynthia Ann's own family members seemed to lose interest as well. Whatever promises they might have made to take her to Comancheria to help find her boys once the Civil War had ended seem to have long been forgotten. As for James Parker, the obsessed uncle who had spent a decade seeking to track down the young people abducted in 1836, there is no record that he ever sought to visit his long-lost niece before his death in Houston County in late 1863. He was buried near his brother Daniel in the Pilgrim Cemetery in Elkhart.

Like so many parts of Cynthia Ann's story, Prairie Flower's death is shrouded in myth and ambiguity. James DeShields in his published history in 1886 claims she died of smallpox, influenza, or one of the other diseases that rampaged across the East Texas countryside sometime in 1863, and a brokenhearted Cynthia Ann—her will to live crushed by her daughter's death—followed within a few months. No one bothered to record the death or write an obituary. In a slight variation of the story, I. D. Parker—Isaac's son and Cynthia Ann's first cousin—who was away fighting in the Civil War from early 1864 until the end of the conflict, claimed that mother and daughter both died in the spring of 1865.

Another legend has it that the Parkers, realizing that a half-breed Indian girl would never find acceptance in the white world, faked the story of Prairie Flower's death, changed her name, and sent her off to be raised in New Orleans. She purportedly married a Spanish sea captain in Houston, moved with him to New Mexico, and raised a family there. A New Mexico woman wrote the Dallas Historical Society in the 1950s saying she had talked to an old man in Las Cruces who claimed to be the son of Prairie Flower. The man said his mother had been killed in an Indian raid, although such attacks would have ceased long before she reached adulthood. Every now and then, someone would emerge and claim to be a grandchild or a distant relative. But no one ever provided proof of the claim.

In fact, the few eyewitness accounts put the date of Cynthia Ann's death as far later, and the only known document from the period supports them. An 1870 census for Anderson County lists Cynthia Ann Parker as a member of the O'Quinn household. It lists her birth year as "abt 1825" and her age as forty-five. J. M. Emerson, a resident of nearby Anderson County who talked to Silas Parker and J. R. O'Quinn many years later, put the year of Prairie Flower's death as 1868, and said Cynthia Ann moved with the O'Quinns to Anderson County and worked in their sawmill. Susan Parker St. John, our most reliable and conscientious contemporary reporter, wrote that Prairie Flower died of brain fever at age nine and was buried in the Fosterville cemetery.

What is clear is that with the death of her darling daughter, Cynthia Ann's own health—physical and spiritual—began to deteriorate. She slashed her arms and breasts with a knife, part of the intense Comanche way of mourning. Her family claimed she turned to Christianity. "Cynthia Ann had united with the Methodist church and insisted on being immersed for baptism," contends Susan St. John, who adds that Cynthia Ann lived for two years after Prairie Flower's death and died in

March 1871 at Orlena's house. She, too, was buried in the Fosterville cemetery "beside her darling."

What's striking is that after all the accounts of her recapture, and the celebrity status that produced big crowds on the streets of Fort Worth and a guest appearance before the Texas legislature, Cynthia Ann and her story fell off the face of the earth. There are no newspaper accounts of her later days, no obituary for her or Prairie Flower, and no reliable way to know exactly when or how she died.

Long afterward, newspapers sought to put the best light on the tragic circumstances of Cynthia Ann's life. "A Romance of the Border" was the headline in the *San Francisco Bulletin*. "Story Is Romantic: Woman Who Liked Indian Life Has Large Place in History," declared the *Lawton (OK) Chronicle*. The *Dallas News* labeled her the "most romantic of Texas heroines." The *Winkler County News* called her a "Symbol of Loyalty and Love of Liberty."

A century later, *Texas Monthly* magazine cast Cynthia Ann as a proto-feminist role model. "Strong as buffalo hide, family-loving and high-spirited despite dire circumstances, Cynthia Ann demonstrated the same qualities that have ennobled iconic Texans from Mary Maverick to Barbara Jordan, Ima Hogg to Lady Bird Johnson," a 2003 article declared. "Maybe the reason we can't let go of Cynthia Ann is because she was the original tough Texas woman."

The truth was less triumphalist and more poignant. Cynthia Ann was not the hardy survivor but rather the ultimate victim of the Texan-Comanche wars, abducted and traumatized by both sides. When she was nine years old, she watched as her father, grandfather, uncle, and family friends were slaughtered before her eyes, and she was ripped from her home by brutal strangers speaking in a foreign tongue who seemed bent on killing her as well. Twenty-four years later, she underwent a similarly horrifying experience at the hands of the U.S. Cavalry and Texas Rangers. The wide gulf of misunderstanding between her and her white relatives was an eerie reflection of the gaping cultural and psychological divide between Comanches and Texans, replayed in one divided family. The fact that she had become the willing partner of a Comanche warrior who had likely been involved in slaughtering her own father, uncle, and grandfather only made her more puzzling and burdensome to her own white family.

Even the patriarch who had returned her to the white world eventually recognized the terrible mistake he had made. In a series of conversations with a young friend, Isaac Parker called Cynthia Ann "the most unhappy person [he] ever saw. She pined for her children and her husband continuously . . . She was as much an Indian as if she had been born one. She knew no other people except as enemies."

Isaac said he had hoped "she would eventually become civilized and her love for her kin return to her, and that she would after a time forget the Indians and be glad to live among her own people." He became tearful at times when he discussed her pain. "She was virtually a prisoner among her own loving kindred, but they did not realize it until too late." Had she been allowed to return to her Comanche home, Isaac said, "she would probably have lived to be an old woman."

The story of Cynthia Ann Parker is partly a story of mothers who lose their children and die without ever knowing the fate of those children. Lucy Duty Parker, Cynthia Ann's mother, died not knowing whether her daughter was safe. Rachel Plummer never learned what happened to her young son James Pratt after her captors pulled him from her grasp. And Cynthia Ann never again saw her two Comanche sons after she and her daughter were captured by soldiers.

Still, if there was one saving grace in the tragedy of Cynthia Ann's final years, it was something she herself never knew about. Only one of her children survived, but he became a heroic figure who helped save the Comanche nation, her adopted people, from destruction.

II

QUANAH

6.

The Warrior (Comancheria, 1865–1871)

Cynthia Ann Parker died believing that all her children were dead as well. But one of her sons survived. His name was Quanah Parker, and he became the next chapter in the Parker legend and the next great storyteller as well. Like the others, he told his mother's story in large part to explain his own.

We know little about his life and times as a son and warrior. Comanches had no written language, and after his surrender in 1875 Quanah had good reasons not to discuss his career as an enemy combatant against the forces of the United States and the sovereign state of Texas. Instead, historians have been left to sort through scraps of information, liberally embroidered with myth and outright falsehood. Quanah emerges in many accounts as the most powerful and skilled of Comanche war chiefs. In some versions, he wreaks vengeance on whites for his white mother's recapture; in others he instructs his followers not to kill white women and children for fear of harming her and his sister, Prairie Flower.

What we know comes from his own carefully selective memory and those of his companions and his foes, all of it recorded long after the events took place. Some of it seems plausible, most of it not. But the portrait of the early Quanah as a well-known and much-feared Comanche war chief is myth: as far as Texans were concerned, he was neither. The indisputable fact is that before 1875 there is no mention of Quanah in any official document or Indian agency record.

One thing he was always clear about: his father, Peta Nocona, was not killed at the Pease River Massacre. According to the most plausible Comanche accounts, Nocona and his two sons were on a hunting trip on the morning of the attack, too far from the besieged encampment to hear or see what was happening—hence Cynthia Ann's extreme anxiety over the fate of her boys after she was captured by the troopers. Nocona heard nothing until a friend tracked him down with the terrible news.

Nocona and his sons made their way to a large Comanche winter encampment. He must have feared the Rangers would come seeking the boys, for he changed both their names to help conceal them. According to one Comanche account, Tseeta, meaning "Eagle," became Quanah, meaning "Sweet Smell," and Pecos became Pee-nah, or "Peanut."

For the first time, Nocona explained to them that their mother was a white woman whom he had captured when she was a girl during a battle in Texas. Quanah said his father became "very morose and unhappy" over the loss of Cynthia Ann and a second wife, a Mexican captive, and "shed many tears."

According to Quanah, his father lived for some five more years. Comanche oral tradition says he died of old war wounds somewhere in the Antelope Hills of Oklahoma.

Quanah would remember the times that followed his father's death as a painful period in which he and his brother, two orphans with no close relatives, had to scrounge for food and clothing with little support from other Comanches. He attributed some of this hardship to the fact that his mother was white. Within a few years his brother died as well from one of the many epidemics that were ravaging the tribe. Quanah was truly on his own.

He was not exactly an outcast but neither was he a cherished member of the tribe. His father had been well respected among Comanches, even legendary, for his prowess as a warrior, but was called "the Wanderer" and was known as a loner with no close friends. The young Quanah, too, traveled alone.

The Staked Plains became his domain. The plains were a parched, brittle, limestone plateau on the western flank of Texas, some 250 miles long and 150 miles wide—as large as Maine. In summer they locked themselves inside a suffocating closet of gray haze—brown, yellow ground with shrubs and dwarfed trees sprinkled throughout like random afterthoughts before the curled blue edges of the hazy horizon. It was a land of high temperatures and low rainfall. Francisco Coronado, who had passed through the area in 1541 on his search for El Dorado, pronounced the plains "so vast that I did not find their limit anywhere I went . . . with no more landmarks than if we had been swallowed up by the sea."

The Spanish called them Llano Estacada—the "Stockade Plains"—a reference either to the fortresslike appearance of their blunt escarpments or to the stakes that one Spanish expedition hammered into the ground so that they could retrace their path through the vast swath of nothingness. On some Texan maps the plains were labeled the Great American Desert, and they might as well have been posted with a skull and crossbones. There was precious little grass and even less water—nothing to keep a horse or a mule or a man alive for very long. Under a canopy of sullen gray sky, the plains were a theater of death. "The land is too much, too empty, claustrophobic in its immensity," wrote the author Timothy Egan.

To the casual observer, the Llano looks like one seamless, arid platform. But Quanah and his fellow Comanches knew that the plains concealed a network of deeply etched canyons like intimate secrets that provided shelter from the winter storms and fragile vegetation and water throughout the rest of the year. The largest is called Palo Duro—"Hard Pole"—a name said to originate in the hardwood wild cherry and plum trees scattered through the hidden valley. At the time of the Civil War no white man had ventured into the area for three hundred years.

Quanah knew intimately the Palo Duro and all of the small depressions, fissures, and hidden seasonal water holes of the Llano. For him each was a haven, a place he could linger and hide without challenge from red men or white. At times he even claimed to have been born on Cedar Lake, the alkaline sea on the eastern edge of the Llano. To an orphan like Quanah, something about the harsh empty desert must have felt like home.

A YOUNG COMANCHE MALE without standing or a patron faced a hard road in attaining stature, prosperity, and a desirable bride. Those fettered by poverty or low rank faced two choices: go along with subordination for an extended period until they could gain a foothold; or strike out on their own. Quanah chose the latter.

From his earliest days, according to oral legend, he showed an untamed romantic streak that violated the norms of Comanche society. After Peta Nocona's death, it was said, a senior chief named Yellow Bear invited Quanah to join his camp. There Quanah fell in love with Yellow Bear's daughter, Weckeah. Quanah knew that a fellow brave named Tannap had first call on Weckeah: Yellow Bear had already made arrangements with Tannap's father, who had offered a string of ponies as a bride price. Yellow Bear pledged that in three nights Weckeah would join Tannap in his teepee to consummate the marriage.

Quanah had other plans. He convinced Weckeah to run away with him the following evening. Some twenty younger warriors decided to join them. The rebels scattered in ten directions to throw off any pursuers, then met up near the headwaters of the Concho River.

For several months Quanah and his comrades raided ranches in West Texas and built a portfolio of stolen horses. Within a year they had established themselves as an offshoot of the Quahadi band. When Yellow Bear tracked them down, elders intervened to prevent open warfare. In the end, Quanah paid twenty ponies to Yellow Bear and nineteen more to Tannap, then staged a two-day feast to smooth over hard feelings. He

This is the first known photograph of Quanah Parker, identified as "Quinine, or Cita, Qua-Ha-Da Comanche," taken by Will Soule at Fort Sill.

and Weckeah were allowed to return, and she became his first wife. Quanah's legend had begun.

THE WORLD QUANAH WAS ENTERING had changed seismically from the one his father had known. Comanche society had been shattered from within and without by plague and continuous warfare. The old clans and traditions were dying out, with nothing to take their place. Meanwhile, the Texans, their mortal enemies, were growing in numbers and firepower. Not for the first time in human history, nor the last, a technologically advanced nation with a growing population and a muscular opinion of its own righteousness asserted its dominance over a smaller, more primitive one.

The Civil War provided a curious hiatus for the Indians and a temporary respite in their demise. Native Americans looked on with amazement as white Unionists and Confederates killed each other with a fervor and determination once reserved for native peoples. Texas sent more than ninety thousand of its young men to fight on eastern battlefields, while the U.S. Army denuded its frontier forts to supply the Union side. Comanche and Kiowa raiders took advantage of the conflict to step up their attacks. More white captives were taken. One Indian agent, I. C. Taylor, reported that the Kiowa chief Satanta and his men boasted "that stealing white women is a more lucrative business than stealing horses."

Still, even as the war was ending, there was little taste in Washington for an all-out assault on the Lords of the Plains. For one thing, Indian fighting was no longer considered a noble undertaking. The slaughter by Union militia under Colonel James Chivington of more than one hundred Cheyenne and Arapaho men, women, and children in southern Colorado in November 1864—known as the Sand Creek Massacre—was a turning point. Chivington's men, ignoring the American flag the Cheyenne villagers were flying, opened fire indiscriminately, then came back later in the day and finished off the wounded, scalping each corpse, cutting off hands and fingers to steal jewelry, and hauling mutilated body parts back to Denver for public display. In the ensuing investigation, witnesses reported having seen the sexual mutilation of men, women, and children's corpses. "In going over the battleground the next day I did not see a body of man, woman or child but was scalped, and in many instances their bodies were mutilated in the most horrible manner—men, women and children's privates cut out, etc.," testified Lieutenant James Connor.

With the Civil War grinding on to its ghastly conclusion and the public grown tired of bloodshed of any kind, Sand Creek caused a wave of popular revulsion and a surge of peace treaties. The first was the Treaty of the Little Arkansas in 1865, in which Kiowas and Comanches ceded their claim to most of East and South Texas in return for annuity payments and the right to continue roaming unfettered through the hunting grounds of the north and west. It was at best a cynical charade: the most warlike bands did not sign, and in any case the federal peace commissioners had no authority to cede Texas state land to Indians. By the following year the raiders were back in the field and so were the Texas Rangers. While the overall numbers of those killed, wounded, or abducted in these attacks were low, the psychological impact of terror was powerful and demoralizing. The Texans may have been winning the war: the forces of population growth and industrialization were firmly on their side. But in the interim they were losing many battles. The population of Wise County in North Texas fell from 3,160 in 1860 to 1,450 a decade later.

If the oral legend is correct, Quanah capitalized on his prowess and his daring and the thinning of Comanche warrior ranks to quickly become a respected warrior. He joined raiding parties rampaging down the familiar trails through the heart of West Texas and into Mexico. Like all young Comanche men, he engaged in rites of passage, such as a vision quest. Every man had his special medicine and connection to the natural and spiritual world, often through animal spirits. Quanah's personal connection was the bear. "Sometimes a Comanche man dreams and a big bear comes and tells him you do this—'You paint your face this way. I help you,'" Quanah later explained. "If he sees bear in his dreams then he makes medicine that way." In battle Quanah would wear a necklace with a bear claw.

The only account Quanah ever gave of a raiding expedition makes the raiders sound like the gang who couldn't shoot straight. As he described it, he and his companions rode south to the Mexican state of Chihuahua and a valley filled with cattle and horses. For nine nights they tried and failed to steal any livestock. "When the white man's houses are thick, they keep the horses hidden and they are hard to find," he explained, rather lamely.

Finally on the tenth night they found some horses and spirited them away. They also stole a calf, which they roasted immediately and wolfed down because no one had eaten for two days. The raiders fled Mexico with a few dozen horses, no scalps, no captives, and no brave stories to tell.

He was raiding in the Staked Plains when he met a small group of fellow Comanches who told him that soldiers were coming into southern Kansas with beef cattle, sugar, coffee, and other cherished goods for those Indians willing to participate in a great peace council. Putting his skepticism aside, Quanah and his small band of warriors rode to the site.

THE "GRAND COUNCIL" MET in a clearing of tall elms near Medicine Lodge Creek in southern Kansas on the morning of October 19, 1867. Chiefs of the Comanche, Kiowa, Arapaho, and Cheyenne nations sat on logs facing the peace commissioners, who sat in a semi-circle of stiff-backed chairs. Fishermore, a Kiowa crier, opened the proceedings at 10:00 a.m. with a loud call for everyone to "do right."

The wily old Kiowa leader, Satanta, was seated on a camp chair in front of the other chiefs. Nearby was a white woman, Virginia Adams, interpreter for the Arapahos, dressed in a crimson gown made especially for the occasion. Behind them was Ten Bears, elder statesman of the Yamparika Comanches. "What I say is law for the Comanches," Ten Bears proclaimed. "But it takes a half dozen to speak for the Kiowas."

Kansas senator John B. Henderson spoke first. He accused the assembled warriors of violating the Treaty of the Little Arkansas forged two years earlier by attacking work crews laying railroad tracks across Indian territory and by killing white women and children. "These reports made the hearts of our people very sad," Henderson told the assembled chiefs.

Nonetheless, said Henderson, the government in Washington wanted "to do justice to the Red Man." He promised the chiefs "all the comforts of civilization, religion, and wealth," including "comfortable homes upon our richest agricultural lands." The government would provide schools and churches as well as livestock and farming tools. All it wanted in return was an Indian agreement to keep the peace and to live a "civilized" existence—in other words, to cease being Indians.

The first chief to respond was Satanta. A large, flamboyant performer who could leap nimbly from arrogance to servility and back again, he buried his hands in the ground, rubbed them with sand, and strolled around the circle shaking hands with each participant. Then he walked into the center and began to speak. Satanta used a timeworn strategy: he blamed other Indians. His young men and those of the Comanches had honored the treaty, he claimed, but the Cheyenne had not. They were the ones responsible for the raids and the depredations. "They did it in broad daylight, so that all could see them," he declared.

But Satanta was also blunt: he had no interest in reservation life. "I have heard that you intend to settle us on a reservation near the mountains," he told the commissioners. "I don't want to settle there. I love to roam over the wide prairie, and when I do it I feel free and happy, but when we settle down, we grow pale and thin."

The soon-to-be-famous British journalist Henry M. Stanley, who witnessed the ceremony, said Satanta's bald rejection "produced a rather blank look upon the faces of the Peace Commissioners." The response they had been looking for from the chiefs was submission to the inevitable, if not gratitude. What they hadn't expected was defiance.

The next morning, they heard even more of it. Ten Bears, the old Comanche warrior chief, gave a ringing address—one of the most poignant and memorable in the history of Native American oratory. Ten Bears said he was glad to come and talk peace because his people had suffered from fighting and the loss of many braves and warriors. He said soldiers had begun the hostilities two years earlier by attacking his young men. The warriors had merely fought back. "The Comanches are not weak and blind like the pups of a dog when seven sleeps old. They are strong and farsighted, like grown horses. We took their road and we went on it. The white women cried, and our women laughed."

Ten Bears had visited Washington recently and said the Great White Father had promised that he and his people could roam free in designated land. But he found unacceptable the puny size of the area now on offer. "If the Texans had kept out of my country, there might have been peace," he told the commissioners. "But that which you now say we must live on is too small."

Ten Bears also rejected the demand that his people move permanently to reservations and live in houses. "I was born upon the prairie," he declared, "where the wind blew free and there was nothing to break the light of the sun. I was born where there were no enclosures, and where everything drew a free breath. I want to die there, and not within walls."

Senator Henderson replied as bluntly as Satanta and Ten Bears. The Indian "must change the road his father trod, or he must suffer, and probably die," he warned. "The whites are settling up all the good lands . . . When they come, they drive out the buffalo. If you oppose them, war must come. They are many, and you are few."

Despite their strong misgivings, both Satanta and Ten Bears did indeed bow to the inevitable by signing the treaty at Medicine Lodge. It allotted large portions of the area south of the Arkansas River—most of Oklahoma and the Texas Panhandle—to the tribes. They were given to understand that white hunters would be prevented from crossing the Arkansas into their designated territory, although this was not put in writing. The treaty's first article was more a promise than an enforceable reality: "From this day forward all war between the parties to this agreement shall forever cease."

The tribes relinquished the right to occupy permanently the territories outside their reservation. They were to allow the peaceful completion of railway lines throughout the region. And they promised to cease raiding white settlements and families. "They will never capture or carry off from the settlement white women or children . . . [and] never kill or scalp white men nor attempt to do them harm." In return, they were allowed "the right to hunt on any lands south of the Arkansas River, so long as the buffalo may range thereon in such numbers as to justify the chase."

Article Three of the treaty committed up to 320 acres for each Kiowa and Comanche family head to be recorded in a land book. The notion was to push the Indians into the alien realm of private property and farming. The nomads of the plains overnight were to become gentlemen farmers—the treaty pledged to each head of family up to $100 in seeds and agricultural implements for the first year and $25 each for the next three, as well as a suit of clothes. And educated as well: Article Seven stated that all the Indian signatories "pledge themselves to compel their children, male and female, between the ages of six and sixteen years, to attend school."

Quanah listened, but he lacked the standing of the Comanche chiefs and was not asked to speak. "I went and heard it—there were many soldiers there," he would recall. ". . . The soldier chief said, '. . . You must remember one thing and hold fast to and that is you must stop going on the warpath . . .'"

The treaty in essence was a story of peace and reconciliation that each side told the other but neither truly believed. Quanah listened to it, but he had no intention of honoring it. Neither he nor any of the Quahadi band signed on. The raiding continued.

AMONG THE PEACE COMMISSIONERS sitting in their hard, stiff-backed wooden chairs that week in southern Kansas was another warrior who was just as skeptical and contemptuous of the proceedings as Quanah. General William T. Sherman, the Civil War's ruthless apostle of total war, was placed in command of the Military Division of the Mississippi in July 1865, three months after the war ended. The position gave him responsibility for military affairs and domestic security from the Mississippi River to the Rocky Mountains, all except for Texas. The Plains Indians—from the Lakota Sioux in the north down through the Comanches and Kiowas in the south—were his special burden. Sherman felt sorry for Indians, but they exasperated him. He had no patience with their recalcitrance nor with the sympathy they engendered back east among those who knew them only from newspaper articles, James Fenimore Cooper novels, and the new phenomenon of dime novels. "He viewed them as stubborn children who needed disciplining," wrote one of Sherman's biographers.

Sherman was widely attributed to have first uttered the saying "The only good Indian is a dead Indian," although he always claimed Miles Standish deserved the credit. Still, he firmly adhered to the idea. He believed the Indian way of life was anarchic and slovenly. Although he did not seek their extermination, he was repelled by their culture. For them to survive in the modern world, he insisted, they would have to become productive and orderly members of society. Indians, he told a graduating class at West Point, refused "to earn their bread by the sweat of their brow." They were a barrier to progress. Some twenty thousand Indians could barely manage to subsist in Nebraska, "while whites will be able to feed two million off its soil."

Still, while they might be living at a mere subsistence level, Indians were a powerful military threat. There were after the Civil War some 100,000 potentially hostile Indians out of a native population of 270,000 nationwide, and they were highly mobile and increasingly well armed. Sherman had but 20,000 soldiers. He knew he had to stay on the offensive and keep his enemy on the run. He had in mind a winter campaign to destroy Indian horses and supplies and harass them into surrender. It was the same strategy that had crippled Georgia and the Deep South during the Civil War. "In the end they must be removed to small and clearly defined reservations or must be killed," Sherman wrote.

Sherman and his soldiers were not exterminationists. Unlike the Texans, they would fight until their enemy was subdued, not destroyed. For the cavalry, the war against the Comanches was a military campaign with strategies and tactics, not a blood feud. Their methods could be brutal and ruthless: soldiers killed women and children, destroyed livestock, and torched homes. But they operated out of a sense of professional duty more than personal hatred. The Comanches themselves could tell the difference.

Some, like Quanah, maintained their fiercely independent, nomadic lives and kept their distance from the reservations and agencies. But other bands settled on the outskirts of the agency, living off government beef and grain in winter. While the older warriors preached peace, many of the young men fed and sheltered over the winter months, fattening their ponies, and then set off south in spring to raid in Texas and Mexico. In a two-and-one-half-year period between 1865 and 1867, thirty-five counties in Texas reported a total of 162 people killed, 24 wounded, and 43 captured, along with more than 30,000 stolen livestock.

The year after Medicine Lodge, 1868—the same year in which the novelist Alan LeMay would later set *The Searchers*—was typical, according to the agents and scouts. The official reports read like a depressing frontier police blotter. In a raid in January, Kiowas killed "several families and took seven children prisoners, who all froze to death," according to Indian scout Phil McCusker's report. In February they killed several people in another raid and took five captives, all of whom were later freed. In May, Comanches plundered and burned a local trading post and warned residents not to cut down any more trees or erect new buildings. That same month Kiowas hauled out to the prairie Colonel Jesse H. Leavenworth, the agent who helped arrange the Medicine Lodge treaty, tied a rope around his neck, and ordered him to abandon his post. He did so promptly, failing to inform his deputy, S. T. Walkley, of his sudden departure. Walkley himself reported that three raiding parties returned from Texas over the summer with a total of thirteen scalps, three captive children, and an unspecified number of horses and mules. In August Comanche bands killed eight Texans, three of them children.

Walkley recovered five white captives over the summer. The older chiefs were "doing all they can to keep not only their own bands but all wild Indians from committing depredations . . . and when their young men have stolen away in the night to go on marauding expeditions to Texas, they have sent after them and brought them back in the morning," Walkley reported to Major General William B. Hazen, the regional commander.

Hazen forwarded these reports on to General Phil Sheridan, Sherman's deputy, along with two letters from grief-stricken parents in Texas seeking the whereabouts of their abducted children. In an accompanying note, Hazen proposed "to hang all the principal participants in this outlawry, and to disarm and dismount the rest." This, he said, was "the mildest remedy that promises a certain cure."

Sheridan agreed. "If a white man commits murder or robs, we hang him or send him to the penitentiary," he wrote. "If an Indian does the same, we have been in the habit of giving him more blankets."

With Sherman's blessing, Sheridan launched the Winter Campaign of 1868–69 against the Cheyenne, Kiowa, and Comanche tribes in their winter quarters, seizing their supplies and livestock, killing those who resisted, and driving the rest back into the reservation. Lieutenant Colonel George Armstrong Custer, the great mythmaker, marching under Sheridan's orders, struck the biggest and most controversial blow in late November in a surprise attack on a Cheyenne and Arapaho encampment on the Washita River near modern-day Cheyenne, Oklahoma. Traveling through a foot of fresh snow, Custer and eight hundred men overran a winter village of fifty-one lodges, killing dozens of men, women, and children. Among the victims were Black Kettle, the Cheyenne chief who was a signatory at Medicine Lodge, and his wife. In an eerie premonition of Custer's own demise at Little Big Horn eight years later, two officers and nineteen enlisted men were killed when they ran into a superior force of Cheyenne, Arapaho, and Kiowa braves coming to Black Kettle's aid. Custer burned the lodges and winter food supply, slaughtered hundreds of Indian ponies and mules, and brought back fifty prisoners.

Sheridan justified the slaughter of Indian women and children by accusing Black Kettle of engaging in the same deeds. Custer's men had found the bodies of two white captives, Clara Blinn and her two-year-old son, Willie, both of whom had been killed by Cheyenne warriors. The troopers, Sheridan, wrote in his report, "had struck a hard blow, and wiped out old Black Kettle and his murderers and rapers of helpless women."

He flung the most hideous of accusations, characterizing whites who sympathized with the Indians as accessories to murder and rape—"the aiders and abettors of savages who murdered, without mercy, men, women, and children; in all cases ravishing the women sometimes as often as forty and fifty times in succession, and while insensible from brutality and exhaustion forced sticks up their persons, and, in one instance, the fortieth or fiftieth savage drew his saber and used it on the person of the woman in the same manner. I do not know exactly how far these humanitarians should be excused on account of their ignorance . . ."

Sheridan believed such women were no longer worth rescuing, having suffered the classic "Fate Worse than Death," and it might be best if they perished by murder, suicide "or the providentially directed bullet of a would-be rescuer."

While it seemed like a deranged and twisted notion, Sheridan's formula captured the nightmares and obsessions of many whites—their need for retribution, yet at the same time their deep-seated belief that women sexually abused in such a fashion were fit only for death. Nearly a century later, the director John Ford would take the same theme and build *The Searchers* around it.

PRESIDENT ULYSSES S. GRANT had seen enough. In an effort to end the Plains Indian wars, he met with a delegation of Quakers shortly after his election to the presidency in 1868 and agreed to appoint their clergy as Indian agents. Grant, as usual, put it simply: "If you can make Quakers out of the Indians it will take the fight out of them," he told the group. "Let us have peace."

Lawrie Tatum, a balding, bearded forty-seven-year-old teacher living on a farm in Iowa, was one of those pressed into government service in the name of Grant's peace policy. Tatum was a prominent Iowan known for his involvement with helping runaway slaves before the Civil War. Despite having no experience in dealing with Indians, he was named Kiowa-Comanche agent in 1869.

Tatum came to the agency in Anadarko with few illusions. Kiowas and Comanches "were still addicted to raiding in Texas, stealing horses and mules, and sometimes committing other depredations . . . ," he wrote. "They were probably the worst Indians east of the Rocky Mountains." The warriors saw themselves at war with Texans, not with the Army. But a prominent Comanche chief told Tatum flatly that "if Washington don't want my young men to raid in Texas, then Washington must move Texas clear away, where my young men can't find it."

Tatum quickly figured out how the warriors were exploiting the reservation system. "They told me a number of times," he wrote, "that the only way that they could get a large supply of annuity goods was to go out onto the warpath, kill some people, steal a good many horses, get the soldiers to chase them awhile, without permitting them to do much harm, and then the Government would give them a large amount of blankets, calico, muslin, etc. to get them to quit!"

From the beginning, the warriors taunted and exploited Tatum's goodwill and naïveté. Comanches stole his horses and his mules. A raiding party killed a man at the agency's beef corral, and killed and scalped another man six miles away. Tatum was forced to move the beef cattle sixty miles east to Chickasaw territory so they would be out of Comanche reach. All the Friends employees fled the agency, including Tatum's wife.

As so often was the case, the showdown came over the question of white captives. In August 1869 a raiding party killed a Texas rancher named Koozier and abducted his wife and five children. The warriors returning to the agency demanded two mules and a carbine as ransom for the family. "I told them that I should give them nothing at that time, and they need not come again for their rations until the captives were brought to me," wrote Tatum.

It was a tense moment. The Indians kept their bows and arrows at their sides as they spoke with Tatum, and one of them ostentatiously took the cartridges out of his breech-loading gun and put them back again. Another one took to whetting a butcher knife in full view, "turning it over from side to side, making all the noise he could with it," Tatum recalled.

"After the council closed an Indian came over to me and ran his hand under my vest over my heart to see if he could 'feel any scare,'" he recalled.

In the end, Tatum got back the captives. The Indians wanted large supplies of coffee and sugar and their usual supply of flour and beef, plus ammunition. He gave them only the usual amount, "and $100 for each captive, as approved by the department." Working this way, bargaining for live bodies one family at a time, Lawrie Tatum recovered a total of twenty-six captives during his four years as Indian agent.

The Quahadis, Quanah's band, did not play these games. For the most part they stayed away from the agency altogether. Their message, said Tatum, was that they "would never go to the agency and shake hands until the soldiers would go there and fight with them; if whipped, they would then go to the agency and shake hands."

SHERMAN WAS INFURIATED by Tatum's reports. After President Grant appointed him overall commander of the army in 1869, Sherman and Army Inspector General Randolph Marcy went to Texas to see the situation for themselves. They left San Antonio on May 1871 on a 430-mile fact-finding mission to the army's freshly established Fort Sill, escorted by seventeen black soldiers from the Tenth Cavalry. Along the way, they observed burned-out ranch houses and abandoned farms. Sherman marveled at how anyone could live in such a dangerous area without expecting to be killed.

On May 18, Sherman's party crossed Salt Creek Prairie under the watchful eyes of 150 Comanche and Kiowa braves led by Satanta, Satank, Big Tree, and a Kiowa medicine man named Mamanti, who was known as the Owl Prophet. The Indians had left the reservation at Fort Sill a few days earlier for their annual spring raiding season in Texas. The night before, Mamanti received a vision foretelling an encounter with two groups of whites the next day; the vision told him to let the first pass unharmed. Thus Sherman and his men rode free. An hour or so later, a small wagon train of a dozen teamsters hauling corn from the railway line to Fort Griffin passed the same spot. This time the warriors struck.

When Sherman heard about the attack, he ordered Colonel Ranald S. Mackenzie, the new commander of the Fourth Cavalry based at Fort Griffin, to rush to the scene. It was a miserable rainy day when Mackenzie and his men arrived. "The poor victims were stripped, scalped, and horribly mutilated; several were beheaded and their brains scooped out," Captain Robert G. Carter, one of Mackenzie's subordinates, recalled. "Their fingers, toes, and private parts had been cut off and stuck in their mouths, and their bodies, now lying in several inches of water and swollen or bloated beyond all chance of recognition, were filled with arrows which made them resemble porcupines. Their bowels had been gashed with knives and carefully heaped upon each exposed abdomen had been placed a mass of live coals . . ."

"One wretched man, Samuel Elliott . . . was found chained between two wagon wheels and, a fire having been made from the wagon pole, he had been slowly roasted to death . . ."

Sherman pushed on to Fort Sill, arriving May 23. When the Kiowa leaders arrived four days later, Satanta freely described to Lawrie Tatum what had happened. He was summoned to a meeting with Sherman at the post commander's house. Standing on the front porch, Sherman signaled his men, and the windows of the house and nearby stables were thrown open. Soldiers trained their guns on Satanta and his followers. The Kiowa chief quickly shifted into servile mode, and sought to walk back his claim: he had only watched the massacre from a distance, he insisted, not participated in it. But Sherman ordered him, Big Tree, and Satank placed in irons.

Lone Wolf came riding up, eager for a showdown. He sat down on the porch with a Winchester cocked defiantly across his lap. For a moment, a replay of the Council House massacre of 1840 seemed imminent, and Sherman would have been caught in the crossfire. But Colonel Benjamin Grierson, Fort Sill's commander, grabbed Lone Wolf's carbine and warned the Indians they had no chance.

Satanta could not quite comprehend why Sherman was so upset, a fact that enraged the general even more. "I answered him that it was a cowardly act for a hundred professed Warriors to attack a dozen Citizen Teamsters, and that all his hundred in time would be hung up like dogs as he would be," Sherman wrote in a letter to his son. "He begged me to take him out now & shoot him, but I told him he should hang in Texas. This they dread terribly."

Sherman ordered Mackenzie to take Satank, Satanta, and Big Tree to Texas for trial. As the journey began, Satank told a Caddo escort named George Washington, "Tell my people that I am dead. I died the first day out from Fort Sill. My bones will be lying on the side of the road. I wish my people to gather them up and take them home."

About a mile from the post, Satank sang a death song. Then, with his back to his guards, he pulled the shackles from his hands, scraping off the skin, drew a butcher knife he had somehow managed to conceal in his clothes, and attacked a guard. The other guards opened fire. "It took him twenty minutes to die," Carter recalled. Mackenzie left the body on the side of the road.

MOODY, THIN-LIPPED, and hobbled by wounds that seemed both physical and emotional, Ranald Slidell Mackenzie came from a family of warriors. His father had been a naval commander, his uncle a Confederate commissioner. His mother was the granddaughter of Revolutionary War soldiers and his brother-in-law was no less than Commodore Matthew C. Perry, the man who opened Japan to the West. One of Mackenzie's brothers attained the rank of lieutenant commander during the Civil War, and another was a navy rear admiral.

Born in New York City in 1840, Mackenzie graduated first in his class at West Point in 1862 and went directly into combat. Before the Civil War ended he received seven brevets for gallantry and was wounded six times, three of them at the battle of Cedar Creek in northern Virginia in October 1864, where he was shot in the heel, then hit again and temporarily paralyzed after his horse was shot in the head and catapulted him to the hard ground. Two fingers on his right hand were shot off during the siege of Petersburg—which led the Indians to call him "Bad Hand." He was present at the Appomattox surrender at the request of Grant, who called him "the most promising young officer in the army."

After the war Mackenzie was promoted to colonel and commanded one of the Buffalo Soldier regiments of black troops and fought Apaches. In February 1871 he took command of the Fourth Cavalry, based at Fort Concho and Fort Richardson in north Texas.

Mackenzie burned with ambition, but he was small, rheumatic, and awkward on horseback. Captain Carter, who became a loyal admirer, called him "fretful, irritable, often times irascible." Lieutenant James Parker, another loyal subordinate, recalled the deep, uncomfortable silences when Mackenzie invited Parker to join him for dinner. "We are full of meditation," wrote Parker, "and we meditate and eat and meditate." Still, these same aides recalled how Mackenzie generously paid off the $500 debt of a junior officer, telling him to pay it back when he could.

In early October 1871, Mackenzie led the Fourth Cavalry into Blanco Canyon in the lower Panhandle, the heart of Quahadi territory, to punish the warriors who refused to submit to reservation rule. Few white men had ventured into this region ever since Coronado's doomed expedition for gold in 1541. Every few miles the canyon widened into a broad valley hemmed in by impassable bluffs and pockmarked with ravines, sand hills, and narrow creeks that fed ponds and lagoons. There were herds of buffalo, flocks of wild ducks, and, according to Carter, "occasionally a majestic swan, whose trumpet notes sounded strange to our hunters."

After several uncomfortable nights, the hungry and exhausted troopers bivouacked in a narrow gap between the canyon walls. Mackenzie allowed them to build campfires, tipping their location. Around midnight a dozen shots rang out in quick succession. Mounted Indians rushed the camp, riding by at full speed, ringing bells, screaming war whoops, and trying to stampede the six hundred horses and mules. The terrified animals strained at their ropes to break loose—"rearing, jumping, plunging, running, and snorting," wrote Carter, "with a strength that terror and brute frenzy alone can inspire. They trembled and groaned in their crazed fright . . ." Officers shouted commands, "Get to your horses!" The panicked horses pulled up the iron picket pins from the ground, sending them hurtling and whistling like bullets. The troopers tried to grab the ropes, "only to be dragged and thrown among the heels of the horses with hands lacerated and burnt by the ropes running rapidly through their fingers." The men secured all that they could as the raiders fled in triumph.

"The hissing and spitting of the bullets sounded viciously," Carter would recall, "and the yells of the retreating Indians from the distance came back on the midnight air with a peculiar, taunting ring." Carter thought to himself, "We found them at last!" And then he realized a more accurate and frightening truth: "*They had found us!*"

The Indians had taken some seventy of the army's horses and mules, including Mackenzie's own fine gray pacer.

At dawn Carter led a patrol to search for the lost horses. A shot rang out in the valley, and through the yellow morning haze Carter and his men spotted several Comanches attempting to make off with a dozen more animals. The troopers gave chase, vaulting an arroyo and pursuing the Indians onto a flat open prairie ascending toward a ridge. Suddenly, as the sun rose high enough to illuminate the plain, Carter made out the forms of dozens of mounted Indians galloping over the ridge straight at him and his twelve men. He had fallen into an ambush.

"It was like an electric shock," he would recall. "All seemed to realize the deadly peril of their situation and to take it in at a glance. For a moment the blood seemed fairly congealed for we realized what the ruse of the Indians had been . . ."

Carter had to choose. He and his men could try to coax their tired mounts back to the ravine, where they could take cover. But Carter knew their horses were too spent to make it. The alternative was to stand and fight where they were and retreat slowly, firing at every step. Carter ordered the men to dismount.

The Comanches moved to encircle the small band of soldiers. The warriors, Carter wrote, "were naked to the waist; were arrayed in all their war paint and trinkets, with head dress or war bonnets of fur or feathers . . . Their ponies, especially the white, cream, dun and clay banks, were striped and otherwise artistically painted and decorated with gaudy stripes of flannel and calico. Bells were jingling, feathers waving, and with jubilant, discordant yells . . . and uttering taunting shouts, they pressed on to what they surely considered to be their legitimate prey."

Somewhere behind the warriors, high up one of the canyon walls, Carter could hear Comanche women ululating in a high-pitched tremolo, urging on their men.

Carter and his men kept firing as they pulled back, then leapt on their horses and broke for the ravine. One of the men, Sergeant Seander Gregg, was riding an exhausted gray horse that stumbled. An Indian, taller and

Quahadi Comanche camp, 1869–74. The Quahadis were the last of the major Comanche groups to surrender to white military rule and take up reservation life.

darker than most, came racing out of the pack on a coal-black horse. He was dressed in a full-length war bonnet and bear claw necklace. "His face was smeared with black war paint, which gave his features a satanic look," Carter wrote. "A large, cruel mouth added to his ferocious appearance."

Forty yards away, Gregg's comrades tried to lay down covering fire. But the warrior pulled his horse behind the hapless sergeant, using him as a shield against the bullets. Carter shouted to Gregg to use his carbine or his six-shooter, but Gregg was too stunned and weakened to force a cartridge into the chamber. The Indian drew his own pistol and shot Gregg point-blank in the head.

Many years later Carter, in his detailed but melodramatic account of the skirmish, would claim that the warrior was Quanah. The claim might be categorized as just another post-incident Quanah myth, except for the fact that Quanah himself later affirmed publicly that he had killed Gregg.

He wheeled his horse around and galloped away with his warriors. At first Carter wondered why, but then he saw Tonkawa scouts riding to his rescue, bearing down toward his position; right behind them were Mackenzie's troopers.

The Comanches, supplied with fresh mounts by their women atop the canyon walls, shouted down taunts and insults. But they did not attack. By the time Mackenzie's troops made it to the top, the Quahadis had melted away.

The next few days were a game of cat and mouse. The Quahadis had fresh ponies and knew intimately the hidden folds and creases of the landscape, but they were carrying hundreds of women and children alongside the warriors. Mackenzie's men and horses, meanwhile, were reaching the point of exhaustion. The day after the ambush the Tonkawas signaled from atop the bluff that they had found a trail. It took the troops hours to scale the narrow path on their spent mounts. When they reached the top, wrote Carter, they came upon "what appeared to be a vast, almost illimitable expanse of prairie. As far as the eye could reach, not a brush or tree, a twig or stone, not an object of any kind or a living thing, was in sight. It stretched out before us—one uninterrupted plain, only to be compared to the ocean in its vastness."

The troopers had come to the edge of the Staked Plains, Quanah's flat, arid, relentless kingdom. They were three thousand feet above sea level on the limestone plateau in mid-October with a cold north wind howling down the treeless prairie.

The Quahadis refused to engage, keeping a steady distance between themselves and the troopers as the afternoon faded to darkness and the wind blew in a cold rain mixed with sleet. The soldiers followed a trail of half-burned campfires and jettisoned lodge poles, stone hammers, mortars, pestles, and buffalo skins. Eventually Carter could see the main body of fleeing women and children about a mile in the distance. He awaited Mackenzie's order to attack, but it never came. Perhaps, Carter surmised, the colonel feared risking his troops against a clever and ruthless enemy some one hundred miles beyond his supply lines, or perhaps he did not have the stomach for slaughtering women and children on a cold October night. Within minutes, the village was gone, its escape hidden by the darkness.

The soldiers were left to huddle in the storm. Mackenzie himself, suffering in immaculate silence from his old war wounds, shivered from exposure until someone threw a buffalo robe over his shaking body.

Faced with flagging morale, tired horses, and a dwindling supply of food, Mackenzie decided to turn back east to Fort Richardson. He was finished, for now, with Quanah, the Staked Plains, and the Quahadis.

But the Quahadis were not quite finished with him. As the column once again pushed its way through Canyon Blanco, someone cried out,

"Indians! Indians!" The Tonkawa scouts broke away from the column, racing toward a small ravine where they had spotted two Comanches leading their horses up the canyon trail. The Tonkawas sealed off the area and went into the ravine for the kill. Mackenzie grew impatient and dismounted. "Just then, a sharp swish, a thud, and a spiked arrow buried itself in the upper fleshy part of Mackenzie's leg," wrote Carter. "He hurried back to the rear and had the spike cut out and the wound dressed." The old warrior had been wounded again.

Mackenzie's troop staggered back into Fort Richardson on November 18, 1871, in the midst of a blizzard. The men had been in the field since May 1 and they were cold, exhausted, and starving. Total war had faltered. Quanah and the Quahadis still roamed free.

7.

The Surrender (Comancheria, 1874–1875)

E ven by the dubious standards of the frontier, buffalo hunters were a breed apart. In the field they were mechanical killers, spending long days mowing down senseless beasts in assembly-line fashion. They worked, ate, and slept among the fly-infested corpses, bathing in nearby creeks when they bathed at all. The skinners were especially filthy, working daily with the putrefying carcasses, covered in blood, fat, and parasites.

They were the meanest of men, and "the meanest man among them," according to a fellow hunter, was Billy Dixon. Born in West Virginia in 1850, orphaned at age twelve, Dixon was working as a teamster in Kansas by the time he was fifteen. He wore his black hair long, stringy, and greasy and it all but concealed his dark brown face. He never lacked for the one prerequisite for survival on the Plains: self-assurance. He described himself as "in perfect health, strong and muscular, with keen eyesight, a natural aptitude for outdoor life . . . an excellent shot [with] a burning desire to experience every phase of adventure to be found on the Plains."

Life on the High Plains was rugged and cheap, and death was ubiquitous. In Leavenworth City, Kansas, which he made home for a time, Dixon would recall, "Shootings were as common as the arrival of a bulltrain, and excited little comment. The man who was quickest on the trigger usually came out ahead—the other fellow was buried, and no questions asked."

The buffalo trade gained momentum slowly. At first, tanneries back east complained that the bison hides were too thick and rough to use for fine leather goods. But by 1872, firms in New York and Pennsylvania had imported European methods of softening the hides, creating a keen demand for raw materials and a new incentive for hunters.

So far as William T. Sherman and his right-hand man, Phil Sheridan, were concerned, the timing of this breakthrough was perfect. The two generals set extermination of the vast herds of American bison on the Great Plains as a policy goal in order to deprive Plains Indians of their primary source of food, clothing, and shelter. Professional hunters, trespassing on Indian land, killed more than four million bison by 1874. When the Texas legislature considered a law banning bison poaching on tribal lands, Sheridan journeyed to Austin to personally testify against the measure. He suggested that the legislature might better give each hunter a medal, engraved with a dead buffalo on one side and a discouraged-looking Indian on the other. The way to solve "the vexed Indian question," Sheridan told the lawmakers, was by destroying "the Indians' commissary."

With a growing market to supply, the buffalo hunter's arsenal rapidly increased in size and accuracy: muzzle loaders, shotguns, and Springfield rifles gave way to Henry and Spencer repeating rifles. The Sharps Rifle Company paved the way with new models specially designed for killing buffalo, led by the Big Fifty, a fifty-caliber rifle that fired a large bullet from a long shell containing a heavy powder charge—ideal for big game. Buffalo were so plentiful, so slow to move, and so oblivious to danger that an efficient hunter could kill between seventy-five and one hundred a day, an average hunter about fifty and even a poor one twenty-five. "I have seen their bodies so thick after being skinned that they would look like logs where a hurricane had passed through a forest," recalled W. S. Glenn, who hunted bison across the Plains in the 1870s. "If they were lying on a hillside, the rays of the sun would make it look like a hundred glass windows."

By 1872, hunters could expect to earn four dollars for each bull hide. A prolific shooter like Billy Dixon would hire two skinners to accompany him on hunts in order to keep up with the frenetic pace he set. Each was expected to prepare up to fifty skins a day. Dixon would pay up to twenty cents a hide to a good skinner.

By the winter of 1872, according to Dixon's memoir, some seventy-five thousand bison had been killed within a sixty-mile radius of Dodge City, the southern hub of organized buffalo hunting. "The noise of the guns of the hunters could be heard on all sides, rumbling and booming hour after hour, as if a heavy battle were being fought," he recalled. The outskirts of town were rank with the sight and smell of rotting carcasses. And the herds began to vanish.

Army colonel Richard Irving Dodge recalled that in May 1871 he had come across an endless chain of buffalo over a twenty-five-mile stretch along the Arkansas River. "The whole country appeared one mass of buffalo, moving slowly to the northward," he wrote.

One year later, "where there were myriads of buffalo the year before, there were now myriads of carcasses. The air was foul with sickening stench, and the vast plain, which only a short twelvemonth before teemed with animal life, was a dead, solitary, putrid desert."

The Arkansas River in North Texas and Oklahoma was the border south of which no hunter could go. "We gazed longingly across the sandy wastes that marked the course of the Arkansas," wrote Dixon. "The oftener we looked the more eager we were to tempt fate." Even the danger of encountering Indians "added spice to the temptation."

The Treaty of Medicine Lodge in 1867 prohibited whites from hunting for buffalo south of the Arkansas. Still, after hunters had eliminated most of the great herds north of the river, they began moving south. Even the hunters themselves were under the impression that the army would try to stop them. Only it didn't. When a group of buffalo men sought his advice, Colonel Dodge offered a cryptic reply. "Boys, if I were a buffalo hunter, I would hunt buffalo where buffalo are," he told them.

A hunter-merchant named J. Wright Mooar got the hint. In March 1874 he helped organize a train of one hundred wagons loaded with hunters, merchants, and camp followers, including himself and Dixon, and headed southwest from Dodge City. They crossed the Arkansas River into Indian Territory and kept going. They stopped eventually at the confluence of two creeks two miles north of the Canadian River, a gently sloping meadow with fresh drinking water and enough tall trees to provide timber. The site was just a mile from the adobe rubble of an older trading post that had been the scene of a bloody confrontation in 1864 between Colonel Kit Carson's New Mexico volunteers and Comanche, Kiowa, and Apache warriors. Carson's small force was lucky to have escaped with their lives. The old trading post was called Adobe Walls.

The new Adobe Walls became the central staging ground for the new generation of white hunters. The newcomers started constructing a complex of sod buildings, including a store, mess hall, and stable, along with an eight-foot-high picket corral to contain livestock. A competing group arrived about a month later and built another store, corral, and outhouse nearby. And someone added a saloon and blacksmith shop to the complex.

By mid-June teamsters were hauling a thousand hides into the trading post every day. Visitors recalled seeing vast piles near the site. "The first idea I had was that there was a small settlement out there in the wilderness . . . ," recalled Seth Hathaway. "[But] on getting closer, what I first took for houses turned out to be piles of buffalo hides stacked up and ready to be hauled to the railroad."

Billy Dixon and the others were now operating in the heart of the hunting grounds claimed by Quanah and the Quahadis. The hunters knew they were pushing their luck by setting up camp inside Comanche territory, but the rewards were too tempting to resist. Instead of two skinners a day, Dixon was now using three, and paying them up to twenty-five cents per skin. He and his men would set up a dugout with a big open fireplace near plenty of water and wood. He would kill thirty-five or forty bulls within a few hours. "No mercy was shown the buffalo when I got back to camp from Adobe Walls," he would recall. "I killed as many as my three men could handle, working them as hard as they were willing to work. This was deadly business, without sentiment; it was dollars against tenderheartedness, and dollars won."

Dixon headed back to Adobe Walls to hire more skinners. The Canadian River was flooded and hard to cross. Along the way he got the news that two hunters had been killed by Kiowas fifteen miles downriver. The Indians had mutilated the two men—broken open the victims' skulls, spilled out their brains and filled the cavities with grass, and cut out their hearts along with their ears, noses, fingers, and toes.

Around the same time, two other hunters, an Englishman and a German, were killed a few miles away.

"Every man of us was dead set against abandoning the buffalo range," Dixon would recall. "The herds were now at hand. And we were in a fair way to make big money." The hunters decided to go out together. "I felt uneasy all the time. Something seemed to be wrong. There was Indian in the air."

THE IDEA OF ATTACKING Adobe Walls started with Quanah, or so he would later claim. His original plan was to avenge the death of a childhood friend who had been killed by Tonkawa Indians, the allies of the Texans. The killing "make my heart hot and I want to make it even," he said, so he recruited warriors for a raid in the time-honored method, going from camp to camp offering his pipe. Those who smoked with him signaled their agreement to go to battle. Quanah visited the No-koni band at the head of Cache Creek and the Quahadis near Elk Creek, then the Kiowas and Cheyennes on the Washita River. "I work one month," Quanah would recall.

He had an unusual partner for his effort. A young Comanche sha-man named Isatai was making his bid to become a messiah by claiming that he could make medicine that would render warriors immune from bullets. Isatai—whose name in Comanche meant "Wolf Droppings"—insisted he possessed miraculous healing powers and could even raise the dead. He accurately predicted the harsh spring and summer drought of 1874. He told followers he had ascended to heaven to visit the Great Spirit "high above that occupied by the white man's Great Spiritual Power" and was empowered to wage war on the whites. He claimed to be able to spit out nearly a wagonload of cartridges at a time—unlimited ammunition for the fighters. To the Comanches, decimated by smallpox and cholera epidemics and running out of options, Isatai's message was impossible to resist.

He and Quanah succeeded in organizing a sun dance for all the Co-manche bands. They gathered sometime in May along the Red River near the mouth of Sweetwater Creek. They even built a mock fort and tore it down in a practice battle. The older chiefs agreed to send their young men on the attack, and they wanted the first target to be Adobe Walls.

As Quanah later recalled, the chiefs told him, "You pretty good fighter, Quanah, but you not know everything. We think you take pipe first against white buffalo hunters—you kill white men [and] make your heart feel good. After that you come back, take all young men and go to Texas warpath."

It was Isatai who turned the plan into a grand scheme to eliminate whites altogether and save the remaining buffalo herds, and who came up with medicine he claimed would protect them from the white man's bullets. "God tell me we going to kill lots white men," Isatai told them, according to Quanah's account. "Bullets not penetrate shirts—we kill them just like old woman."

More than two hundred warriors—the number is still in dispute among historians—rode west for several days, then stopped in the late afternoon, made medicine, painted their faces, donned war bonnets, and crossed the Canadian River. They approached the trading post on foot; some slept for a few hours while others stayed awake talking and smoking. Then, just as daylight began to creep through the eastern sky, they mounted their horses.

THE NIGHT OF JUNE 26 was sultry and dry, part of the prolonged drought that gripped the southern plains that summer. Inside Adobe Walls twenty-eight men and one woman—Mrs. William Olds, who had come from Dodge City with her husband to operate a dining room in the rear of the trading store—bedded down after midnight following some spirited carousing. All of the doors and windows were left wide open in the hope of catching a breeze. Billy Dixon slept on the ground outside to be near his wagon and horses. At around 2:00 a.m. pressure from the heavy sod covering the roof of Hanrahan's saloon cracked the cottonwood ridgepole in its center, producing a loud, sharp report like a gunshot. Hanrahan ordered everyone out of the building for fear it would collapse.

Dixon helped shore up the roof. By the time they got the ridgepole back in place, the sky was growing red. Figuring it was too late to get back to sleep, Dixon decided to move on. He picked up his rifle and sauntered toward his horses. Just beyond them, at the edge of the tree line, he could make out objects moving in his direction. "Then I was thunderstruck," he recalled. "The black body of moving objects suddenly spread out like a fan, and from it went up one single, solid yell—a war-whoop that seemed to shake the very air of the early morning." Then came the thundering roar of Indian ponies and more bloodcurdling war cries.

Dixon dashed for his saddle horse, tied it to his wagon, aimed his rifle and fired off one quick shot, then fled toward the closest shelter, Hanrahan's saloon. He sprinted through the door just before a wave of Indians engulfed the compound. Two brothers, Jacob and Isaac Scheidler, were not so lucky. They had been asleep in their wagon and had no chance to run. The warriors hacked them to pieces, scalped them, and even cut a piece of hide from the bloody corpse of their black Newfoundland dog.

The sleep-deprived defenders in three buildings grabbed their guns, threw up makeshift barricades of sacks of flour and grain and packing crates, and opened fire. Many fought the entire day in their underwear.

The first half hour was a close-in gun battle. Quanah and his warriors punched holes in the adobe walls of the saloon and tried to break down the doors, but a steady rain of gunfire forced them to retreat. Next they tried to climb the roof, but once again the gunfire was too intense. Isatai's medicine failed to protect them from the hunters' bullets. "I am sure that we surprised the Indians as badly as they surprised us," Dixon recalled.

After the defenders fought off the assault, the warriors pulled back and laid siege to the compound throughout the day, launching periodic attacks on the buildings but never breaking through. The hunters, despite their small numbers, simply wielded too much firepower.

Wearing his long, flowing war bonnet, Quanah circled the site on his gray pony, seeking to rally the warriors. He fell from his horse during heavy gunfire and took shelter behind an old buffalo carcass. While lying there, he felt a searing stab of pain between his shoulder blade and his neck. It felt like he had been hit by a rock, but he realized quickly it must have been a ricocheting bullet. He crawled to a plum thicket, where other warriors pulled him to safety. "The white men had big guns," Quanah would recall, and Isatai's magic proved to be "polecat medicine."

After that, the warriors pulled back even farther, trading shots with the hunters until evening.

The siege continued for a second day. The Indians killed or ran off all the hunters' horses, leaving them no way to escape or seek help from the outside. But toward the end of the day two teams of hunters punched through the Indian encirclement from the outside and made their way to the compound.

By the third day, the hunters with their long-range rifles began to get a bead on their attackers. Memories and boasts were notoriously unreliable, but Billy Dixon claimed to have taken aim with his .50-caliber Sharps rifle and gotten off three shots at someone crawling in the tall grass some eight hundred yards away. After the battle ended, the hunters found a dead Indian lying flat on his stomach. "They killed us," Quanah would recall.

By mid-afternoon the Indians retreated. An angry swarm of Cheyennes grabbed Isatai by the throat and demanded he be killed, but the Comanches argued he had been disgraced enough by his failure. Isatai's messiah days were over.

Over the years Isatai offered several explanations for his failure to ward off bullets. He said that on their way to Adobe Walls the warriors had killed a skunk, whose spirit had somehow neutralized the power of his medicine. He told someone else that he had concocted the medicine to sabotage the guns at Fort Dodge and had not considered that it would not work at Adobe Walls. In truth, he had sold his own myth so powerfully to his fellow warriors that he himself had come to believe it.

Three whites were killed and thirteen warriors were found dead at the site, although the Indians may have carried off the bodies of another dozen. A fourth white man, Mrs. Olds's hapless husband, William, died when he slipped on a ladder with a loaded gun cradled in his arm and blew off his own head. When a relief column finally arrived, the troops found thirteen severed Indian heads staring blindly from the posts of the corral gate.

THE ATTACK ON ADOBE WALLS was the moment the army had been waiting for. Secretary of War W. W. Belknap took the reins off Sherman, instructing him to punish all hostile Indians, including those living on reservations. Sherman, in turn, ordered Sheridan "to act with vindictive earnestness and to make every Kiowa and Comanche knuckle down."

Sheridan dispatched five columns totaling three thousand troops who entered the Panhandle from five different directions in a pincer movement to squeeze the warriors. A series of fourteen skirmishes and small battles ensued, known collectively as the Red River War. There were few casualties, but each violent encounter reduced the Indians' supply of food, horses, and shelter.

Ranald Mackenzie's column of 640 men entered the canyon country of the eastern Panhandle in mid-September. A group of newspaper reporters demanded permission to accompany him, but Bad Hand was not interested in publicity. Sherman had called for a full-scale assault. "The more Indians we can kill this year, the less will have to be killed the next," he declared. But Mackenzie believed that the most effective way to defeat the Comanches was not to attempt to mow them down but to destroy their means of survival.

Mackenzie's men beat off an attack by 250 warriors after dark on September 26, at the head of Tule Canyon. Aware that he and his men were being watched, Mackenzie set off after the warriors, who were moving away from Palo Duro canyon. But when darkness fell, he changed direction, pushing his men all night thirty miles south toward the spot where Cita Blanca and Palo Duro canyons meet. At daybreak the troopers stormed the Quahadi winter stronghold on the canyon floor. Most of the Comanches escaped—the soldiers killed only three warriors—but they left behind teepees, food, blankets, saddles, and 1,424 horses and ponies. Mackenzie ordered the animals slaughtered. It was a crushing blow to the Comanches. When it rained the next night, the Indians were forced to sleep "in puddles of mud and water like swine," Mackenzie wrote.

For the next two months, Mackenzie trailed the Comanches in relentless pursuit of his crippled foe. Through increasing sleet and rain, Mackenzie and his men doggedly stalked Quanah and the Quahadis, who were slowed by hundreds of cold, hungry, and exhausted women and children. "It is important to give the Indians as little rest as possible," Mackenzie wrote his superiors on October 29. The Comanches eventually retreated into the Staked Plains. Mackenzie followed until sheer exhaustion and lack of food forced him and his men to quit around Christmastime. But unlike the soldiers, the Indians had no safe haven to retreat to.

FACED WITH A WINTER without shelter and with little food, other Comanche and Kiowa bands were calling it quits. Satanta and Big Tree surrendered on October 4, 1874, to Lieutenant Colonel Thomas H. Neill of the Sixth Cavalry, bringing in 145 Kiowa warriors and their families. "I came in here to give myself up and do as the white chief wishes," proclaimed Satanta. Predictably blaming the Comanches for Adobe Walls, he claimed, "I have done no fighting against the whites, have killed no white men, and committed no depredations since I left Fort Sill."

Mackenzie returned to Fort Sill in March 1875. One month later, 3 Comanche leaders, 35 braves, and 140 women and children surrendered themselves at the fort with some 700 horses. But the Quahadis were still on the loose.

Mackenzie began preparing for a new spring offensive to hunt them down, but first he wanted to see if he could coax them into surrender. He sent out an emissary: Jacob J. Sturm, the same man who had brought home young Bianca Babb from her Comanche abductors a decade earlier. Sturm was a self-styled "pioneer physician," Army scout, and interpreter who had married a local Caddo woman. Accompanied by three reservation Comanches, he set out from Fort Sill on April 23. According to Sturm's journal, it took them a week to travel roughly 250 miles through territory where white men had once feared to tread. Now the land seemed empty of people and wildlife.

Sturm's party eventually encountered a friendly Quahadi band, led by Black Beard, a chief with fifteen to twenty lodges. Black Beard was happy to see Sturm, fed him a dinner of buffalo meat, shared a pipe, and then got down to business, saying he and his followers were tired of war and ready to come to Fort Sill. The main Quahadi camp, he told Sturm, was "two sleeps" away. To cement his friendship and sincerity, Black Beard bestowed upon Sturm any mule of his choice.

It took several more days for Sturm's little party to ascend the timbered bushland and emerge onto the eastern edge of the empty, windswept Staked Plains—"a barren waste unfit for habitation of civilized men," according to Sturm. There they finally caught up to the main Quahadi camp, under the leadership of the much-maligned Isatai. Sturm and his men introduced themselves as messengers of peace and shared their supplies of tobacco, coffee, and sugar with the Comanches.

The Indians told Sturm they were no longer seeking to fight anyone and were doing their best to keep out of the way of those whites who still wanted to fight them. Isatai said he was inclined to take his people to Fort Sill, but could not make a final decision until the return of thirty men who were out on a buffalo hunt. He and Sturm met again the next day, and this time he brought along a tall young warrior named Quanah, whom Sturm described as "a young man of much influence with his people." The young warrior expressed his support for surrendering. Isatai "then told his people they must all prepare to come in to Fort Sill and as his authority seems to be absolute they all agreed to start tomorrow," wrote Sturm.

They broke camp the next day and started northeast to Fort Sill, leaving a message for the hunters to catch up to them on a piece of buffalo skin stuck on a pole.

It was, Sturm writes, an extraordinary sight: hundreds of warriors, women, and children, trekking through the High Plains in a great snaking line that strung out for miles. They were traveling from their hunting grounds and a harsh, unsustainable freedom to a form of captivity and an unknown future. There was nothing joyous or exciting about the journey; they were making it because they had no choice. They were in no hurry: they killed a handful of buffalo along the way, stripped the corpses of their meat, and waited two days while meat and hides dried in the sun.

At one point near sundown, Sturm spotted a single rider moving through the plains like a sailboat on an open, placid sea, "coming out of this vastness of the great plain, without any path to keep him from getting lost nor road to guide him, but coming up to our camp on a beeline." It was an Apache who said that more than forty lodges of his tribesmen—perhaps three hundred people—were also prepared to surrender. "I told him I was not instructed to bring in Apaches but was sure that General Mackenzie would be much pleased if they would all come in."

The next night the Comanches staged a medicine dance—"the last . . . they ever expect to have [on] these broad Plains." They were gripped by fear, hope, and resignation. "They say they will abandon their roving life and try to learn to live as white people do," wrote Sturm.

The next day the caravan climbed a rocky bluff and ascended onto "the great high plain wonderful and grand in its vastness." It was clear to Sturm that Isatai, not Quanah, was in charge. "When he says move, we move, and when he says stop, we stop, and if I ask any one when we will start they refer me to him always."

With the main body of Quahadis winding slowly through the plains, Sturm sent an advance party of three Comanches on ahead. They arrived at Fort Sill on May 13. With Horace Jones interpreting, the men told the colonel that the Quahadis would keep their word and surrender as promised. The main body was moving slowly because their horses were weak and there were women, children, and old people among them. But it would arrive in a few weeks.

After the warriors finished, one of them—an unusually tall and powerful-looking man with striking gray eyes—took Jones aside for a lengthy discussion, after which the interpreter turned to Mackenzie and conveyed a highly unusual request. Jones told him the warrior's name was Quanah and he wanted the colonel's help in locating his white mother and his sister. As a child he had been called Tseeta or Citra, and these were the names by which his mother might recognize him. Her white name, Jones added, was Cynthia Ann Parker. Jones, who had met Cynthia Ann after her recapture fifteen years earlier and had also spoken with her Comanche husband, Peta Nocona, knew her story well and filled in the details for the colonel.

Mackenzie respected the Quahadis. He admired the fact that, unlike his other Indian foes, they had never played the double game of camping at the reservation for food and shelter during the winter months and then returning to raiding in the spring and summer. He wanted to help them. "I think better of this band than of any other on the reservation as they have been steadily out and now come in at a most unusual time," he wrote. "I shall let them down as easily as I can."

Mackenzie listened carefully to Quanah's request. He said he would try to help.

8.

The Go-between (Fort Sill, 1875–1886)

In *End of the Trail* (1915), James Earle Fraser's doleful statue of a Native American rider and horse, the heads of both are bowed in defeat. This was the tragic and romantic portrait of the Noble but Doomed Savage at the beginning of the twentieth century, vanquished and displaced by the modern world, the tip of his war lance turned downward in submission. But its message was misleading: Indians did not vanish, their story was not over, and their trail did not end when they lost their struggle against white domination. Their struggle to survive continued, only in many ways it was harder and more complex than the one they had waged in battle.

The long, thin caravan of Quahadi men, women, and children—the last significant group of hostile Comanches on the High Plains—finally trickled into the Signal Station, six miles west of Fort Sill, on June 2, 1875. The official count was 427 people and 1,500 horses. The old people, women, and children proceeded to an appointed campground, while the men quietly laid down their arms and trudged under military escort to their place of confinement at the fort, a roofless icehouse with a stone floor, 150 by 40 feet, already crammed with 130 Comanche, Kiowa, and Cheyenne prisoners. At meal times soldiers would throw chunks of raw meat over the high walls. "They fed us like we were lions," said Gotebo, a Kiowa warrior. Quanah was spared this indignity and allowed to camp with his wives and children west of the fort, along the banks of Cache Creek.

Many of the Quahadis who rode into Fort Sill to surrender in the summer of 1875 likely believed they could ride out again and resume their nomadic warrior life whenever they chose to, as they had in the past.

Quanah, by contrast, seemed to understand from the beginning that his life had been irrevocably altered, and he began to adjust accordingly.

For one thing, the Comanche population had been decimated by war, epidemic, starvation, and the grim realities of fugitive life on the unyielding plains. When the nineteenth century began, there had been between twenty thousand and thirty thousand Comanches. But James M. Haworth, head of the Kiowa-Comanche-Apache agency at the fort, registered only 1,475 in 1877, along with 1,120 Kiowas and 344 Apaches. A few hundred more were huddled in remote corners of the Staked Plains or in the foothills of the Rockies. The assembly-line extermination of the buffalo over the past decade meant that the Comanches had lost not only most of their own community but also their sole traditional means of replenishing it.

Open resistance was futile. Quanah knew well the fate of Satank, Satanta, Big Tree, and the other chiefs who had been hunted down, imprisoned, or condemned to a never-ending life on the run. Quanah was a proud man but a practical one. He harbored no taste for martyrdom.

He decided to recast his own narrative. Not that he thought of it in exactly those terms, but Quanah was a storyteller. His old story was about a proud, independent warrior, beholden to no one, who had held out as long as he could. Now he had a different tale to tell—about a man who was half-white and half-Comanche, and who longed to bring those two worlds together, explaining each to the other and linking the two, just as they were linked in his own bloodstream. The Man of Peace. The White Comanche. The Noble Savage. It was, always, a work in progress. But almost from the moment his captivity began, it is clear that this was the role he had decided to play.

From the day he arrived at Fort Sill, Quanah chose to make himself useful to the men who were now in charge of his fate, Colonel Ranald Mackenzie and Indian agent Haworth. Twice that summer Quanah volunteered to round up Comanche stragglers and deliver them to the fort; each time Mackenzie sent along a document of authorization to give Quanah a modicum of protection from trigger-happy whites inclined to kill any Comanche they encountered.

Texas was a dangerous place for any Indian to venture into. A Texas congressman attached a rider to an appropriation bill that year forbidding Indian hunting parties from entering the state even when escorted by troops. Perhaps he was thinking of their safety. Five Indians who crossed into Jack County in northeastern Texas in April 1875 were surrounded by white settlers, gunned down, and beheaded. "I understand the heads are now preserved in alcohol in Jacksboro," wrote Haworth in his annual report to Washington.

On his first run as an agent of the United States government, Quanah brought back a party of twenty-one Comanches whom he located on the Pecos River. This was "excellent conduct in a dangerous expedition," Mackenzie reported to his superiors. The returned fugitives were stripped of their weapons and horses and dispatched to the icehouse. But Quanah insisted that they not be shipped off to a military prison. This earned him the gratitude of the former fugitives. Already he was learning how to serve as a bridge between the two sides, white and Indian.

It was not long before Mackenzie sent out Quanah again, this time to find and bring back a small band of Quahadis still lurking in the familiar, well-worn creases of the Texas Panhandle. Quanah left on July 12 with three men, three women, and several pack mules loaded with supplies. He carried a white flag and a stern letter from Mackenzie warning anyone they encountered not to interfere with him or his mission.

One of the renegades was Herman Lehmann, a teenage white captive turned Comanche warrior. He and his fellow warriors, determined to live by the old ways, scoured the desolate plateau for the last remnants of wild game while avoiding the soldiers and Texas Rangers who were in turn hunting for them. But their main enemies were the buffalo hunters who were engaged in eliminating the last of the herds. Everywhere they rode, the Quahadis came across stinking mounds of rotting carcasses. "The plains were literally alive with buffalo hunters," Lehmann would recall.

Some of the warriors had fought in the debacle at Adobe Walls and did not yearn for another. For the most part they shied away from the hunters, who were armed with long-range Sharps rifles. But early in 1877 the nomads joined forces with warriors under Black Horse, a Quahadi chief who had obtained permission from Haworth for a hunting expedition in the Panhandle. When Black Horse and his increasingly frustrated followers could not find any buffalo to kill, they decided to hunt the hunters instead. One morning in early February they came across a lone buffalo man named Marshall Sewell, who was working the Salt Fork of the Brazos River. They watched unseen from a distance as Sewell brought down beast after beast in mechanical fashion with his rifle. When he finally ran out of bullets, they moved in. One of the Indians shot him in the thigh. Sewell frantically hobbled back toward his camp but Lehmann and the others cut him off and finished him.

The Comanches pillaged the camp, taking weapons, tools, and food, defacing the hides with their knives and setting them on fire. They scalped Sewell's corpse, cut a gash in each temple and stuck a sharp stick through his stomach, then set fire to his wagon. No white hunter could miss the message.

Seeking revenge, about four dozen buffalo men set out in early March to hunt down the Comanches. They found the Indians camped in Yellow House Canyon, a few miles east of present-day Lubbock. The gun battle lasted all day—one hunter and three Indians were killed—until the badly outnumbered hunters were forced to withdraw. The skirmish constituted the last organized battle between whites and Indians in the state of Texas. A few weeks later a cavalry troop from Fort Griffin quietly rounded up most of the Quahadi stragglers and escorted them back to Fort Sill. Lehmann and a ragtag handful eluded capture and continued to roam the Staked Plains until Quanah tracked them down that summer along the Pecos River in eastern New Mexico.

To these hardened, defiant, but exhausted stragglers, Quanah did not try to preach peace, love, or reconciliation, just practical arithmetic. They were, he told them, outnumbered. He "told us that it was useless for us to fight longer," Lehmann would recall, "for the white people would kill all of us if we kept on fighting . . . He said the white men had us completely surrounded; that they would come in on us from every side, and we had better give up."

Some of the men, including Herman, wanted to hold out longer, but they all reluctantly agreed to come with Quanah. He moved them across the hostile Panhandle under cover of darkness, abandoning three hundred horses and mules along the way. During the daytime Quanah used a pair of army field glasses to search the landscape for buffalo hunters. In his past life as a warrior, he had ferociously hunted these men; now he sought to hide from them.

Lehmann came in with Quanah but refused to surrender. Quanah concealed him for a time among Quanah's own household, but then told him he must return to his white family. Lehmann grew angry; he even threatened to kill Horace Jones, the Comanche interpreter, when Jones summoned him to Fort Sill for a talk. Quanah took Lehmann back to his lodge, fed him, and persuaded him to go home to Texas. Quanah promised to look after Lehmann's horses and to welcome him back if things didn't work out with his white relatives. This was a subject Quanah knew something about, for he had started searching for white relatives of his own.

RANALD MACKENZIE HAD BEEN A TACTICIAN of brutal efficiency, but now he was keen to help his former Comanche foes survive. This was not purely altruism on his part. With winter approaching, he wrote to his superiors, "the emergency is pressing, and unless these Indians are fed and the obligations of the Indian Department to them fulfilled, we may expect certainly a stampede of the Kiowas and Comanches from their reservation." Hungry Indians storming back onto the warpath was not a pleasant image to contemplate.

Mackenzie gave back to the Comanches more than five hundred of their horses and mules seized during the Red River campaign, and he sold the rest for $27,000 and established a Pony Fund. He used the money to buy 3,500 head of sheep, hoping the Comanches would learn to harvest the wool and eat the meat. The experiment was an utter failure: Comanches, it turned out, hated mutton. In any event, most of the sheep died of exposure that first winter. Cattle were the only realistic option.

Mackenzie's efforts at family reunification were no more successful. Six days after Quanah first arrived at Fort Sill, Mackenzie wrote to the quartermaster at Denison, Texas, seeking information on Cynthia Ann and Prairie Flower. The letter was published in several Texas newspapers and aroused much interest. Eventually Mackenzie received a reply from Benjamin Parker, one of Cynthia Ann's first cousins and the son of the late Reverend Daniel Parker, informing him that she and Prairie Flower had died. There would be no mother and child reunion.

Mackenzie went off to the Dakotas to fight Dull Knife, chief of the northern Cheyenne. When he returned to Fort Sill two years later he wrote to Isaac Parker, Quanah's uncle and the man who had taken Cynthia Ann home after she was recaptured in 1860, telling him of Quanah's efforts to contact his Texas relatives. "He has been here two years, and none of his cousins or other relations have been here to see him," Mackenzie told Isaac. ". . . He rather thinks that they do not wish to see him."

He described Quanah as "a man whom it is worth trying to do something with," and pleaded with Isaac that Quanah "certainly should not be held responsible for the sins of a former generation of Comanches."

Quanah's motives for a reunion with his Texas relatives were not just sentimental: he hoped they could rescue him from captivity and enrich him as well. "After an Indian custom," Mackenzie's letter added, Quanah wanted to receive a small gift from his relatives as a signal that they would welcome him for a visit. Mackenzie pleaded on Quanah's behalf "that he has heard his uncle is well off, and that he is poor and trying to live like a white man, and that he would like him to give him a light wagon, if this is the case."

There is no record that Isaac Parker ever responded. Cynthia Ann had been such an embarrassment to her white family that no one seemed willing to contemplate welcoming her wild Comanche son into their Texas home.

Still, in some ways, Quanah's opportunities were better in the new world than in the old. As a half-white Comanche orphan, he had possessed limited stature in a shattered tribal community disintegrating under military pressure and disease. Now he had new patrons and potential allies. He frequently invoked Mackenzie and Haworth's paternal advice: "Follow the white man's path."

Mackenzie soon left Fort Sill again for another assignment. His life would be cut short by illnesses both physical and mental. Haworth, too, was eventually reassigned. When Philemon B. Hunt, the new agent, arrived to take Haworth's place, Quanah was quick to curry his favor as well. "Even though I am here with my friends yet there is but one council I listen to, and that is yours," he wrote Hunt in a letter. "I do not listen to any foolish talks. I wait and listen to you alone, you are my agent."

Hunt soon fell under Quanah's spell, and even tried to help him claim his rightful share of his late mother's legacy: the league of land pledged to her by the Texas state assembly in 1861. The agent wrote to Benjamin Parker and engaged a lawyer and a land agent in Texas, all to no avail. The Texas land office ruled Cynthia Ann's warrant invalid because her uncle and brother, after originally applying for the land certificate in 1861, had failed to pursue the matter until the Civil War ended in 1865. "By then, all acts of the previous legislature had been considered void because they occurred during the rebellion," the lawyer L. H. Miller told Hunt. The only way to obtain the land, Miller added, was by a new act of the legislature. Hunt had raised Quanah's expectations in vain.

Still, the former warrior was beginning to invoke his mother's story in telling his own—and in explaining why Comanches and whites must learn to live together in peace. And he did something that was very un-Comanche-like: he began to use her last name.

From now on he was Quanah Parker.

EVEN IN THEIR NEW STATE of semicaptivity, the Comanches were not a displaced people. The reservation they had been allotted under the Treaty of Medicine Lodge was located on land that held deep meaning in their history. Its myths were just as strong for them as the myth of the frontier was for whites. Cache Creek, where most of the Comanches pitched their teepees, had been a favorite hunting and watering spot for more than a century. A few miles to the north were the Wichita Mountains, the place where they believed the world had begun. The largest of the Wichitas was Mount Scott, more than two thousand feet tall, which towered protectively like a somber, brooding sentinel above the animated prairie. The mountain was the sacred site from which, according to Kiowa legend, the buffalo had first emerged thousands of years ago to populate the earth—and had retreated to in recent years to escape the white hunters. The buffalo would emerge again someday once the danger had passed.

To the east was Medicine Bluff, a holy ground of sharp granite ridges and rocky outcroppings where priests communed with the Great Spirit and gathered their magic and power. And to the south was Big Pasture—nearly one million acres of flat, unpopulated grass and scrub suitable for grazing, an unruly kingdom of wild game, migratory birds, and wolves. This land, too, was part of the Kiowa-Comanche-Apache preserve.

The reservation was a complex and treacherous place riddled with politics, corruption, and special interests. For predatory whites it was rich with possibilities for larceny and self-enrichment. Unscrupulous "squaw men" married Indian women and then claimed the right to a share of whatever allocations their wives were entitled to. White merchants exploited Indian ignorance about cash and credit. Quanah helped run down thieves who raided the four thousand Indian-owned horses grazing the unfenced pastures of greater Fort Sill as if it was their private preserve.

But outright theft was the least of the problems. The Kiowa-Comanche-Apache agency was beholden to Congress and to a byzantine bureaucracy, both of which had their own goals and imperatives; concern for the safety and welfare of its Indian wards was far down the list. As stipulated by the Medicine Lodge treaty, Indians were expected to embrace white schools, private property, and Christian values. Having defeated the Indians in battle, the white world was now determined to obliterate their identity as well. The agency was supposed to ease their transition from nomadic warriors to gentleman farmers yet was stunningly ill equipped for the task. The land allotted for agriculture was barely arable, subject to regular drought and lurking insects, and unsuitable for growing corn, the main staple. Its poor quality served only to reinforce the traditional Comanche aversion to farming. Government rations, as promised at Medicine Lodge, were essential for the Indians' survival, yet Fort Sill was 165 miles from the nearest railhead. The government was supposed to deliver 10,000 pounds of flour, 2,000 pounds of bacon, 825 pounds of coffee, and 1,650 pounds of sugar as well as a beef ration to the 3,000 Indians each week. But the supplies came erratically, if at all, and were subject to profiteers who delivered maggot-riddled staples and spoiled meat. Medicine Lodge had also stipulated annuities worth $30,000 per year in useful goods such as axes, frying pans, and butcher knives, plus a special allotment of clothing. Indians desperate for cash promptly resold many of the items to whites at a fraction of their value.

Indians gathered twice a month at the commissary on Issue Day to receive their supplies. The most exciting moment came when the cattle were brought out for distribution. "The steers were penned in a big corral and the braves sat on horses outside, with their Winchesters resting across their saddle horn," recalled R. A. Sneed, an Indian trader at Fort Sill. "When the big gate was opened and a steer came bolting out, they all started after it in hot pursuit, thus reproducing to some extent the thrill of the old buffalo hunting days."

Once the men succeeded in shooting down the animal, women, children, and dogs descended in a mad rush. "The herd rushes out, scattering widely over the plain, each animal followed by half a dozen yelling Indians," wrote Colonel Dodge. "In ten to twenty minutes all are down, riddled with bullets and arrows . . . No sooner are the cattle down, than the squaws are at them. An officer told me that he had seen the tongue cut out of a beef while it was yet alive."

After the Indian affairs bureau banned these "hunts," the Comanches developed a new name for the issue station at Cache Creek: *pesenah-dumun*, "the place of putrid meat."

THE MEDICINE LODGE TREATY entitled reservation Indians to hunt to supplement their rations, but the extermination of the buffalo, the

Palo Duro Canyon, the former Comanche stronghold in the Texas Panhandle.

decline of wild game due to overhunting, and the introduction of barbed-wire fencing made hunting increasingly futile. Quanah and his men found this out for themselves in the fall of 1878 when he organized a buffalo hunt around Palo Duro Canyon. The Indians were bored at Fort Sill, tired of the attempt to convert them into farmers and livestock herders, and eager to fill their bellies in the old-fashioned warrior manner. Fall traditionally was the time when they gathered meat and hides for the long winter. The Indians knew the buffalo herds had been greatly thinned, but they hoped to find remnants on the floor of the canyon, one of their ancient hunting grounds. A few dozen Comanche and Kiowas set out for the Panhandle, nearly a two-hundred-mile journey, without first seeking permission from the authorities at the fort. Many brought along their wives and children: they had no intention of returning to the reservation.

Palo Duro had irrevocably changed. After Mackenzie had chased the Comanches from the canyon in the fall of 1874, former Texas Ranger Charles Goodnight and his business partner, John G. Adair, had moved in, staking claim to the property and renaming it the JA Ranch. It was one of the biggest spreads in Texas. Their ranch hands slaughtered or drove off the remaining buffalo to make space for cattle to graze. By the time Quanah and his hunting party arrived in early December, there were no buffalo, just JA steers and an early layer of snow. Restless and hungry, the Indians began helping themselves to prime beef.

Goodnight was a crusty, irascible rancher: at forty-two he was already known far and wide as "the Old Man." He had seen the worst of the Indian wars in North Texas and New Mexico and had fought without quarter, participating in the Pease River massacre eighteen years earlier in which Quanah's mother and little sister had been captured. But the Old Man had no interest in shedding more blood. He and his men approached the Comanche camp with their guns holstered. When Goodnight asked to speak to their leader, Quanah appeared, and when Goodnight asked his name, he replied, "Maybe so two names—Mr. Parker or Quanah." Already Quanah was trying out his new hybrid identity on the white man.

The exchange did not start out well. The Indians formed a circle around Goodnight and his interpreter and pelted him with wary, hostile questions: What were they doing there? Had they killed off all of the Indians' buffalo?

"No," he told them, "I have plenty of fat cattle, and buffaloes aren't much good."

Didn't Goodnight know this country was the Indians'? the Comanches asked. Goodnight replied that he and Adair had bought the land from the state of Texas, and if the Indians had a complaint they should take it up with the state government.

Next they wanted to know if Goodnight was from Texas. Knowing their bitterness toward Texans, he figured it was safer to tell them he was from Colorado. They then asked him a number of questions about Colorado to see whether he knew the area. Goodnight didn't care for the belligerent tone. He told them he had weapons and bullets, "but I don't want to fight you unless you force me to."

Finally they relented. What did Goodnight have to offer? one of them demanded.

Goodnight addressed his reply directly to Quanah. "You keep order and behave yourself, protect my property and let it alone, and I'll give you two beeves every other day until you find out where the buffaloes are." Quanah accepted.

The two men sat around the campfire and talked, sealing the arrangement and initiating a friendship in the process. Each filled in some of the blanks in the other's knowledge. Quanah told Goodnight the true story of Peta Nocona's death. Goodnight in turn could offer Quanah a detailed account of how the Rangers had captured his mother and of how she had been treated after she was taken prisoner.

Quanah told Goodnight that the Indians at Fort Sill were not given half the beef that was due them and what they did receive was often inedible. And so Quanah and his men had decided to flee to the Staked Plains. But over days of talking around the campfire, Quanah mellowed. When a detachment of cavalry from Fort Sill arrived at the JA in early January with a wagonload of rations, Quanah accepted the food and agreed to accompany the troops back to the fort. "He told me that if his people were not properly fed he would leave again," Goodnight recalled.

Quanah quickly saw that Goodnight could serve as a powerful ally, someone with influence in the white world because of his wealth and connections. Perhaps Quanah could also see that the old former warrior shared with him a similar outlook. There was much irony here; after all, it was Goodnight and the other megaranchers of North Texas who were moving into the lands vacated by the Comanches and other nomadic tribes, prospering from the destruction of the Indian way of life. Yet these illegitimate heirs were in some ways the Indians' most natural allies. It was a partnership of profit and convenience, but underlying it was a deep, almost mystical respect for the land and those who roamed it.

QUANAH NEXT STRUCK up a friendship with S. B. "Burk" Burnett, an enterprising Fort Worth cattleman. Like Goodnight, Burnett took advantage of the newly opened lands from which the Comanches had been driven to establish a cattle empire with his business partner, W. T. Waggoner. They worked the 1,200-mile Chisholm Trail, which passed through Indian Territory just east of Big Pasture. They would cross the Red River in spring and graze their cattle for weeks in the grasslands, fattening the steers for the long haul to Abilene and Topeka. Indian bands roaming the area would steal a beeve or two or demand gifts and bribes to allow the cattle drive to pass without interference. Quanah was one of the original offenders. Even while he was reporting to Philemon Hunt on those Kiowas who were extorting cattle from the herds, he obtained a letter from the agent enabling him to practice a similar form of extortion. He would doff his hat, show the paper, identify himself as a Comanche chief, offer advice on the best route with good grass and water, and then, by the way, politely demand a few head in payment.

Like Goodnight before him, Burnett found in Quanah a kindred spirit. Early on, Burnett gave Quanah a Model 1873 Colt .45 with an ornate hand-tooled leather holster and belt. It hung from Quanah's bedpost throughout his lifetime. Burnett also gave Quanah a dignified and elaborate horse-drawn carriage that the chief used for his trips to Fort Sill and the Indian agency offices. "I got one good friend, Burk Burnett," Quanah once told a crowd. "He big heart, rich man, cow man. Help my people good deal."

Between 1880 and 1883, competition among white ranchers for the right to graze their herds on reservation grass became the dominant issue in tribal politics. A bad drought in 1881 forced matters: the ranchers parked thousands of steers on the grasslands and kept them there all summer. At first Quanah strongly opposed this practice, demanding that the cattle trails be closed off. But Burnett and his fellow cattlemen went to work cultivating relationships with the Indian agent, influential squaw men, and Indian leaders such as Quanah. In 1883 the Harrold & Ikard outfit out of Illinois hired Quanah and three other Quahadis and gave them some three hundred head of cattle over eighteen months in payment. Other ranchers followed suit. Quanah became particularly close to the Big Five: Burnett, Waggoner, E. C. Sugg, J. P. Addington, and C. T. Herring. At his urging, they came up with a scheme to lease annual grazing rights for more than a million acres from the Comanches and Kiowas who were its ostensible owners.

Quanah parlayed his growing influence with Burnett and the other cattlemen into his first trip to Washington in August 1884, paid for by the ranchers, to witness the signing of the first lease agreement. He assured Interior Department and Indian Bureau officials that a majority of Kiowas and Comanches favored leasing. He shrewdly insisted that the "grass money," as the scheme became known, be paid directly to Indians so that it would not get mixed in with the government's annuity payments. The Kiowa-Comanche-Apache agency's own informal poll on the reservation indicated that, contrary to Quanah's claim, the anti-leasing faction had a clear majority. But when the lease agreement was drawn up, most Indians signed on.

Quanah mocked and disparaged opponents of the agreement. "I cannot tell what objection they have to it, unless they have not got sense," Quanah told officials in Washington. "They are kind of old fogy, on the wild road yet, unless they have not got brains enough to *sabe* the advantage there is in it."

By providing the entire reservation community with an annual payment, the leases gave Indians a small degree of prosperity, although not any real power or control. The terms and the amounts were dictated by the Bureau of Indian Affairs in Washington. The money became a source of division among Kiowas and Comanches, and Quanah became a favorite target of the anti-leasing faction. His critics claimed Quanah had been "bought by the cattlemen, and don't come and talk with the rest of us chiefs," called him a "half-breed," and demanded he be re-placed as spokesman for the Comanches. Echoing bits and pieces of oral legend, they spread rumors that his father was not Nocona but a Mexi-can captive, and that therefore he lacked any Indian blood. Thirty-seven prominent Comanches signed a petition endorsing Quanah's dismissal. But the anti-leasers lacked the support of the enterprising and politically adept white ranchers, nor did they have a leader with the energy and charisma of Quanah.

Quanah returned to Washington the following February with a del-egation that met with Secretary of the Interior Henry M. Teller. When the Department of the Interior formulated rules a year later for leasing the ranges through the agency in Anadarko, the Indians received six cents per acre per year for six years.

Despite opposition from fellow tribesmen, Quanah emerged as the clear winner of the controversy over grass money. He was now accepted by whites and by many Indians as the spokesman for the reservation's native population. He ordered new stationery. It read: "Principal Chief of the Comanche Indians."

9.

The Chief
(Fort Sill, Oklahoma, 1887–92)

He was tall—at six foot two he towered over most Comanches—erect, and dignified, with piercing gray-blue eyes. The height and the eye color were inherited from his white mother, but the rest was all Comanche. In photographs, he always looks solemn and intense, posing on his horse or in the buggy he used to travel with his wives and children.

"He was a fine specimen of physical manhood, tall, muscular and straight as an arrow . . . the envy of feminine hearts," wrote his cousin Susan Parker St. John after meeting him in 1886. "Quanah looked you straight in the eyes; had dark copper skin, perfect white teeth with heavy raven black hair. This he wore hanging in two rolls wrapped around with red cloth. He parted his hair in the middle with a scalplock, the size of a dollar, plaited and tangled, hung down in front, signifying: If you want a fight, you can have it."

The grass money deals solidified Quanah's position as a classic middleman between the two worlds—enriching himself even as he protected his community—and made him more of a magnet for resentment and criticism from fellow Comanches. The more they needed him, the less they liked him. And his racial origins—half-white, half-Comanche—compounded his rivals' distaste.

There were death threats: Quanah eventually built a barbed-wire fence around his home for protection. And he was quick to go on the offensive, seeking to taunt a rival chief into a showdown. "Quanah Parker started the fight by slapping Lone Wolf, but the latter did not move," one newspaper reported. "Then Quanah hit Lone Wolf over the head with a six-shooter, but still the Kiowa chief refused to offer resistance or strike back at his assailant. Nothing Quanah would do would provoke Lone Wolf to fight."

There were many conflicts of interest: agents, squaw men, and interpreters who worked for the cattlemen directly or otherwise stood to profit from the deals—Quanah among them. He drew a minimum of thirty-five dollars per month on Colonel B. B. Groom's payroll, plus Groom's promise of five hundred head of cattle. The cattlemen also kept Quanah loyal by gifts and junkets to Dallas and Fort Worth. He shared this largesse, of course, with family members and with the tribe at large. But like a shrewd middleman, he always took his cut.

Burk Burnett invited Quanah and his men frequently to Fort Worth to appear in the annual Fat Stock Show. "There is one thing that you can say to all the Indians," Burnett wrote to Quanah. "That they will have a bully good time and not be out a cent of their money, as all expenses are to be paid coming and going and while they are here."

In 1883 the *Fort Worth Gazette* reported on one such visit. Its correspondent noticed a large, swarthy, well-dressed man with flowing black hair sitting by the fireplace of the Commercial Hotel. The man was dressed in a black cashmere suit, and wore a large white hat, a fine pair of boots, wrist-warmers, a gold watch and chain, and a stiff collar and cravat. He sat for an hour and spoke not a word, until the hotel owner's little girl came up to him, "when he commenced stroking her hair softly and speaking in a low soft tone to her."

Quanah had just been to visit with his cousin I. D. Parker, the oldest son of Isaac Parker, the uncle who brought Cynthia Ann "home" to Texas. Isaac had died eight months earlier, at age eighty-nine. This visit marked the first time a white member of the far-flung Parker clan had agreed to meet with Quanah. After they met, I.D. placed a newspaper notice on Quanah's behalf seeking a copy of the photograph taken of Cynthia Ann and Prairie Flower in Fort Worth in 1861. The legend of Cynthia Ann Parker, dormant for more than a decade, was beginning to reassert its power, thanks to the ardent efforts of her surviving son.

Quanah extended his personal generosity to all his white relatives. Knox Beal's mother was one of Cynthia Ann's cousins. As a young man Beal worked for a traveling circus and was suffering from a bout of extreme homesickness when he met Quanah outside San Antonio in 1884. Quanah invited Beal to come live with him in Oklahoma, and Beal remained there for some six years, eventually settling permanently in the area. "He certainly was a wonderful friend and counselor to me," Beal would recall, "and I have never regretted the day I came home with him."

Soon after, with Indian agent Hunt's enthusiastic support, the Bureau of Indian Affairs formally recognized Quanah as "chief" of the Comanche nation. Comanches had always been a loosely knit group of communities that shared language, customs, and kinship ties, but they had never recognized any one leader as their chief. Many were not happy when Quanah accepted this role; some denounced him as a usurper and a white stooge. None of this deterred him. But he yearned for a substantive symbol of his new position.

A great chief, Quanah decided, needed a great house.

QUANAH FIRST PROPOSED the idea to Philemon Hunt in 1882. Originally he had in mind a simple two-room structure like the ones many Comanches were building in the pastures near Cache Creek. But as Quanah's stature grew, his idea evolved into something far grander: a house of unprecedented size for an Indian that would overlook the cabins, teepees, and lodges of his fellow Comanches. His repeated efforts to extract money from Washington for the project were rejected or ignored. Indian commissioner Thomas J. Morgan, a fervent Baptist, told the new Indian agent, Charles E. Adams, that the idea was a nonstarter. "While at your agency I stated to you personally that I did not deem it wise for the government to contribute money to assist in building a house for an Indian who has five wives," Morgan wrote. "I do not think the proposition admits of discussion."

For the next eight years Quanah remained in his teepee, moving to the traditional bush arbor in summer. But he never abandoned the idea of presiding over a big house. With Burk Burnett's help, Quanah bought a thousand dollars' worth of lumber in Texas, had it shipped in wagons across the Red River, and contracted for a grand two-story, ten-room house. It took two years to build, and Quanah estimated the cost at $2,000. No one ever offered a definitive account of who paid for what.

The Star House became Quanah's showcase and seat of power. Sitting by itself atop a slight ridge on an empty stretch of pasture, it was an unmistakable monument to the man who lived within. He insisted upon painting twelve stars on the roof so that he could outrank any general who came to visit. Each year the two wings of the house seemed to grow in length as Quanah added rooms for his seven wives and nineteen children and also for the many hangers-on, white and red, whom he collected as he and his entourage traveled through Oklahoma and Texas.

The Star House, built by Quanah Parker, on the grounds of Fort Sill, outside Cache, Oklahoma, ca. 1911.

Quanah wined and dined countless guests in the long dining room, including Theodore Roosevelt and James Bryce, the British ambassador to the United States. He even played host to Geronimo after the old Apache war chief was transferred to Fort Sill from a prison camp in Florida. Neda Parker Birdsong, one of Quanah's daughters, recalled Geronimo's first visit to the Star House: "On the table at dinner was a big bucket of molasses. Geronimo dipped in and liked it so much that he appropriated the bucket and spooned every bit of it up."

Quanah, who prided himself on following the traditions of Comanche hospitality, used the Star House to prove to his white guests that he was indeed "civilized." C. H. Detrick, a prosperous Kansas merchant, arrived unexpectedly late one evening with a party of fellow businessmen. Quanah invited them in and, hearing they had had no dinner, roused his household and ordered up a hearty meal of steak, potatoes, biscuits, honey, and butter. He put the men up for the night and then fed them breakfast the next morning. "In doing the honors of his home, his manners were as finished and courteous as those of a grand gentleman, which he, indeed, was," Detrick would recall.

Some whites never overcame the suspicion that the hostile Indian raiders who had once ruled the plains and their nightmares were waiting for an opportunity to rise up and strike again. New Indian uprisings became a staple of press coverage. "Comanches on the War-Path"

Quanah Parker on the porch of his new house, ca. 1890.

read a typical dispatch in the *St. Louis Globe-Democrat* in March 1886, accusing Quanah and an alleged band of 1,300 men, women, and children of invading North Texas, setting wildfires and killing 40 to 50 cattle.

To allay white fears, Quanah was willing to play the role of enforcer of the white man's laws and rules on the reservation. When it suited his purpose, he even played the informer. In a note dated April 7, 1887, handwritten for him by his son-in-law Emmett Cox, Quanah warned Captain Lee Hall, the chief Indian agent in Anadarko, that Kiowa leaders "had been making medicine on Elk Creek" and had decided "to make a war break on Fort Sill in the middle of the summer." They asked Quanah to join with them. "Me and my people have quit fighting long ago and we have no desire to join anyone in war again," wrote Quanah, who signed the note "respectfully, Quanah Parker." Two years later, when the government established a "Court of Indian Offenses," Quanah was appointed presiding judge, a position that gave him formal police powers and the right to adjudicate disputes.

In the early 1890s the Ghost Dance craze, which began among Sioux Indians in the Dakotas, set off a wave of panic in Oklahoma and the Texas Panhandle. Indians, despite their recent exposure to Christianity, reverted to their barbaric, animistic past, or so many whites believed. One night in 1891 a group of ranch hands in Collingsworth County, Texas, fired off several shots to kill a steer, which rampaged blindly through their encampment and toppled the campfire. A woman in a nearby settler's dugout heard the shots and the yelling and saw the smoke. Assuming it was Indians, the panic-stricken woman saddled her horse, took her two babies to a nearby farm, and triggered an alarm that spread from Clarendon to Amarillo. Townsfolk built barricades and wagonloads of settlers poured into towns from the rural areas seeking shelter from a Red Peril that did not exist. It took several days for calm to return.

Quanah and his moderate Kiowa ally, Apiatin, worked hard to convince their fellow Indians that the Ghost Dance had no value. Apiatin even journeyed to the Pine Ridge reservation in South Dakota to meet the purported messiah behind the movement, and reported back to Oklahoma that the man was a fraud.

The same kind of panic occurred in 1898 at the start of the Spanish-American War, when most of the garrison at Fort Sill was ordered to report to the Gulf Coast on short notice, leaving only twenty-one soldiers at the fort. A rumor soon spread that Geronimo and the handful of Apaches who were living on the grounds were planning to rise up and seize the fort. In response, Quanah rounded up his own men and set up a protective ring around the fort's corral and guardhouse. The panic soon dissipated. But the Apaches were bemused to see Comanches—the former Lords of the Plains—mobilized to protect a U.S. Army facility from other Indians.

THE SAD TRUTH was that when it came to whites, Indians had more to fear from their friends than from their enemies. It was their friends, after all, who sought to destroy Native American culture, belief systems, language, and family structures, and seize control of the upbringing and education of Native American children, all in the name of progress and the Indians' own best interests.

Former warriors and hunters were expected to become docile farmers. Their children were required to attend government schools where their Comanche identity, culture, and language were banned or denigrated. Christian ministers, seeking to save souls, challenged the Comanche animistic faith and their practice of polygamy. Even their diet came under attack: Thomas J. Morgan, the chief Indian commissioner, sought to ban the eating of blood and intestines—"a savage and filthy practice," he wrote in a letter to subordinates. "It serves to nourish brutal instincts and . . . [is] a fruitful source of disease."

For Quanah, Morgan was a formidable opponent. A devout Baptist schoolteacher from Indiana, he had served as a commander of African-American troops during the Civil War, and he saw himself as a champion of racial equality. But his notion of equality was total assimilation: Indians, like Negroes, needed to lose their identity as a distinctive ethnic group and become proper little white folks. He even banned Indian participation in Wild West shows, believing that the exhibitions helped sustain the stereotype of the bloodthirsty savage that Indians needed to overcome.

"The Indians are destined to be absorbed into the national life, not as Indians but as Americans," Morgan wrote to Indian agents and school superintendents throughout the country. "In all proper ways teachers in Indian schools should endeavor to appeal to the highest elements of manhood, and womanhood in their pupils . . . and they should carefully avoid any unnecessary reference to the fact that they are Indians."

Reformers such as Richard Henry Pratt, a former army officer placed in charge of Kiowa and Comanche prisoners sent to Florida after the Red River War, were openly determined to destroy Indian culture. As Pratt put it, the goal was to "kill the Indian and save the man." Pratt founded the Carlisle School in Pennsylvania, which became the best-known of the many Indian boarding schools. He dressed his charges in "civilized" outfits—high-buttoned coats and stove-pipe trousers for the boys, dresses and smocks for the girls—chopped off their braids, and banned their native languages. This was ruthless pragmatism in the service of a higher good, according to Pratt: "The sooner all tribal relations are broken up; the sooner the Indian loses all his Indian ways, even his language, the better it will be for him and for the government and the greater will be the economy for both."

Faced with this cultural onslaught, Quanah fought a careful rearguard action. He was willing to accept white religion and education, but was determined to preserve Comanche culture and identity. He authorized Christian missionaries to open churches and schools in Comanche territory, but only those who first came to seek his permission. He eventually sent his own children to white-organized schools, both the Fort Sill Indian School locally and the Carlisle Indian Industrial School.

In time, Quanah came to believe that Indian children needed to learn the same skills as whites if they were to survive in a white-dominated world. "Me no like Indian school for my people," he said. "Indian boy go to Indian school, stay like Indian; go white school, be like white . . ."

All of this became part of the image that Quanah carefully constructed as a reformed warrior who was ready and willing to travel the white man's road. "Like slaves on a plantation, the Comanches quickly learned, and none better than Quanah, the necessity of telling the white man what he wanted to hear, while preserving as much of the old way of life as possible," wrote the historian William Hagan.

Still, there were parts of Quanah's life that he refused to compromise or change. While he wore business suits in public, he would not cut off his warrior braids. Similarly, he refused to abandon polygamy, arguing that it was an essential part of the Comanche way of life. When asked by an official to provide leadership by choosing one among his wives, Quanah teased that he himself was willing to pick one, "but you must tell the others."

His first wife was To-ha-yea, a Mescalero Apache, but the marriage quickly unraveled. Next he married Weckeah ("Hunting for Something"), the woman he had eloped with back in the 1860s. Their daughter Nahmukuh married Emmett Cox, the white ranch hand whom Quanah helped to get a job at the Indian agency and who became one of Quanah's most trusted advisers. Then came Cho-ny ("Going with the Wind"), followed by A-er-wuth-takum ("She Fell with a Wound"), each of whom had four children. By 1892, Quanah had six wives and seventeen children. Each wife had a specific set of household duties focused on the Star House. One handled his personal papers, one took care of his riding horses, one was in charge of his clothing, one ran the kitchen, and one carried water, chopped wood, and cleaned the yard. Each had her own room on the main floor and took turns sharing Quanah's bed, while the children slept upstairs dormitory-style.

Quanah, by all accounts, took delight in his children's accomplishments, especially the literacy and education of his daughters. Several of the girls served as his personal secretary over the years, writing his letters and keeping track of the books. There are no stories of him beating or otherwise abusing his children, and many tales of his care and concern. When his son White got into trouble at the Chilocco Indian school in northern Oklahoma and was confined to the guardhouse, Quanah wrote to the superintendent, S. M. Cowan: "I cannot, Mr. Cowan, ask you to turn him loose even if it could be done that way, but I do want you to wire me if he is ill during his confinement." He added, "I want you to make a good boy out of him if you can . . ."

Still, there were times when Quanah's public mask slipped, giving a glimpse of the man hiding behind it. For several months he met clandestinely with a young Comanche woman named Tonarcy—she quickly earned the nickname Too-Nicey—who had been married off as a young girl along with her sister to Cruz Portillo, an older Comanche. Tonarcy pleaded with Quanah to allow her to come live with him at the Star House, but he warned her that her husband would kill her if she did. This was no idle threat: when Cruz had suspected another man of paying too much attention to one of his wives, he arranged to have the man killed, according to Comanche lore.

One night after a quarrel with her husband, Tonarcy knocked on the window of Quanah's bedroom on the first floor of the Star House. He did not let her in but sent her down the road to the home of his sharecropper, David Granthum. The following day, Quanah headed off in his buggy without telling anyone. He picked up Tonarcy and rode to a nearby ranch of white friends, then crossed the Red River to the small Texas town of Vernon and rode on to Mexico. At first his wives and friends feared he had been murdered. But when Tonarcy's husband reported her missing as well, the truth became obvious.

The incident inflamed Quanah's enemies among the Comanches. "Now it's time to kill that white man," one of them said, referring to Quanah's mixed blood. "He's caused enough trouble, and now it's getting worse."

The Mexico trip became a key moment in the Quanah Parker legend. Some storytellers say it was on this trip that he first became acquainted with peyote and its healing powers and brought this strong medicine back to his people. Others contend that Quanah and Tonarcy found a haven at the Mexican ranch of his uncle John Parker, Cynthia Ann's younger brother, who had purportedly settled there with his wife after failing to find a home in either Texan or Comanche society. Neither of these tales is even remotely documented.

What is clear is that after several weeks, agents for the United States and Mexican governments tracked down Quanah and convinced him to return home. When he and Tonarcy came back, his wives were furious. Weckeah packed her clothes and children and stormed out, never to return. The other wives, angry but wary, forced him to cede to them a large proportion of his horses, cattle, and other possessions. He also had to pay Tonarcy's aggrieved husband a team of horses, a buggy, and one hundred dollars cash. Tonarcy moved into the Star House, married Quanah in September 1894, and became his "show wife," the one he took on trips to Washington and other cities. Tonarcy was unable to have children, and so a few years later Quanah added yet another wife, Topay ("Something Fell"), with whom he had three more children.

The press was fascinated by the beauty and multiplicity of Quanah's wives. It fit the white notion of the Indian as a sexually voracious animal with no sense of moral decency—the same psychosexual theme underpinning the captivity narrative. A correspondent for the *Daily Oklahoman* retold the tale of the elopement with Tonarcy and described in loving detail her appearance and the apparent wealth of her husband as if they were American nobility: "The seventh Mrs. Parker is one of the finest Indian women in America and Chief Parker is proud of her . . . He never allows her to go out of his sight . . . She wears a blue velvet waist with what is known as a bat wing cape and moccasins that are very rich. The costume which she wore the last time she was here cost, it is said, over $1,500, the beads and other ornaments being very costly."

THE PEYOTE PLANT is a small, spineless cactus found mostly in northern Mexico and South Texas. It contains a powerful hallucinogen whose effects can be relaxing and euphoric. Accounts of the original Spanish explorers to the region describe native peyote rituals of frenzied dancing with knives and hooks. From its earliest days in Mexico, leaders of the Catholic Church saw peyote worship as an idolatrous evil that needed to be eradicated. They never quite succeeded.

In their longstanding raiding and trading forays into northern Mexico, Comanches and Kiowas were exposed to peyote and its spiritual and medicinal powers. But it seems to have gained traction among these tribes only after they were consigned to the reservation. A new generation of prophets and holy men emerged who blended Christian theology with traditional Native American music and rituals. John Wilson, a Caddo-Delaware, recounted a vision in which Christ took Wilson down the road he had walked after the crucifixion from his tomb to the moon on his way to heaven. Those who traveled the Peyote Road, preached Wilson, would themselves follow Christ to heaven.

Peyote worship was a direct result of white man's demands and innovations. The reservation system threw Comanches and Kiowas together with Mescalero and Lipan Apaches who had practiced peyote worship and brought the rituals to the reservation. Quanah first learned these rituals from two Apaches who ran all-night meetings in a big teepee with a fire pit in the middle. And it was a technological breakthrough, the railroad, that facilitated the introduction of peyote worship by enabling Indians to travel efficiently to Mexico and bring back dried peyote buttons. The loss of their old way of life and their difficulties in adjusting to reservation life created a spiritual void for many Indians. Some turned to Christianity for answers. But others found peyotism more in keeping with their spiritual identity. It was, above all, uniquely *theirs*, not another forced import from the white world.

Quanah helped introduce peyote to his tribe, protected it from those seeking to ban it, and preached about its healing powers even while maintaining friendships with white Christian missionaries and officials who opposed it. Even when it came to myths and legends, Quanah was willing to split the difference, blending Christian ritual with Indian traditions. "The white man goes into his church house and talks about Jesus," said Quanah, "but the Indian goes into his teepee and talks *to* Jesus."

In 1888, Special Agent E. E. White posted a written order prohibiting the use of peyote. White anticipated resistance, but Quanah paid him a visit claiming to carry a message from the other chiefs and headmen expressing their understanding that White "had taken the step solely for their own good and that they had almost entirely quit using [peyote]." White was not immovable, and Quanah quickly learned how to move him. Two months later White reported that he had reached an agreement with Quanah "to permit Indians to use peyote one night at each full moon for the next three to four months" until the supply ran out. Apparently it never did.

James Mooney, an Indiana newspaper reporter who became an ethnologist for the Smithsonian Institution, attended several all-night peyote rituals in the early 1890s. He was allowed to participate, he wrote, "so that on my return I could tell the government and the white men that it was all good and not bad, and that it was the religion of the Indians in which they believed, and which was as dear to them as ours to us."

Still, to many whites, peyote was just another way for Indians to get high. J. J. Methvin, a Methodist missionary who befriended Quanah, approached a teepee near the agency one evening and found two of Quanah's wives stretched out on the grass. When he asked what was going on, one of them motioned for him to enter the tent. He took a seat among a circle of worshippers who had their eyes shut tight and were beating tom-toms, rattling gourds, and chanting wildly. "Quanah opened his eyes and discovered me; he smiled his recognition and welcome."

Quanah explained that peyote helped Indians be inspired by the Great Father, just as whites were inspired from the Bible. "All the same God, both ways good," he told Methvin. But the preacher was not buying this line. "This is not the Indian's old religion and indeed cannot properly be called a religion at all," Methvin wrote. "It is a drug habit under the guise of religion."

When the Oklahoma territorial legislature proposed banning peyote, Quanah led a delegation of chiefs in opposition. He told the lawmakers that peyote use was healthy and helped some Indians quit drinking. "My Indians use what they call pectus; some call it mescal. All my Indian people use that for medicine . . . It is no poison and we want to keep that medicine. I use that and I use the white doctor's medicine, and my people use it too . . . My ways in time will wear out, and in time this medicine will wear out too.

". . . I do not think this Legislature should interfere with a man's religion," he concluded. The lawmakers agreed: the bill failed.

QUANAH SELDOM GAVE INTERVIEWS: early on he seemed to grasp the danger of speaking freely to white people. But in 1901 he sat down with an anonymous correspondent from the *Oklahoman* newspaper. The reporter was clearly fixated on the number of Quanah's wives. He noted that each wife had her own bedroom and sewing machine, and that they took turns attending Quanah in the master bedroom. The reporter could not conceal his surprise to learn that a former Comanche nomad kept carpets on the floors, as well as bureaus, chiffoniers, lamps, and other articles of furniture.

The article reported that Quanah had many enemies among Comanches who spread rumors about him. "Some of the old people among the Comanches do not like me," he acknowledged to the man from the *Oklahoman*. "They call me a white man. They are like all old people . . . They want to do now what they did fifty years ago. That's no good anymore."

Quanah dressed in traditional garb that day: a white eagle feather in his hair, his scalp painted yellow and parted in the middle, his long hair braided and wrapped in rich beaver skin on both sides of his head. He wore a colorful blanket around his waist, a standing linen collar, and a heavy silk tie fastened to the collar with a sunburst amethyst pin. But when the reporter asked to take his photo, Quanah asked if he could first change into modern clothes.

As the generation that had experienced the Comanche wars began to die off and the wars themselves became enshrined in myth, Quanah became a familiar figure at state fairs, rodeos, and parades, where he and his former warriors would stage "raids" and entertain the same whites whose parents they had once terrorized. A new Texas town near the Oklahoma border, just a few miles north of the site of the Pease River massacre, was named for him, as was the local railroad line. Quanah gave his namesake town his blessing: "May the Great Spirit smile on your town; may the rains fall in season; and under the warmth of the sunshine after the rain may the earth yield bountifully; may peace and contentment be with you and your children forever."

He returned to Quanah, Texas, a few years later to attend Fourth of July celebrations, along with 225 braves, women, and children; they rode in the parade and he gave a speech. "I am not a bad man and have not done many of the things told about me," he told the crowd. "My mother raised me like your mothers raised their children, but my father taught me to be brave and learn to fight to become chief of my people. But we want to fight no more."

Even old enemies became allies. Sul Ross, the former Texas Ranger captain who had helped recapture Cynthia Ann at the Pease River, became a benefactor. Ross was elected governor of Texas in 1886 and re-elected two years later in part because of his reputation as the legendary Indian fighter who had rescued Cynthia Ann Parker. When Ross saw the advertisement for a photo of Cynthia Ann that Quanah had placed in the *Fort Worth Gazette*, he sent Quanah a copy of the daguerreotype of her nursing Prairie Flower that she had reluctantly posed for at A. F. Corning's studio in Fort Worth in 1861. Quanah framed the picture, struck it on an easel, placed it in his parlor, and posed for photos sitting next to it.

By this time a new generation of Texas historians had rediscovered the Parker saga. John Henry Brown had first met Cynthia Ann in Austin in 1861 when her uncle Isaac brought her to the secessionist legislative session seeking an annuity for her and Prairie Flower, and his wife had helped dress her and escorted her to the gallery during the session. Brown, a former Texas Ranger, state legislator, newspaper publisher, and collector of pioneer tales, later wrote a brief history of the Parker family after being asked to introduce Isaac at a political gathering in Dallas in 1874. And he later recounted the tale of Parker's Fort in his 762-page magnum opus, *Indian Wars and Pioneers of Texas*, originally published in 1880. Brown, who by then was mayor of Dallas, wrote that

Quanah Parker in his bedroom with the photograph of his mother, Cynthia Ann, and sister, Prairie Flower, a photo sent to him by Texas governor Sul Ross.

Ross had killed a warrior named Mohee, "chief of the band," at the Pease River.

Next came James T. DeShields, a twenty-three-year-old book sales-man and amateur historian who contacted and collected material from Brown, Ross, Ross's newspaper friend Victor M. Rose, Quanah, and Quanah's cousin Ben Parker, and put together the first detailed account of the massacre, the fate of Cynthia Ann, and the emergence of her sur-viving child. *Cynthia Ann Parker: The Story of Her Capture*, first pub-lished in 1886, became the definitive version of her life. DeShields put the declaration "Truth is Stranger than Fiction" on the title page and dedicated the book to Ross.

DeShields promised his readers a "narrative of plain, unvarnished facts," but he could not resist fanciful details and commentary. He claimed the Indian attack on Fort Parker involved five hundred warriors who, despite their vast numbers, used treachery against the worthy pioneers, making "such pleas with all the servile sycophancy of a slave, like the Italian who embraces his victim ere plunging the poniard into his heart."

The young self-styled historian also used his imagination to portray Cynthia Ann's "budding charms" as the white captive of dark-skinned savages.

"Doubtless the heart of more than one warrior was pierced by the Ulyssean darts from her laughing eyes, or charmed by the silvery ripple of her joyous laughter," he wrote. No doubt she had fallen in love with Peta Nocona, "performing for her imperious lord all the slavish offices which savageism and Indian custom assigns as the duty of a wife. She bore him children and we are assured loved him with a species of fierce passion and wifely devotion."

DeShields even claimed that Cynthia Ann rode alongside Peta Nocona and five hundred Comanches who sought to rescue the warriors trapped by Rip Ford's raiders in Indian Territory in 1858. "Doubtless," DeShields quotes Victor Rose, "Cynthia Ann rode from this ill-starred field with her infant daughter pressed to her bosom and her sons . . . at her side."

By now a politician aspiring for the governor's mansion, Ross assured DeShields that "my early life was one of constant danger from [Indian] forays." He changed the identity of the warrior he killed at the Pease River from the little-known Mohee to "the chief of the party, Peta Nocona, a noted warrior of great repute."

"It was a short but desperate conflict," wrote DeShields of Ross's clash with the Comanche chief. "Victory trembled in the balance . . . The two chiefs engaged in a personal encounter, which must result in the death of one or the other. Peta Nocona fell, and his last sigh was taken up in mournful wailings on the wings of defeat."

Victor Rose, who served as Ross's campaign strategist and biographer, undoubtedly had a hand in the rewrite. DeShields helped the campaign by transforming a brief, tawdry massacre into a heroic triumph: "the great Comanche confederacy was forever broken." He also stated as fact I. D. Parker's claim that Cynthia Ann and Prairie Flower, "her little barbarian," had died in 1864.

Despite its many inaccuracies, DeShields's account became enshrined in one of the most enduring of the Indian war histories, *Indian Depredations in Texas*, published in 1889. John Wesley Wilbarger's 691-page book is an exhaustive compendium of Indian attacks on pioneers and their families, most of them drawn from firsthand accounts and previously published stories. He reprinted DeShields's version of events without fact-checking a single sentence. The book helped establish DeShields's work as the accepted official account of the Cynthia Ann saga, handed down through the generations and incorporated into the state of Texas's public school history curriculum.

Brown, DeShields, and Wilbarger all depicted Comanches as savage killers shorn of all humanity—"these wild Ishmaelites of the prairie," in DeShields's words. Wilbarger was especially scornful of "maudlin, sentimental writers" who failed to recognize the brutality of the Indians. Such writers, he surmised, "never had their fathers, mothers, brothers, or sisters butchered by them in cold blood; never had their little sons and daughters carried away by them into captivity, to be brought up as savages . . . and certainly they never themselves had their own limbs beaten, bruised, burnt, and tortured with fiendish ingenuity by 'ye gentle savages,' nor their scalps ruthlessly torn from their bleeding heads."

His own view of the Indian, said Wilbarger, was: "We are glad he is gone, and that there are no Indians now in Texas except 'good ones,' who are as dead as Julius Caesar."

At the same time, each author praised Quanah, and their books contributed to his growing celebrity as the Noble Savage. Brown's book includes a photo of Quanah and describes him as "a popular and trustworthy chief of the Comanches . . . a fine looking and dignified son of the plains."

Each of these male authors created and buffed the macho frontier legend using whatever facts fit their vision and discarding those that were less convenient. But occasionally someone came along who gathered a more modest, fact-based account.

John Henry Brown's daughter Marion spent three months at Fort Sill beginning in November 1886. Marion was a vivacious and unmarried twenty-nine-year-old seeking to restore her health in the dry climes of central Oklahoma, and she spent a lot of her time at parties, playing whist with the officer's wives, and attending "hops" on the arms of various young officers. But her father had another mission in mind for her. "I sent you plenty of paper, pens, etc. and hope you will go into the Fort Sill history with a will to succeed," he wrote in a letter addressed to "Dear Baby" just before Christmas. "The main point is to get the facts in clear shape."

After the Christmas holidays ended, Marion Brown set out to do just that. She was introduced to Quanah through the old scout Horace Jones. In letters home, Marion expressed her surprise at hearing from both Jones and Quanah that Sul Ross had not killed Peta Nocona at the Pease River. Jones complained that Ross was getting too much glory for the massacre. Marion wrote of Jones, "I think him an old —— but everyone here seems to consider him reliable in all Indian history . . . I can scarcely understand anything he says, everything ends in a grunt."

Still, Jones provided Marion with her most important evidence that Peta Nocona had survived the Pease River massacre. He told her that Nocona, hearing that Jones had seen and talked with Cynthia Ann after her recapture by the Texas Rangers, had sought him out at Fort Cobb, one of the northern stockades, where Jones was working as an interpreter after the army abandoned the ruined Camp Cooper. The two men sat out in the yard at Fort Cobb under a large walnut tree. Before they spoke, Nocona rubbed his hands in the dust, then on his chest, took out a pipe, lit it, and took a few puffs before passing it to Jones. "Now I want to hear the truth," he declared.

Jones told him of Cynthia Ann's capture and how she had been taken to her uncle's house to live. Jones in turn asked Nocona about his two sons. His answer was suitably elusive. "They are way out on the prairie where you cannot see them," Nocona replied, "but some day you may."

Jones reckoned that the meeting took place in either the fall of 1861 or 1862. He never saw Peta Nocona again, but later heard that Nocona had lived several more years.

Marion avidly reported the details to her parents. She rather savored the prospect of discomfiting the newly elected governor of Texas. "What will Sul Ross say about Puttack Nocona?" Marion wrote. "I rather enjoy it myself. It will surprise people." Indeed, it might have, but Marion Brown's account was not published until 1970. Her father, perhaps for political reasons, made no attempt to print her story, although he ambiguously altered his own *Indian Wars and Pioneers of Texas* in its 1896 edition. In the section "The Fall of Parker's Fort," he credits Ross with killing "Mohee, chief of the band." But in his portrait of Ross some 250 pages later, he writes that Ross "killed Peta Nocona, the last of the great Comanche chieftains."

Marion was charmed by Quanah, but not taken in. The man she described was very much a performer. She noticed upon shaking hands that "his were softer than mine. He had his hair arranged in the Indian style, with an eagle feather standing up straight from his head, his face was painted, moccasins adorned his feet, the blanket was thrown carelessly around him and the remainder of his costume was strictly Indian with the exception of a neat pair of driving gloves." He was so quiet and expressionless during their first meeting that Marion assumed he could not speak English. Then, after she told him she wanted to see him dressed as an Indian, he smiled widely, laughed, and replied, "No like to come this way. Come another time when can stay longer." When one of her gentlemen friends called on her later that evening, he noted that Quanah already had five wives. "He asked if Quanah had asked me to be number six."

Like any effective leader, Quanah intuitively grasped the importance of a clean public image. He was careful not to discuss the things he had seen and done as a warrior, and he discouraged other Comanches from talking about the past. He knew the state of Texas was conducting "depredation courts," where residents could make claims for damages for destruction of property and loss of life and limb during the Indian wars. He feared such proceedings could evolve into criminal trials.

Quanah knew that Sul Ross's claim that he had killed Peta Nocona at the Pease River was a falsehood, that his father had not been present during the battle, but despite what he said privately to Marion Brown, he refused to publicly contradict Ross. "Out of respect to the family of General Ross, do not deny that he killed Peta Nocona," he wrote to his daughter Neda, who served for a time as Quanah's personal secretary. "If he felt that it was any credit to him to have killed my father, let his people continue to believe that he did so."

BY THE EARLY 1890s, Quanah was at the pinnacle of his success. His holdings consisted of a farm of 150 acres, 425 cattle, 200 hogs, 160 horses, 3 wagons, a buggy, and the newly completed Star House. He also controlled 44,000 acres of Big Pasture, thousands of which he privately leased to his rancher partners. He was presiding judge of the Court of Indian Offenses. He had outsmarted and outmaneuvered his opponents, white and red. He possessed the title of Chief of the Comanches while keeping his peyote faith and his polygamous family intact. No Native American in the United States enjoyed the same level of respect and admiration. None was as welcome in the white world. Even the Parkers were beginning to embrace him as an exotic but useful member of their extended family.

But at that very moment, it all began to unravel. And at the heart of the matter, as was so often true in relations between whites and Native Americans, was land.

10.

Mother and Son
(Cache, Oklahoma, 1892–1911)

Indian Territory contained hundreds of thousands of untapped acres. The Treaty of Medicine Lodge in 1867 had pledged the land to the Indians of the reservations, but by and large they neither farmed nor raised livestock on most of the acreage. Meanwhile, thousands of aspiring white homesteaders and land agents saw it as the last frontier— something that should belong to them.

Some of the Indians' purported friends—men such as Indian affairs commissioner Thomas J. Morgan, Quanah's old nemesis—believed that the vast collective holdings were impeding the process of assimilation. They argued that reservation Indians possessed far more land than they knew what to do with and were plagued by unscrupulous white intruders who exploited their ignorance and naïveté. The best solution for native people, these critics argued, was to concentrate them on tracts sufficient for their personal use and sell off the rest. "The Indian does not want to work and he will not do so unless compelled," Morgan pronounced.

As it happened, of course, this was also the best solution for land-hungry white homesteaders known as Boomers, and the phalanx of railroad interests, land speculators, lawyers, and politicians who forged an irresistible political and economic coalition of convenience as the Twin Territories of Oklahoma—the Indian half and the white half— lurched toward statehood. Congress agreed and, in 1887, passed the Dawes Severalty Act authorizing the allotment of small holdings to individual Indians while selling off the vast tracts around them. The profits were supposed to be used on the Indians' behalf to build schools, purchase livestock, and fund other useful pursuits. Commissioner Morgan designated February 8, when the bill was signed, to be observed in Indian schools as "the possible turning point in Indian history" when "Indians may strike out from tribal and reservation life and enter American citizenship."

As part of the new act, Congress established a three-man commission to adjudicate the process, chaired by former Michigan governor David H. Jerome. A solemn man with short clipped hair and a long, flowing beard, Jerome had been a forty-niner during the California gold rush and owner of a large hardware store in Saginaw. After a brief term as governor, he had settled into the role of Christian philanthropist, which made him prime material for a seat on the non-salaried federal Board of Indian Commissioners. Jerome and his three-man panel traveled throughout Indian Territory holding public hearings to determine the size and price of the acreage. Their mandate was to get control of the lands as cheaply as possible. They first pressured the Cherokees and the other so-called civilized tribes in the eastern half of the territory, then turned their attention to the Comanches and Kiowas in the southwest.

Quanah could see early on what was coming. He was not opposed in principle to allotting small parcels to individual Indians, but he knew that the sell-off of surplus land would mean the end of the grass money partnership with his cattlemen allies. They, too, were opposed to anything that would impinge on the special deal they had with Quanah and the Comanches. Both groups knew they lacked the political power to repeal the Dawes Act, but they had every intention of delaying its impact. The ranchers dispatched Quanah to Washington in 1889, accompanied by one of their lawyers, to stall the commission's first planned visit to Comanche territory. He made eight more visits over the coming decade.

Quanah did his job so well that the commissioners did not get to Fort Sill until September 19, 1892. They held eight days of meetings haggling with Indian leaders. Chairman Jerome sought to portray the panel's role in simple, paternalistic terms. "The Commissioners are not here to deal sharply with the Indians or to wring the Indians or do anything that a father would not do with his child," Jerome solemnly declared on the session's opening day. "But we are here to talk to you patiently, slowly and quietly to the end that you may know exactly what the wishes of the Great Father are and that we may know what the wishes of the Indians are."

Although respectful in his tone, Quanah had no time for such platitudes. He told Jerome that he had advised his fellow Indians, "Do not go at this thing like you were riding a swift horse . . . do not go into this thing recklessly." He said Indian commissioner Morgan had warned him that the commissioners "have not got any money but want to buy it with mouth-shoot."

He demanded of Jerome, "How much will be paid for one acre, what the terms will be and when it will be paid?"

Jerome replied that the details would be revealed "by and by."

Unimpressed, Quanah announced that he needed to supervise work on a new two-story porch for the Star House and would not be attending the next day's session. He might return, he said, "in a few days."

Various other Comanche and Kiowa leaders spoke up, most of them expressing extreme reluctance to sell their lands. One of the most revealing was White Eagle, the adopted name of Isatai, the former shaman of the battle of Adobe Walls. He and Quanah had been rivals ever since Isatai had botched the magic potion seventeen years earlier and caused the Indian defeat. But White Eagle now backed Quanah's stand and neatly summed up the chief's importance to the Comanche leadership: "What he learns from the Government he writes on his tongue and we learn from him."

The new porch, apparently, could wait. Quanah showed up for the next day's session. Of all the Indian leaders who spoke during the meetings, he was the only one who demanded plain and simple answers in acres of land and dollars and cents.

Commissioner Warren G. Sayre had promised payments totaling $2 million for the surplus land—the equivalent of $665 for every man, woman, and child on the reservation. But Quanah insisted on breaking it down to simple terms.

"How much per acre?" he asked Sayre.

"I cannot tell you," Sayre replied.

"How do you arrive at the figure of [two] million dollars if you do not know?"

"We just guess at it."

Having wrung this startling admission, Quanah pointed out that some tribes in prior negotiations with the commission had received $1.25 per acre, while others had gotten only fifty cents. Sayre said the commission couldn't say for sure how much the Comanches and Kiowas would get because the calculations depended on the quality of land, the number of owners, and other unknown factors. The meeting ended in stalemate.

Quanah invited the commissioners to the Star House, where he fed them dinner and put them up for the night. Jerome returned praising

Quanah's hospitality. He noted Quanah's livestock holdings and implied that any Indian could enjoy similar prosperity in the future—ignoring the fact that much of Quanah's wealth came from grass money he received from the cattlemen.

Eventually the commission offered $2 million for approximately 2.5 million acres of reservation lands and agreed to leave to Congress the question of an additional $500,000 payment to make up for the lost grass money. Each Indian was to receive four forty-acre tracts. Quanah had fought the Jerome Commission with every means at his disposal, but in the end he and his allies acquiesced. They signed on October 6, 1892. He felt he had gotten the best deal he could, but he continued to obstruct the final settlement for the next nine years.

The commission then needed to win approval from at least three-fourths of the adult male Indian population. To help it along, the commission stipulated that eighteen whites "be entitled to all the benefits of land and money conferred by this agreement." The whites, who included Emmett Cox, Quanah's son-in-law, were all influential and popular members of the reservation community. With their support, the commission managed to obtain signatures from 456 of 562 adult males.

One of Quanah's advisers in this matter was Lieutenant Hugh L. Scott of the Seventh Cavalry, a West Point graduate who fancied himself an Indian expert. At Fort Lincoln, in the Dakota Territory, Scott had worked to cultivate the Sioux prisoners, win their confidence, and learn their sign language. After his unit was transferred to Fort Sill, he became commander of a troop of Indian scouts. He became an influential peacemaker and was often sent out to talk to malcontent tribesmen. He was considered a knowledgeable observer who took a rare interest in the Indians he oversaw. His notebooks include notes from one of the rare interviews with Quanah in which the chief seems to be speaking frankly about his past, his role in the Adobe Walls battle, and his views on leadership. But the two men fell out in the aftermath of the Jerome Commission.

By 1898, Quanah had come around to favoring ratification of the agreement and arranged for a congressional hearing in Washington to speak in favor. But the anti-Quanah forces among the Kiowas and Comanches decided to send their own delegation to Washington to speak out against the deal and appointed Scott as their spokesman. Quanah was outraged when Scott appeared to testify. "Quanah jumped up in a great rage and said he wouldn't have any white man speak for him or his people," Scott later recalled. After Scott testified, the two sides argued throughout the afternoon and the committee put off making a decision. When it was over, wrote Scott, "Quanah announced his intention of killing me before I could get back to Fort Sill."

Scott survived, but his motives and loyalties remained in doubt. When the Jerome Commission's report was ratified, Scott's name appeared as one of the whites eligible for a 160-acre grant, although he later withdrew it. In 1901, he sold for $3,000 Quanah's war bonnet and other valuable artifacts to the Bancroft collection at the University of California at Berkeley.

Kiowa opponents foolishly appealed the Jerome Commission's ruling to the Supreme Court, which issued a disastrous ruling in 1903 that rendered Indian land rights as essentially nonexistent. In *Lone Wolf v. Hitchcock*, the court affirmed the power of Congress to allot reservation lands in any way it saw fit, effectively endorsing the disenfranchisement of Native Americans. Big Pasture was carved up and allotted to white interests in 1906. The Kiowa chiefs had sought the protection of the white man's judicial system, only to find it was no protection at all. Their failure vindicated Quanah's less confrontational approach.

IN ANTICIPATION of the August 6, 1901, opening of the reservation's surplus lands, some 50,000 Boomers poured into the reservation illegally, staking out land claims and wildcatting for minerals in the Wichita Mountains. Between July 10 and early August, more than 165,000 people registered at El Reno and Lawton for 13,000 homesteads. Tent cities of 10,000 people each sprang up outside Lawton and Anadarko, accompanied by crime, drunkenness, unsanitary conditions, and disease.

Men and women mingled freely. "They slept in cots under tents that had no sides. They took naps in chairs on the sidewalks; they spent the night upon the grass of the parkings, glad to find a place to rest." Temperatures rose past one hundred degrees. On the morning of August 6, officials accompanied by witnesses and newspapermen arrived before a stunning sight, according to one observer.

> Massed upon a sloping hillside, standing shoulder to shoulder, were people from every section of the Nation. Women, thousands of them, were in the eager throng . . . On the edges of the crowd was a fringe of prairie schooners bearing the men and women who had made the greatest sacrifice to enter the lists. To them, or some of them, the drawing meant everything. Brooding over the mighty

gathering was a spirit of tense nervousness that affected even the members of the Commission, and the officer's hand trembled when he lifted up to view the first bits of paper by which Fate distributed fortune to her favorites.

The commissioners read out the list of 13,000 winners among 167,000 applicants. Those holding lucky numbers raced across the prairie in a mad marathon of horses, mules, wagons, and buggies—anything with wheels—to claim their homesteads. Quanah had made the best deal he could. But the reservation was history, and its dismantling shattered the last promise white men had made to red in what six years later became the state of Oklahoma.

THEODORE ROOSEVELT was a naturalist, historian, progressive, imperialist, and outdoorsman, the kind of president who ordered bison heads to be carved on the mantel in the state dining room at the White House. He was also a storyteller, mythmaker, and showman—just like Quanah Parker.

One thing he wasn't was an Indian lover. In his seven-volume opus, *The Winning of the West*, first published in 1894, the future president depicted the settling of the American frontier as a contest between a superior white race and inferior dark-skinned natives. For him the West was a Darwinian theater where the fittest triumphed and the losers were subordinated or destroyed. "Unless we were willing that the whole continent west of the Alleghenies should remain an un-peopled waste, *war was inevitable* . . . ," he wrote in the first volume. "It is wholly impossible to avoid conflicts with the weaker race."

For Roosevelt, violence was a purifying act, both cleansing and mythical. He had no time for those "foolish sentimentalists" who sought to protect and preserve Indian culture.

Above all, he believed that character was destiny and that strong men made their own history. He loved natural men who could ride, shoot, hunt, and thrive in the wilderness. Thus a special man such as Quanah Parker—an Indian, yet with his mother's Anglo-Saxon blood coursing through his veins—appealed to Roosevelt's celebration of "a race of heroes."

Quanah first came to Roosevelt's attention through Francis E. Leeup, a New York journalist and Indian rights lobbyist who became part of Roosevelt's inner circle. The president dispatched Leeup to the Kiowa-

Comanche-Apache agency in Anadarko in 1903 to investigate allegations of corruption against the Indian agent James Randlett, one of Quanah's closest allies. Leeup uncovered a nest of jealousy, double-dealing, theft, and vicious in-fighting among white merchants, land speculators, squaw men, and chiefs, but he exonerated the agent. As for Quanah, Leeup wrote approvingly that the Comanche chief was "always conscious that he is Indian, but never forgetful that the white civilization is supreme, and that the Indian's wisest course is to adapt himself to it as fast as he can."

Leeup had observed politicians in Washington over the years and believed he knew leadership when he saw it. "If ever Nature stamped a man with the seal of headship she did it in his case," he wrote. "Quanah would have been a leader and a governor in any circle where fate might have cast him. It is in his blood . . . Even those who are restive under his rule recognize its supremacy."

Quanah's national fame was cemented at the St. Louis World's Fair in 1904, where he participated in a celebration of the American West. It was followed by an invitation to Roosevelt's March 4, 1905, inauguration, along with Geronimo, Buckskin Charlie of the Utes, Hollow Horn Bear of the Rosebud Sioux, American Horse of the Brule Sioux, and Little Plume of the Blackfeet. In what the historian Douglas Brinkley called "Roosevelt's own Buffalo Bill production," pioneers, cowboys, Rough Riders, the cowboy star Tom Mix, and the Indian chiefs all gathered to parade in a light snow.

The authorities ordered Quanah to appear "fully equipped with Indian clothing as gorgeous as possible in its make-up and complete in its representation of old Indian dress," wrote Captain W. A. Mercer, superintendent at the Carlisle Indian School, to Randlett. Quanah was to epitomize "the progressive Indian, one who is in accord with the efforts of the Government to better the condition of the race."

Not everyone approved of Quanah's place of honor. Retired Army captain Robert G. Carter, who had served in the Fourth Cavalry under Mackenzie during the Red River War, was incensed that Roosevelt had invited Quanah and the other "good Indians . . . most of whom had dipped their hands in many a white settler's blood." Carter was equally angered that Texas towns had been named after Quanah and his father, Nocona. Had any towns been named for one of the cavalrymen, Carter wondered, "who risked their lives and sacrificed their health and future happiness here on earth in more than one effort to drive out that same Quahada Comanche band and open up that wild and desolate region to settlement?" But Carter's was a minority view. Having been thoroughly vanquished and defanged, Native Americans were now fair subjects for popular admiration.

One month after the inauguration, Roosevelt decided to take up an invitation to go wolf hunting in southwestern Oklahoma, and he made the territory one of the stops on a five-week tour of the West. When he arrived at the train station in Frederick on April 8, Roosevelt invited Quanah to join him on the speaker's stand. "Give the red man the same chance as the white," the president told the small crowd. "The country is founded on a doctrine of giving each man a fair show to see what there is in him."

Quanah showed up with twelve of his men and wore his six-shooter strapped to his waist—"afraid somebody might try to kill President," he explained.

Burk Burnett and his son Tom—two of Quanah's white benefactors— were the president's main hosts, along with Guy Waggoner, Burnett's business partner. They brought with them Jack "Catch 'Em Alive" Abernathy, a Texas-born wolf hunter. They took the president and his party south to Big Pasture, setting up camp at Deep Red Creek, which empties into the Red River, under the shade of elms and pecan trees. They were serenaded by cardinals and mockingbirds—"the most individual and delightful of all birds in voice and manner," declared Roosevelt.

"The weather was good, we were in the saddle from morning until night, and our camp was in all respects all that a camp should be," the president exulted. "So how could we help enjoying ourselves?"

They spent four days there, killed seventeen wolves, and ate and slept outdoors. On the third day, three of Quanah's wives and two of his children joined them. "It was a thoroughly congenial company all through," Roosevelt wrote. When it ended, Quanah invited Roosevelt to the Star House for dinner. While talking with Quanah that evening, Roosevelt mentioned the idea of establishing a bison refuge, populated by buffalo currently residing at the Bronx Zoo in New York, in the newly created Wichita Mountain Wildlife Refuge, a few miles north of the Star House. Quanah was almost speechless with excitement at the prospect of seeing buffalo again near his home.

Anna Birdsong Dean, one of Quanah's granddaughters, recalled hearing from her mother about Roosevelt's visit to the house. "My mother's job was to see if everything was done properly," Anna recalled. She checked the dining room table before the president was to arrive and chastised Quanah for filling large goblets to the brim with wine.

"Grandfather replied that when he went to Washington the President served wine in small glasses and he wanted to give the President more wine than Roosevelt gave him."

It took more than two years for the paperwork to go through. But on October 11, 1907, seven bison bulls and eight cows were loaded onto fifteen padded compartments at Fordham Station, accompanied by three zoo officials for the two-thousand-mile journey to the Wichita refuge. Three of the bison were named for Lone Wolf, Geronimo, and Quanah.

Dressed in full war feathers, Quanah awaited their arrival in Cache. He and his men helped load the bison into wagons for the thirteen-mile journey to the refuge. It was as if the ancient Kiowa vision had been realized: the bison again came roaring out of Mount Scott, even if only a remnant.

BY NOW QUANAH HAD BECOME the most important and influential Native American of his generation. He was the Man to See when it came to Comanche affairs, a reliable ally and a formidable enemy. He was also the white man's favorite Indian, in no small part because he was the son of a white woman.

A certificate from Indian commissioner W. A. Jones recognized his power and authority even while reflecting just how fragile the entire arrangement was: "This is to certify that Quanah Parker is recognized as the chief of the Comanches, and has promised his Great Father to be always friendly towards white men, and any white man to whom he may show this Paper is requested by the Government to treaty him in a friendly manner, and to be careful to give him no cause to break his promise."

His relations with the long parade of white officials who ran the Kiowa-Comanche-Apache Indian agency were friendly but measured. Many developed a genuine affection for Quanah and his family. James Randlett, who became his closest ally among the agents, arranged to have one of the first telephones in the Oklahoma territory installed at the Star House and helped with jobs and housing for many of Quanah's vast brood. When one of the periodic smallpox epidemics broke out, Randlett wrote one of his subordinates: "I wish you to go over to Quanah's to find out how he is fixed and if anything can be done for him . . . After you get this I want you to write me every day so long as smallpox is in Quanah's family, and tell me how they are and if anything can be done for them."

Yet, while the agents sought to respect Quanah's pride and dignity, the portrait that emerges from the agency's files is of a man who was still a ward of the state. Every expense, no matter how trivial, was scrutinized. Quanah could not spend his own private funds to buy building materials for his house or purchase a new cow without agency permission. Often the agent had to pass these requests up the chain of command to the Bureau of Indian Affairs in Washington. Nor could Quanah travel to Washington without permission from the commissioner of Indian Affairs. Once when Quanah sought fifty dollars' reimbursement for the expenses of his wife Pohpondy for a trip to Washington, an Interior Department bureaucrat rejected the request by noting he had not seen proof that Pohpondy was Quanah's legal spouse.

For Quanah, there were two worlds: the Comanche world he came from and identified with, and the white world that found him fascinating and acceptable so long as he was careful and obsequious. He alone moved between these worlds, yet at the same time he knew to keep them separate, and he seldom let his guard down in either one.

"My grandfather never trusted a white man," Baldwin Parker Jr., a grandson, once told an interviewer. "He was smart enough to live with them. He could live in both worlds at the same time. His whiteness and red-ness worked for him instead of against him. The two had become one."

Quanah's celebrity continued to grow. He hosted two major pow-wows near his home that attracted thousands of visitors. The highlight in 1903 was a staged attack by three hundred warriors on a Frisco passenger train just arriving at the station in Cache. "Painted, brandishing their bows and arrows and shrieking their war cries, the Indians produced near-panic on the train, and passengers screamed and fainted in the coaches," reported one newspaper account.

His fame became a passport that allowed him to enter worlds that other Indians were not welcome in. Once in Texas, he recalled to his cousin Susan St. John, he had sat down in a train coach across from some white businessmen. He was always careful when he rode the train to dress in his finest dark wool suit from the haberdashers in Electra, Texas, but he never hid his warrior's braids, which gave him away as a Comanche just as his pale blue eyes betrayed his white origins. The men wanted this obvious Indian evicted from the coach and some of them went to get a conductor, who proceeded to inform them that the man in question was the famous Quanah Parker. Suddenly the mood changed.

The men shook his hand and engaged him in conversation. As far as they were concerned, Quanah Parker was a celebrity.

Still, some doors remained closed. When Quanah sought to enroll one of his sons in the Cache public schools, the boy was rejected by order of the Republican-dominated school board. The board ruled the boy was not a bona fide resident of Cache, but a personal investigation by the *Oklahoman*'s special correspondent reported, "The real reason is because he is an Indian."

Quanah went to J. A. Johnson, an old friend who was superintendent of schools in Comanche County, and asked Johnson to organize a new school district in Quanah's area. The chief donated the land, built the school, and ensured that residents paid a school tax. Quanah was elected head of the board in June 1908.

Cache held a "great Quanah Parker celebration" that same year, with bronco busting, horse races, Indian dances, stagecoach robbery enactments, and oratory. Quanah loved the hoopla, but he insisted upon his dignity. When two businessmen approached him the following year and offered him $5,000 for six months if he agreed to appear in a Wild West show in New York, he said no. "You put me in little pen," he told them. "I no monkey."

THROUGH IT ALL, Quanah maintained a burning interest in his mother and her fate. His obsession stemmed from both a sincere longing and a canny assessment of the stature and protection white blood offered at a time when the white world was seeking to destroy what was left of Comanche culture and identity. It also gave him a soothing story to tell: the fierce Indian warrior now transformed into an ambassador for peace and reconciliation because of his love for his white mother.

His white relatives may not have been eager to welcome him to Texas, but he always welcomed them to Oklahoma. Adam Parker of Weatherford, Texas, one of Uncle Isaac's sons, spent two weeks at the Star House in 1902 and wrote to his cousin Susan Parker St. John that Quanah was "a most interesting character . . . He boasts of his ancestral white blood and delights in the entertainment of Cynthiann's [*sic*] relations." He concluded: "You should visit him."

Two years later, she took up the suggestion. Susan was a daughter of Nathaniel Parker, one of the sons of Elder John who chose not to migrate to Texas with his father and brothers. Thus she was a first cousin of Cynthia Ann. She recalled growing up listening to her father tell stories of Cynthia Ann's capture. "Being a little girl myself Cynthia Ann's fate appealed most strongly of all to me," she wrote.

Susan had married John P. St. John, who became governor of Kansas, and she ventured periodically from her home in Olathe, Kansas, to Oklahoma and Texas interviewing survivors and gathering firsthand accounts of the life and times of Cynthia Ann and Quanah for a family memoir she planned to publish.

She and a woman friend traveled to Lawton, where Quanah came to greet them at a local hotel. He himself drove his coach, drawn by four mules, up to the front entrance. "Quanah is a man worth looking at," she later told an interviewer. "He is a magnificent-looking man and his bearing and manner is that of a cavalier. He was dressed in the latest style of civilization and, as he strode into the hotel, I was just proud of him."

Quanah stared at her as she came forward.

"Is this the cousin?" he asked.

"This is the cousin," she replied.

Then he took Susan's hand and kissed it, she recalled, "as cousinly and gently as if he had learned the art in some finishing school for gentlemen. And, only to think of it, not so many years ago this man was a bloodthirsty, scalping wild Indian."

Later, he told her she looked like his mother.

Susan Parker St. John, first cousin of Cynthia Ann, interviewed family members and other sources and visited with Quanah Parker. Her unpublished notes are one of the most reliable sources of information about Cynthia Ann's life and death after her recapture in 1860.

He took the two women to the Star House. The house was handsomely furnished and scrupulously clean—"just as the house of any white man of wealth and refinement," Susan would recall.

Susan was especially impressed with Quanah's kindness to his wife Topay. When a fierce storm lit up the evening sky, he ushered everyone inside for their safety. "Quanah showed us how the windows bolted and doors locked, said the big gate . . . was locked . . . [N]o one could get in. [He] told us he slept in the next room and if we needed anything or was afraid to rap on his door." He asked Susan if Topay, who had recently lost a baby, could stay with her during the storm. "He seems so thoughtful of his wives. I suppose that's why he brought her in our room."

Susan in her account captured Quanah's virtue and his vanity. "He is a fine looking man proud as a peacock and vain as a . . . pretty girl," she recalled, "[who] likes to have you tell him what a great man he is."

QUANAH HAD LOST his mother when she was alive; now he wanted to claim her in death by having her remains removed from Texas and reburied in the homeland of the native people she had embraced as her own. He knew he would never obtain permission from the Texas legislature for such a project, so instead he asked his rancher friends Burnett and Goodnight to lobby in Washington. In 1909, Congress passed a bill authorizing the transfer and appropriating $1,000 for the purpose.

On Department of Interior letterhead, Quanah petitioned Texas governor Thomas Mitchell Campbell for his personal protection: "Dear Sir, Congress has set aside money for me to remove the body of my mother Cynthia Ann Parker and build a monument and some time past I was hunting in Texas and they accused me [of] killing antelope and I was afraid to come for fear they might make some trouble for me because of a dislike to a friend of mine in Texas, would you protect me if I was to come to Austin and neighborhood to remove my mother's body some time soon."

There is no record of a reply from Campbell. But Quanah did get an offer of help, handwritten in pencil, from J. R. O'Quinn, a first cousin:

Sir:

I see your advertisement in reguard to your Mother Cytnia An Parkers grave and its where bouts I aught to no how she was.

She was my mothers sister that makes her my own aunt. And she was living with my father and mother when she died. You said you wanted to find her grave if you do we aught to no where it is and if you will come down I think we can site you to the place my father written to you some 8 or 10 days ago but miss address not doing the exact Post office the address to Lawton. Well I have written to a cousin that I never have seen, waiting to hear from you soon.

Yours Respectfully,
JR O'Quinn

Other members of the Texas Parkers were not so accommodating. "The relatives of Cynthia Ann and the friends of the Parkers did not want to see her removed, they said they thought she had suffered enough from the Indians, and they didn't want her taken up and buried among them," recalled Ambrosia Miller, a cousin. "The Parkers helped make Texas and they thought they had more right to Cynthia Ann's body than the Indians."

In the fall of 1910, Quanah dispatched son-in-law Aubrey C. Birdsong, who was married to his daughter Neda, to East Texas. Birdsong visited small-town cemeteries in Groesbeck, Canton, Mineola, Athens, and several other sites, but despite O'Quinn's offer of help, he could not locate Cynthia Ann's grave. At first he could not even find anyone who had attended her funeral. But eventually he found his way to a local judge named John Parker. The judge in turn sent him to the small town of Poynor to meet Bob and Joe Padgett.

The Padgetts had known Cynthia Ann in the last year of her life; Bob and Joe told Birdsong they had assisted in her burial. Joe's wife recalled dressing the body and pinning up Cynthia Ann's hair with a bone hairpin. The brothers escorted Birdsong to an unmarked grave in the nearby Fosterville cemetery, described by one relative as "the most desolate and forsaken cemetery I have ever seen." Birdsong located the grave on Thanksgiving Day.

When he dug up Cynthia Ann's remains, Birdsong was surprised to find a small skeleton in the grave lying beside her. He surmised that this was Prairie Flower. Although he had no legal authority to do so, Birdsong decided to put the bones in the same casket with Cynthia Ann "with the little girl's remains placed as if she were in the arms of her mother."

"I felt that this meant so much to Quanah Parker that I was doing a most humane act, a sort of an unwritten law," Birdsong recalled in an interview with a Fort Sill archivist forty-nine years later. He worked surreptitiously. "I knew if I'd try to obtain permission from Texas authorities I would be arrested for going as far as I did without permission, and I'd never get the remains out of the State."

Birdsong spirited the remains to Oklahoma, where they were placed in a coffin that was displayed at the Post Oak Mission near the Star House. A photograph taken inside the Post Oak Mission hall shows a somber Quanah Parker staring down at a small white coffin strewn with flowers and propped between two chairs. Quanah, dressed in a formal dark suit, stands stiffly, hands by his side.

"Are you sure this is my little white mother?" Quanah asked his son-in-law.

Birdsong said he was sure.

"I look for her long time," Quanah told him. "Now I'm done."

At the funeral Quanah spoke twice about Cynthia Ann, once in Comanche and once in English. His mother, Quanah said, "love Indians so much she no want to go back folks. All same people anyway, God say."

Then he explained himself by evoking Cynthia Ann. "I love my mother. I like white folks. Got great heart. I want my people to follow after white way, get educate, know work, make living. When people die today, tomorrow, ten years, I want them be ready like my mother. Then we all lie together again.

"That's why when government give money for monument and new grave, I have this funeral and ask whites to help. Me glad so many Indians and white people come. That's all."

After a ceremony, the casket was lifted by four pallbearers to the grave site. Quanah solemnly followed. He lingered at the site for a long time. He "stood in tears and deep agony over the lowered casket," wrote his daughter Neda.

Man and myth had finally come together.

OVER THE DECADES, Quanah's partnership with ranchers such as Charles Goodnight and Burk Burnett never faded. Burnett felt especially protective and paternalistic toward his Comanche friend. Each November he invited Quanah to bring his warriors to the Matador Ranch in East Texas for hunting. But he warned the chief to be careful when traveling into the state, because "as you know there is considerable prejudice among the white people of that country against your Indians hunting out there."

Burnett helped arrange for what turned out to be Quanah's last foray into Texas. When the construction of the Quanah, Acme, and Pacific Railway was complete, the company held a "Quanah Route Day" celebration at the Texas State Fair in Dallas in October 1910. Although no one could say for certain, Quanah by this time was probably around sixty-five years old, and he had suffered for several years from rheumatism, a painful inflammation of the joints. Still, he dressed in full Comanche war regalia for the event and entered the fairgrounds on horseback, followed by his extended family and a collection of aging former warriors.

Quanah spoke to the crowd. Sul Ross had died twelve years earlier, and Quanah was no longer quite so reticent about discussing his past life as a warrior. He stated explicitly that the old story that Sul Ross had killed his father was pure fiction. "The Texas history says General Ross killed my father. The old Indian told me no so. He no kill my father . . . After that—two year, three year maybe—my father sick. I see him die. I want to get that in Texas history straight up."

For the first time, he also publicly described his killing of Trooper Gregg at Blanco Canyon in 1871. "I tell my men stand up behind hill, holler, shoot, and run. I run to one side and use this knife. I came up right side and killed man sergeant and scalp. You see how bad man I at that time?"

But his message now was one of peace and reconciliation. And he emphasized that despite their bloodstained past and all the wrongs that had been done, Comanches and Texans shared a common identity and a common national enterprise. "You look at me," he told them. "I put on this war bonnet. This is my war trinket. Ladies and gentlemen, I used to be a bad man. Now I am a citizen of the United States. I pay taxes the same as you people do. We are the same people now. We used to give you some trouble, but we are the same people now."

He never stopped searching for his mother's long-lost legacy of land in Texas. No doubt this quest was partly because the land had monetary value. But there was more to it than that. A piece of Texas land from his mother would have objectified his connection to her and to the state he and his fellow Comanches had fought against for so long. It would have resolved the conflict in a meaningful material way. And for a man who had been orphaned by history, it could have provided the home he never had. His father had been a loner and a wanderer by choice, his mother by force of violent circumstances. Quanah, too, was a man apart—never a white man but never quite a full Comanche, either. Viewed from this angle, his life was a quest to find for himself, his family, and his people a place to call home. Quanah was a searcher.

In a letter to Goodnight dated January 7, 1911, Quanah again asked his rancher friend's help in taking up the matter, He also promised to visit Goodnight's ranch in the near future. "I am going to bring some old Indians to your place and see your buffalo and make these old Indians glad."

He never made it.

FOR SEVERAL WEEKS Quanah had been feeling sick to his stomach as well as aching in his joints, and Laura Parker Birdsong, his devoted eldest daughter, believed the rheumatism had spread to his heart. Still, he insisted on making a train trip to participate in a peyote ceremony with Cheyenne friends. He must have stayed up all night for the ritual before boarding a train home. On the way back he had trouble breathing and his temperature spiked. By the time Emmet Cox met the train at nearby Indiahoma, Quanah was unconscious.

A doctor at the station revived him with a heart stimulant, and Cox rushed him to the Star House in his car. Tonarcy and Topay were waiting for him there. They laid him down on the couch. He got up unaided while Knox Beal helped remove his outer garments.

The two wives seemed to understand the end was near. They had Beal and the white doctor leave the room, then summoned a medicine man named Quasei. "Father in heaven, this is our brother coming," he prayed. Placing an arm around Quanah, Quasei flapped his hands and imitated the call of the Great Eagle. He thrust an eagle bone down Quanah's throat to open it, and Tonarcy squirted water into his mouth. "He coughed, gasped, moved his lips feebly, and died, just twenty minutes after his arrival," reported the *Lawton Daily News*.

They laid out his body in full Indian costume. His wives cut the buttons from their moccasins, burned their quilts, and threw away their new clothing while his body lay in state in a casket in his bedroom.

He was buried next to his mother's grave, just as he had planned. There were perhaps 1,200 people at the ceremony, evenly divided between Indians and whites—far too many for the small sanctuary of the Post Oak Mission church. "Every automobile that could be rented in Lawton" was at the site, reported the *Cache Register*. The mourners sang "Nearer My God to Thee" and the Indian women wailed.

Quanah Parker's funeral in Cache, Oklahoma, February 24, 1911.

Laura fainted and had to be carried outside. "It just seemed as if my heart was cut from my body to give him up," she said later. Tonarcy, the "show wife" whom he always took with him on his trips to Washington, rode in an automobile, while other wives and family members squatted in the bed of a horse-drawn farm wagon.

It was a day of powerful contrasts and strange juxtapositions, the reflection of a man who had straddled two worlds, two cultures, and two centuries. Motorcars puffed and puttered alongside cow ponies and horse-drawn wagons. White men in stiff black suits mingled with Indian women with papooses on their backs. At a restaurant in Cache an Indian couple ate dinner before the ceremony, the man dressed in a neatly pressed black serge suit with white shirt and collar, the woman in blankets and buckskins. Before they ate, the woman offered a Christian prayer for Quanah's soul.

His red granite headstone, quarried from the sacred Wichita Mountains, read: "Resting Here Until Day Breaks and Shadows Fall and Darkness Disappears Is Quanah Parker Last Chief of the Comanches."

The man was dead. But the legend of the last Comanche warrior and his beloved white mother was just beginning.

11.

The Legend
(Oklahoma and Texas, 1911–52)

Quanah's surviving relatives sat down in May, three months after his death, and divided his assets. He had seventeen lawful heirs, including Tonarcy, his only legally recognized wife. The Star House and the property around it were appraised at $2,540. He had additional assets of $500.52 and debts of $347.12. Topay got the house, while she and Tonarcy split the land allotment. The possessions were divided among sixteen children.

The "richest Indian in America," as he was often called, turned out to be worth less than three thousand dollars. It was just one fantasy among many that had shaped and defined Quanah's image to white Americans.

The money may have been scarce, but the praise poured out in buckets. The *Christian Herald* extolled "the Indian Who Made Good," in an article dripping with fantasy and condescension:

> It was Quanah's pride that he had been obedient to every order of the government since coming under their charge. The white settlers near him respected and esteemed him, while his sovereignty over the Comanches was absolute. He was to them as a father; his home was the spot towards which each Comanche set his face when he needed advice; they knew him as honest and just in all his dealings, therefore his word was their law.
>
> Now that he has gone, it must be admitted that one at least of the too often despised race "made good," and deserves the tardy recommendation, "well done."

The *Herald*'s encomium was unusual in one respect: it made no reference to Quanah's half-white parentage. Virtually every other tribute took pains to point out that what made this ordinary redskin such an extraordinary man was the blood and civilizing touch of his white mother. The state of Oklahoma dedicated a monument at his burial site, and James C. Nance, speaker of the state house of representatives, hailed Quanah as "a beacon of light to a wandering people. It was the loving touch of the white woman's hand that developed the character of Quanah Parker."

With few solid facts to go on, the saga of Cynthia Ann and Quanah evolved according to the needs and sensibilities of each succeeding generation. Olive King Dixon, a prominent Panhandle schoolteacher and newspaper reporter—and widow of the late buffalo hunter Billy Dixon of Adobe Walls fame—helped spread the legend with an article titled "Fearless and Effective Foe, He Spared Women and Children Always." Far from being an outcast among the Comanches because he was an orphan with white blood, her Quanah was a full-fledged war chief who struck fear into the hearts of Texans even while playing the role of the ultimate Noble Savage. "He was never known to break a promise and if he said he would do a thing he did it," she wrote. "He claimed he never allowed any woman or children to be killed in his battles. As the red blood in his veins dominated in his youth, so the white strain began to show itself more strongly as the years passed."

A caption of a photo of the Star House published with the article reported that Quanah "is said to have possessed the cunning of a white man and the brutality of a savage."

This little passage goes to the heart of Quanah's appeal to whites. They were able to claim him as one of theirs. The brain was a white man's brain, even if the body was all red. They took pride in his achievements and admired the clever way he managed to circumnavigate the white world after his surrender.

Inevitably he and his mother became easy subjects for melodrama. There were operas, choral symphonies, one-act plays, novels, and eventually a comic book called *White Chief of the Comanches*. Its cover depicts a massive Indian with bulging muscles swinging down from a tree to rescue a helpless blonde white woman in a canoe heading toward a waterfall.

The opera, *Cynthia Parker* by Julia Smith, first performed in 1939, is no less fanciful. The saga gets a full-bodied fictional treatment, as if the true story weren't tragic enough. The first two acts are relatively straightforward. But Act III opens to the hoot of an owl and the cry of a wolf, signaling that Quanah and his men have come to rescue Cynthia Ann and his sister from their white captors. In the ensuing skirmish, Cynthia Ann is accidentally struck by an arrow from one of her putative rescuers. She dies in the arms of Quanah and Prairie Flower, after which the Indians carry her body back to Oklahoma.

The world premiere was held at North Texas State Teachers' College in Denton. Quanah's son White Parker attended, as did Topay, Quanah's surviving wife, who was dressed in full Indian costume. James DeShields, the most ubiquitous purveyor of the Parker legend, nearing eighty but still mobile, was also on hand. The opera's tale, after all, was not much more fanciful than his own published work.

But the main architects of the Cynthia Ann–Quanah legend have been the Parkers themselves, both the Comanche and Texan sides of the family. Quanah had tried and failed to bring them together during his lifetime, but after his death they began to coalesce.

In the 1890s, Araminta McClellan, the Reverend Daniel Parker's great-great-granddaughter, met and married a young man named Joseph Taulman in Hubbard City in East Texas, just thirty-five miles from the site of Parker's Fort. As a young man, Joe Taulman worked as a printer, saddle and harness maker, and cowboy. In 1893 he opened a photography studio in Hubbard City and remained in that business until 1919. He moved his family to Fort Worth in 1920, and he worked as a linotype operator for the *Ft. Worth Star-Telegram* from 1925 until his death in 1946. But Joe and Araminta's true passion was collecting and recording family histories, and the vast, extended Parker family with its close ties to the founding and history of the state of Texas became their full-time passion.

In the early days before cars and telephones, they did it the old-fashioned way, with letters and telegrams. They constructed a family tree, collecting as many documents as possible, including the Articles of Faith of the Pilgrim Predestinarian Regular Baptist Church—signed at Lamotte, Illinois, in 1833 by Daniel Parker, his family, and other congregants—and Benjamin Parker's original family Bible, discovered amid the wreckage of Parker's Fort after the massacre. Other documents relate to the establishment of the church in Texas, where it was the first organized Baptist church. The Taulmans also collected property deeds from North Carolina, Illinois, and Tennessee, where the Parkers lived before coming to Texas, as well as original land grants from the Republic and the state of Texas, and a Mexican land grant to

Daniel Parker. The Briscoe Center for American History at the University of Texas at Austin has nearly forty feet of files, 2,800 photographs, and 600 negatives that Joe and Araminta collected over their lifetimes.

The Taulmans had little recorded information to work with. Joe carried on a regular correspondence with fellow amateur historians such as DeShields. Unlike Susan Parker St. John, there's no record that the Taulmans ever ventured up to Cache to meet their famous Comanche cousin, although they encouraged Susan to do so. Later Joe pleaded with Mrs. Aubrey C. Birdsong, one of Quanah's daughters, to help him piece together the true story. "So many wrong statements have been printed in the newspapers in the past, and are still being printed, in regard to Cynthia Ann and her family that I think it is time that an authentic history was prepared and published," he told her.

It's clear from her reply that the Comanche side of the family was still hoping to locate the elusive league of land that Texas legislators had promised Cynthia Ann in 1861. "I wonder if you are fortunate enough to have record or negative record of any kind of the 'land grant' given Cynthia Ann Parker by the state of Texas," she wrote Joe. "After her death, who were next of kin?"

Araminta had her own aspirations. She wrote a manuscript titled *Twice a Captive*, a short account of Cynthia Ann's life that she sent in 1935 to Adeline M. Alvord, a Hollywood agent. Alvord was encouraging at first, saying the studios were feverishly buying up good historical material. But nothing ever developed. A year later Alvord returned the manuscript. "The market for historical scenarios has been very inactive and shows little disposition to pick up," she told Araminta.

Still, even though they never published their own account, the Taulmans managed to put together factual material that was often far more reliable than the feverish myth-spinning of James DeShields and his fellow historians. In 1925, Araminta tracked down and interviewed the women who had sat with Cynthia Ann in 1861 at the photographic studio in Fort Worth where her famous portrait was taken. The Taulmans also collected the various handwritten notes of Susan St. John, the cousin who interviewed Cynthia Ann's white relatives after her death and first established that both she and Prairie Flower had lived well beyond 1864, the date recorded in DeShields's unreliable saga. Susan had hoped to write her own book for the extended Parker family, but she never finished it; she died in a fire in a nursing home in Los Angeles in 1925.

Despite the best efforts of the Taulmans and Susan Parker St. John, other members of the Parker family were as prone as James DeShields to historical fantasy. When three of James Parker's descendants reprinted Rachel Plummer's narrative in 1926, they added a remarkable account in the foreword of Quanah's bravery that manages to invoke the familiar trope of his white blood:

"On one occasion the Redmen declared war on the paleface; Quanah alone opposed the war and they held another council and because of the Paleface blood in his veins they declared him a traitor to the Redmen, and condemned him to be put to death. He told them, 'the Palefaces have many braves; we have only a few braves; our braves will all be killed by the many Paleface braves . . .'"

Faced with Quanah's courage, his enemies back down and peace triumphs: "In this one act, he no doubt averted war and preserved many lives of both tribes, as well as much suffering and distress."

In this fable, the author of the Battle of Adobe Walls becomes the apostle of peace.

AFTER QUANAH'S DEATH, the white and Comanche Parkers generally kept their distance from each other. The big event that brought them together was the 1936 centennial marking both Texas independence and the raid on Parker's Fort. The state funded a replica of the fort built on the original site on the outskirts of Groesbeck, and the town sponsored memorial festivities at which representatives of both sides of the family gathered to reenact both the raid and Cynthia Ann's subsequent recapture twenty-four years later. "Cynthia Ann Parker Is Rescued from the Indians" proclaimed the full-page ad in the *Groesbeck Journal*'s Pioneer Edition of May 15, 1936. "Come See Texas History in the Making . . . A Gigantic, Stupendous Spectacle! You'll Regret It All Your Life If You Miss It!"

The ad promised a cast of four hundred "depicting the strange life of Cynthia Ann Parker, famous Texas History Character." Admission was twenty-five or fifty cents, with the added attraction of Jack Bothwell's Famous Centennial Rodeo, featuring Miss Ruth Wood, "internationally known Cow Girl, riding the wildest of broncos."

It was a curiously American celebration—after all, this was a vast and disparate family welded together by a traumatic moment when one side had pillaged, murdered, and raped the other. It was also a quintessential commercial opportunity: the local Texaco station, Dr. Cox's Hospital, the R. E. Cox Dry Goods Company, and Palestine Pig Salt were among dozens of businesses that took out ads in the *Journal* welcoming visitors to town. Cayton's Drug Store advertised "Cynthia Ann Ice Cream manufactured and sold exclusively at our fountain" in six varieties. It also offered a Cynthia Ann Frozen Malt and a Cynthia Ann Lime Cooler.

There was no mention of Quanah. Instead, the focus was on the brave pioneers who had made their stand against Indian barbarism. The *Journal* reprinted in full "The Fall of Parker's Fort," DeShields's imaginative and hyperbolic account excerpted from his *Border Wars of Texas*, first published in 1912 and dedicated to "the Sons and Daughters of Those Noble Pioneer Fathers and Mothers who . . . battled so bravely for supremacy and . . . made possible all the glorious blessings that have followed."

AFTER THE CENTENNIAL, the Parkers left Groesbeck and returned to their respective corners of Texas and Oklahoma. But in the early 1950s a primary school teacher in nearby Mexia, Texas, named Elsie Hamill had one of the young Parkers in her class. He told her the amazing tale of Cynthia Ann and Quanah. Hamill, who was fascinated, eventually wrote to Wanada Parker Page, another of Quanah's daughters, to check the facts.

Elsie's original letter no longer exists, but Wanada's pencil-written reply is in a file in the Baylor University library in Waco. It's easy to sense from her answers just how naïve Elsie's questions were—and how by 1952 the perceptual gap between whites and Indians could often be far larger than the cultural one:

Dear Mrs. Hamill,

First I will begin by telling you that the Comanche Indians and most all Oklahoma Indians live and have practically the same customs of their white friends. Many of them have modern homes, drive good automobiles, and most of the young Indians are well-educated.

We do have a few "very few" of the older Indians who still clings to some of the old customs & beliefs, but they are passing away at a rapid pace and within a very short time we will not have a Comanche Indian who cannot understand and talk the English language.

According to my father he was about 12 years old when he last saw his mother.

I cannot tell you what was the cause of Cynthia Ann baby girls death.
I do not know but we have heard many times that Cynthia Ann died
of a broken heart longing to be back with the Indians again.

You can almost hear the walls of ignorance and prejudice crumbling as Wanada writes her amused and commonsense answers to Elsie's questions. Elsie clearly isn't certain whom she is dealing with; she asks in her letter whether Wanada might feel anxious about meeting with white people. "I'm not afraid of white people," Wanada responds. "After all, I've been married to one for forty years."

Wanada's letter is a ringing antidote to the myths of prejudice and ignorance concerning Native Americans. "Yes Indians are very affectionate to their children," she tells Elsie, putting to rest the old saw that Indians were anything but.

Elsie proved to be ready and willing to learn. She and her husband drove up to Cache that summer, visited Wanada, and stayed at her home. The two women put together a two-day family reunion for Indians and whites at the replica of Old Fort Parker in July 1953.

Since then, the two families have sent representatives to attend each other's annual family events. Someone on the Texan side commissioned a silver bowl with the Texas and Oklahoma state flags and the legend "Yesterday, Today, and Tomorrow" inscribed over a peace pipe. The bowl has been passed back and forth each year from one side to the other.

EVEN THE BODIES of Cynthia Ann, Quanah, and Prairie Flower, buried side by side in the modest cemetery at the Post Oak Mission near the Star House, were not allowed to rest in peace. A few years after the first reunion, the army decided it needed the land to build a firing range for its new atomic cannon and it seized a seven-square-mile strip on the west side of Fort Sill, a patch that included the Star House, the Post Oak Mission, several ranches, and the Craterville amusement park. It proposed jacking up the houses and relocating them to nearby Cache, and digging up and reburying the graves as well. The Parker family and the Comanche community in general were torn. Many had fought in World War Two, and they felt a deep sense of pride and respect for the military. At the same time, they revered the burial places of their tribal elders. General Thomas E. de Shazo, commander of Fort Sill, enlisted Gillett Griswold, director of the fort's history museum, and Anne Powell, a civilian employee of the information office, to campaign among the Comanches for the reburial.

Neda Birdsong, one of Quanah's surviving daughters, was the closest thing to a family leader. Educated at the Carlisle Indian School, she had composed the epitaph on Quanah's granite gravestone, and she was deeply disturbed at the prospect of digging up her father's and his mother's remains. "If we were in a war . . . and I were asked to give my father's house, I would walk out of this door without one word," she told an interviewer at the time. "But in a time of peace it seems to me they could take a little more thought and make some better plans."

The army eventually came up with a plan. Anne Powell made the first approach, offering to rebury Cynthia Ann and Quanah at Fort Sill's main cemetery. After several visits, Mrs. Birdsong agreed to meet with de Shazo. She came along with a half-dozen family members to his office and inspected the proposed site. They agreed to the reinterment with full military honors, which took place in a public ceremony in August 1957.

New monuments of Wichita red granite were erected. The Parkers were given pride of place, in front of the graves for Santanta and other celebrated warriors in a spot now known as the Chiefs' Knoll. It is the only military cemetery in the United States where whites and Indians are buried side by side.

But the new grave site was not yet complete. In 1965, Prairie Flower's remains purportedly were disinterred and reburied at Fort Sill alongside those of her mother and her older brother. Nothing about the event was

The gravestones of Wichita red granite for Quanah Parker, Cynthia Ann, and Prairie Flower on the Chief's Knoll at Fort Sill, Oklahoma. It is reputedly the only U.S. military cemetery where whites and Indians are buried side by side.

straightforward. Quanah's son-in-law Aubrey Birdsong, now eighty-seven, insisted he had dug up Prairie Flower's remains in Cynthia Ann's grave site in 1910 when he had found her bones and those of a small child in the Fosterville Cemetery, and other accounts from that era supported his claim. But the disinterment permit from the Texas State Department of Health claimed Prairie Flower had died on or about December 15, 1863, of "influenza-pneumonia" and had been buried in the Asbury Cemetery near Edom in Van Zandt County, Texas. Where the date came from no one could say, and when the Rangers went to dig up and remove the remains, they found only a few strands of hair and sand, which they dropped into a cloth sack and carried off to Oklahoma.

"To tell the truth, Captain," wrote Stan Redding, a Ranger historian who was part of the reburial detail, to his commanding officer, "I didn't really deliver no body, just some east Texas sand and a legend. The sand and some bits of wood that might have been part of her coffin was all that was left when we dug her up . . ."

The army had no solution for the slowly rotting Star House. The Corps of Engineers offered to buy it for demolition, or to move it. Mrs. Birdsong and the family chose the latter. Engineers divided it into two sections, jacked it up onto two flatbed trucks, and deposited it on the main road. They left it there for a winter, then moved it to a vacant lot in Cache. The house caught fire twice during the next two years, and volunteer firemen rushed out to save it. But with no concrete foundation to provide stability, it seemed doomed to collapse. Then, on Easter Sunday, 1958, Mrs. Birdsong drove to the house of a local businessman named Herbert Woesner, whom she had known for many years. She did not get out of her car, just honked until he came out to greet her. "She told him, 'Son, if this house is to be saved, it looks like it's going to be up to you,'" recalled Woesner's sister Kathy. He agreed to buy it from her in trade for the house of the high school basketball coach, who was leaving town for another job. They drew up the papers the following day. Woesner's men jacked up the house again and moved it a half mile to a large lot in the back of his property, just a few dozen feet from Cache Creek. "It was one of the happiest moments in my life," Herbert Woesner said at the time.

Like the Star House and the remains of the principals themselves, the legend of Cynthia Ann and Quanah was transplanted to fresher soil and reconsecrated. She remained the tragic figure, unable to bridge the gap between two warring civilizations. But her son had managed to build a bridge between the two worlds, and his children strengthened and deepened those links.

AROUND THE SAME TIME Elsie Hamill was making contact with Wanada Parker Page, a Western novelist and screenplay writer showed up in East Texas asking questions about the original abduction of Cynthia Ann and the events that followed.

Alan LeMay had known about the Parkers and Cynthia Ann at least since his sojourn to the Texas Panhandle, once the heart of Comancheria, to shoot a B Western titled *The Sundowners* in 1950. As a new novel began to take shape in his mind, he journeyed to Elkhart, where the Parkers had built their Baptist church in the 1830s and where descendants of Cynthia Ann's family still lived. He visited there with Ben Parker, the eighty-four-year-old patriarch of the family and keeper of the blue trunk that had held family documents for generations.

Ben was born in 1868, which made him old enough to have met as a boy some of the survivors of the original massacre, including Abram Anglin, who was still alive and recounting the story well into the 1880s. A farmer, Ben became deputy sheriff of Anderson County and worked for a time in a sawmill, for which he showed no particular talent, as evidenced by his nickname, "Five Finger Ben," because by the time he left its employ that was all the fingers he had left on his two hands.

Ben had helped with the reconstruction of Parker's Fort for the centennial of the massacre in 1936, basing his knowledge of the size and shape of the fort on what he had heard as a child. He also helped build a replica of the original Pilgrim Church, the first Protestant church established in the colony of Texas, founded by his great-uncle Daniel Parker. Each day after Ben retired, his son would come pick him up and drive him to town, where he would hold court at the lone grocery store on Parker Street. In tolerable weather, he would plant himself atop an old tin bread box in front of the store, smoking his pipe and talking to anyone who came by. Ben was a proud Parker: his relatives reckoned that 90 percent of his conversation in his later years centered around family history and lore.

LeMay visited Ben at his modest farmhouse, where Ben sat in his rocking chair near the fireplace. There are no surviving notes of their conversation, but Ben said later he was surprised that LeMay wasn't so much interested in Cynthia Ann but rather in the problematic and long-forgotten character who had searched for her for eight years after her abduction: her angry, vindictive, self-justifying uncle James.

III

ALAN LEMAY

12.

The Author (Hollywood, 1952)

When Alan LeMay first began writing fiction for a living in the early 1920s, the Western novel was already as entrenched in popular culture as jazz or baseball or gangster stories. James Fenimore Cooper's enormously well-read literary novels of the American frontier had evolved—or, more accurately, deteriorated—into the orange-backed dime novels of the 1860s, launching the Western to an even higher level of popularity, with total sales reaching five million copies by 1865. The cowboys were taking over from the pioneers. Wise and resourceful backwoods heroes like Daniel Boone, Davy Crockett, Kit Carson, and Cooper's fictional equivalent, Natty Bumppo, were supplanted by gunfighters and lawmen such as Deadwood Dick, Buffalo Bill Cody, Wild Bill Hickok, Wyatt Earp, and Doc Holliday. And a new generation of outlaws based loosely on real-life characters—Jesse and Frank James, Billy the Kid, Butch Cassidy, and the Dalton Gang—was emerging and adding a new layer of moral ambiguity to the entire enterprise.

Women characters were transformed as well, from Cooper's delicate and passive objects of desire to rough-and-ready gals who could handle themselves in any situation. One recurring character was the purported Indian girl of great physical ability—she rides and shoots better than any man—who turns out to be an upper-class white girl who had been abducted as a child by Indians.

Buffalo Bill himself took the next step, turning literature into live entertainment, bringing real cowboys, Indians, horses, cattle, and even stagecoaches and buffalo onstage for his Wild West Show.

The cowboy was Natty Bumppo's natural heir: a rugged man, freed from the phony gentility of East Coast society and transformed into a two-gunned, two-fisted man with his own moral code. Sometimes he himself was an outlaw or had been one in the past, and he was not always readily distinguishable from the bad guys he fought against. And fight he did: gun violence was his means of taming and purifying the wilderness. Almost every story ended with a triumphant gunfight.

The first great cowboy novel, Owen Wister's *The Virginian*, published in 1902 and dedicated to his good friend Theodore Roosevelt, sold nearly two hundred thousand copies in its first year. The Virginian is a transplanted Easterner who has become a cowhand in Wyoming: a natural man, supremely competent, suspicious of city folks and their silly, impatient, sharp-dealing ways. He is not too fond of foreigners or of Jews, two of whom he unceremoniously evicts from a flophouse late one evening to make more room for himself. The narrator, a visitor from the East, describes him in Nietzsche-like, homoerotic terms as "a slim young giant, more beautiful than pictures. His broad, soft hat was pushed back; a loose-knotted, dull-scarlet handkerchief sagged from his throat; and one casual thumb was hooked in the cartridge-belt that slanted across his hips. He had plainly come many miles from somewhere across the vast horizon, as the dust upon him showed . . . The weather-beaten bloom of his face shone through it duskily, as the ripe peaches look upon their trees in a dry season. But no dinginess of travel or shabbiness of attire could tarnish the splendor that radiated from his youth and strength."

The Virginian—we never learn his real name—is a laconic superman who slays the bad guy, wins the heart of the pretty schoolteacher, and rides off with her into the sunset.

Popular fiction writers such as Zane Grey, Max Brand, N. M. Bower, and Ernest Haycox would follow. Americans liked stories about themselves, and they especially admired mythic ones. Whatever the particular plotline, the Western was grounded in the enduring foundational myth that the American frontier was an untouched, pure new world, and a place to test one's mettle and faith. The land was a metaphor for the mission: taming the savage wilderness, after all, meant taming one's own soul. It was a place to celebrate the great American values: self-reliance, individualism, and democracy. And the wilderness could be made safe for white women and children only when Indians, with their chaotic violence and barbaric rapacity, had been subdued. The classic Man Who Knows Indians—a white man raised to understand the lore, mind-set, and weaknesses of red men—led the path to civilization.

The Western consistently outsold all other genres, including its closest competitor, the detective story—whose protagonist was, after all, just another version of the Western hero clothed in a double-breasted suit and sent forth into the urban wilderness minus the horse and saddle.

Men wrote and published most of the books, of course, both nonfiction and novels, and they presented a vision of the American West as an exclusively male domain where women served either as victims or as objects of purity rather than desire. It would take many years for a different and more ambiguous version of the settlement of the West to emerge: a female counternarrative that emphasized family and community over the lone heroic gunman. The characters created by Laura Ingalls Wilder and Willa Cather had to fight for their place alongside Wild Bill Hickok and Billy the Kid. Even Annie Oakley and Calamity Jane, the great sharpshooter and gunslinger, were women of manly virtues.

AN UNSENTIMENTAL MAN, Alan LeMay always claimed that his motives for writing Westerns were strictly monetary. But this was misleading. In focusing on the Western, he was writing what he knew best, honoring his own family history and his understanding of the struggle between white civilization and Indian culture.

His ancestors were pioneers, searching for a promised land on the Great Plains of Kansas, guided by faith and opportunity—not unlike the Parkers of Texas some forty years earlier. LeMay's ancestors settled in Kansas in the days when buffalo herds were still a common sight and Cheyennes and Kiowas still a tangible threat. Indian abductions were a common theme: two white women, Anna White and Sarah Morgan, had been taken by Sioux and Cheyenne in 1868 and rescued the following year by troops under George Armstrong Custer. Anna White had become pregnant during her time in captivity, and after she gave birth to a half-Indian son her white husband threw her out—standard behavior toward a "polluted" former captive.

Alan's paternal grandmother came to Kansas from Denmark in 1870 when she was nineteen. Karen Sophia Jensen was part of a small band of congregants who followed their minister, the Reverend Nels Nelson, across the Atlantic by freighter and then by the new transcontinental railroad to Jamestown, Kansas, where she was one of eleven founding members of the Scandinavian Baptist Church and where she met Oliver Lamay (the spelling would change with the next generation to fit the pronunciation), a hunter and harness maker from nearby Concordia.

The couple married on June 24, 1872, and homesteaded 155 acres in a one-room sod house just outside Jamestown. The last major Indian attack took place 140 miles away on September 30, 1878, when Cheyennes rampaged through western Kansas, killing some thirty homesteaders outside the town of Oberlin. These Indians were not the confident, brazen Comanches of the 1830s but desperate escapees seeking to flee captivity on a reservation in Oklahoma and return to their native homeland in the north. No matter. For those in their path, the results were just as lethal.

Oliver wasn't much of a farmer, but he was a crack rifleman, reputedly the best in Kansas. Buffalo herds would occasionally storm by on their migration south, and one day Oliver grabbed his rifle and shot a buffalo not far from his front door. The animal rose and charged him, and Oliver threw himself into a gulley. The beast rode over him, collapsed a few paces farther, and died.

Early death was no stranger. Oliver and Sophia's three sons survived to adulthood, but their daughter died in infancy. Oliver himself got caught in a blizzard on a hunting trip and developed pneumonia. He died in 1879 at age twenty-six. Sophia, who had no formal education, raised the boys alone, putting all three through high school and college. Her grit and determination clearly served as model traits for Alan's strong, capable women characters.

Dan Brown, Alan's maternal grandfather, was an Indiana boy who lied about his age to join the Indiana Volunteers and went off to fight the Civil War when he was sixteen. He was wounded in the Battle of Kennesaw Mountain in June 1864 and carried to a crowded slave cabin that served as a makeshift field hospital. Dan lay in the sodden clothes in which he had been wounded on bed straw that was never changed, and subsisted on a diet of hardtack and sowbelly. When he was discharged from the hospital three weeks later, he weighed sixty-seven pounds. But he recovered, survived the war, and married an Indiana girl in 1867; Alan's mother, Maude, was born in LaPorte, Indiana, six years later. As an old man, Dan told Civil War stories to his attentive grandson, who learned that there was nothing romantic or redeeming about shooting a man or getting shot yourself.

In 1879 the Browns moved to Concordia on the Republican River in Cloud County, Kansas, where Dan opened a law office, ran for mayor, and bought and sold farmland. It was here that Sophia's eldest son, John LeMay, met Dan Brown's daughter, Maude. They were married in 1897 in Indianapolis; Alan was born two years later on North Illinois

Alan LeMay in 1921, age twenty-two, on a schooner off the coast of Colombia, before he became a full-time author.

Street. He grew up there, graduated high school, and then served as a shave-tail infantry lieutenant during World War One—"in which I accomplished nothing," he later recalled, having never left the States.

After the war he worked a wide variety of jobs: horse wrangler in Colorado, swamper in Wisconsin, fisherman in Florida, crew member on a schooner in the Caribbean, geologist in Colombia, sparring partner for a welterweight boxer in Chicago. "I've also tried several other things," he later wrote, "none of them for very long, but each, I was told, for long enough."

Perhaps it was the breadth of his recent experiences—or perhaps his driving need to find something he was good at—that drove him to become a writer. In any event, within a few months after he entered the University of Chicago in 1919 he was writing stories for money. He sold his first short story to *Detective Story* magazine in December 1919 and never looked back. Two months after he graduated in 1922, he married Esther Skinner, a girl from back home, and took a job at the *Aurora*

Beacon News, figuring to make a career as a reporter. But he quickly determined that fiction was more his line. He sold a few more short stories, then started on a novel.

It was, of course, a Western.

PAINTED PONIES IS SET ON THE PLATTE RIVER in western Kansas, and the heart of the story is the trek of the Cheyennes fleeing the wasteland of the Oklahoma reservation for Nebraska and Wyoming.

The novel's hero is a young cowhand named Ben "Slide" Morgan, who shuttles between the prosperous, ever-expanding white world of cowboys, ranch hands, and pioneers and the dying world of the nomadic Cheyenne, unsure whether he himself is white or Indian. The book has an elegiac tone and a rare and intense sympathy for both sides, Indians and pioneers.

The basic characters and the arc of the plot are ones that LeMay would return to time and again. There is the likable, ruggedly handsome cowboy hero, with a straight, bony nose, prominent cheekbones, and "a face as friendly in expression as that of a six-months pup." Slide Morgan is a talented rider and a straight shooter who can handle himself in almost any situation that requires nerve, determination, or gunplay. But he is frustratingly tongue-tied when he tries to address the woman who is the object of his affection. Nancy Chase is eighteen, fair-skinned, spunky, and practical, a young woman willing to wait for the man she loves to realize he loves her too. LeMay lingers like a lover himself over his first fictional female creation: "It was a face of gently rounded lines, with quiet lips, and smiling eyes of a hazel color, as if the brown-green of the sage were shot through with flecks of sunlight. Her hair was of the color of misting rain when the sun faintly touches it with a breath of gold."

These are characters whose very physical appearance is at one with the unspoiled, natural land they call home.

But what makes *Painted Ponies* stand out above the pulp fiction of its era is its powerful and sensitive portrait of Native Americans. Morgan first happens upon a scouting party of Cheyenne while he is fleeing vigilantes after killing a man in self-defense. The Indians spare his life because he speaks fluent Cheyenne and convinces them that he himself is Cheyenne by birth. They take him to their camp, where he meets Morning Star and Little Wolf, leaders of the procession of families heading north in a last-ditch attempt to return to their homeland. Seeing them for the first time is for Morgan "perhaps the deepest thrill he had ever known. Here was a fighting people in the saddle, riding out of a land of death through a gauntlet of United States troops—fighting their way home!"

Morgan rides with the Cheyenne for several weeks as they make their bid for freedom. The Indian characters are sympathetically drawn, including a young widow, Antelope Woman, and her small son, Little Frog, whose moccasin Morgan repairs using a small piece of leather from his own. LeMay makes no attempt to turn Morgan into a white savior. Morgan admires the Cheyenne's ways and their doomed crusade, but he has no influence over them, and when they reach territory near his ranch, he breaks off and returns to his own affairs, leaving the Cheyenne to their fate. The Indians fight pitched battles and wage a deft if ultimately hopeless guerrilla campaign against federal troops until the last 149 Indians are rounded up and imprisoned at Fort Robinson. There they go on a hunger strike to protest being sent back to Oklahoma, then stage a breakout with a handful of smuggled rifles, killing their guards and attempting to flee. All of the Cheyenne are killed—men, women, and children alike, including Antelope Woman and Little Frog—cut down and slaughtered in the snow by soldiers grimly following orders. The victims lose their lives but not their dignity. The Western novel formula strains against something deeper, darker, more complex, and quite modern for its time.

"To march in the zero weather would have meant death to many," LeMay writes. "To arrive safely in the southern land would have meant slow death to many more, perhaps all . . . Morning Star had pledged himself never to return there alive. No surrender! Death might come to them at this place, but it would find them unbending."

The other element that makes *Painted Ponies* surprising and unusual is the ambiguity that LeMay creates around Slide Morgan's racial identity. Morgan has high cheekbones and dark skin. White vigilantes type him for "a breed" and pursue him murderously. He is drawn to the Cheyenne, who act with honor, as opposed to whites, who kill out of greed or ego. "For all practical purposes, Slide Morgan had gone red," LeMay writes. Yet LeMay doesn't steer this plotline to its logical conclusion. Slide inevitably discovers he is indeed white; the reason he knows the Cheyenne language is because he was taught as a small child by a family friend who believed that learning native tongues would foster understanding between red people and white. Still, Slide Morgan's journey between separate worlds and sensibilities and his own confused identity became a theme that Alan LeMay would return to again and again. No matter how formulaic his plots sometimes became, his stories were always *about* something. Facts and myths both fascinated him: he used the former to create the latter.

Painted Ponies was published in 1926 and serialized in four parts in *Adventure* magazine in 1927. It received decent reviews and sold well enough to get Alan another book contract. After Esther gave birth to their first child, a girl named Jody, the LeMays moved to New Orleans, where Alan worked on two novels about the Mississippi River and the delta region, *Old Father of Waters* and *Pelican Coast*. But by the late 1920s he decided that Westerns were his future. He and Esther picked up and moved to San Diego. He broke into the high-end magazines in early 1929 when *Collier's* published a short story titled "Cowboys Will Be Cowboys." He knew he had arrived as a professional writer two years later when *Collier's* announced on its cover a serialization of "*Gunsight Trail*, A New Novel by Alan LeMay."

By now he was selling most of his short stories to *Collier's*, *Cosmopolitan*, and the *Saturday Evening Post*. The ones that weren't sophisticated enough for those venues he farmed out under a pseudonym to *Argosy*, *Adventure*, and other potboiler magazines. His rates began to rise: from eighteen cents per word in 1931 to thirty-five cents in 1936. His son Dan calculates that his father published close to sixty short stories in that six-year stretch, plus seven novels and countless serializations. His work was well received. In 1935 the *New York Herald Tribune* heralded his new novel, *The Smoky Years*, as "a completely literate Western . . . Naturally there is a slight trace of formula in *The Smoky Years*, since it is meant for readers who appear to dote on rubber stamps, but Mr. LeMay has dressed his necessary gambits with generous amounts of good sense and good writing."

Success brought rewards. Alan hired a secretary with a British accent for his professional work and an experienced ranch hand for his growing collection of livestock, and started raising horses and playing polo. There were parties, cruises, stylish clothes, a canary-yellow Buick convertible, a Great Dane, and trips to Mexico and Waikiki.

Inevitably he cooked up a scheme for a dream house—a horse farm, actually, on a twenty-acre rectangular plot outside La Jolla, with an old adobe ranch house, a reservoir, and a peach and apple orchard. He named the two dirt roads bordering the property Boardwalk and Park Place. He bought it in 1936, named it Rancho Una Vaca—"One Cow Ranch"—invested in twenty white-face heifers and a bull, and proceeded to go bust, thanks to the Depression and his own extravagant plans.

Alan LeMay could write about Western myths, but he couldn't create his own. "I am now thirty-eight years old," he wrote to his parents in June 1937. "In review, it seems to me that I have spent most of the thirty-eight years worrying."

He was an energetic buzz saw of a man, five-foot-six, with a big head, thick chest, and wide shoulders atop truncated legs. The hand-tooled, high-heeled cowboy boots he always wore added two more inches. His blunt features—bushy eyebrows, sharp nose and chin, steel-gray hair combed back from his forehead—added to the sense of a small, powerful, and explosive package. When he drank too much, the explosions were more likely. Starting in college, where he smoked to stay awake so that he could study and write through the night, he was a two-pack-a-day man with a seemingly permanent cough. When the family doctor prescribed Parliaments, one of the early filtered cigarettes with a small wad of cotton at the end, Alan tried them once and then gave up. "Dad said they tasted like a steam kettle," Dan LeMay recalled. "He immediately went back to Camels."

Pugnacious and constantly in motion, Alan was an amateur boxer, polo player, and—an avocation he suddenly chose to acquire in his mid-fifties—race car driver. The kind of man who, when he discovered he was afraid of flying, willed himself to take aviation lessons to conquer what he called "this shameful cowardice."

He was highly critical of his own work and scathing about other people's. He refused to read anyone else's manuscript: those naïve neophytes who foolishly sent him theirs in hope of receiving a helpful critique or encouragement got their envelopes back unopened. As he explained to Dan, why give away his valuable insights for free?

Even when Alan was writing, he couldn't stop moving, pacing the floor in his study and fashioning giant chains of paper clips. He was always working, always looking for the next great project and the big payday. Vacations were just a drain; he couldn't afford either the time or the money. Yet for all his outward purposefulness and steely determination, he was a finicky writer, endlessly overhauling entire manuscripts and stalling out from his own self-doubt. "The deadline I believe would actually be a help," he once wrote to his literary agent in New York, Max Wilkinson, "for it would put a check on the infinite shuffling and reshuffling of the possibilities to which I seem prone. I have a notion that any improvement achieved by countless substitutions of components, all to the same effect, is purely accidental. It's a rut I get into; but I can make up my mind when I have to."

By the late 1930s he and Esther were drinking heavily and fighting constantly, and later that year they separated. Alan moved back to his parents' house in Aurora, Illinois, with Jody and Dan. Within months he'd met another girl from Illinois, Arlene Hoffman, manager of a local radio station where Alan worked part-time as an engineer. After the divorce from Esther was finalized, he and Arlene got married in Las Vegas in July 1939. He had a new wife, two kids, and a monthly alimony bill, at a time when the magazine business was drying up along with book sales.

Alan LeMay decided to go where the money was: he moved to Hollywood.

WESTERN MOVIES HAD SUFFERED a long creative hiatus in the early days of sound, when they were largely exiled to the cheaper studios and the realm of B movies and children's Saturday matinees. But now they were in the midst of a major comeback and on the brink of a golden age. A-list directors such as Raoul Walsh and John Ford were returning to the genre and carving out a visual style of storytelling that fit the demands of the form, and actors like Gary Cooper, Errol Flynn, Randolph Scott, Henry Fonda, and a relative newcomer named John Wayne were thriving.

Alan had never written a screenplay, but Cecil B. DeMille at Paramount offered him a job as a story consultant. DeMille was looking for "a more primal tint of virility on his palette," according to Jesse Lasky Jr., one of his regular screenwriters, and Alan's ability to turn out alpha-male Westerns seemed like just what the self-styled great showman of the cinema was looking for. The job was like a velvet coffin: DeMille paid well but in return demanded sycophancy and trafficked in insult and humiliation.

DeMille liked to launch a new scriptwriting project with a marathon session aboard his yacht, the *Seaward*. He summoned Alan just days after the wedding to Arlene—prompting her to tell friends that they had spent their honeymoon on Cecil B. DeMille's yacht, only she didn't get to go. The movie at hand was *North West Mounted Police*, starring Gary Cooper, Madeleine Carroll, and Paulette Goddard, a melodrama about a Texas Ranger, dispatched to Canada to hunt down an outlaw, who falls in love with a nurse who is involved with a Mountie, who in turn . . . etcetera. Alan's first screenplay—he shared the credit with Lasky and C. Gardner Sullivan—became a box office hit, but one that

he described to his parents as "a hashed-over product, every line hammered down into plastic pulp and cast into some synthetic shape."

Still, DeMille admired Alan's work enough to hire him again for
Reap the Wild Wind, another lusty drama, this one set off the Florida
Keys, complete with shipwrecks and underwater combat with a giant
squid. It starred Ray Milland, Goddard, and Wayne, a veteran B-movie
actor fresh from his recent success in John Ford's *Stagecoach*. Again, the
work began on DeMille's yacht; Alan described to his parents a sumptu-
ous dinner of Hungarian goose liver, oxtail soup, birch partridge, and
peach blanch mango in a rare old kirsch. "In social moments, as at dinner, DeMille becomes a host of the superlative, old southern gentleman
type, in violent contrast to his angry tornadoing at all other times,"
Alan wrote them.

After working intensely to churn out a script he was proud of, Alan
was bitterly disappointed by the picture itself. The giant squid looked
like "the world's most bewildered inner tube" despite all the money
DeMille spent on special effects. The best faint praise that Alan could
offer: "It is definitely not as bad as *North West Mounted*."

Despite Alan's disdain, the credits with DeMille opened up a world of
steady, lucrative work. Alan was an independent scriptwriter—he never
knew where his next paycheck might come from—but a well-paid one. In
the mid-1940s he spent a year on contract at Warner Brothers, where he
contributed to various second-tier Westerns. He became known as an
"outdoor writer," yet one who could write meaty parts for women.

Even though he was working more steadily than most independent
screenwriters, Alan LeMay still careened from prosperity to famine and
back again. In 1945 he reported he had an eight-month cushion of sav-
ings. A year later he had to borrow money to pay the bills. In June 1947
he was still in trouble, yet eighteen months later he was able to produce
an early television pilot with his own surplus funds.

Alan and Arlene's lifestyle was affluent, although a serious notch below Hollywood aristocracy. They lived in a succession of comfortable
houses, starting with an elaborate rental on Lookout Mountain that
was formerly occupied by Errol Flynn. In 1951 they bought a house on a
quiet block of Toyopa Drive in Pacific Palisades. It was a sensible two-
story affair, with gnarly camphor trees slouching like twisted sentries on
both sides of the front door walk. Charlton Heston lived across the
street, and Walter Matthau, Mel Blanc, and Audrey Hepburn eventually
moved nearby. The great Frank Sinatra rented a house near the beach
for himself and Ava Gardner in 1950 at a time when he was struggling as

an actor and a voice. The LeMay house was designed by Paul Williams, an African-American architect who not only drew up plans for opulent mansions for celebrities but also designed reliable middle-class houses for people like the LeMays. The purchase price was $37,500.

Arlene wanted children, and the LeMays wound up adopting two newborns—Molly and Mark—in the mid-1940s. Alan made clear that this second round of parenthood wasn't his idea; nonetheless, he held up his end as a father.

By then he had figured out that the real money in Hollywood didn't lie in screenwriting, and he pressed various studios to give him a shot at producing or directing. But he was too much in demand as a writer. When studios showed an interest in his comic novel *The Useless Cowboy*, Alan tried for a producer's credit, but Gary Cooper intervened and took it for himself. The result, *Along Came Jones*, became one of Cooper's biggest hits. Next, Alan formed an independent production company with his friend George Templeton. Together they took a cast and crew to the Texas Panhandle and filmed two low-budget Westerns with screenplays based on Alan's novels: *The Sundowners* (1949), directed by Templeton and starring Robert Preston, Robert Sterling, and Chill Wills; and *High Lonesome* (1950), which Alan directed as well as produced. Neither made any money, and Alan's direction of *High Lonesome* was panned by reviewers as stiff and unconvincing. But he enjoyed

Alan LeMay directing on the set of *High Lonesome* in Palo Duro Canyon, Texas, in 1950.

working on location, and both films featured fabulous shots of Palo Duro Canyon, the former Comanche stronghold, now overrun by white men in cowboy outfits firing pistols with blank cartridges while the movie cameras rolled.

Still, an independent screenwriter was only as good as his last picture, and Alan was struggling. He was fed up, disillusioned, and slightly broke. In a moment of uncharacteristic self-pity, he wrote to his father back home in Indiana that although he had directed one movie, produced two, and written seventeen, "I am now totally unknown and can start over at the bottom."

His melancholy conclusion: *"All I want of this business and this town is out of it."*

In the late 1940s, he had written an original screenplay treatment called *African Pitfall*, set in southern Africa in the 1890s, about a soldier of fortune named Charlie Frye who searches for and ultimately rescues a white girl abducted by Matabele warriors and raised in a chief's kraal. It was a Western captivity narrative transplanted in African soil: the abduction of a white virgin by savages who adopt her as one of their own. The theme, which had long resonated in American literature, now caught Alan's imagination as well. Although *African Pitfall* was never made into a movie, he didn't forget.

It wasn't long before he found another, similar story. Most likely it was while on the film shoot in the Panhandle that he heard about Cynthia Ann Parker. Her story had many of the elements he was looking for: pioneer families on the brink of danger, Comanche raiders, a captive white girl, and the uncle who seeks to get her back. Alan was interested in all these themes, but he was especially intrigued by the search to find and restore Cynthia Ann to her original family. He was also desperate to stop writing second-tier screenplays and return to a form he knew well, one that he—not the producers, nor the directors, nor the money people, nor the actors—could control: the Western novel.

He rented office space about a mile up the hill from the house, just across West Sunset Boulevard, in a corner room behind the House of Lee Chinese restaurant. Its two windows oversaw a rear parking lot, but in the distance the Santa Monica Mountains glowed orange in the sunset. It was there that Alan LeMay set to work on *The Searchers*.

13.

The Novel (Pacific Palisades, California, 1953)

S upper is over and a bloodred sun is setting outside the ranch house. Henry Edwards is taking a last look around the extended yard before dark, cradling his light shotgun, but it's not game fowl he's seeking. He fears the worst—that somewhere beyond the faint roll of the prairie, just out of sight, a Comanche raiding party is preparing to attack.

The year is 1869 and the Edwards family lives at the sharp edge of pioneer country, "holding the back door of Texas" in the northwest corner of the state. Comanches and Kiowas are punishing the range, killing and burning out settlers, making a mockery of the so-called peace policy that President Grant and the Quakers serving as his Indian agents are seeking to establish on the High Plains. Despite a series of massacres, a few pioneer families are staying put, trusting that their luck will hold, but Henry Edwards's luck has run out. The night before, he sent off his brother Amos and his adopted son Martin to help a posse hunt down purported cattle thieves who had struck a neighbor's herd. But now it's clear that the thievery was just a ruse by Indians whose real goal is a murder raid. Having tricked their pursuers into a wild-goose chase, the killers are about to strike.

So begins *The Searchers*, Alan LeMay's thirteenth novel, one of the most memorable Westerns of the 1950s. It is the story of two men, Amos Edwards and his adopted nephew, Martin Pauley, and their epic search for Amos's niece Debbie, the sole survivor of the raid on the Edwards's ranch house that LeMay so dramatically sets up in his opening chapter. Set in post–Civil War Texas, *The Searchers* is an odyssey through the last years of the Comanche-Texan wars, told from Martin's point of view. It captures the magnificent heroism and endurance of the settlers who carried on in the face of overwhelming odds, but it also reflects their deep racial hatred of Comanches, who are portrayed as savage murderers and rapists true only to their own barbaric code. Harrowing, grim, and un-relenting, the book reflects LeMay's abiding verdict that life is inescap-ably tragic and even the dead do not rest in peace.

The Searchers is an inverted captivity narrative. It focuses not on the victims nor on their Indian captors but rather on the pursuers, Amos and Martin, who embark upon a quest to rescue the captives and take vengeance on those responsible. Debbie, the object of their search, is nine years old when the story begins—the same age as Cynthia Ann Parker when she was abducted.

Alan LeMay was intrigued by the fact that James Parker, Cynthia Ann's uncle, was a backwoodsman of dubious reputation and an unre-pentant Indian hater. The novelist proceeded to build his own fictional character, Amos Edwards, from the bare bones of James's life and quest. He created a second fictional searcher in Martin Pauley, whose own family had been slaughtered by Comanches when he was a baby. And LeMay updated the tale: instead of taking place in 1836, the raid and abduction occur after the end of the Civil War, which allowed LeMay to turn Amos into a disgruntled Confederate war veteran and to track the decline and final defeat of the Comanches by the U.S. Army as he tells the saga of Amos and Martin's search for a fictionalized version of Cyn-thia Ann.

A meticulous researcher, LeMay collected information on sixty-four Indian abductions, including Cynthia Ann's; his notes show references both to her and to her Comanche son Quanah. He compiled ten pages of typed and handwritten notes about abductions, battles, and Coman-che bands. In the end he freely cherry-picked and mashed together fea-tures from several true stories to create his fictional one.

Amos Edwards is forty, "a big burly figure on a strong but speedless horse," with heavy reddish brown hair and a short, silent fuse. "He was liable to be pulled back into his shell between rare outbursts of temper." He is a drifter on the frontier: his résumé includes two years as a Texas Ranger, four years in the Confederate cavalry, and two long cattle drives working as a cowhand up the Chisholm Trail. Yet he always finds his way back home to work for his younger brother Henry on the ranch, and no one can quite figure out why. Amos's secret is that he is in love with Martha, Henry's wife. Amos tells no one; not even Martha sus-pects the truth.

Martin Pauley, his fellow searcher, is "a quiet boy, dark as an Indian except for his light eyes; he never did feel he cut much of a figure among the blond and easy-laughing people with whom he was raised." Martin's parents had settled the territory alongside two other families, the Mathisons and Edwardses, two decades earlier. Martin was a baby when his family was wiped out in a Comanche murder raid in the early 1850s. Henry Edwards found him lying under a bush where his parents hid him from the warriors, and Henry and Martha took him in and raised him as one of their own.

LeMay's Texas frontier is a frightening place where families risk annihilation at the hands of savages, and those who remain do so because they feel they have no choice. It is a land where only the strongest and most stubborn seek to hold on. "It was Martha who would not quit," writes LeMay, "and she had a will that could jump and blaze like a grass fire. How do you take a woman back to the poverty of the cotton rows against her will? They stayed."

Martha's insistence that she and her family remain on the frontier eventually leads to their destruction. No one blames her, however. It is the land itself that is truly at fault. "This is a rough country," Amos tells Martin. "It's a country knows how to scour a human man right off the face of itself. A Texan is nothing but a human man way out on a limb. This year, and next year, and maybe for a hundred more. But I don't think it'll be forever. Some day this country will be a fine good place to be. Maybe it needs our bones in the ground before that time can come."

When the posse figures out they've been duped by the Comanches, Amos and Martin race back to the Edwards homestead to find the butchered corpses of Henry, Martha, and their two young sons. The Comanche raiders have abducted Debbie and her older sister, Lucy. The pioneers hastily bury the victims, and Amos, Martin, and five neighbors set out to try to find and rescue the girls. James Parker took weeks to get a posse going, while Amos and Martin are able to launch theirs at once.

They track the raiding party for five days, then realize that the Comanches have sucked them into an ambush. The Texans hold off a large force of Comanches in a gun battle at the Cat-Tails marsh, after which Amos, Martin, and Brad Mathison, Lucy's ardent young suitor, continue the search alone.

Amos breaks off at one point to follow tracks up a narrow canyon, then catches up to the others minus a saddle blanket. Brad scouts ahead, finds the Indian camp, and reports back that he has spotted Lucy there. But Amos tells him that what he saw was a Comanche buck wearing

Lucy's dress. Amos found Lucy's body the day before and buried her in his blanket. When Brad asks, "Did they—was she?" Amos explodes: "Shut up! Never ask me what more I seen!"

Despite the attempts of the others to stop him, a crazed Brad charges into the Comanche camp on his own and is killed and mutilated. Amos and Martin continue their pursuit for several more weeks, but break it off as winter closes in. "This don't change anything," Amos pledges. "If she's alive, she's safe by now, and they've kept her to raise . . . We'll find them in the end; I promise you that . . . We'll catch up to 'em, just as sure as the turning of the earth!"

The two men strike out for Indian Territory, just as James Parker did in real life. But after months of false leads and endless frustration, they return to the Mathison homestead. Amos is determined to continue the search on his own. Young Laurie Mathison loves Martin and begs him to stay behind, telling him that Amos will find Debbie without his help. "That's what scares me, Laurie," he replies. "I've seen all the fires of hell come up in his eyes when he so much as thinks about getting a Comanche in his sights." Martin fears for Debbie's life. He knows Comanches often kill their white captives when under attack. "What I counted on, I hoped I'd be there to stop him, if such thing come."

The tension is established that drives forward the rest of the narrative. Amos Edwards is an angry, implacable man bent upon revenge. Even though Debbie is the daughter of Martha, the only woman he has ever loved, Amos doesn't care if she lives or dies. His goal is to avenge Martha's rape and murder, and to destroy the world of those who have destroyed his. His sole motivation is hate.

When it comes to Comanches, Martin is no less hateful. He embraces the Texan idea of a war of extermination. "I see now why the Comanches murder our women when they raid—brain our babies even," he tells a fellow pioneer. ". . . It's so we won't breed. They want us off the earth. I understand that, because that's what I want for them. I want them dead. All of them. I want them cleaned off the face of the world."

But Martin's hatred has its limits. It extends to all Comanches, but not to Debbie, even if she has grown up to become one of them. Martin values kinship above all else. Because Debbie is his sister, his obligation to her is clear, unbreakable, and nonnegotiable. While the world around him seems crazed with bloodlust and vengeance, his own moral compass remains firm.

The Searchers is a journey of discovery. Martin Pauley grows from a terrified, callow teenager into an adept, experienced, and grimly determined tracker and huntsman. His convictions harden and his willingness to challenge his elders—and most specifically Amos Edwards—evolves into a moral certainty. Even Amos comes to recognize Martin's willingness to go all the way to defend Debbie. "I believe you'd do it," he tells Martin, with grudging admiration. "I believe you'd kill me in the bat of an eye if it comes to that."

Their search goes on for five years, echoing incidents that occurred in James Parker's hunt for Cynthia Ann. Just as James received unreliable information from several traders in Indian Territory, so, too, must LeMay's searchers deal with the machinations of an unscrupulous trading post owner. And just as James and a companion had to shoot their way out of an Indian ambush, so must Amos and Martin escape several attacks.

But their main antagonist is the land itself, the relentless High Plains of North Texas and the Panhandle, the flat, endless, natural habitat of the Comanches and a place where white men can expect to find death or a kind of malevolent, spirit-sucking black magic. "That country seemed to have some kind of weird spell upon it," writes LeMay, "so that you could travel in one spot all day long, and never gain a mile . . . If a man could have seen the vastness in which he was a speck, the heart would have gone out of him; and if his horse could have seen it, the animal would have died."

There are times when nature seems to want to kill Amos and Martin even more than the Comanches do. They are trapped by a sudden blizzard that takes them by surprise, blinds them in its white fury, and buries them alive. The storm is like a murderous animal: "It tore at them, snatching their breaths from their mouths, and its gusts buffeted their backs as solidly as thrown sacks of grain." It renders them "sightless and deafened in the howling chaos," and it plunges them down a twelve-foot gulley, breaking the neck of Amos's pony. They shelter under a newly downed willow, dig a small bare spot for a fire, and spend sixty hours huddled over it, taking turns staying awake to keep from drifting into a frozen death. Finally, they emerge from their snowbound prison, their lips cracked and blackened, their beards frostbitten, and trek 110 miles to the fragile safety of Fort Sill.

They finally locate Debbie living in the encampment of a Comanche chief named Scar. They arrive claiming to be traders, but Scar knows who they really are. They keep their cool and ride off, but Debbie intercepts them outside the village and warns them to flee, that Scar is planning to kill them. She refuses to go with them: she is betrothed to a young warrior and considers the Comanches her people, even though Martin tries to explain that it was Scar who led the raid that killed her family—just as Cynthia Ann's Comanche husband, Peta Nocona, had led the murder raid on Parker's Fort in 1836. The scene mirrors that of Cynthia Ann when white scouts came across her in 1846 but she refused to consider leaving the Comanches to return to her Texas family.

In the novel, Amos and Martin meet up with a contingent of Texas Rangers, U.S. Cavalry, and their Tonkawa Indian allies who aim to attack Scar's encampment. Martin also runs into Charlie MacCorry, a local cowhand and Texas Ranger, who informs Martin that he and Laurie have gotten married.

The Texans and soldiers attack Scar's village and overcome the defenders—not unlike the Ranger attack at the Pease River in 1860. Amos sees a Comanche girl who looks like Debbie, reaches for his pistol, but at the last minute chooses to rescue her. But it isn't Debbie. The girl pulls a gun from the fold of her outfit and shoots him dead.

Martin searches in vain for Debbie among the wreckage of the village, then trails her to the remote northwest, where he finds her cold, exhausted, and dying of thirst and cold. He warms her body with his own and keeps her alive. She tells him that she ran away from Scar and the Comanches after discovering that what Amos and Martin had said was true: the Indians had killed her family. Now she has no family, no people, and no hope. "I have no place," she tells him. "It is empty. Nobody is there."

Martin promises he will stay with her. "I'll be there, Debbie."

He begs her to remember the past. "I remember," she tells him. "I remember it all. But you the most. I remember how hard I loved you."

Love and memory have the last word. But there is no way to know how these two orphans will fare in such a merciless land. Martin's possibility of happiness with Laurie has been shattered, while Debbie has lost her home and her people. Their only hope now is each other.

The Searchers is a story of courage and endurance, of people who refuse to give up even when the odds are ruthlessly stacked against them. But it is a hard, pessimistic book, as unyielding as the landscape it takes places in. In its sense of despair, its emotions echo those of Cynthia Ann Parker after she was purportedly liberated in 1860.

Alan LeMay dedicated the book to his Kansas ancestors. The book jacket, adapted from a letter Alan wrote his publisher in July 1954, explains: "These people had a kind of courage that may be the finest gift of man: the courage of those who simply keep on, doing the next thing, far beyond all reasonable endurance, seldom thinking of themselves as martyred, and never thinking of themselves as brave."

In this hard land, the most destructive force is the Comanches themselves. Unlike in *Painted Ponies*, LeMay's first novel, there are no Noble Savages in *The Searchers* and not one sympathetic or admirable Indian character. The Comanches are brutal, duplicitous, and merciless. They ruthlessly take advantage of the U.S. government's naïve peace policy to shelter during the winter in government reservations in Indian territory, then resume raiding and pillaging vulnerable pioneer families in Texas in springtime. They literally spit upon and try to intimidate the benevolent Indian agents who seek to help them. They are unstoppable, unappeasable, and fundamentally inhuman. All of their actions and instincts are unpredictable and confounding. "I ain't larned but one thing about an Indian," says Amos. "Whatever you know you'd do in his place—he ain't going to do that."

Even the gift of language—one of the fundamental attributes of humankind—seems beyond them. "The Comanches themselves seemed unable, or perhaps unwilling, to explain themselves any more exactly," writes LeMay. ". . . Nothing else existed but various kinds of enemies which The People had to get rid of. They were working on it now."

The idealistic young novelist who wrote so sympathetically about the Cheyenne Indians in *Painted Ponies* twenty-five years earlier had hardened into the remorseless creator of *The Searchers*. Alan himself explained his antipathy to the Comanches as his attempt to even up the literary box score. "A great deal has been written about historic injustices to the Indian," he wrote one reader. "I myself once wrote a book highly partisan to the Northern Cheyennes. I thought it was time somebody showed that in the case of the Texans, at least, there were two sides to it, and that the settlers had understandable reasons to be sore."

But the real depths of LeMay's hard-earned pessimism are evident in his portrayal of Laurie Mathison, Martin's lost love. In most of LeMay's novels and screenplays, the hero gets the girl, and vice versa. Not so in *The Searchers*. Martin loses Laurie for the noble reason that he won't abandon his sacred mission for the sake of their personal happiness. Laurie tries to be as virtuous as he is; she waits patiently for years and helps him however she can. But in the end she surrenders to despair and marries Charlie MacCorry. Before she does so, she endorses the idea of an honor killing—that because Debbie has been defiled by savages, she must be killed to restore her own purity and her family's honor. Debbie has "had time to be with half the Comanche bucks in creation by now," Laurie tells Martin. ". . . Sold time and again to the highest bidder . . . got savage brats of her own, most like."

"Do you know what Amos will do if he finds Deborah Edwards?" she adds. "It will be a right thing, a good thing—and I tell you Martha would want it now. He'll put a bullet in her brain."

As she speaks these hateful words, Laurie's beautiful face hardens, and "the eyes were lighted with the same fires of war [Martin] had seen in Amos' eyes the times he had stomped Comanche scalps into the dirt."

Martin refuses to accept Debbie's death as a just solution. "Only if I'm dead," he tells Laurie, and leaves her behind one last time in order to rescue his adopted sister. For Martin, kinship is stronger than love or hate.

The Searchers was Alan's first serious literary effort in ten years, and it was a painful and painstaking labor that took him nearly eighteen months to write. "In all I wrote about 2,000 pages, mostly no good, to get the 200 pages we used," he told one letter writer.

When another letter writer suggested he write a novel about Cynthia Ann Parker, Alan replied with a gentle refusal. *The Searchers*, he wrote, "represents about all I have to contribute on this particular subject." It was as close as Alan LeMay would come to acknowledging the connection between Cynthia Ann's story and his novel.

Alan first wrote the novel in five serialized pieces, titled "The Avenging Texans," which his New York agent, Max Wilkinson, sold to the *Saturday Evening Post* for an undisclosed sum. Next, Wilkinson took it around to book publishers. He and Alan settled on Harper & Row and an experienced and empathetic editor named Evan Thomas, who would later become famous for editing John F. Kennedy's *Profiles in Courage* and William Manchester's *The Death of a President*.

In the end *The Searchers* can be read not just as Alan LeMay's tribute to his ancestors and his purest and most personal expression of the American Western founding myth, but also as an exploration of his own hardened psyche. LeMay felt he had barely survived Hollywood, hanging on to a piece of his soul in a predatory environment where only the strongest and most cunning could survive. He himself had become a searcher for his own autonomous place in a difficult world. His kinship with his hardy ancestors was not just a blood tie but a link forged by grim experience. In this sense—as with all storytellers—Alan's story is about himself.

The book was a critical success. "Its simplicity is one of subtle art," wrote the literary critic Orville Prescott in the *New York Times*, "suggestive, charged with emotion and the feel of the land and the time."

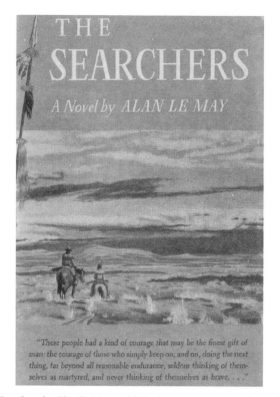

The Searchers, by Alan LeMay, published in 1954 by Harper & Brothers.

The hardcover book sold more than fourteen thousand copies, and has continued to sell in various reprints and paperback editions for more than a half century. It garnered a lot of gratifying attention, which Evan Thomas eagerly reported back to his author. "One of the White House correspondents tells me that Eisenhower is reading the book, with great pleasure," Thomas wrote to Alan in February 1955.

Reader's Digest bought the rights for $50,000, half of which went to Alan and half to Harper. But the most important sale was to Cornelius Vanderbilt Whitney, a playboy businessman and heir to the immense Vanderbilt-Whitney fortune. Whitney had just formed a film company and hired Merian C. Cooper as his executive producer. Cooper's other business partner was the famed film director John Ford.

Alan returned home to Pacific Palisades from two weeks of researching his next novel among the Kiowas in Oklahoma to learn the good news that H. N. Swanson, the legendary Hollywood literary agent who once boasted F. Scott Fitzgerald as a client, had sold the movie rights to C. V. Whitney Productions for $60,000. The amount, "I am told (not too reliably), ties the record for the year," an ecstatic LeMay wrote to Thomas, "the whole thing being made possible by the rewrite under your coaching."

Still, despite his years of experience as a screenwriter—or more likely because of them—Alan wanted to have nothing to do with the movie. He told his son Dan that he had sold the rights with the stipulation that he would not have to write the screenplay or even see the film. Having survived working for Cecil B. DeMille for a half-dozen years, the last thing LeMay wanted was to get involved in making a movie with John Ford, who was by reputation another famous tyrant and scourge of screenwriters. LeMay had been in Hollywood long enough to know how Ford liked to work. He would probably use his own in-house screenwriter, Frank Nugent, and film the picture in Ford's personal Western playground: Monument Valley, the stunningly beautiful Navajo tribal park on the Arizona-Utah border. It was a ridiculous notion to film a story set in the flat, high plains of Texas in the lunar mesa dreamscape of Monument Valley. But when it came to making Westerns, nobody, especially a lowly novelist and screenwriter, could tell John Ford what to do. Better, thought Alan LeMay, to get out of the way.

The Searchers was John Ford's baby now.

IV

PAPPY AND THE DUKE

14.

The Director (Hollywood, 1954)

As John Ford liked to point out, movies and Westerns grew up together, a natural marriage of medium and genre. The first moving
picture in the United States was a series of still photographs in 1878 of a
horse racing down a track south of San Francisco on the grounds of
what became Stanford University, stitched together by Eadweard Muy-
bridge to prove that horses did indeed gallop with all four feet off the
ground. From that time on, horses and pictures seemed to go together,
as Ford himself once noted: "A running horse remains one of the finest
subjects for a movie camera."

The official end of the American Frontier, solemnly announced like a
death in the family in 1890 by the Office of the Census, virtually coincided
with the birth of motion pictures. Frederick Jackson Turner's frontier
thesis—that the West had provided a safety valve that had defused social
tensions and class conflict during the American nation's adolescence—
became a template for the Western film, which was from its beginnings a
form of elegy for a time and place that had already vanished.

After *The Great Train Robbery* in 1903, the genre slowly took shape
over the course of a decade, overlapping with genuine remnants of the
past. Ford himself befriended the legendary lawman and gunslinger
Wyatt Earp, who spent his final years loitering around Hollywood film
sets. Buffalo Bill Cody, Frank James, the surviving Younger brothers,
the former Comanche captive Herman Lehmann—all appeared in various cinematic accounts of their life and times, adding a dab of color,
showmanship, and faux authenticity.

The first moving pictures of Indians were likely made by Thomas
Edison in 1894 for a small kinetoscope called *Sioux Ghost Dance*, an

immediate hit on the penny arcade circuit. The early films were makeshift and improvisatory. They used real locations and real Indians. One of the first was a short called *The Bank Robbery*, filmed in 1908 in Cache, Oklahoma, in the heart of the former Comanche reservation by the Oklahoma Mutoscope Company. One of its stars was the former Comanche warrior turned peace chief, Quanah Parker. After outlaws rob the bank at Cache, Quanah rides with the posse that tracks them to their hideout in the Wichita Mountains. Quanah is involved in a shootout in which all of the robbers are either gunned down or captured. The money is restored to the bank and the outlaws are hauled off to jail. Despite his Comanche ethnicity, Quanah Parker is undifferentiated from the rest of the volunteer lawmen—just a good citizen doing his duty.

But that notion of the Indian as ordinary community member was quickly supplanted. As the Western film and its storytelling evolved, it quickly adopted a fixed set of ideas and images about Native Americans from nineteenth-century literature, theater, and legend. There were two dominant stereotypes. The first was the Noble Savage: the Indian who

John Ford, ca. 1940.

appreciated the benefits of the white man's civilization, wished to live in peace, and was often more heroic and moral than the craven whites he had to contend with. This was the role Quanah Parker had sought to play after his surrender in 1875, both to protect his people and to enhance his own stature.

In Hollywood's first full-length feature film—Cecil B. DeMille's *The Squaw Man*, made in 1914—an English nobleman journeys to the American West to create a new life for himself after taking the rap back home for a crime he didn't commit. He falls in love with a beautiful Ute maiden who kills an evil rancher to save the nobleman's life. They marry and have a child, but when a determined sheriff comes to arrest her for the killing six years later, the doomed maiden kills herself to protect her family and prevent an Indian war. *The Squaw Man*, which was remade several times over the next few decades, presents two enduring social lessons: consensual sex across racial lines is almost always fatal to the Indian participant; and the Noble Savage is far too noble to survive in the modern world ruled by whites.

Over time this stock figure was pushed aside by a frightening and dramatically more potent stereotype: the treacherous, untamable, sexually voracious Cruel Barbarian, abductor and murderer of white women and children, and obstacle to civilization. This Indian was a much better fit for the needs and imperatives of feature-length films. And just as Indian characters helped shape movies, so did movies help shape our modern image of the Indian. The old myths about Indians from frontier days were readily transferred to the new medium of film, writes Wilcomb E. Washburn, a cultural historian with the Smithsonian Institution, "because the characteristics that define American Indians are all dramatically conveyed by film. In violent, exotic and dramatic terms—savage, cruel, with special identity, villain, hero, worthy foe. Objects of fantasy and fable."

One of the first films of D. W. Griffith, founding father of American cinema, was *The Battle at Elderbush Gulch* (1913), a twenty-nine minute short starring Mae Marsh and Lillian Gish, in which a band of drunken Indians launch a war against white settlers after a misunderstanding leads to the death of an Indian prince. The Indians kill a white woman and murder an infant by crushing its skull. Marsh's character saves another white baby by racing onto a battlefield to take the infant from the arms of a dead settler and crawling back to safety. The Indians then besiege a small cabin of settlers and the end seems near; one man aims a gun at the head of Gish's character to spare her the classic Fate Worse than Death of rape by savages. But the cavalry arrives in a nick of time to save the small band of settlers, mother, baby, waifs, and puppy dogs.

Almost from the moment he got off the train at Union Station in Los Angeles in 1914, the young John Ford worked in Westerns, first as a stuntman, cameraman, and actor. *Tornado* (1917), the first film he directed, was a Western, and he once estimated that perhaps one-fourth of his total output of movies were in the same genre. He groomed and cultivated Western film stars like Harry Carey, George O'Brien, Henry Fonda, and, of course, the greatest of them all, John Wayne. His entourage included wranglers, stuntmen, and Native Americans, and he eventually came upon Monument Valley, a remote and breathtakingly beautiful corner of Utah and Arizona, and used it as the setting for a half dozen of his finest films. His greatest silent movie, *The Iron Horse* (1924), was an epic Western, as was *Stagecoach* (1939), the film that revitalized the genre artistically and commercially after a decade of stagnation and helped make a star of Wayne. These films were rip-roaring adventure stories, with good guys and bad guys, Indian attacks and gunplay. But they were also fables about how America became great.

"A director can put his whole heart and soul into a picture with a great theme, for example, like the winning of the West," he told one newspaper interviewer at the height of his silent-film career in 1925, and you can hear the enthusiasm spilling out from the page. Movies like *The Iron Horse*, he proclaimed, "display something besides entertainment; something which may be characterized as spirit, something ranking just a little bit higher than amusement." The heights that film creators can achieve, he added, "are governed only by their own limitations."

HE WAS BORN John Martin Feeney in February 1894 in Cape Elizabeth, Maine, of Irish immigrants, the tenth of eleven children, six of whom survived to adulthood, and he grew up in nearby Portland. As he built his myth about America, so, too, would he construct his own personal myth, beginning with his own name. He would claim to have been born Sean Aloysius O'Feeney—a more emphatically Irish name. It was the first of many small fictions. "When the legend becomes fact, print the legend," a newspaper editor opines in *The Man Who Shot Liberty Valance* (1962), Ford's last great Western. It could have served as his personal motto.

His brother Francis, twelve years his senior, left home early, changed his last name to Ford, and migrated to the newly hatched moving-picture business in Los Angeles as an actor and director. Francis acted in and helped direct some of the first Westerns, two-reelers such as *War on the Plains* (1912) and *Custer's Last Fight* (1912) that early studio mogul Thomas Ince shot at a ranch in Santa Ynez Canyon overlooking Santa Monica. After graduating high school in 1914, John was rejected by the U.S. Naval Academy, then dropped out of the University of Maine after just a few days on campus. Before the year was out he joined his older brother in the new promised land of Southern California. Francis got him work: in one of his earliest roles he played a Ku Klux Klansman on horseback in D. W. Griffith's *The Birth of a Nation* in 1915. Two years later Carl Laemmle, president of Universal Studios, decided that Ford had the self-assurance, commanding presence, and loud voice required to direct a film crew. *The Tornado* was a two-reel, thirty-minute Western, and Ford, who was a gangly, awkward, pasty-faced six-footer with little physical charisma, was both star and director. The former role was a flop; the latter proved to be his destiny.

Hollywood was bursting at its seams. Gone were the barley fields that Horace Henderson Wilcox, a real estate developer from Kansas, had first carved into imaginary avenues and boulevards in 1887. The construction in 1904 of a trolley car line from central Los Angeles seven miles to the east and the incorporation of the distant village into the city six years later brought cheap municipal water and sewage and the budding film industry, which found Hollywood's open spaces and benign climate conducive to outdoor work. It was far easier logistically to film Westerns here than in the real West. Already the illusion was being spun.

Young John Ford arrived in Hollywood in time to watch pioneering filmmakers like Griffith and DeMille create the foundations of modern cinema, and he learned the craft from the bottom up. He saw quickly that Westerns would be his ticket to success. Soon after he started working at Universal, he teamed up with a dark-eyed actor from the Bronx with a long, soulful face. Harry Carey was a law school graduate, semi-pro baseball player, actor, and writer who had come out to Hollywood from Long Island City with Griffith's Biograph company in 1913. Carey was sixteen years older than Ford and knew his way around film sets, ranches, and horses. The two men ground out a series of low-budget, twenty-five-minute two-reelers, then defied their bosses by making *Straight Shooting*, a full-length feature, without prior permission. Carey plays Cheyenne Harry, a hired gun who starts out working for a corrupt cattle boss but changes sides to support a beleaguered farmer. Carey's character is deliberate, solemn, measured, and thoughtful. There are no wasted gestures or actorly flourishes. He wears an unadorned dark shirt, crumpled hat, and rolled-up denims. Ford admired Carey's naturalistic style—as did a strapping teenager named Marion Morrison growing up in nearby Glendale who, after watching Carey's films, began to adopt it as his own.

When Universal's moneymen found out what Ford and Carey had done, they wanted to cut the film to two reels and fire both men. But Irving Thalberg, executive assistant to studio head Laemmle, intervened, and *Straight Shooting* became Ford and Carey's first hit. The two men went on to make a total of twenty-three Westerns using classic dime-novel plots with titles like *Three Mounted Men*, *The Phantom Riders*, *Hell Bent*, and *Roped*. "They weren't shoot-'em-ups, they were character stories," Ford later recalled. "Carey was a great actor, and we didn't dress him up like the cowboys you see on TV."

The partnership eventually fell apart over money, jealousy, and competition for recognition—recurring themes in many of Ford's wrecked friendships. But his work with Carey established Ford as a dependable action film director, and his career flourished. When his contract with Universal expired, he moved to Fox, a bigger and more respectable studio.

In 1920 he met and married a dark-haired Irish woman named Mary McBryde Smith, and they moved into an unassuming stucco house on Odin Street in the Majestic Heights section of Hollywood. They quickly had two children, Patrick, born in April 1921, and Barbara, in December 1922. Life seemed good. Ford worked steadily at Fox, grinding out feature-length Westerns according to a tried-and-true formula, including two films with cowboy star Tom Mix. By 1923 he was making almost $45,000 per year. But his restless ambition pushed him further. In 1924 he made *The Iron Horse*, an epic tale of the building of the first transcontinental railroad. It set the story of a young man's quest for revenge for the murder of his father against the backdrop of a great historical event that celebrated national pride and manifest destiny.

Ford had found his future. *The Iron Horse* is pure entertainment, crammed with evocative compositions and action scenes, patriotic fervor and passionate hokum. It's got buffalo herds, cattle drives, stampedes, drunken brawls, shootouts, crass humor, easy women, villainous businessmen, new towns springing out of the barren Plains, Buffalo

Bill, and Abraham Lincoln. And it's got Indians—brutal, treacherous, and picturesque symbols of a way of life being pushed inevitably toward extinction.

Early on in *The Iron Horse* there is a harrowing scene in which the leader of a band of Cheyenne Indians cruelly murders a white man with an axe while the man's young son watches from hiding. Ford stretches the moment for maximum terror, crosscutting between the smiling, sadistic killer swinging the axe in his hand, the cowering soon-to-be victim, and the horrified young onlooker. After the killer strikes, he rips off his victim's scalp and the frenzied Cheyenne celebrate with an orgy of dancing and elation. It is one of the ugliest moments in early American cinema and one that seems calculated to make Indians seem at once both fiendish and pathetic. Their leader turns out to be a renegade white man who goads his Indian followers into acts of barbarism and serves the will of a villainous white entrepreneur seeking to sabotage the railroad project. The Indians are obstacles to progress and they are doomed. Ford used hundreds of Sioux, Cheyennes, and Pawnees for *The Iron Horse*, most of them outfitted in their own native garb. They are a breathtaking sight careening down the warpath to attack the railroad construction crew. Still, whatever reverence or respect Ford would later hold for Native Americans, something more malign is on display in *The Iron Horse*.

After *The Iron Horse*, Ford continued to alternate studio potboilers and more ambitious works such as *3 Bad Men* and *Four Sons*. By 1927 he had directed some sixty films, nearly three-quarters of them Westerns. He prided himself on his productivity and the iron control he wielded on his film sets. "When he walked on the set, he knew that he was God," said director Andrew McLaglen, whose father Victor became one of Ford's favorite actors.

Many silent film directors found it difficult to adjust to the new era of sound, which inevitably changed the character of visual setups and the nature of film acting. Ford was only thirty-three when *The Jazz Singer* premiered in October 1927, but some of the studio bosses considered him washed up. He had a few more small hits, but he was developing a reputation as a serious drinker and a difficult man to work with. When Fox loaned him out to the Goldwyn Company in 1931 to shoot the Sinclair Lewis novel *Arrowsmith*, Ford got into a creative dispute with Sam Goldwyn, stormed off the set, and later showed up for work "bruised and battered, spoke incoherently, and couldn't remember what had been said minutes before," according to a Goldwyn Company memo. Goldwyn not only fired Ford, he forced Fox to refund $4,100 of the money he had paid for Ford's services.

John Ford needed a rescuer—and not for the first nor last time in his life, one appeared.

MERIAN CALDWELL COOPER COULD BOAST of the kind of dashing, daredevil biography that Ford envied and wished for himself. Born in Georgia of southern aristocrats who were long on pedigree but short on cash, Cooper dropped out of the Naval Academy during his senior year to join the Merchant Marine. He served as an aerial observer during World War One, was shot down in a dogfight when his plane caught fire, and wound up in a German prisoner-of-war hospital. After the war, he joined the Polish Air Force and fought against the Red Army. Shot down again, he escaped after a year in prison and was decorated by the president of Poland. After a brief spell as a newspaper reporter in New York, he set out to explore the world with a motion-picture camera. Working with Ernest B. Schoedsack, a newsreel cameraman, Cooper made his first film, *Grass* (1925), a documentary about the summer migration of Bakhtiari tribesmen. Two years later they made *Chang* (1927), about a family living in the jungle in northern Siam. And in 1929 the two men made their first Hollywood feature, *The Four Feathers*, one of the last great silent films, set in colonial India in the 1850s.

Affable, chatty, and impulsive, Cooper was a self-styled visionary and hard-charging self-promoter, a showman who claimed to have first paired Fred Astaire and Ginger Rogers, and an early pioneer of Technicolor, which he described with characteristic humility as "a panacea for all industrial ills." He so hated to be unproductive that if he was reading a paperback book and had to go downtown on the subway, he would tear out enough pages to last him for the trip. He talked at a relentless machine-gun pace, spraying ideas and enthusiasm just like he sprayed tobacco leaves and ash from the pipe he was constantly relighting.

Cooper went to work for David O. Selznick at RKO Studios in 1931 as an executive producer. Two years later Cooper made *King Kong*, an iconic adventure film that expanded the imaginative possibilities of what movies could be. That same year he listened as Winfield Sheehan at MGM complained that John Ford was a washed-up hack who couldn't get the feel of talking pictures and drank too much. "That's too bad," said Cooper, who happened to believe that Ford was one of Hollywood's greatest talents. He proceeded to invite Ford to RKO for a meeting at which the director arrived "with a chip on his shoulder which I immediately put at ease." The two men hit it off. Cooper told Ford he could make any picture he wanted, provided he also made a second one chosen by Cooper. With Cooper at his side, Ford drank a little less, at least while working, and tried a little harder to please the studio bosses. Over time Cooper became the middleman between Ford and the studio system, freeing the director to do some of his best work.

With Cooper's help, Ford delivered *The Lost Patrol* (1934) and *The Informer* (1935). The latter was a major work—a dark drama of betrayal set in Dublin but filmed on an RKO soundstage in shadows and fog that reflected the style of the German Expressionists. It won Ford his first Academy Award for best director, plus Oscars for Best Actor (Victor McLaglen), Best Screenplay (Dudley Nichols), and Best Musical Score (Max Steiner).

Back at Fox, Ford answered to Darryl F. Zanuck, the autocratic executive producer who controlled virtually every part of the filmmaking process. Under Zanuck's guidance, Ford directed popular stars like Shirley Temple and Will Rogers, making films set in small-town America that celebrated the values and sensibilities of a simpler world that was already fading from view, if it ever indeed existed. This period culminated in one of his most classic works, *Young Mr. Lincoln* (1939), his first picture starring Fonda. It was followed by a trio of films—*The Grapes of Wrath* (1940), *The Long Voyage Home* (1940), and *How Green Was My Valley* (1941)—that most truly define Ford as a film artist. The films are brilliantly composed and lovingly photographed, and each one comes to a melancholy conclusion about the meaning of life and the demands of family, friendship, and community. Tom Joad in *The Grapes of Wrath* must separate himself from his family and become a fugitive. Driscoll in *Long Voyage* surrenders his freedom while protecting his comrades and dies a martyr to the cause of friendship. The Morgan family in *Valley* disintegrates, as does its Welsh coal-mining village, in the face of economic and social forces beyond its control.

Ford nursed similarly painful passions in his own life. Even after he married Mary, he conducted a number of affairs with young actresses, the most intense of which was with Katharine Hepburn. As he grew older, his flirtations grew more and more pathetic—ostentatiously ogling young starlets and blurting out crude remarks. He also collected handsome young men, although here the sexual component was repressed. He nurtured his community of actors, stuntmen, and crew members whom he used in picture after picture—the John Ford Stock Company, as they informally dubbed themselves. It was his version of a rural Irish village, with himself as the stern but loving *squireen*. But when his mood turned dark, as it did at some point during nearly every picture he made, he could turn cruel and abusive, seeking easy targets for his wrath. "There was an essence of fear in every Ford camp," said Frank Baker, a character actor who worked with him often in the early years. "He always picked on somebody at the beginning of a picture, and he'd let them have it . . . You couldn't do anything right. And he just sat there with that flat voice, and he would attack you; he would humiliate you. He'd make you grovel."

Ford's father had been a saloon manager, and alcohol seemed embedded in the family DNA. Ford, his wife, Mary, and both his children, Patrick and Barbara, were all heavy drinkers. He pledged never to drink while working on a film. But when a project ended, he would let loose. "Daddy is what we called in those days a periodic," Barbara recalled. "He would come to my mother and say 'I filmed the picture, I've cut the picture, music is okayed . . . it's shipped for negative, now call the bootlegger. And here is $1,000 for you to do what you want,' and then he got drunk. And he drank for three weeks." The reason? Barbara, who herself struggled with alcoholism all her life, knew the answer: "Escape. Oblivion, you know. He had done his job."

As time went on, the drinking got worse. Mark Armistead, a Navy lieutenant commander on a PT boat who worked with Ford during World War Two, recalled that Ford would sometimes go on a bender for no particular reason. "One drink—he's the type of person that one drink is one too many and a thousand is not enough."

Armistead, who recalled his time with Ford with great warmth laced with despair, described him as an easily distracted man who always needed to be looked after, especially when he traveled. "The only thing he carried in his pocket was the rabbit's foot, a handkerchief and a pocket knife, never any money . . . Never give him a baggage check because in thirty seconds he would lose it."

He was, ultimately, a profoundly lonely man. Philip Dunne, one of his early screenwriters, told biographer Joseph McBride that Ford had no true friends. "They'd go on his yacht and drink and play cards, but there was a lack of intimacy," said McBride. "I think Ford had serious problems with intimacy all his life."

The luminous young actress Maureen O'Hara thought she had become friends with Ford when he cast her in *How Green Was My Valley* in one of her first starring roles. They bonded over their shared Irish heritage: O'Hara had been born in Dublin and could dish out the blarney with a vigor that delighted Ford. She loved the conviviality of his family dinner table, although she noticed early on that he could be casually insulting to Mary. O'Hara described Ford on the *Valley* film set as a combination of tyrant and magician, slouched in his director's chair as if on a troubled throne. Although he was only forty-seven, he looked older and unhealthy to O'Hara. His "thick eyeglasses protruded from under the rim of a weather-beaten hat, and his rumpled clothes looked as though they never made it to the cleaners . . . Commanding and demanding, his dictatorial manner was matched only by the ease of his competence."

To O'Hara, Ford was a visual master who painstakingly composed every frame. She recalled how in an early scene he had a kitchen chair placed so that its shadow was bigger than the actors. "I looked at its enormity, its imposing presence, and thought, My God, look what's he's doing. It's magnificent."

Over time O'Hara became close to Ford and his family. Then at a Christmas party at the Odin Street house, she let slip a casual remark that offended Ford—she could not even recall its content—and he leaned back and punched her in the jaw. "I felt my head snap back and heard the gasps of everyone there as each of them stared at me in disbelief and shock," she recalled. No one said a word. She got up and silently left the house. The incident was never mentioned again. But it was one of several that convinced Maureen O'Hara that there was an ugly streak of anger lurking behind Pappy Ford's front of benevolence. Ford, she concluded, "built walls of secrecy, lies, and aggression."

A decade later, O'Hara would claim, she walked into Ford's office without knocking one day and found him kissing a man—"one of the most famous leading men in the picture business." O'Hara does not name the actor, although it's likely from the context that she was referring to Tyrone Power, who was making *The Long Gray Line* with Ford at the time.

Harry Carey Jr., whom Ford often treated like a favorite nephew, experienced two sides of Uncle Jack. Ford could be a kind, gracious, and avuncular mentor. "I didn't really feel I could act until I worked for John Ford," said Carey. "I didn't know I was capable of doing what he made me do."

At the same time, Ford instinctively smelled out weakness and

John Ford in the garden at the family home on Peak's Island, Maine, ca. 1926.

ambivalence and pounced upon those too vulnerable to fight back. Periodically on a film set he would order Carey to bend over and then deliver a swift kick to Carey's exposed rear end. On occasion he would insist that John Wayne mete out the kick—something that Wayne detested doing, yet performed on demand. "Ford was a bully, he loved to intimidate people," Carey recalled. ". . . He was always testing me." Yet, Carey added, "I couldn't help but love him."

He was a man of big emotions, unspoken but not hard to see. After their estrangement, Ford still visited his old friend and film partner Harry Carey Sr. on occasion, but in twenty-five years he hired Carey only once for a part in one of his films. Yet when Carey was dying of cancer in 1948, Ford rushed to his bedside and was there when Carey died. "I remember Jack came out and he took a hold of me and put his head on my breast and cried and the whole front of my sweater was sopping wet all the way down the front," Carey's wife, Olive, recalled. "He cried for at least fifteen or twenty minutes, just solid sobbing . . ."

* * *

JOHN FORD ALWAYS INSISTED his films were "a job of work," nothing more, and throughout the 1930s he worked as a master craftsman laboring in the studio system. He made comedies, tragedies, costume dramas, historical pieces, and adventure stories. But the one genre he could not seem to return to was the one he loved best.

The Western had fallen on hard times by the early 1930s. Part of the problem was the new technology of sound. Westerns looked stiff and artificial on studio soundstages, but authentic audio was hard to record in the great outdoors. In any event, location shooting was costly and complicated, as Ford had found out when he filmed large portions of *The Iron Horse* in the Sierra Nevadas. Westerns were exiled to the land of the B movie, where they grew undernourished on thin plots, thinner scripts, and actors who often looked ridiculous on horseback. For a while singing cowboys were the rage: Gene Autry, Tex Ritter, and Roy Rogers all became Western movie icons. Children may have squealed with delight, but few adults bothered to watch. The Western became a minor, cut-rate genre.

Ford felt differently. He loved Westerns and was keen to make another. On a long cross-country train trip, his son Pat, then sixteen, read "Stage to Lordsburg," a short story published in *Collier's* magazine by the Western novelist Ernest Haycox. "Read this," Pat told his father. "I think it's a movie."

Haycox's story was a taut narrative about a handful of disparate stagecoach passengers forced to travel together on a tense journey through hostile Apache territory. Ford saw its possibilities as a thrilling action movie as well as a comedy of manners and social commentary pitting two young iconoclasts—an outlaw and a prostitute—against their purported elders and betters. Ford hoped to film it on an authentic location somewhere away from Hollywood. He set to work with Dudley Nichols, his favorite screenwriter.

Merian Cooper loved the idea of shooting an exciting Western on location, and he arranged a dinner meeting between Ford and David O. Selznick, Cooper's boss at RKO. At first, Selznick was adamantly opposed to Ford's wasting his time and talent on what Selznick called "just another Western." But as Ford and Cooper talked about the project, Selznick slowly began to melt. By the end of the evening, Cooper believed that they had won Selznick's approval.

"I went into Dave's office at Pathé [next morning], thinking everything on *Stagecoach* was just fine," Cooper recalled thirty years later. "It wasn't."

Selznick's ultimate objection wasn't to the story but to the cast. He insisted that the picture would fail to "get its print costs back unless we put stars into the two leads." Selznick suggested Gary Cooper and Marlene Dietrich, both at the height of their careers. Cooper would play the young outlaw, seeking revenge for a brother gunned down by bad men, and Dietrich the kindhearted prostitute who falls in love with him. Both were a little old for their roles, but Selznick was quite certain they would ensure box-office success. John Ford was a great director, Selznick conceded, maybe the greatest, but he didn't know how to pick the most commercially viable material or package it the right way.

But Ford had already committed to two lesser-known actors. The female lead, Claire Trevor, was a well-respected character actress with impressive credits but hardly the draw that Dietrich could have been. As for the male lead, Ford was proposing to jump off an even higher cliff by choosing a strapping young B-movie actor who was a virtual unknown in the mainstream studios and whose only starring role in a major motion picture, nine years earlier, had proved to be a certified box-office disaster.

Selznick was adamantly opposed. John Wayne, he insisted, could never carry a feature-length film.

15.

The Actor (Hollywood, 1954)

By the late 1930s, improved technology was breathing new life into the oldest of American genres. Better motion picture cameras; crisper, more realistic sound; fresh vistas; and a nostalgic sense of longing by filmgoers for simpler times and a sepia-toned America that had never quite existed all helped feed the Western movie's comeback. Emerging from the Great Depression and facing a global challenge that was inevitably pulling them into another world war, Americans were rediscovering their own history and reimagining it as a glorious and patriotic enterprise. John Ford's *Drums Along the Mohawk* and *Young Mr. Lincoln* were part of this nascent movement, as was *Stagecoach*. All three were released in 1939.

But the key to rebuilding the myth of the American frontier was the character. Popular culture had always latched onto the rugged male hero—whether backwoodsmen or gunslingers or lawmen or outlaws—as the focus of its collective fantasy.

Many of the early Western stars, such as Tom Mix, Hoot Gibson, and Ken Maynard, were showmen who rode fancy horses, dressed flamboyantly, and twirled their pistols like batons. Their elaborate clothing never got dirty and their bodies never broke a sweat. They were entertaining performers but they lacked the grit and authenticity that the new technology could capture and that audiences demanded. Gary Cooper, whose breakthrough as a film star was in the title role of *The Virginian* in 1929, had the necessary attributes of stoicism, modesty, and intensity, but meaty parts in good Westerns were few in the 1930s.

Throughout the decade, an amiable, slow-moving, tall young actor named John Wayne searched for a foothold, churning out a steady flow of cheap, disposable B Westerns that occupied the bottom halves of double bills and Saturday morning matinees for children. He took an early and misguided turn as Singin' Sandy Saunders in *Riders of Destiny* (1933), crooning from the back of a white horse while pretending to strum a guitar, and he later played Stony Brook, one of *The Three Mesquiteers*, in a series of memorably forgettable movies. With a wife and four children to support, Wayne needed a steady income, and he made dozens of two-reelers, running under sixty minutes, for $500 each.

Still, even in the cheesiest of settings, Wayne was learning how to act, honing his craft, and carving out a persona. He was deep in the process, on and off the screen, of becoming John Wayne. There were times when he could be self-deprecating and cynical in describing the character he constructed. "When I started, I knew I was no actor, and I went to work on this Wayne thing," he recalled in an unusually candid interview some thirty years later. "It was as deliberate and studied a project as you'll ever see. I figured I needed a gimmick, so I dreamed up the drawl, the squint and a way of moving meant to suggest that I wasn't looking for trouble but would just as soon throw a bottle at your head as not. It was a hit-or-miss project for a while but it began to develop."

Our modern image of Wayne has been shaped and distorted by the final decade of his career, when he became the symbol and spokesman for a simplistic, militaristic, macho-driven vision of the United States amid the debacle of the Vietnam War. It was a decade when, working mostly with second-string directors and screenwriters, Wayne the actor was a bulky, plodding, toupee-wearing self-parody, repeating himself in role after role. But before he became John Wayne, Inc., Wayne was something more. Working with John Ford and Howard Hawks, two of Hollywood's finest directors, Wayne created a range of distinctly American characters and a unique film persona of charm, menace, and physical grace. Contrary to popular belief, Wayne was more than just a passive lump of clay that Ford and Hawks sculpted. Wayne himself was a storyteller and a mythmaker. He did not invent the roles he played, but he did invent the man who played them. The story he told was about the settling of the American West, and the central character was a cowboy played by another character, a man named John Wayne.

WAYNE WAS BORN Marion Morrison in Winterset, Iowa, in 1907. When he was six years old, his pharmacist father moved the family to Southern

California in pursuit of ranchland and a bid for financial independence. The journey was an early-twentieth-century replay of the Parker family saga, minus the religious fervor and the hostile Indians—a pioneer family heading west in search of new opportunities in a promised land. But Clyde Morrison, an amiable but ineffectual man, failed to develop his small stake in the parched hills outside Bakersfield into a productive ranch. Eventually Clyde, his imperiously critical wife, Molly, and their two sons fled to Glendale, a distant suburb of Los Angeles, and Clyde wound up back behind a pharmacy counter working for other people for the rest of his life.

Young Duke Morrison—he always claimed he picked up the nickname from the family Airedale—grew up with a gnawing sense of grievance. He knew what it was like to try to scrape by in a family always ill at ease because of lack of money and an ever-simmering struggle between father and mother. He didn't care for horses and had no great interest in ranching or cowboys. He was a good student and very much a charmer—tall, powerfully built, and instantly likable, with a shy smile and curly dark hair. His voice was high-pitched and thin, but he had an engagingly slow way of speaking that was friendly and vulnerable without seeming soft. All of which was enough to earn him a football scholarship to the University of Southern California.

He met John Ford in 1926 on the back lot at Twentieth Century-Fox, where Ford was directing and the strapping nineteen-year-old Morrison was working as a stagehand, thanks to USC's powerful alumni corps. The two men bantered and, according to legend, egged each other on. Ford, who was thirteen years older, had been a football lineman in high school, and he challenged Morrison to tackle him. The younger man knocked him on his butt, a brave thing to do. Ford liked it. Thus, Wayne said later, "the beginning of the finest relationship in my life."

Ford gave Morrison various odd jobs on the set. The younger man quickly came to admire Ford and his work—the way he organized the set each day, and the way he handled people, getting the best out of every actor—and developed an interest in becoming a director himself. "I'd never seen a genius at work before," Wayne later recalled, "but I knew I was seeing one now." When Morrison injured his shoulder and was suspended from football, costing him his scholarship, he turned to Ford for advice.

"I poured out my troubles to him," Duke later recalled. "He said, 'Why don't you stay out of school a year? Give the shoulder a chance to heal. Then maybe you can start playing again. You can come work for me when school lets out. I'll find something for you to do—propping or acting.'"

Duke was heartened by Ford's offer. But when Duke reported for work, Ford said he had no movie in the works and wouldn't be ready to start a new one for two months. It was as if he had never talked to Duke before. "I walked out of the gate feeling like the whole world was against me," Wayne later recalled.

Ford eventually found odd jobs for Duke as a stagehand and stunt-man. The two men always described their budding friendship as the close relationship of a wise and generous mentor and an eager young acolyte. But the details Wayne divulged over the years suggest that Ford often exploited the goodwill and naïveté of his young friend. Like Ford himself when he worked for his brother Francis, Duke took on the most ar-duous and at times most dangerous tasks. For example, Ford promised Duke seventy-five dollars for every risky stunt dive he did during the filming of *Men Without Women* (1930), a submarine picture. After per-forming a half dozen, Duke figured he was owed a total of $450, but when the assistant director added only $7.50 to his regular paycheck of $35 a week, he kept quiet. "I should have complained to Ford but I didn't," Wayne recalled. "I was still a shy, timid person, always embarrassed about speaking up for my rights."

Wayne always believed that Ford suggested his name to the director Raoul Walsh when Walsh was looking for a new talent to star in *The Big Trail* (1930), the epic Western that Fox was putting together. But Walsh claimed that Ford never mentioned Morrison. Instead, Walsh said, he came across Morrison by happenstance.

"We looked high and low and I was walking by the property depart-ment on Western [Avenue], this big warehouse building, and there's a young guy carrying some furniture, it was one of those overstuffed chairs. He had a good height. He was bare breasted. It was a hot day. He wasn't wearing a shirt. He was a good looking boy." Walsh asked him, "Where did you get all that muscle?" Duke replied, "I used to play foot-ball at USC."

Walsh said he liked the sound of Morrison's voice and the way he moved. "He had a certain western hang to his shoulders. I know that does not make sense to you, maybe, but, a certain way of holding your-self and walking is typical of a real westerner and he had it." Walsh screen-tested him, and liked what he saw. The studio gave the young man a new name. "They came up with John Wayne," Duke recalled thirty-five years later. "I didn't have any say in it, but I think it's a great name . . . It took me a long time to get used to it, though. I still don't recognize it when somebody calls me John."

With *The Big Trail*, Wayne began shaping his persona as a mythic Western hero. Wayne's character in the film, Breck Coleman, is a natural man who has lived among Indians and knows their lore, is dedicated to justice, and is a determined hunter of bad men. "I never quit a job in the middle," Breck declares, and we believe him. Although not a slick ladies' man, he's alluring and irresistible to women. He's honest, self-reliant, and friendly, and he adheres to a moral code. Physically, he looks graceful, thin, and almost angelic—clean, white, and glowing. He is an innocent young man, strong and fluid in his movements, with a classical *controposto* stance and posture—one leg relaxed, the other rigid—echoing Michelangelo's statue of David.

Still, Breck Coleman is a work in progress and not yet the classic John Wayne character of later years. He comes across as a bit nervous, eager, and naïve, slumps on his horse, wears fancy leather clothes, uses a knife rather than a gun as his lethal weapon of choice, clenches his jaw as he waits to speak his lines, and walks tentatively. All were traits that Wayne later discarded or refined.

A flop at the box office, *The Big Trail* failed to propel Wayne into the ranks of movie stars. It also cost him for a time his friendship with John Ford, who didn't speak to him for two years after the film was made. Wayne never knew whether Ford's boycott stemmed from jealousy or from Ford's sense that Wayne somehow had violated the rules of their friendship by going to work for a rival director. Forty years later, this treatment still rankled Wayne. "Instead of facing me with it and saying what the hell are you doing, he just quit talking to me, and so I quit talking to him," Wayne told Ford's grandson Dan.

The silence ended abruptly when Ford ran into Wayne at a bar called Christian's Hut on Catalina Island. Ford sent his eleven-year-old daughter, Barbara, to summon Wayne to his table, then invited Wayne to dinner. Nothing more was ever said about the freeze-out.

After that, the two men were inseparable. They took saunas together at the Hollywood Athletic Club, played cards at least once a week, drank and dined together, spent weekends on Ford's yacht, the *Araner*, and sailed to Mexico for fishing, beer, and the local cantinas. Wayne became part of Ford's inner circle of cronies, along with fellow USC dropout Ward Bond, Henry Fonda, and the screenwriter Dudley Nichols. They called Ford "Pappy," looked up to him, followed his lead, and obeyed his commands. According to Dan Ford, who wrote an intimate biographical memoir of his grandfather, John Ford "did not surround himself with his creative peers, but rather with sycophants who were willing to serve him and obey his every whim." Wayne, who could hold his liquor under any circumstance, became the hard-drinking, hell-raising, hardworking son Ford had always wanted.

Still, despite his friendship with Ford, Wayne was an outlier in Hollywood, a proletarian among the cinematic aristocracy. For most of the 1930s, he rarely worked at the upscale studios like MGM, Paramount, or Twentieth Century-Fox, making his living at smaller shops like Monogram, RKO, and Republic—known collectively as "Poverty Row"—grinding out dozens of cheap, forgettable features while laboring to master his craft.

An eager student and a quick study, Wayne had the best of mentors. He started by modeling himself after the Western star Harry Carey, Ford's former movie partner. Wayne admired Carey's slow, soulful manner: the audience could see Carey in the act of thinking before he sprang into action. Wayne got to know Carey and his wife, Olive, through Ford and other members of Hollywood's "cowboy posse" of Western actors, stuntmen, and wranglers in the 1930s, and Carey was a generous teacher.

The Gower Gulch cowboys were named for the corner of Gower Street and Sunset Boulevard, where they gathered early in the morning while waiting for film studio work. Those who could afford it ate breakfast and drank coffee at the lunch counter of the local drugstore dressed in their cowboy denims. These were hard men who knew how to ride a horse, rope a steer, and fall off an animal in full flight without breaking a serious limb—essential abilities in a genre whose most enduring dramatic elements were horse riding and gun violence. Wayne was never one of these men; he preferred golf to horseback riding and tailored suits to cowboy duds. But he respected what they did and studied them and their moves with utmost care.

The one he watched most was Yakima Canutt, a well-known stuntman and occasional actor. A native of the Snake River hills in southwest Washington State, Canutt had arrived in Hollywood in 1919 after winning every major prize as a bronco buster on the Western rodeo circuit. He wasn't much of an actor, but he was the real thing as a cowboy. "I studied him for many weeks, the way he walked and talked and rode a horse and pulled a gun," Wayne recalled. "I noted that the angrier he got, the more he lowered his voice and slowed up his delivery. I guess unconscious, even today, I try to say my lines slow and strong the way Yak did."

The two men worked together in a dozen or more B Westerns, with Canutt usually cast as the bad guy. Together they developed an innovative approach to the fistfight, a classic moment in every B Western. "Before I came along it was standard practice that the hero must always fight clean," Wayne recalled. "The heavy was allowed to hit the hero on the head with a chair or throw a kerosene lamp at him or kick him in the stomach, but the hero could only knock the villain down politely and then wait until he rose. I changed all that. I threw chairs and lamps. I fought hard and I fought dirty. I fought to win."

From watching Carey and Canutt and listening to Ford, Wayne learned the basic lesson that appearing natural on-screen is in fact an artifice. He slowed his cadence and deepened his voice. He picked up little physical and verbal clues from the wranglers and stuntmen he met—not only how they talked but how they walked.

The character actor Paul Fix, whose daughter Marilyn married Carey's son, helped Wayne work it through. Paul "coached him, he taught him how to walk," Harry Carey Jr. recalled. "Wayne became very graceful because he worked at it so hard. In those early movies you can see he looks cumbersome. Wayne said he couldn't stand to watch himself on the screen. So Paul said 'point your toes into the ground when you walk, and swivel your hips.'"

"Duke's basic problem was coordinating himself physically to his part—getting his body in gear with his motions and with the lines he had to speak," said Fix. "Acting natural the way Duke can act does not come naturally. He had to work hard to learn to look as natural as he does. And he was anxious to improve himself and very smart. So he kept getting better all the time . . ."

By the end of his first eight-picture deal with Monogram, Wayne had established his basic screen persona—the lean, tough loner, impatient with small talk, keen for justice, protector of women and children—as well as the physical mannerisms to go with it. He walked and talked slowly and deliberately, pausing in mid-sentence. He believed the pause helped rivet the audience's attention, making them wonder what he was thinking. It also added to a sense of vulnerability and tentativeness. But behind his smile was a hint of menace and unpredictability. This was a man who was dangerous to cross.

Wayne was developing into more than just a competent actor. He was becoming a movie star at a time when stars were emerging as magnets and plot points for filmgoers and as the organizing principle of films. Unlike onstage, where the audience maintained a physical distance from the performers that even the most powerful opera glasses could not overcome, the camera's lens could move in for a close-up, creating the illusion of intimacy and identification between actor and viewer. Viewers became fans, and actors became stars. Filmgoers imitated, worshipped, and identified with stars—were in effect seduced by them.

Essential to the process was a feeling of authenticity. Movie stars, as opposed to theatrical performers, were supposed to be *real*. As Jeanine Basinger writes in her history of Hollywood star making, no one expects Laurence Olivier onstage as Hamlet to be accurately depicting the dilemmas and life choices of an indecisive young Danish nobleman. But they do expect the actor in a film—whether it's Humphrey Bogart as Sam Spade or Harrison Ford as Indiana Jones or John Wayne as Ethan Edwards—to somehow be the real thing. The actor and the role need to meet and overlap. Young John Wayne's crowning achievement was to recognize intuitively this evolving truth and learn how to use it. His characters were largely representations of the man he thought himself to be, and he became the man whom other men wanted to emulate and identify with.

"I've found the character the average man wants himself, his brother or his kid to be," Wayne explained. "It's the same type of guy the average wife wants for her husband. Always walk with your head held high. Look everybody straight in the eye. Never double-cross a pal. This is the heart I have and the sentiment I feel. There's too much knavery and underhanded stuff in the world without my adding to it. I refuse to play the heel."

Because they were classic natural men, Wayne's characters were often steeped in Indian lore and customs, but they usually treated Native Americans with deep suspicion and heightened vigilance. In the conquest of the American West, Indians were another obstacle to overcome. In real life as well, Wayne's view of Native Americans reflected the manifest destiny vision of men like William T. Sherman and Teddy Roosevelt. "I don't feel we did wrong in taking this great country away from them," Wayne once told *Playboy* magazine. ". . . There were great numbers of people who needed new land, and the Indians were selfishly trying to keep it for themselves."

Wayne went on to claim that, contrary to the opinion of certain liberals, his Westerns were actually too sympathetic to Indians. "We treated them as if they had the same moral code that the American people wish every American had," he told another interviewer, "and we gave them a nobility that was worthy of a king, when actually we know that they were, you know, savage, treacherous, competent warriors with little or no pity or mercy . . ."

John Wayne, the man who played the Man Who Knew Indians, did not believe in one of the Western's other most cherished myths, the Noble Savage.

But Indians were only bit players in the persona that the young man from Glendale was constructing for himself as an icon of American masculine power and integrity. John Wayne played the part so well that he was more than a star. He became in effect his own myth—something that was true, as Garry Wills later wrote, because people needed it to be true.

JOHN FORD TENDED TO TREAT people he was fond of with dry, mirthful derision, and he was slow at first to pick up on the transformation of his favorite young drinking buddy. "Christ, if you learned to act you'd get better parts," Ford would tell Wayne in front of other people.

When Ford came up with the idea of making *Stagecoach* (1939), he toyed with Wayne for a while, asking him to name some actors he felt could play the role of the Ringo Kid. After Wayne made a few half-hearted suggestions, Ford barked, "You idiot, couldn't you play it?" Which is what Ford had in mind all along.

Ford was so certain that Wayne was right for the role, he and Merian Cooper walked away from a potential deal with David O. Selznick, and Ford ended up making the film with the independent producer Walter Wanger. The Ringo Kid rescued Wayne from the B-Western movie factory, and he was eternally grateful to Ford for the chance. Still, the old man baited him mercilessly during the filming. "Can't you wash your fucking face?" Ford demanded while filming one scene, making Wayne do it over and over again until his face was almost raw. Ford called him "a big oaf" and "dumb bastard."

Ford also had no use for Wayne's rolling way of walking. "Can't you walk, for Chrissake, instead of skipping like a goddamn fairy?"

"Ford took Duke by the chin and shook him," costar Claire Trevor recalled. "Why are you moving your mouth so much? Don't you know that you don't act with your mouth in pictures? You act with your eyes."

Wayne kept quiet at the time, although he later told an interviewer, "I was so fucking mad I wanted to kill him." All the abuse, Wayne later would insist, was a calculated move by Ford designed to elicit sympathy and respect for Wayne from the other, more experienced actors in the cast, such as Trevor, Thomas Mitchell, and John Carradine. But it was a pattern that Ford repeated in every film the two men made together—and that Wayne generally suffered without complaint.

Still, the payoff for Wayne was enormous. The Ringo Kid doesn't make his first appearance until around the ten-minute mark, but Ford made sure it was a memorable one. Wayne is atop a small hill, holding his saddle in one hand and waving his rifle with the other as the stagecoach pulls up. In one of Ford's most striking cinematic flourishes, the camera moves toward Wayne, slips briefly out of focus, and comes back in as if suddenly seeing for the first time the magnetic young man standing before it. It is one of the classic introductions in American cinema, a visual announcement of a star being born.

Wayne put up with all of Ford's abuse in part because of a sense of loyalty and deference to an older man who had taken an interest in him, and in part no doubt because Ford was the stern, demanding father that the easygoing but constantly thwarted Clyde Morrison had never been. But it was

John Ford, John Wayne, and a mutual friend during one of the annual Christmas parties at the Field Photo Farm in Reseda, Los Angeles, in the late 1940s.

also because Wayne knew how good Ford was at making movies and constructing myths—and how good he was at making Wayne look good as well. *Stagecoach* helped revive the Western as a respectable—and box-office-worthy—film genre and earned Ford his second Oscar nomination for best director. But it also established John Wayne as their mutual project, Ford's and Wayne's.

Like Breck Coleman in *The Big Trail*, the Ringo Kid is another version of Daniel Boone, Davy Crockett, and Kit Carson, the untamed natural men of American legend. But this time Wayne has traded the moccasins and fringe leather blouse that he wore in *The Big Trail* for cowboy boots and Harry Carey's unadorned dark shirt. He wears a crooked smile and a temperament that is calm, lighthearted, and benign, yet capable of quick, decisive action. As with all of Ford's sympathetic characters in *Stagecoach*, Wayne's eyes twinkle brightly throughout the film. Just like Humphrey Bogart, whose star began to rise at roughly the same time, Wayne had toiled for years in relative obscurity until the right role came along.

Stagecoach embraced all the Western clichés and reinvented them, both with its characters—the benevolent outlaw, the hooker with a heart of gold, the drunken sawbones doctor, the greedy, dishonest banker—and with its iconic moments: the Indian attack, the cavalry to the rescue, and the showdown with three bad guys. And perhaps the ultimate cliché: the malevolent, threatening savages.

The Apaches of *Stagecoach* are murderers and rapists, and the movie subscribes to the notion that for a white woman to be captured by Indians is a Fate Worse than Death. In a grim early scene, the stagecoach and its passengers come across the site of a massacre, and one of the passengers, a former Confederate army officer named Hatfield, removes his cloak to cover the half-naked body of a murdered woman. It's clear from the awkward way the body is draped over a wooden board that she has been raped. It is a stunning stab of visual realism—and a warning of the fate that awaits any white woman unlucky enough to fall into Indian hands. In a later scene, when the stagecoach is engulfed by attacking Apaches, Hatfield aims his gun at the head of a female passenger to spare her from being captured—a moment replayed from D. W. Griffith's *Battle at Elderbush Gulch*—but is himself killed before he can shoot her.

Later the Indians will chase the stagecoach for several thundering minutes until the passengers are rescued by the cavalry. "One thing I can't understand about it, Jack," the film critic and screenwriter Frank Nugent once asked Ford. "In the chase, why didn't the Indians just shoot the horses pulling the stagecoach?"

"In actual fact that's probably what *did* happen, Frank," Ford replied, "but if they had, it would have been the end of the picture, wouldn't it?" Ford was never inclined to let reality interfere with a thrilling narrative.

Nugent, who later became Ford's trusted screenwriter, got the idea. "Mr. Ford is not one of your subtle directors," he wrote in the *New York Times* when *Stagecoach* premiered. "When his Redskins bite the dust, he expects to hear the thud and see the dirt spurt up. Above all, he likes to have things happen out in the open, where his camera can keep them in view."

EVEN AFTER *STAGECOACH*, John Wayne's ascendancy to stardom was bumpy. There were occasional hits such as *Dark Command* and *Reap the Wild Wind*, but also more B Westerns for Republic over the next year. Ford, meanwhile, made three of his very best films, including *The Long Voyage Home,* which costarred Wayne.

Then came the war. Ford, who was forty-seven on Pearl Harbor Day, first served in an informal capacity as a spy for U.S. naval intelligence monitoring Japanese infiltration along the Pacific coast south of the Mexican border, then became commander of the Field Photographic Branch. While officially a member of the navy, Ford was assigned to work for Wild Bill Donovan's office, which later became the Office of Strategic Services, forerunner to the CIA. Ford personally filmed the B-25B bombers taking off from an aircraft carrier in the Pacific for Jimmy Doolittle's 1942 raid on Tokyo. A few weeks later he got to Midway Island in time to witness and film the war's most pivotal naval battle. When Japanese planes attacked the airfield he was visiting, he grabbed a camera, climbed atop an exposed water tower, and started shooting. At one point a fragmentation bomb exploded nearby, driving steel shards into Ford's arm. The camera jumps. Ford keeps filming.

Robert Parrish, a Hollywood film editor who served in the unit, described how Ford showed up at the Washington headquarters after the battle, unshaven, his left arm still bandaged, looking like he hadn't slept in a week. He was carrying eight cans of 16mm color film that he had managed to smuggle past the navy censors. He ordered Parrish to hand-deliver the film to Hollywood, entreated Dudley Nichols and James Kevin McGuinness to write a script, got Henry Fonda and actress Jane Darwell among others to do the narration, and put together a twenty-minute documentary within a few days. When Parrish asked Ford what he should do if navy officers demanded the film be returned, Ford replied,

"It's against the law for an enlisted man to even handle top-secret material . . . [Y]our best bet is to tell 'em to fuck off and not open the door."

In effect, Ford had cast himself as his own Western hero: a lone wolf, fearless, dedicated, and defiant of authority yet committed to the cause. He was, in other words, playing the John Wayne role. He was never happier than during his time in the military. The war gave him a sense of purpose that Hollywood filmmaking never had.

When Ford showed the finished product at the White House a few weeks later, it made Eleanor Roosevelt cry. "I want every mother in America to see this picture," her husband declared. *The Battle of Midway* won the navy an Oscar as best documentary short subject of 1942. The following year, the navy won another for *December 7th*, Ford's docudrama about Pearl Harbor.

While Ford was filming the real war, John Wayne was waging his own battles on the screen, becoming America's new cinematic war hero. Wayne, who was thirty-four when the war began, insisted that he wanted to serve in the military, but he had four kids and a troubled marriage and was keen to make money while his newfound stardom lasted. The hits kept coming: *Flying Tigers* (1942), *The Fighting Seabees* (1944), and *Back to Bataan* (1945) all cemented his status as a rising star and put him in the forefront of the celluloid war effort. Ford was unimpressed: he wanted Wayne to serve in the real thing. Ford sought to arrange for the OSS to take in Wayne. The office sent Wayne a letter saying they were running out of places and urging him to sign on without delay, but Wayne claimed that Josephine, his estranged first wife, hid it from him. "I never got it," he later told Dan Ford. Wayne also blamed Herbert Yates, head of Republic pictures, who he said had threatened to sue him if he didn't fulfill his contractual obligations—although it's hard to imagine any Hollywood studio being foolish enough to sue a star for enlisting during World War Two. Wayne also claimed to be hindered by old football injuries to his back and shoulders.

Finally, like any recalcitrant movie star, Wayne blamed the military itself for not offering him a big enough role. He later explained to Dan Ford that he was told he could enlist in the OSS but only as a private. "Well Jesus, I'm forty years old and of fair standing and I didn't feel I could go in as a private, I felt I could do more good going around on tours and things . . ." It was the young guys in the front lines, Wayne insisted, whom he was thinking of. "I was America to them. They had taken their sweethearts to that Saturday matinee and held hands over a

Wayne Western. So I wore a big hat and I thought it was better. And it was better than to take just any kind of position."

Even General Douglas MacArthur agreed. "You represent the American serviceman better than the American serviceman himself," he declared in a speech to an American Legion convention, suggesting that the mythic figure created by Wayne was more valid than the real thing. More than three decades later Congress would agree by authorizing a John Wayne Congressional Gold Medal, honoring this lifelong civilian as "the embodiment of American military virtue," in the words of the cultural historian Richard Slotkin. Wayne effectively made the transition from the guy who didn't enlist in the war to the guy who won it.

The gap between reality and legend was too much even for John Ford, the ultimate legend maker. He was scathing about Wayne's dodging of the war effort and he took it out on his star on the set of *They Were Expendable*, the war film they teamed up to make in 1945. Ford berated Wayne at every turn. "Duke, can't you manage a salute that at least looks like you've been in the service?" Ford demanded. The abuse got so bad that costar Robert Montgomery, who had earned his hero's status during the war as a PT boat commander, walked over to the director's chair one day and rebuked Ford. "Don't ever talk to Duke like that," he told Ford. "You ought to be ashamed." Ford broke down in tears. But *Expendable* became one of Ford's greatest films—a melancholy meditation on victory, defeat, and personal sacrifice.

AFTER THEY RAN AGROUND with David O. Selznick over *Stagecoach*, John Ford and Merian C. Cooper decided to form their own independent production company in the hope they would no longer have to answer to anyone but themselves. They called it Argosy Pictures, with Cooper as president and Ford as chairman of the board. It became a forerunner of modern Hollywood, where anyone with stature seeks their own production company.

Argosy, which was partly bankrolled by former OSS chief Donovan and friends, snagged a four-picture distribution deal with RKO in 1946 that gave the company full creative control and ownership of its films. Ford chose to start with *The Fugitive* (1947), a story of the betrayal of a Catholic priest, based on *The Power and the Glory*, one of Graham Greene's greatest novels. It was far too dark and idiosyncratic to do much at the box office. Chastened and chagrined, Ford turned to a sure thing: a John Wayne Western.

Wayne was already a box-office draw, but his true breakthrough years—both as an actor and as a star—were the late 1940s. They began with Howard Hawks's *Red River* (1948), in which Wayne plays Thomas Dunson, a Texas ranch owner and trail boss determined to get his cattle herd to market no matter the cost. Like Breck Coleman and the Ringo Kid, Dunson is a force of nature, but he's an older, more troubled, and more damaged version. Wayne looks weighed down and inert. As his character ages in the course of the film, Wayne slows down his tempo even more, magnifying his strength. For the first time with Wayne, the audience sees and hears the weight of experience, the voice of authority and of history. When Dunson's adopted son, Matt, played by Montgomery Clift, crosses him and takes away the herd for his own good, Dunson declares, "I'm gonna kill you." Wayne delivers this line as a statement of fact more than a threat, all the more powerful because it is so low-key.

In *Red River*, Wayne is starting to become larger-than-life on the screen. He's a very dangerous man, one who doesn't fall even when shot, and he deals out his own personal brand of justice to other men, often unfairly. Yet he's not a villain but a figure of tragedy. In the final showdown, he storms across the screen, pushing his way through man and beast until he reaches the son he means to kill. The ending is silly: Dunson and Matt trade punches until the woman who cares for each of them pulls a gun and forces them to realize how much they love each other. But it doesn't detract from the Oedipus-in-reverse power of what precedes it.

If *Stagecoach* established Wayne as a star, *Red River* established him as an actor. Even John Ford was amazed. "I never knew the big son of a bitch could act," he told Hawks.

"I don't think he ever really had any kind of respect for me as an actor until I made *Red River*," Wayne once observed. ". . . Even then, I was never quite sure."

Inspired in part by what Hawks had captured on film, Ford proceeded to challenge his star with a more complex and nuanced role than any he had offered Wayne before. *She Wore a Yellow Ribbon* was one of three Westerns filmed by Ford in the late 1940s and early '50s, all starring Wayne and all focusing on the U.S. Cavalry in the Indian-fighting days after the Civil War. Although set in the past, they were Ford's monument to his experiences in World War Two, as well as a parable for the Cold War struggle against communism that many Americans were processing through the same defenders-of-civilization-versus-barbarians prism through which they viewed the Indian wars. The films became known as the Cavalry Trilogy, and each of the three has a Kiplingesque sense of love for duty, honor, and empire and Ford's trademark fondness for the imagined community of officers, enlisted men, and their families.

Wayne plays Captain Nathan Brittles, a veteran commander pushing sixty and on the brink of retirement. Brittles is a fount of wisdom and experience who cares deeply for his men and tries to forestall a new Indian war, first by seeking a rapprochement with an old Indian ally and later by a ruse that allows him and his men to capture the warriors' pony herd and force them to return to the reservation. Brittles's men love him and yet he is alone—a widower with no children and no home except the cavalry he is being compelled to leave. It was one of Wayne's favorite roles, the one that he believed finally proved to Pappy and anyone else who mattered that he truly could give a great performance.

One of Wayne's most memorable scenes comes toward the end at Brittles's retirement ceremony, when his troopers give him a silver watch and chain. The awkward, moving speech he gives was not in the original screenplay but was improvised on the spot. "It was an emotional reaction rather than a studied response," Wayne would recall. "Pappy was very conscious of each actor that he had, their sensitivity, he knew the paint he was using when he put me in that scene. So he knew my reaction would be simplistic and deeply moving, which I think it was."

Finally, there was *Sands of Iwo Jima* (1949), directed by Allan Dwan, in which Wayne plays Sergeant John Stryker, a tough-as-nails marine officer who gets the best out of his men even while humiliating and angering them. Stryker trains them with his superior know-how and his fists, leads them into battle, and wins their loyalty and admiration. He is a warrior of personal charisma and almost superhuman powers. He is also the moral compass that men heed and measure themselves against. His kind is necessary to win the war, but there is no place for him in the postwar world. In the end he is killed by a Japanese sniper just as victory is at hand. Wayne is hard to kill in movies, even when a storyline seems to proceed logically toward his death. He is simply too strong to perish. *Sands of Iwo Jima* is the exception that proves the rule.

In *Red River*, *Yellow Ribbon*, and *Sands*, Wayne gives three contrasting performances. Sometimes he plays an older man, sometimes a younger one. In each he uses his body and voice differently. Yet he is always John Wayne, the melancholy authority figure—not the existential rebel like Bogart, Cagney, Gable, or Brando. No longer the outsider, he is now the charismatic leader of men, and yet somehow still solitary.

As Wayne's character grows into middle age, he becomes burdened with responsibilities and command. He has lost his wife or fiancé to death, divorce, or estrangement. The American West was a man's world, in the view of the Wayne persona, with no time or psychic space for women. The John Wayne hero walks alone.

John Ford's Westerns are also male-dominated, yet there are subtle differences. Even in a male genre, Ford always seems to find room for strong women characters: Dallas in *Stagecoach*, Mrs. McKlennar in *Drums Along the Mohawk*, Mrs. Allshard in *She Wore a Yellow Ribbon*, and Kathleen Yorke in *Rio Grande*. In retrospect, these characters are setting the stage for the women who are essential to the drama and meaning of *The Searchers*.

In a 1952 cover story, *Time* magazine declared that Wayne was "not the world's greatest actor—indeed, the only character he plays is John Wayne." What *Time*'s cultural commissars failed to grasp was that the character known as John Wayne was a subtle and varied creature. He carried the predictable toolkit of manly virtues and the ability to resort to physical action. But Wayne delivered something much deeper. "There is enough unacknowledged sorrow in his broad features, and enough uncontrolled anger in that slow, hesitant phrasing, to make him seem dangerous, unpredictable: someone to watch," wrote the *New York Times* critic A. O. Scott in 2006, with the benefit of a half century of further consideration. "He is never quite who you think he will be."

Behind Wayne's iron façade was a well of vulnerability, within his certainty a deep pocket of something far less certain. This was the heart of Wayne's art. He came on direct, angry, and unbending, daring you to test him and prepared to deposit your ass on the ground with a punch to the jaw. Yet there was a certain sadness to the whole enterprise. Wayne's character seemed to be constantly looking back, searching for something—a way of life, a code of honor—that had ceased to exist.

Unlike Wayne, who thoroughly enjoyed his box-office stature, Ford kept his distance from the Hollywood crowd, expressing profound disdain for banquets, balls, and black-tie affairs. Still, he wanted it both ways—to remain an outsider to the film community while commanding its respect.

That same ambivalence was evident in his politics. Ford called himself "a rock-ribbed Republican from the state of Maine," yet he supported Franklin Roosevelt and directed *The Grapes of Wrath*, one of the most pro-socialist films ever made in Hollywood. At the same time, Ford associated with Wayne and Bond, two ardent right-wingers who helped lead the witch hunt against purported Communists and fellow travelers during the McCarthy era.

Wayne took credit for helping expose alleged Hollywood Communists such as writer and producer Carl Foreman and director Edward Dmytryk. In 1948, Wayne became president of the stridently right-wing Motion Picture Alliance, succeeding Bond. In the harsh judgment of author Garry Wills, Wayne avoided combat in the ideological struggle between Communists and anti-Communists until the battle had been won, just as he had avoided genuine combat in World War Two. "His role, finally, was to emerge after the battle and shoot the wounded," writes Wills.

Ford's own signature moment came in October 1950 when Cecil B. DeMille, one of the enforcers of Hollywood's blacklist of suspected Communists, called a special meeting of the Directors Guild, held in the Crystal Room of the Beverly Hills Hotel, to seek to oust Joseph Mankiewicz as president because of Mankiewicz's supposed leftist leanings. Ford sat quietly through several hours of discussion. He finally rose and introduced himself. "My name is John Ford," he declared. "I am a director of Westerns."

First he praised DeMille as a filmmaker. "I don't think there's anyone in this room who knows more about what the American public wants than Cecil B. DeMille—and he certainly knows how to give it to them." Then Ford turned and looked directly at DeMille. "But I don't like you, C.B.," he said, "and I don't like what you've been saying here tonight." He proceeded to blast DeMille's proposal: "I don't think we should put ourselves in a position of putting out derogatory information about a director, whether he is a Communist, beats his mother-in-law, or beats dogs . . .

"Now I move we give Joe a vote of confidence," Ford concluded, "and let's all go home and get some sleep."

The vote in favor of Mankiewicz was decisive. John Ford, casting himself as the unassuming, solitary hero, had gunned down Cecil B. DeMille.

THE 1952 *TIME* MAGAZINE story officially validated John Wayne's iconic status. "The Wages of Virtue" portrays Wayne as an ironfisted businessman "who probably exercises a tighter control over the films he appears in than any other top star in Hollywood. He insists on simple stories, sympathetic parts that fit his personality, and dialogue that he can speak convincingly."

Chata Wayne, his second wife, ruefully describes her husband to *Time* as "one of the few persons who is always interested in his business. He talks of it constantly. When he reads, it's scripts. Our dinner guests always talk business. And he spends all his time working, discussing work, or planning work."

Wayne, who had become a producer at Republic Pictures, would pace the floor, temper boiling over, then apologize for his periodic outbursts. "He has acquired that final badge of executive success," reported *Time*, "a gastric ulcer."

One person remained a constant in his life. "John Ford still treats him as a clumsy sophomore and bawls him out unmercifully when they work together. Wayne takes it like a scolded schoolboy and murmurs, 'Sorry, Coach,' with abject hero-worship."

Besides his other commitments, wrote *Time*, "Wayne has an unwritten agreement with Producer-Director John Ford to star in any movie for which Ford may want him."

By 1954, John Wayne had been on the list of the top ten film stars in the Quigley Poll for five consecutive years—on his way to a record twenty-five out of twenty-six years. His latest hit movie was *The High and the Mighty*, the story of a crowded commercial airliner that limps home to safety despite two damaged engines, a star-laden vehicle that anticipated the disaster films of the 1970s. Wayne was making more than $100,000 per film, plus a percentage of the profits. He had his own independent production company, a string of employees, and a mob of sycophantic admirers. It could be said that he owed nothing to anyone. Yet there was one man who could pick up the phone and summon Wayne for any project he so desired. Whether the assignment was to stage a Christmas pageant for a favorite charity or to star in a major motion picture, John Ford still had John Wayne's number.

Most stars at the height of their careers are unwilling to tinker with their screen personas, and Wayne was no different: in the hands of second-string directors he often took control of the set and insisted on operating within a narrow range of character and emotion. But despite the verbal abuse he was compelled to endure, Wayne trusted Ford and was willing to do whatever Ford demanded of him as an actor.

Wayne was forty-eight now, and it showed. The years of good living had fattened his cheeks and put a beer gut below his barrel chest. His hair had thinned to the point where he wore a hairpiece for every role. The three to six packs of cigarettes he ravenously burned through each day had scorched his voice into a raspy growl. He could barely catch his breath—which slowed down his speech even more and put deep punctuation marks between his thoughts and his phrases. But his physical grace remained intact. He still could move like a panther, spin a revolver like a baton twirler, and pivot on his toes like a ballet dancer.

Most of all, Wayne still trusted his "Coach" to take him somewhere deep and not betray him. He was willing to go wherever Ford directed him to, even to the darkest of places, where a hero could resolve to slaughter an innocent maiden, and an uncle could seek to kill his own niece.

Wayne had already fulfilled his debt to Ford by starring in *The Quiet Man*. For that matter, Ford could have found someone else to star in *The Searchers*: Kirk Douglas, then coming into his prime, lobbied hard for the role. But from the beginning John Ford wanted only Wayne— and John Wayne reported for duty.

"My dad had tremendous loyalty to Ford," said Patrick Wayne. "He also had an overwhelming respect for Ford's talents . . . I can't say whether my father wanted to do the film or not. Basically, when Ford asked, my father said yes."

16.

The Production (Hollywood, 1955)

Merian Cooper was correct in figuring that once he had lined up John Ford's talent, John Wayne's charisma, and Sonny Whitney's money, selling a big film studio on *The Searchers* was a sure thing. By 1954 the Western had become Hollywood's most reliably bankable genre— the one product C. V. Whitney Productions could offer that no savvy studio could turn down. Two years earlier, *High Noon* had grossed $18 million worldwide and won four Oscars, including Best Actor for Gary Cooper. The following year, *Shane* grossed $20 million in the United States alone. By one estimate, Westerns by the mid-1950s accounted for one-third of the output of the major studios and half the output of the smaller independents. Besides Wayne, several name-brand movie stars had made or revived their careers by making Westerns, including Cooper, Clark Gable, Gregory Peck, Henry Fonda, Joel McCrea, Randolph Scott, Robert Taylor, James Stewart, and Alan Ladd. The Western was starting to dominate the young medium of television as well, bringing forth a fresh crop of young actors such as James Garner, Steve McQueen, Richard Boone, Clint Eastwood, Robert Culp, and Michael Landon. Anytime someone in Hollywood moaned at the prospect of financing yet another Western, the rejoinder was simple economics: "No Western picture has ever lost money." Western novels were also an unassailable product. Of the 300 million paperbacks sold in 1956, one-third were Westerns.

Scholars have turned millions of trees into paper seeking to explain why the Western was such a popular postwar phenomenon. It surely filled the need for what the cultural historian Richard Slotkin calls an "informing mythology": at a time of rising Cold War tensions and thermonuclear anxiety, the Western offered a comforting pseudohistorical narrative of America as an exceptional and triumphant nation, built on a foundation of frontier values of rugged independence, rough justice, and moral certitude. And in the hands of skillful writers, directors, and actors, it also proved to be rousing and very profitable entertainment.

The Searchers has all the elements of the classic Western. It begins with the slaughter of a family and the abduction of a white girl by hostile savages. Then a rugged hero and his young understudy leave what is left of their home to undertake a perilous journey, crossing borders, overcoming challenges, confronting the enemy and rescuing the loved one in a climactic gun battle, and returning home in triumph. Most of the stock characters and themes are here: the Man Who Knows Indians and the Indian Hater (rolled into one person, to be played by the strongest actor of them all); the evil war chief; the captivity narrative; and the Fate Worse than Death, with all of its psychosexual fears brought to the surface.

Merian Cooper signed a five-year deal to become executive producer in C. V. Whitney Productions, Sonny's newly formed film company. Then he approached various studios for a distribution deal. MGM offered a 50-50 split of the profits, while Columbia trumped its rival by offering a 65-35 split favorable to Whitney Productions. But Warner Brothers offered the same split along with an agreement to forgo some of its studio overhead charges. Whatever lingering grievances Jack Warner may have had over *Mister Roberts*, he was eager to get *The Searchers*. Warner also agreed to fund one-third of the projected $1.5 million budget, with Whitney supplying the rest. John Ford got a flat fee of $175,000 to direct.

Ford had his gallbladder surgery in late October 1954. By December he felt well enough to visit Europe for the Christmas holidays with Mary, Barbara, and Barbara's second husband, the handsome actor-singer Ken Curtis. ("Oh my God! That's for me!" Barbara Ford had said when she first laid eyes on Curtis, ignoring the technical inconvenience that he was married to someone else at the time.) By January, Ford was back in the office, working on the new project.

"We are busy working on the script of *The Searchers*," he wrote his Irish friend Michael Killanin. "It is a tough, arduous job as I want it to be good. I've been longing to do a Western for quite some time. It's good for my health, spirit and morale and also good for the physical health of my numerous Feeney Peasantry, of whom I am surrounded."

Ford had intended to make a film about Quanah Parker before World

War Two, and had discussed a script with his longtime screenwriter Dudley Nichols and with Lamar Trotti, screenwriter of *Young Mr. Lincoln*, but the war intervened and Ford never returned to the project. Now he pored through Alan LeMay's novel, making a few quick notes in the margins. The fact that the story was set in Texas made no difference to him: from the beginning he planned to shoot the outdoor scenes in Monument Valley, his favorite location and one that Western fans identified with his work.

"I go out to Arizona, I breathe fresh air, I get out of the smog and the fog and it gives you a different view on life," he told an interviewer. "I can relax and I sleep better at night and I eat better. And that is why occasionally I like to do Westerns."

THE SEARCHERS would be the ultimate creative collaboration between John Ford and John Wayne, and the director and his star tower over the finished product like two of the hulking mesas that dominate the landscape at Monument Valley. But two other men, both long forgotten, were crucial to the film's character and sensibility: Patrick Ford and Frank S. Nugent.

Pat was John Ford's eldest child and only son. He had worked for his father at Argosy for a decade as a screenwriter, production manager, and associate producer. Tall, talkative, and tightly wound, with a mop of dark curly hair and a thin frame, Pat inherited his father's impatience, bitter sense of humor, and weakness for alcohol, but he lacked the creative spark that made John Ford a great artist. Pat trusted no one and had a gift for making enemies. He resented his famous father, yet could never escape John Ford's cold, eternal shadow. Seven years after his father's death, Pat expressed those resentments in his only known interview, with the Ford scholar James D'Arc. Pat described his father as "a very strange man. He was . . . a man with the ability to concentrate almost wholly on his profession, excluding a lot else. My conversations with him as his only son—that I know of—was 'Yes Sir,' until one day I said 'No sir,' and then I was no longer around. I mean, our relationship was . . . in fact our family life was pretty much like that of a shipmaster and his crew, or a wagon master and his people. He gave the orders, and we carried them out."

"That I know of" is the tipoff: the phrase is at once cynical, irreverent, wary, and derogatory of his father and, perhaps, of his mother as well. Pat Ford, by his own testimony, did not feel loved.

"He was a good American, that he was," Pat concluded. Merian Cooper had used a similar phrase in praising Ford to Sonny Whitney, but Pat made it sound like a condemnation. "He was a lousy father, but he was a good movie director and a good American."

"Pat was an able guy, [but] he wanted to be John Ford," Pat's son Dan recalled. "And that kind of spoiled him. You know, he was so close to the golden ring and yet it wasn't his ring. It was someone else's. He was along for the ride. At one moment he wanted to be in the big picture . . . and the other he wanted to be his own man. And these were two conflicting things."

John Ford, in turn, could be withering about his son's talent and manhood. Maureen O'Hara says he called Pat "that capon son of a bitch." (A capon is a castrated cock.) "It was a horrible thing to call his own son," she recalled.

His conflicts with his father would eventually drive Pat from the family fold altogether. But at the time of *The Searchers*, he was a crucial if undervalued member of his father's stock company of assistants, crew

Father and son, John Ford and Patrick Ford, in the late 1940s.

members, and players, entrusted both with helping his father and Frank Nugent develop the concepts and characters for the film's screenplay, and with coming up with a workable plan for shooting an ambitious movie within a six-month time frame. His primary task was to eliminate as much of the risk as possible.

Pat's preproduction notes—addressed to his father, Cooper, Nugent, and Frank Beetson, the men's wardrobe coordinator—read like a performance. They are full of insight, bombast, and contradiction. Yet they are the only written blueprint we have to the thought process behind the making of one of Hollywood's greatest movies. John Ford said little about his work and wrote even less. Often what he did say was a lie or an exaggeration designed to throw his interrogator off the scent. Even with interviewers he admired—like his grandson Dan or the young Peter Bogdanovich, a film critic who was in the process of becoming a director—Ford could not help but falsify or conceal. He was a mythmaker whose greatest myth was John Ford.

Pat thoroughly read through Alan LeMay's novel and located guideposts and themes to help translate a 230-page novel into a two-hour movie. "The novel is a narrative that organizes itself in the world, while the cinema is a world that organizes itself into a narrative," wrote the French film critic Jean Mitry, and Pat's role was to launch the process by which this mystical transformation was to occur.

In memos in January 1955, Pat captures the sense of isolation that grips the frontier families in LeMay's novel. "There is no communal life on this frontier. Each family holds tenaciously to its holdings . . . There is nothing pleasant about their lives, and they themselves could not tell you why they submit to such hardships."

Amos Edwards and Martin Pauley are the products of this grim milieu. "They are not nice people," writes Pat. "They are only a shade less barbaric than the savages they follow."

Amos Edwards, Pat observes, is "relentless in his hatred of Indians, and of all things pertaining them." He is "a silently bitter, hard-hating man," cruel yet self-confident. "He would see every Comanche dead if he had his way."

Yet Pat grasps the paradox at the heart of Amos's character. "There is much to dislike about Amos," Pat continues. "Sometimes his treatment of Martin verges on the sadistic . . . A modern man would find much about him that is psychopathic. But there is greatness in him, too. His courage, relentlessness and frontier skill are magnificent. He achieves his goal where more stable men fail."

Pat also understands the strength of Martin's character as only a long-underestimated son could. "In his own way he is as persistent as Amos," he writes of Martin.

As for the Comanches, Pat makes clear that he and his father have a singular goal in mind: "We hope to portray the Comanches with as much barbarism and savagery as possible." Indeed, John Ford later uses the exact same sentence in his own brief story notes. Still, a touch of sympathy creeps in.

"Their villages . . . are scenes of utter squalor," Pat writes. "They were poor, filthy and smelled bad . . . The reservation should not be pictured as a place of barbaric beauty but should symbolize the degradation and hopelessness the Indians hoped to escape."

Both Pat and his father express great aspirations for authenticity in their depiction of the Comanches. "It is our hope to portray the Western Plains Indians as they really were, and as they have seldom been pictured on the screen," writes Pat. "They were a hard-riding, hard-fighting race of mixed blood—White, Mexican, Kiowa, Comanche, and Jicarilla Apache, all intermixed with southern Cheyennes to form a fierce coalition known as the Comanche."

Everyone involved shared the conceit that *The Searchers* would somehow offer an accurate and evenhanded portrait of the Comanches. "The Indians were to be treated fairly for a change," said Sonny Whitney's wife, Eleanor Searle Whitney, echoing the mind-set of her husband, Cooper, and Ford.

But Pat Ford makes clear that the real goal is not authenticity or fairness—just the *appearance* of them for the sake of the story. When it comes to horsemanship, for example, Pat writes, "Though they were famous bareback riders, we know from past experience that few modern Indians, or even stunt men, can perform adequately for the camera without saddles. Our Indians will have saddles."

The same goes for Indian outfits. Rather than authentic Comanche outfits, Pat calls for Navajo-Apache-style boot moccasins and blanket leggings tied at the waist to "heighten the barbaric effect we hope to achieve."

"It is important that the costumes of the Comanches be not exactly authentic."

AFTER PAT HELPED shape the story, he devised a plan to shoot at different locations in different seasons, varying from dry summer heat to intense winter snow. Pat, who served as the film's associate producer, took his father, Sonny Whitney, and a small film crew to Gunnison, Colorado, to film the winter scenes, using the stuntmen Terry Wilson and Chuck Hayward as doubles for the actors playing Amos and Martin.

Pat traveled to Gunnison first to set up the shoot, including a scene of the ruins of an Indian village after a raid by Custer's Seventh Cavalry. "If we're in luck, we hope a new snow fall has partially obliterated the camp and the wreckage," Pat wrote. "If it hasn't we'll have to use the wind machines."

John Ford began shooting on March 1, 1955. For four days he shot in below-freezing temperatures scenes of the destroyed village, prisoners being herded into a fort, a troop of cavalrymen crossing a freezing stream, and Amos and Martin trekking through snow country. Ford knew what he wanted. He described the winter sequence at the fort as "rough . . . rugged . . . cold . . . frozen . . . [I]f possible let's try to get the horses blowing vapor from their nostrils."

Three weeks later, Pat took a small crew up to Edmonton, Alberta, Canada, to shoot footage of a buffalo herd in winter. He filmed a stampede in classic John Ford style, with one camera in a pit dug in the frozen ground to capture the buffalo as they thundered above it, and the second on a truck running parallel to the frenzied herd.

Pat's shooting scheme allowed his father to get sweeping winter shots into the can before setting out for Monument Valley for the main film shoot in June. It also allowed Whitney's production company to boast grandiosely that *The Searchers* covered a wider range of geography and temperatures than any previous movie: 1,500 miles from Alberta, Canada, to Monument Valley, and more than 100 degrees Fahrenheit from the below-zero frozen tundra of Canada to the blistering hot temperatures of summer in the valley. Sonny Whitney, after all, had made himself clear: he didn't want just a movie; he wanted an epic.

THE OTHER KEY CREATIVE MEMBER of Ford's inner circle was his screenwriter—a Screen Writers Guild card–carrying member of a breed that Ford always claimed to abhor. Frank Stanley Nugent was an affable, voluble, nearsighted former journalist with a chunky torso, ruddy complexion, graying curly hair, and the owlish, wire-rimmed glasses of a scholar. "He was just a little early in the style of Donald O'Connor dressed up as Ethel Merman's secretary in *Call Me Madam*," recalled Katherine Cliffton, Ford's story and research editor at *Argosy*. Nugent had few pretensions and lacked the well-tended ego and pomposity of many of his peers in Hollywood—a place where, as one observer noted, the $1,000-per-week writers refused to socialize with the $500-per-week ones. "Nugent was a very knowable man," Cliffton added. ". . . I hate to use the word *pal*, but if you were working with him, you got the feeling we were all in this together."

Born in New York City to an Irish father and Jewish mother, Nugent liked to talk even more than he liked to write. "'Tis not my talent to conceal my thoughts" was written below his name in the 1925 yearbook at Regis High School, along with the labels "class poet" and "ironic joke teller." He graduated from the school of journalism at Columbia University and got a job as a cub reporter at the *New York Times* in 1929. Seven years later he was promoted to film critic and feature writer. He was known for his acerbic wit and poison-tipped pen, and even his news articles had verve and voice; his features were chatty, clever, and intimate, if occasionally smug. One of the few directors he admired was John Ford. Nugent's reviews of *Stagecoach* and *The Grapes of Wrath* were extravagant in their praise. "*The Grapes of Wrath*," he told readers of the *Times*, "is just about as good as any picture has a right to be; if it were any better, we just wouldn't believe our eyes."

His review caught the eye of the film's producer, Darryl F. Zanuck, czar of production at Twentieth Century-Fox, who offered him $400 a week—"a very exorbitant salary," as Nugent himself put it—to defect from the ranks of the critics in 1940 and become a screenwriter. This was around the same time that another gifted storyteller, Alan LeMay, was starting work for Cecil B. DeMille.

Nugent's ensuing four years at Fox were a disaster. He didn't earn a single screen credit. Zanuck used Nugent's acerbic critical eye and ability to spot flaws in scripts as a weapon against his other writers, and Nugent naïvely embraced the role with heedless abandon. "My opinion of this script is unchanged," he told Zanuck in a May 20, 1942, memo about a script called *White-Collar Girl*. "So far as I'm concerned, there's nothing wrong with it that a waste basket can't cure."

Nugent later acknowledged his mistake. "I stepped on everyone's toes, and most writers avoided me like the plague," he recalled.

Zanuck let Nugent go in 1944 with a "Dear Frank" letter that bemoaned the writer's "unfortunate break . . . I want you to know that I regret exceedingly the fact that you were never able to properly display your writing talents. I mean this sincerely." He signed off, "Kindest regards, Darryl." That was the way Hollywood worked: lots of warm and sentimental adverbs as they showed you to the door.

Nugent was miserable and knew it. He had continued writing Hollywood profiles for the *New York Times* all through his time at Fox. He even tried unsuccessfully to convince the *Times* to send him overseas during the war as a foreign correspondent. Meanwhile, John Ford was looking for a new in-house screenwriter. His longtime partnership with Dudley Nichols was coming to its inevitable end. Nichols, a cerebral dramatist who aspired to the stature of Eugene O'Neill, had lost patience with Ford's irascible mistreatment, while Ford wanted a writer more inclined to do whatever the hell Ford told him to do. Nugent, coming off his humiliating experience at Fox, was a more pliable and less demanding writing partner.

Ford, who knew about Nugent's favorable reviews of his films, first approached the writer in 1947 to work on the screenplay for *Fort Apache*, the first film in what became the Cavalry Trilogy. Nugent was flattered but surprised. He'd grown up riding the Staten Island Ferry, not horses, and he knew as much about the cavalry in post–Civil War Arizona as he did about thermonuclear physics. The loose informality of the West was alien to him; his son Kevin remembered Nugent keeping his tie on after he got home from work, even wearing it under his apron when he barbecued. Ford launched him on a tutorial, giving him dozens of books to read, then dispatched him to Apache country "to get the smell and feel of the land." Nugent hired an anthropology student at the University of Arizona to show him around. When he reported back to Hollywood, he told Ford he felt he'd done enough research. "Good," Ford told him. "Now, just forget everything you've read and we'll start writing a movie."

Ford commanded Nugent to write out biographical sketches for every character—in some cases a typewritten, single-spaced full page or more. Then Ford told him to throw them out and write the script. The two men worked closely together developing the draft, both in the office and aboard Ford's yacht, the *Araner*. Sometimes Ford was "groping like a musician who has a theme but doesn't quite know how to develop it," Nugent recalled. "Then if I come up with the next notes and they're what he wanted, he beams and says that's right, that's what he was trying to get over."

Despite his affable exterior, Nugent was a perfectionist when it came to writing, and he and Ford were frequently at odds. "He used to fight your grandfather tooth and nail," the writer James Warner Bellah told Ford's grandson Dan. "Well, that was one of your grandfather's methods—make 'em mad and they'll work harder."

Nugent understood he had struck a devil's bargain. In return for working with a master filmmaker, he paid a price in routine humiliation. "He can be rude and frequently insulting; he can also be affable, charming, genial, and generous in his praise (I prefer not to tell you what the percentage is)." But once the script was finished, Nugent added, the writer had better stay out of Ford's way. Ford never invited Nugent to his film sets or to studio screenings—not even those to which stuntmen and crew were invited. "I don't profess to understand this," Nugent ruefully confessed. Still, he wrote, it was "a small price to pay for the privilege of working with the best director in Hollywood."

A chatty, affable man in public, Nugent concealed a darker set of emotions. In his personal diaries he revealed an acidic reservoir of contempt for himself and the women he met after he and his first wife separated. "I am full of bitterness, self-dislike, and dislike of others," he wrote in a 1947 entry. "I want to lash out and wound as I have been hurt—even if most of my wounds are self-inflicted . . . It's as though my skin has been worn raw so that the least contrary breath stings and makes me strike out in my own pain and anger."

Like the diaries, Nugent's best screenplays push deeply into the emotional danger zone between men and women. While critics often pummeled Ford for his lack of subtlety in depicting male-female relationships, Nugent created for the old man two exceptionally complex partnerships between wounded, estranged, yet inextricably bound husbands and wives in *Rio Grande* and *The Quiet Man*, played in both films by John Wayne and Maureen O'Hara. He also tempered some of Ford's patriotic bombast and latent racism. Many critics have noted the jingoistic overlay of the Cavalry Trilogy, much of it attributable to the short stories on which they were based, written by James Bellah, a right-wing ideologue whose politics, according to his own son, "were just a little right of Attila. He was a fascist, a racist and a world-class bigot." Yet Nugent's screenplays for *Fort Apache* and *She Wore a Yellow Ribbon* showed respect and even admiration for some of their Indian characters. By contrast, *Rio Grande*, which Nugent did not work on, was riddled with racism.

Besides those first two screenplays, Nugent cowrote with Pat the script for *Wagon Master* (1950), a rocky collaboration at best. Nugent clearly resented having to share a writing credit with the director's son, and John Ford himself was slyly disparaging. "I liked your script, boys," Ford told them afterward. "In fact, I actually shot a few pages of it." Two years later, Nugent got a full screen credit and an Academy Award nomination for *The Quiet Man*, one of Ford's greatest films.

Ford refused to be impressed with Nugent's craft. "There's no such thing as a good script really," he told Peter Bogdanovich. "Scripts are dialogue, and I don't like all that talk. I've always tried to get things across visually. I don't like to do books or plays. I prefer to take a short story and expand it, rather than take a novel and try to condense it."

Later in life, Ford professed disdain for Nugent, calling him his favorite "body and fender man." He denied he was ever close to Nugent, whom he described as "a very unsophisticated person." But he saved his most hurtful criticism for Nugent's writing. "He was always putting in cute little pieces of business which I always cut out," the great man recalled. "Which annoyed him greatly."

With *The Searchers*, Nugent broadened the novel by increasing the number of characters and weaving comedy into the tragic framework. Nugent's son Kevin says his father's special gift was his feel for people. "The difference between his Westerns and other Westerns was such an intense character establishment," said Kevin Nugent. "One of the reasons I thought *The Searchers* didn't do so well at the time was because it was way too much character, too much John Wayne really feeling revenge and stuff, when gee, we went to see John Wayne shoot the Indians."

Frank Nugent said he learned a lot from John Ford. "Character is not shown so much by what is said as by what is done," Nugent wrote when he first started working with Ford. "Characters must make decisions."

"Ford never has formally surrendered to the talkies. His writers are under standing orders to keep dialogue to an 'irreducible minimum'. Ford usually manages to trim the 'irreducible' still more. He always works with his writers on a script, but never lets them forget who holds the whip hand."

"Ford detests exposition," Nugent concluded. It was a trait—a gift, really—Ford would demonstrate over and over again in making *The Searchers*.

ALAN LEMAY'S NOVEL was a spare, taut narrative that moved with speed and economy, with few extraneous characters and no subplots. Its opening scene—Aaron Edwards cautiously stepping off his porch to reconnoiter the area around his ranch house, fearful that Comanche raiders are gathering nearby—is near perfect. There is action, suspense, and a growing sense of dread as Aaron and his family come to realize they will soon be under attack.

After years of doing newspaper journalism and churning out screenplays for Ford, Nugent had boiled down narrative writing to certain firm principles. A story occurs when the status quo is upset. "There is a situation or a condition," Nugent writes. "Something happens to upset it; the disturbance is the story; and the story ends when another status quo is attained." The writer's primary job, he adds, is simple: "To look long and hard at his story and see whether it can be reduced to terms of the upsetting of the status quo."

With this in mind, Nugent and Ford discussed LeMay's opening for several days, and although they both admired it, they decided to hold back the scene until later in the film. Instead, they chose to begin, as in many Ford pictures, with an arrival: a lone horseman riding up to the Edwards house. This was Ford's way of starting out by introducing the new element rather than by establishing the existing situation. "It is no accident that most Ford pictures open with a figure in motion," wrote Nugent: a stagecoach, or a train pulling into a station in *The Quiet Man*, or a bus dropping off a passenger at an Oklahoma crossroads in *The Grapes of Wrath*.

The opening scene that they devised is formal, almost silent, and highly ambiguous. The horseman is identified only as "Uncle Ethan" (they dropped the name "Amos" because of *Amos 'n' Andy*, the radio and TV comedy show). It is not clear where he has come from, whether he is a highwayman or a soldier of fortune, or whether he is in love with his brother's wife, Martha, or she with him. Nor do we know why he displays an instant dislike for Martin Pauley, the part-Cherokee seventeen-year-old who has been living as an adopted child at Aaron and Martha's house after Martin's own family had been slaughtered by Comanches.

"The picture never answered all the questions," wrote Nugent. "We never meant that it should. But we drew a character of interest and speculation, and we met a family that was to be massacred or taken captive in the next reel or two.

"But when you look at it closely, you will see that we had been employing the time-honored technique; we had begun in motion, with an arrival, and we had established the status quo that soon was to be upset by a Comanche raid."

There was, of course, another reason to change the opening: it didn't feature the star attraction. *The Searchers* was first and foremost a John Wayne movie, and audiences expected to see him early and expected that the story would be built around him.

Nugent's opening took full advantage of Wayne's power and presence. His screenplay describes Ethan as "a man as hard as the country he is crossing. Ethan is in his forties, with a three-day stubble of beard. Dust is caked in the lines of his face and powders his clothing. He wears a long Confederate overcoat."

Like a suit in need of major alterations, Ethan's character had to be expanded and deepened to fit Wayne. Nugent had written for Wayne before, and understood his nuances and power. He believed that writing for Wayne was different than for any other star: it was almost a throwback to the old days of studio contract players, when "story problems were solved by writing for specific actors. Today this is true only to a degree. I know John Wayne is a certain type of man—terse, laconic and so physically capable that you hardly have to show it—and I use that as a prop."

JOHN FORD HAD NOTED little things in Alan LeMay's novel that he thought might give an added dash of drama and tension. In his personal copy of the book, he underlined the paragraph in which Aaron Edwards observes that the "bedded-down meadow lark sprang into the air, circled uncertainly, then drifted away . . . [A] covey of quail went up." Knowing the birds have been disturbed by invaders, Aaron turns and runs for the house. Similarly, in the film birds fly up, giving Aaron a fright.

Ford underlined a quote from the novel that Ethan Edwards speaks word for word in the film about the chances of tracking down the Indians who have abducted Debbie even though they have a head start of several days: "Yes . . . we got a chance . . . An Indian will chase a thing until he thinks he's chased it enough. Then he quits. So the same when he runs . . . He never learns there's such a thing as a critter that might just keep coming on."

He did the same with a quote eloquently characterizing the pioneers. "A Texan is nothing but a human man way out on a limb," the Ethan Edwards character says in the book. "This year, and next year, and maybe for a hundred more. But I don't think it'll be forever. Someday this country will be a fine good place to be. Maybe it needs our bones in the ground before that time can come." But it's much too philosophical a quote for a man of action and few words like John Wayne, and so Ford and Nugent transferred it instead to Mrs. Jorgensen, a pioneer wife.

In the novel, Amos Edwards's love for Martha is a secret known only to himself. Ford and Nugent chose to make it achingly mutual, unspoken and kept from others, yet hidden in plain sight. After Ethan offers his brother a bag of freshly minted Yankee gold dollars, he turns to Martha and takes her hands gently in his own, remarking that she has cut one of her fingers. She tries to hide her hands from him and their eyes meet—"a world of sadness and hopelessness is in the look," says

Nugent's screenplay. Afterward, she retreats to the bedroom as Ethan heads outside. He sits out on the porch and glances back to see Aaron closing the bedroom door. Martha may love Ethan, but she belongs to his brother.

This mutual but forbidden love is one of the ways that Ford and Nugent bring to the surface the hidden sexual context of LeMay's story. In the novel, Scar, the warrior who leads the massacre of the Edwards family, later becomes a father figure to Debbie, who is just entering marriageable age as her uncle and adopted brother search for her. But in the movie Debbie becomes one of Scar's wives—just as Cynthia Ann married Peta Nocona.

Some of the biggest changes in the script involve enhancing and darkening Ethan—and in the process molding him into a character strong enough yet complex enough for John Wayne. The moral center of gravity in the novel is Martin Pauley, the young adopted brother who grows in stature and experience as he searches for Debbie, his abducted sister. But in the film, Martin is eclipsed by his deeply troubled yet charismatic uncle. The narrative tension centers around Ethan's divided personality and his motives in conducting his obsessive seven-year search for his niece. In the novel, Amos Edwards has no conscious desire or intent to kill Debbie; but Ethan in the film sees Debbie's submission to Scar as her husband and lover, whether willing or not, as a stain on the family honor that can be redeemed only by her death.

The writer and the director also added a more overt racial element to the story. They changed Martin into "a breed"—part-Indian—which highlights Ethan's racism and explains his instant dislike for the younger man when they first meet. The hostility begins at the dinner table on Ethan's first night home at the Edwards ranch house when he says to Martin, "Fella could mistake you for a half-breed," and it continues for much of the film.

"Come on, blankethead," Ethan addresses Martin on the trail. Later when Martin insists on continuing the hunt for Debbie because she's his sister, Ethan retorts, "She's your *nothin'*. She's no kin to you at all."

It's impossible to know who came up with the concept of changing Martin into part-Indian: LeMay notes in the novel that Martin's skin is dark and that he had always felt alienated from his fair-skinned peers in the pioneer community. But Nugent and Ford concretize this sense of otherness and add resonance to the racial divide.

Finally, in the novel Amos dies, killed by a young Comanche woman whom he mistakes for Debbie in the climactic battle scene. But in the film, Ethan survives. He cannot be killed, if for no other reason than because he is John Wayne, the indestructible force.

Midway through the script, Nugent constructs an elaborate narrative within the narrative to give a sense of time passing. Using a letter that Martin writes to Laurie, his fiancé, Nugent encapsulates two years of the search and narrates Martin's growing doubts about Ethan's sanity and his dawning realization that Ethan intends to kill Debbie when he finds her.

Ford and Nugent also inject a large dose of Ford's trademark cornball humor to leaven the grimness of the main plot and theme. They turn some of the minor characters from the novel into comic figures and they add a young cavalry officer called Lieutenant Greenhill whose bumbling sincerity and awkward flourishing of his sword make him the butt of several jokes. And they use Martin for humor as well, most pointedly when he inadvertently trades goods for a Comanche wife he names Look, and again during the cantina scene when he and Ethan find a man who can lead them to the Indian camp where the now grown Debbie is living. Some of Martin's scenes with Laurie are also played for laughs.

By the time Ford and Nugent finished their work, the outline of the story and some of the main characters of *The Searchers* remained the same as in LeMay's novel, but the meaning and many of the details had decisively changed.

"Frank worked awfully hard on that movie," his wife, Jean Nugent, recalled to Ford biographer Scott Eyman.

"He'd come home at night exhausted and grumpy," Nugent's son Kevin told me. "They were making art and it was contentious."

Like many of his contemporaries, including Ford and Wayne, Frank Nugent smoked—at least two packs of Kents a day, according to his son—and drank steadily, although without Ford's self-destructive conviction. He suffered a heart attack in the late 1950s and another one two years later, and he died in 1965 at age fifty-seven from congestive heart failure. Jean Nugent blamed Ford for working her husband to death and, perhaps worse, for a profound lack of gratitude for Nugent's contribution to some of his greatest films. "When [Ford] and Cooper sold out, they didn't give Frank a bottle of scotch," she told Eyman. "That's the kind of guy Jack Ford was."

It's a harsh verdict. But by Nugent's own account, he found working with Ford demanding yet rewarding. The price was high, but the result was worth it.

* * *

MOST FILM PRODUCTIONS USED a casting director to line up candidates for roles and help determine which actor would be best in a given part. Not Ford. He insisted on controlling the entire process. Rather than send out a casting call, he simply put out the word among friends and employees and waited for the usual crew to report for duty. No one dared ask Ford directly for a part. Instead, they engaged in an elaborate and oftentimes humiliating ritual. "What you did was simple, once you caught on," Harry Carey Jr. recalled. "When word got out that the Old Man was going to start a picture, you simply went over to the office for a visit, and he'd tell you whether you were in it or not."

Ford set himself up in a suite of offices at the Warner Brothers studio. Actors arrived to the smell of freshly brewed coffee from a large urn in the front office. One by one, the old regulars showed up: Carey, Hank Worden, John Qualen, Jack Pennick, Mae Marsh, Ruth Clifford, plus the stuntmen and the wranglers whom Ford loved to work with, led by Cliff Lyons. "There was absolutely no chain of command with John Ford," said Carey. "There was him, and there was us."

Ford was smart enough to know he couldn't get by simply with the old stalwarts. He needed fresh and attractive actors to draw younger moviegoers. He had two plum parts for young actresses: Laurie Jorgensen (Ford changed the name from Mathison in the novel) and Debbie Edwards. With Cooper's help, he chose carefully. For Laurie they picked twenty-five-year-old Vera Miles, a relative unknown whose latest and largest role was the love interest (not named Jane) in *Tarzan's Hidden Jungle*. "I was dropped by the best studios in town," she later recalled with pride. Miles was pretty but not impossibly beautiful, rail-thin, and spunky—perfect for Laurie, Martin Pauley's fiancé, an attractive tomboy who grows into an angry, impatient, full-blooded woman as the plot progresses.

For Debbie they chose Natalie Wood, who was under contract with Warner Brothers and easy to requisition for the role. A veteran child actress now about to turn seventeen, she had just completed performing the lead female role in *Rebel Without a Cause*, which would win her an Academy Award nomination for best supporting actress. Natalie's mother consented after Ford agreed to take Natalie's nine-year-old sister, Lana, to play the young Debbie in the film's early scenes.

But the key supporting role was that of Martin Pauley, and it was heavily sought after. Fess Parker, fresh off his performance as Davy Crockett in a three-part TV series for Walt Disney Studios that began broadcasting in December 1954, was eager for the part. Ford put Parker through a bizarre kind of screen test at a dinner party one evening at the apartment of Olive Carey, Harry's widow. On the buffet line, Ford swiped several forkfuls of food from Parker's plate, then twice elbowed the young actor hard in the ribs. Parker just walked away. The response seemed to have worked.

"They wanted you for that [role]," Walt Disney later told Parker. But Disney refused to lend him out. "I wasn't consulted," Parker recalled bitterly. He always regretted not getting the part. It would have been "a badge of honor to work with the old man," he said.

John Agar, the ex-husband of Shirley Temple, who had appeared in significant roles in two parts of the Cavalry Trilogy, lobbied Ford unsuccessfully for the part. So did Robert Wagner, who had costarred in Ford's version of *What Price Glory* in 1952. Tall, handsome, and pleasant to his elders, Wagner was one of Hollywood's young princes. Ford could have cared less, and Wagner knew it. Still, Wagner swallowed his pride after he read Frank Nugent's script and went to Ford's office.

"You'd like to play the part, wouldn't you?" Ford asked Wagner.

"Yes, Mr. Ford."

"Well, you're not going to."

Wagner got up and headed for the door.

"Boob? You *really* want to play the part?"

"Very much, Mr. Ford."

"Well, you're still not going to."

In fact, Ford had already chosen his Martin Pauley: one of Wagner's best friends, another impossibly handsome young actor named Jeffrey Hunter, who was under contract to Twentieth Century-Fox. Hunter was born Henry Herman McKinnies Jr. in New Orleans in 1926 and grew up in Milwaukee, the only child of a sales engineer and his wife. He served in the navy just after World War Two—a military stint that surely must have endeared him to retired admiral John Ford—got a bachelor's degree in speech at Northwestern University on the GI Bill, and then headed west to UCLA seeking a master's in radio broadcasting. With his piercing blue eyes, high cheekbones, easy smile, and taut, muscular physique, Hunter was far too pretty to hide behind a radio microphone. He was quickly spotted by a Hollywood talent scout in a school production of Arthur Miller's *All My Sons* and signed by Fox. His first mainstream film appearance was a small part in *Fourteen Hours* (1951), which was also Grace Kelly's first picture.

When Hunter found out through his agent about *The Searchers*, Ford told him over the phone he was "nowhere near the type" to play Martin.

But Hunter refused to take no for an answer. He showed up at Ford's office the next day with his hair slicked back to make it appear darker and an open-necked sports shirt that displayed a deep-brown suntan. Ford, he recalled later, was puffing on a large cigar when he arrived.

"He stared at me for what seemed an endless time, then grunted, 'Take your shirt off!'"

Hunter complied. After another long stare, Ford grunted again. "I'll let you know," he said.

Hunter was certain it was just another brush-off, but Ford added, "Don't cut your hair until you hear from me." Hunter felt then he was in.

Ford also made sure all of his favorite stock company members got parts. He expanded the role of Texas Ranger leader Sam Clayton from the novel to accommodate his old drinking buddy Ward Bond. Clayton in the screenplay became both a Ranger captain and a preacher, a dual role that neatly encapsulates the duality of the American frontier project— gun in one hand, Bible in the other.

WHILE FORD WAS PUTTING TOGETHER the cast and crew, Merian Cooper was nursing the moneyman. Cornelius Vanderbilt Whitney was one of those improbable men of vast wealth who occasionally make their way to the film industry attracted by the glamour and the sycophancy and the chance to add to their fame and their importance. Sometimes they bed a starlet or two or ten along the way. Like a skilled con artist, Hollywood flatters, humors, and cajoles them for a while, relieves them of their wallets, and then moves on to the next improbable man. Whitney possessed a huge fortune inherited from two of America's wealthiest dynasties, the Vanderbilts and the Whitneys, a proven record of business success, a high opinion of his own financial acumen, and a roaring furnace of patriotic fervor. He longed to get into films; he had developed elaborate plans for an American history trilogy, based upon a *Saturday Evening Post* serial called "The Valiant Virginians" by James Warner Bellah, who had written the short stories Ford had used for his Cavalry Trilogy in the late 1940s. Who better to direct such an ambitious project than John Ford, the director who had made American history his prime subject? But before Whitney placed such a large and expensive triple bet, Cooper wanted to ease him into the motion picture business with a sure thing.

Whitney, Cooper's old army pal, was a cofounder of Pan American

Airways and had served as chairman of the board during the era when Pan Am grew from a small commuter line to the world's largest commercial transport system. Tall and lean, with dark, curly hair and sky-blue eyes, Whitney could be affable and informal, yet he was never quite comfortable around ordinary people and seemed insecure about his money and his place in the world. His vast wealth opened doors to new worlds for him yet barred him from ever fully entering those worlds. Despite his achievements, Whitney was typecast as a dabbler and a dilettante; he was not always taken seriously, but his money was.

He was born in New York and graduated from Yale. He invested early on in Cooper's Technicolor concept in the late 1920s, took a stake in Selznick International Pictures in the 1930s (giving him a piece of *Gone With the Wind* that was still paying annual dividends to his widow, Marylou, in 2010), and lost in a landslide for the House of Representatives as a Democrat in 1932 in a bluestocking Long Island district at the same time Franklin Delano Roosevelt was crushing Herbert Hoover at the top of the ticket. In the early 1950s, at Cooper's behest, he agreed to invest $5 million in Cooper's Cinerama project. Cooper and his backers believed that bigger, wider, deeper, and louder were the solution to declining movie ticket sales. Using a three-screen-wide visual presentation and seven-channel stereo sound, Cinerama sought to re-create the movie theater experience as spectacle in an attempt to hold television at bay. When the other directors of Cinerama refused to give Whitney a seat on the board, he and Cooper walked out. They formed a new film company, C. V. Whitney Productions, and announced a program of films celebrating America's history.

Like John Ford, Whitney saw himself as a mythmaker. His passion was the American dream as he himself defined it. Driven by Cold War fervor, he wanted to educate the masses in the glories of the American past in order to mobilize them to fight the Soviet empire. While the frontier was gone, Whitney argued, its values endured. But he lacked Ford's artistry. All through the making of *The Searchers* he would bombard Ford with unsubtle, bombastic suggestions to turn the movie into an elaborate history lesson, all of which Ford dutifully ignored.

Whitney was prepared to use his connections and his vast wealth get into the motion picture business—"not for self-aggrandizement, but because he believes he can help make a contribution to the motion picture and to better understanding of America abroad," reported the *New York Times*, which seemed curiously eager to accept Whitney's claims at face value.

Whitney quickly compiled a to-do list of four American epics, including *The Valiant Virginians*; *William Liberty*, an unpublished manuscript by Frank Clemensen; a biography of test pilot Chuck Yeager; and a "human document of Americana" focusing on Midwest farming communities.

Whitney was full of ambition and hyperbole. *William Liberty*, he confidently and erroneously predicted to the *Times*, "will do for the West what *Gone With the Wind* did for the South."

On January 29, 1955, Cooper declared to Whitney that "Jack Ford is back and raring to go. *The Searchers* will be a tough picture physically, but in my opinion can be a very fine one and a very profitable one. It is with that thought that I am going ahead fill tilt." But Whitney already had reservations about the direction of the project. In a February telegram sent to Cooper from the Camelback Inn in Phoenix, he called for a special meeting of the staff in Brentwood for February 23. "Prior to this meeting I want no work done on script of *Searchers*" other than the planned Colorado winter sequence, Whitney commanded.

What followed were a series of demands from Whitney to change the original concept, put his personal stamp on *The Searchers*, and turn it into something more grandiose. He followed up the meeting in Brentwood with a letter to Cooper outlining his thinking. *The Searchers*, Whitney decreed, was to become the first of a collection of films that he wanted to call the American Series. "I wish to again emphasize to you the importance which I place upon speed and urgency in the production of this series of pictures."

This was Whitney at his most imperious, issuing orders and making demands. When it came to dealing with Ford, however, Whitney was more diffident. He admired and envied Ford's creativity, and was intimidated by Ford's war record and string of Academy Awards. He knew he couldn't push Ford around and respected him too much to try. "My husband admired Ford so much, just loved his pictures, loved the man," recalled Marylou Whitney, who became Sonny's fourth wife after he divorced Eleanor. "Sonny would never want to get into a fight with someone like Ford; he was so totally different than anybody [Sonny] had been brought up with. For a man who had relatively little education, he was unbelievably brilliant."

Still, Whitney was determined to tinker with the *Searchers* script, and he insisted on Ford's attention. In a telegram dated February 21, Whitney warned Ford, HAVE BEEN WORKING INTENSIVELY HERE FOR TWO WEEKS ON PROBLEMS MY PIX COMPANY IT IS MOST IMPORTANT

I DISCUSS THESE WITH YOU EARLIEST OPPORTUNITY AS CERTAIN TREATMENTS ON THE SEARCHERS WILL BE DIRECTLY AFFECTED.

Whitney insisted on accompanying Ford on location in Colorado for the winter sequences in March 1955. When he came back from the film shoot, he started peppering Ford and Cooper with new ideas for enhancing the film by loading it with overt patriotic themes. He pleaded with Ford to make the movie the first part of an American history trilogy. He also wanted to, as he put it, "dignify or broaden the story" by changing the title to *The Searchers for Freedom* and adding a prologue and epilogue to strengthen the theme. In essence, Whitney, too, wanted to become a mythmaker, using the story of Cynthia Ann Parker as his foundation stone. His purposes were no different from those of Alan LeMay, John Ford, and Frank Nugent—each of whom understood the mythic proportions of the material they were shaping—but Whitney's sensibility was far less artistic or subtle. Rather than tell a story, he wanted to force-feed the audience with patriotic fervor.

There is no record that Ford answered Whitney's notes or honored any of his requests. None of which dissuaded Whitney from trying again, this time in a handwritten letter to Ford from his mansion in Old Westbury, Long Island. "It seems that the market is being flooded with 'Westerns,'" Whitney told his director. "This continues to challenge me as to how we can raise *Searchers* above the rest." Once again, Whitney pleaded with Ford to consider his ideas for a trilogy and an expansion of the theme. "Do I make myself clear?" he demanded at one point. Still, he stopped short of issuing an ultimatum to Ford. "Whether you take any of my ideas or not, I know you will make a fine picture, and I will also know that you gave the ideas consideration, and then acted according to your best judgment."

Once again Ford's response, other than silence, has never been recorded. He made no mention of Whitney's proposals in any surviving letter, memo, or note, and none of Whitney's ideas ever appeared in the movie. It is as if they never happened. Still, Ford grew irritated.

Sonny Whitney "could afford to be a very nice man . . . I mean, he doesn't even know about money, it's just this huge, giant corporation," recalled Pat Ford. "And he'd come around, and he'd want certain things done on pictures, and Ford would just con him out of it, and resented it. Resented having to do it."

"C. V. Whitney was a guy that got $20 million as his twenty-first birthday present, and John Ford was a guy whom for his twenty-first birthday present got thrown out of the house and sent to the Navy. So how in hell are you going to compare the two—how are they going to be friends?"

Yet somehow they managed. John Ford himself never disparaged Sonny Whitney in public. "A man with that many millions," he told his grandson Dan, "can't be an idiot."

Idiot or not, Ford understood that Whitney's millions were the reason Ford could make *The Searchers* without having to worry about demands from Jack Warner and his studio boys. If the requirement was that he tolerate the flights of fancy of a spoiled rich man, it was a price John Ford was more than willing to pay.

17.

The Valley, Part One
(Monument Valley, June 1955)

Just as every storyteller needs characters and a plot, he also needs a setting. Dickens has London, Raymond Chandler's knight-errant detective works out of Los Angeles, and Anne Tyler's moody introverts haunt Baltimore. John Ford's greatest Westerns purportedly took place all over the Southwest, but they were all filmed in one place. Like Shakespeare and the Globe Theatre, Ford used one mythic setting for his stage.

Tucked into the continental crease where southeast Utah rubs shoulders with northwest Arizona, Monument Valley is one of America's most dramatic and remote locales. Its sandstone buttes and mesas soar like cathedral spires into the vacant desert sky. It was ninety miles from the nearest paved road and reputed to be the farthest point in the continental United States from a railroad line. There was nothing cheap about this kind of location work. Film crews had to cart in their own generators, gasoline, groceries, and water tanks. But Ford was keen. He believed that Westerns filmed on a soundstage or in the near suburbs of Hollywood looked drab and artificial. He wanted to capture on film the dust, grit, and sweat of the real thing, and he wanted a dramatic backdrop that would thrill and entertain audiences. In his silent movie heyday, he'd shot *The Iron Horse* in the Sierra Nevadas of California and Nevada, and in Mexico and New Mexico, and he'd shot the Revolutionary War drama *Drums Along the Mohawk* outside Cedar City, Utah. But Monument Valley was even more of a challenge. It was a virtual no-man's-land of little water and hot, reluctant sand, and no one outside of a handful of hardy Navajos lived there. Even livestock shunned it. But Ford loved it. His crews built towns, forts, ranch houses, and Indian villages. He made the valley his personal film set.

John Ford Point, the director's favorite spot in Monument Valley, his favorite locale for shooting Westerns, photographed in 2008 by Peter McBride.

"My favorite location is Monument Valley," Ford declared. "It has rivers, mountains, plains, desert, everything the land can offer. I feel at peace here. I have been all over the world, but I consider this the most complete, beautiful, and peaceful place on earth."

The Searchers was Ford's fifth Monument Valley production. He used the scenery like some modern directors use special effects—to create drama and stun the audience. For *The Searchers*, some of Ford's most dramatic shots evoked the watercolors of Charles M. Russell, a turn-of-the-century painter who was particularly adept at capturing Native Americans and cowboys atop small hillocks as if they were on a pedestal against a vast natural backdrop. "I think you can say that the real star of my Westerns has always been the land," he said.

IT HAD BEEN SEVENTEEN YEARS since Ford first discovered Monument Valley, and like everything else he deemed important in his life, he cloaked in myth the truth of how he first decided to shoot his Westerns there. He told Peter Bogdanovich that he himself had come across the area while driving through Arizona on his way to Santa Fe. But John Wayne said he had told Ford about the valley after working on a film nearby, while the actor George O'Brien claimed that he was the one who first mentioned it to Ford. Still, the story that Harry Goulding and his wife, Leone, told for many decades seems the most plausible.

Harry was a sheepherder's son from Colorado who first laid eyes on the valley in 1921 and never stopped marveling at its raw beauty. Geologists don't know exactly how Monument Valley happened: some twenty million years ago the massive continental plate under most of western North America apparently overrode its neighbor farther to the west, which may have sunk or shifted east. Erosion went to work, hollowing out the soft spots and leaving hard granite towers of red sedimentary rock. Willa Cather wrote of the "incompleteness" of the West's great mesas—"as if, with all the materials for world-making assembled, the Creator had desisted, gone away and left everything on the point of being brought together, on the eve of being arranged into mountain, plain." Monument Valley, by her telling, was one of God's unfinished construction sites.

Its first known inhabitants were Anasazi tribesmen who left behind hollowed-out ruins and hundreds of petroglyphs to mark their time there. No one knows why they fled or where they went, but by the sixteenth century they were gone. Navajo tribesmen emerged to take their place.

Captivated by what he had seen, Harry Goulding came back in 1923 with his new bride, Leone, a pretty young woman from Utah whom Harry nicknamed Mike because, he claimed, he could never remember how to spell her real name. For three years they operated a makeshift trading post from a large canvas tent, swapping coffee, flour, salt, sugar, and other staples with the Indians for rugs, skins, and old coins. The Navajos loved canned tomatoes: they would pry open the lid, sprinkle sugar on the top, eat the sweet, cold contents with a spoon, and pass around the can. They also loved candy and brightly colored soda pop in flavors like strawberry or orange—never Coke, which was too drab in color. Eventually the Gouldings built a two-story stone house in the shadow of Black Rock, one of the area's most dramatic mesas. Then they managed to buy a 640-acre parcel of land from the state of Utah, despite the fact that this was tribal property and supposedly the sole domain of the Navajo people.

Navajo territory comprised twenty-seven thousand square miles—the country's largest Indian reservation—and forty thousand people spread across Arizona, New Mexico, and Utah. The Navajos had fought the Apaches, Paiutes, and Spanish to a standoff, but succumbed inevitably to the overwhelming firepower of American settlers and soldiers. After the main tribe surrendered to Kit Carson in the 1860s, a handful of Navajos fled to the valley and had maintained a foothold ever since.

The Navajos had a well-honed suspicion of outsiders, and at first they viewed Harry and Mike as interlopers. "It was their lands," Harry told Samuel Moon, his biographer, "and they had the atmosphere that they was wanting us to leave. They didn't *ask* us to leave, they just wanted to know *when* we was going to leave."

But the Gouldings had no intention of going away, and eventually they won the grudging respect of many of the Indians. Harry and Mike witnessed the hard times that the Navajos suffered during the Depression and, most especially, during the federal government's brutal livestock reduction program in the 1930s, when bureaucrats sought to kill off what they saw as an unsustainable surplus of Navajo cattle and other animals. Harry and Mike also watched as well-meaning government officials forced Navajo parents to send their children to federally run boarding schools where the students were encouraged to discard their culture and punished if they were caught speaking their native tongue. It was the same misguided philosophy that Quanah Parker's children had faced at the Carlisle Indian School in Pennsylvania three decades earlier.

In 1938, Harry heard that a Hollywood movie company was exploring the area around Flagstaff for a new Western. He and Mike extracted $80 from their meager savings and drove their old pickup truck 650 miles to Los Angeles. Harry forced his way into John Ford's office at United Artists and showed him a set of stunning photographs taken by the German photographer Joseph G. Muench, a frequent visitor to the valley. Harry "just wandered in, a big old guy with a great rube act," recalled Pat Ford, himself a professional skeptic. "And he wasn't near the rube he pretended to be but he sure could play it . . . He was a likable guy, we all liked Harry. We said 'Harry, you've got the best shit-kicking act going.'"

Pat's father was entranced by the photos—and also by Harry's claim that there were hundreds of Navajos available to work cheaply as crew members, carpenters, and film extras. To Harry's amazement, John Ford chartered a plane and flew out to visit the site the next day, then came back, had producer Walter Wanger cut a check for $5,000, and sent Harry back to Monument Valley to line up provisions, food, and tents for the crew. Goulding had no way to cash the check until he got back to

Flagstaff; a filling station owner along the way gave him a fill-up on credit and even loaned him a twenty-dollar bill.

During that first outing to the valley, Ford and his crew shot for only seven days and he wound up using only about ninety seconds of the footage in *Stagecoach*. Ford and his crew stayed not at the Gouldings' but at the inn and trading post run by John Wetherill and his wife in Kayenta, twenty five miles to the south. But when Ford came back after World War Two to make *My Darling Clementine*, he stayed in the guest room on the second floor above Goulding's trading post, and later still Harry and Mike built Ford a cabin of his own. By 1955 they had added a small motor lodge with nine rooms along the ledge above the valley, and they gave number nine to Ford. It had a double bed and a small refrigerator that they stocked with fruit juices at his instruction—no beer this time. For the duration of the film shoot, John Ford was officially on the wagon and Monument Valley was his personal rehab center.

"It gives me a chance to get away from the smog, to get away from this town, to get away from people who would like to tell me how to make pictures," Ford told fellow director Burt Kennedy. "You're working with nice people—cowboys, stuntmen, that kind of person. You get up early in the morning and go out on location and work hard all day and then you get home and you go to bed early. It's a great life—just like a paid vacation."

FORD AND HIS CAST AND CREW BOARDED the famed Santa Fe Super Chief at Union Station in Los Angeles early Tuesday afternoon, June 14, 1955, for the seventeen-hour, all-night train ride to Flagstaff, Arizona. Already they were behind schedule: bad weather in Arizona had delayed their departure by a day. Ford was so anxious, he couldn't sleep that night aboard the train.

Flagship of the Santa Fe line, the Super Chief was the appropriate vessel for Ford's new venture: the gleaming, stainless-steel face of its diesel locomotive was painted crimson red, with trailing yellow and black trim, in the style of an Indian war bonnet. Its elegant interior featured Navajo patterns and motifs in turquoise and copper. Ford held court in the dining car most of the evening. Henry Brandon, the German-born, Stanford University–educated actor hired to play Scar, the Comanche war chief who abducts the young Debbie Edwards, recalled finding Ford there late in the night poring over Frank Nugent's final shooting script.

As soon as they arrived at 6:45 on Wednesday morning, Ford and his son Pat boarded a small plane for Monument Valley. When the plane touched down, he wasted no time. Harry Goulding met him at the airstrip in an ancient station wagon. Ford and Pat hopped in and off they went, navigating the bone-rattling dirt roads and dried creek beds, scouting locations for the opening day's shoot. John Wayne arrived later in his own private plane, while most of the other crew members endured the six-hour drive from Flagstaff on largely unpaved roads.

The making of a Western movie on location was a giant, complex, and costly enterprise. There were hundreds of moving parts: people, vehicles, horses, cameras. John Ford had spent years gathering a collection of actors, cameramen, soundmen, wardrobe designers, support crew, wranglers, stuntmen, and extras who would obey his commands and perform the work with passionate dedication and reasonable efficiency. Ford had the kind of control over the script, the casting, and the editing of his films that most directors could only dream of. Still, so much was beyond even his control, subject to the whims and uncertainties of man and nature.

"A shooting schedule on as rough a location as Monument Valley is really catch-as-catch-can, and depends on Ford's imagination and resourceful genius . . . just an educated guess on paper," Merian Cooper wrote to Sonny Whitney. "On every picture I have done with Ford, such a schedule always has to be revised. It is like fighting a battle. You can plan what you are going to do, but you don't know what the enemy is going to do. And our enemies are the myriad things that can happen on location."

It had been seven years since Ford and Cooper had last mounted a film production in Monument Valley, but little had changed. The Navajos had long since dismantled the previous movie sets Ford had bequeathed them, using the precious lumber for their dwellings and roadside stands and selling off the rest. There were still no phones, no public water system or electrical grid, and only one semipaved road.

After nearly a month on the site, the road and construction crews had completed most of their work. Some two dozen trucks and bulldozers, noisily clawing the ground like mechanical ants in front of the silent, brooding mesas, had smoothed a flat surface on the valley floor just north of Goulding's lodge, and crews had erected some fifty large canvas tents to house three hundred people, wardrobes, and other essentials. They carved roadways and paths between the structures, and planted a street sign in the middle that read "Hollywood and Vine." A late-spring desert wind promptly knocked it over.

Most of the cast and crew lived in the tent city, while Ford, Wayne, the female stars, and their families stayed at the lodge up the hill. Alongside the tent city was a makeshift airstrip, which ferried the principals to the site and carried daily film footage down to Flagstaff every afternoon for the evening train to Los Angeles. Ford's religious insistence on not looking at the dailies would serve him well on this location; there was no time nor facilities to do so before the flight.

In the first days the work crew got their water from Lyster bags, thirty-six-gallon canvas contraptions developed for the U.S. Army that hung by ropes on sturdy tripods. Then Whitney's construction company brought in a heavy-duty pump to service a primitive Indian well, providing the first electrically pumped water ever supplied to the valley.

They erected a canvas mess hall seating two hundred people and shipped in fresh food and ice daily from Monticello, Utah, sixty miles away. They set up a 20,000-kilowatt generator for electricity and portable water tanks. Still, Pippa Scott, a nineteen-year-old actress in her first film role, said it was all "quite primitive." "The women were installed [at the lodge]," she recalled, and "all the men were down in the valley floor in a huge sort of tent city that glowed at night with campfires and, well, frankly, a certain amount of drinking and gambling and carousing. Great fun!"

There were no phones, just a shortwave radio. They set up a three-legged system: a receiver and sender at the Hotel Monte Vista in Flagstaff, 185 miles to the southeast; a second 30 miles from camp atop Black Mesa, the highest point between Flagstaff and Goulding's; and the third at the lodge itself. They took a radio jeep on location wherever they went.

Average temperatures were supposed to be in the high eighties in June, but someone forgot to tell the sun, which was in a vindictive mood. By noon each day the mercury often exceeded 100 degrees. "Wind was an enemy," a film production press release noted. "It raised hob with the roads, obliterating them on a single afternoon's blow. Red dust was in everything, making it especially difficult for the cameramen to keep their lenses clean."

The crew also built two large ranch houses—one for the Edwards family, the other for the Jorgensens. They sank telephone poles as corner braces to keep the flimsy shells from blowing away. Ford in a preproduction note said he wanted the Edwards home to look like "adobe, whitewashed but with the bricks showing through the white in places. It is almost a fortress. It sits alone in a vast expanse." From a distance, the ranch house, nestled just below the trademark butte known as West Mitten, looked exactly as he had projected.

WHILE THE CAST AND CREW WERE ARRIVING, hundreds of Navajo men, women, and children quietly descended on the valley by jeep, horseback, and foot. They established camps on the fringes of the movie set with their tent openings always facing east toward the rising sun, and reported for work as film crew men, construction workers, and movie extras. Lana Wood recalled seeing their campfires each night and hearing their singing wafting up. (She also recalled the discomfort of those who watched her sister sunbathing on the rocks during the day in a skimpy leopard-skin swimsuit.) The men earned $15 a day, women $10, and children $5, plus a free lunch for everyone and time-and-a-half after eight hours, all of it considered a fine day's pay by Navajo standards. Women, often with babies strapped tightly to their backs, took jobs as housekeepers and laundresses. This was the first major film production to hit the valley since *She Wore a Yellow Ribbon* seven years earlier, and the Navajos had no intention of missing the opportunity.

"A lot of people came from Kayenta and Tuba City, some people who lived here tried to be part," recalled Susie Yazzie, a Navajo woman who worked on the set as an extra. "Harry Goulding was the one who asked me to participate." Susie, one of the tribe's most skilled rug weavers, worked for about a month. "We used to eat a lot, we worked in different places. There was a lot of money."

Ford liked to frame his decision to go to Monument Valley in terms of personal benevolence toward the Navajo:

"When we first went into the Indian reservations, they were poor and starving. The pay from the shooting of *Stagecoach* helped put them on their feet . . . I don't mean we should take too much credit for this, or that it makes up for our treatment of them on film, but it is a fact, and it's been important to them."

Ford had no patience for bleeding hearts who bemoaned the Indians' tragic fate but did nothing concrete to improve their economic status. "People have said that on the screen I like having Redskins killed. But today other people in the cinema feel sorry for them, make humanist pamphlets, declarations of their intentions, without ever, *ever* putting a hand in a wallet. Myself, more humbly, I gave them work."

Ford believed in Navajo medicine, or at least, as a good Catholic, he believed in the power of ritual. When Ford first queried Goulding about the weather, Harry told him about an old medicine man named Hosteen Tso. "You let me know what you want about four o'clock in the evening, and he'll fix you up with the weather the next day," Goulding told Ford.

The first day out filming *Stagecoach*, Ford asked for "a few theatrical clouds."

"I can't send that to him," Goulding replied. "I don't know what a theatrical cloud is."

"Just pretty, fluffy clouds," Ford added.

"We'll get it off," said Goulding.

And indeed, they did. The clouds appeared promptly in the afternoon.

After that, Goulding brought Hosteen Tso—Ford nicknamed him "Fatso" for reasons that were abundantly apparent—to visit Ford every afternoon at around four. Ford would give the old man a glass of whiskey and hand in his request for the next day's weather. Ford paid him fifteen dollars a day and claimed that Fatso never let him down.

Ford believed in the Navajos and he believed in Monument Valley, and his sense of responsibility for their welfare was genuine even if paternalistic. He could have filmed *My Darling Clementine* anywhere—it takes place in a mythical Tombstone, Arizona, during the time of Wyatt Earp—but insisted on returning to the valley despite the high cost of transporting and housing a movie crew there. After he finished making the movie, he donated to the Navajos the wooden sets, timber being a highly valued commodity in treeless Monument Valley. Two years later, after he finished making *She Wore a Yellow Ribbon*, the valley was buried by a massive snowfall the Indians called "Two Men Deep." Ford used his military connections to arrange for "Operation Haylift," airdrops of food, grain, and other supplies.

In a letter to James Warner Bellah, Ford made clear just how handy the Indians were for his Westerns: "At Monument Valley I have my own personal tribe of Navajo Indians who are great riders, swell actors . . . have long hair and best of all they believe in me. We can braid their long hair in the Cheyenne, Kiowa, Comanche or whatever hair-dress we desire . . . They are tall, sinewy and as the poor bastards never get enough to eat unless I make a picture there, they have no excess fat on them . . ."

Ford insisted that he treated Indians with dignity in his life and in his films. "They were a very dignified people—even when they were being defeated. Of course, it's not very popular in the United States. The audience likes to see Indians get killed. They don't consider them as human beings—with a great culture of their own—quite different from ours."

He told another interviewer, "My sympathy was always with the Indians."

Still, there was nothing dignified about the way Ford portrayed Indians in his early Monument Valley Westerns. In *Stagecoach* they were stock villains whose sole narrative purpose was to present a challenge that the protagonists had to overcome.

A scene in *My Darling Clementine*, Ford's first Western after returning from the war, was equally callous. Wyatt Earp, the movie's hero, arrests a drunken Indian who is shooting up the town of Tombstone by knocking him on the head and then kicking him in the rear. "Indian, get out of town and stay out," Earp commands.

But Ford's attitude toward Indians was beginning to soften. Cochise in *Fort Apache* (1948) is an honorable leader seeking a peaceful accommodation with whites, but his honor is affronted by Lieutenant Colonel Owen Thursday (played by Henry Fonda), the callous, arrogant commander modeled after George Armstrong Custer who goads the Indians into military confrontation. In *Yellow Ribbon* (1949), John Wayne's Captain Nathan Brittles beseeches an old Indian ally with whom he has enjoyed a longstanding friendship to help him prevent an all-out war. The effort fails, but the scene between Brittles and the Indian chief— played with emphatic dignity by Chief John Big Tree, a Seneca Indian who appeared in at least four of Ford's films—is powerful and affecting. Then in *Rio Grande* (1950) two years later, the Indians once more are savage murderers who kidnap a band of white children and prepare to slaughter them, until John Wayne and the cavalry come to the rescue. There's a horrifying scene where Wayne and his troopers discover the body of a soldier's wife who had been abducted with the children and then raped and mutilated. Ford doesn't show us the corpse, but we see the face of the officer who finds her, the wagon wheel to which she was tied and tortured, and a steaming pool of water—all of it laid out, notes the cultural historian Richard Slotkin, like a horror movie.

"I find it troubling that he makes *Fort Apache* which I just love and is, among other things, pro-Indian, and then he turns around two years later and makes *Rio Grande*, which is a racist hate movie about Indians," said Ford biographer Joseph McBride.

The Navajos, who played Indians from all tribes in Ford's films, did not mind being depicted as villains. In fact, they grew angry when Ford brought in actual Apaches to play some of the Indian roles in *Stagecoach*. "It was a job and we just didn't concern ourselves about that," Navajo medicine man Billy Yellow told McBride about playing villains. "Ford was a very generous man. He fed all the Navajos there. The pay was good."

The Navajos liked Ford's generosity, his sense of humor, his patience, and the way he talked and consulted with them at the end of the day's shooting. And they liked the fact that he didn't do too many takes and wear out their horses. All of his favorite Navajo horsemen—the three Stanley brothers, Bob Many Mules, Harry Black Horse, Pete Grey Eyes, and Billy Yellow—were there to serve him for *The Searchers*. Stuntman Chuck Roberson recalled how Ford would chase ten-year-old Dolly Stanley around the wooden dining tables, growling and grimacing. "The Indian children looked on him with awe," wrote Roberson.

The Navajos liked John Wayne as well. Although few of them ever got to see a Western movie, they knew Wayne was a big star and they felt flattered that he spoke to them regularly and treated them with respect. Early on in the filming of *The Searchers*, he volunteered his private Cessna to fly a two-year-old Navajo girl with measles and double pneumonia to the hospital in Tuba City, one hundred miles away. Wayne personally carried the little girl to his plane and placed her inside. "So overnight, Wayne, the actor with the Big Eagle, has become a heap big hero to the local Navajos," read the film company's breathlessly condescending press release.

ONCE THE ACTORS AND FILM CREW ARRIVED in the valley, Ford wasted no time. On Thursday, June 16, the first day of shooting, he filmed eleven setups from eight different scenes in less than four hours on a blistering hot afternoon, finishing up at 5:59 p.m. The first ones were the opening shots of the film, with Wayne as Ethan Edwards riding along a ridge and slowly making his way through an arid sea of sagebrush to his brother Aaron's farmhouse for a bittersweet homecoming. Ford also shot scenes of Ethan and Mose, a fellow settler, galloping past a horseless Martin on their way back to the burning ranch house, and shots of Ethan and Martin escaping the Comanches after first seeing Debbie many years later.

From the beginning Ford was forced to improvise. The original shooting scheme was laid out before he and Pat knew that Jeff Hunter would be delayed a week to finish a previous film. Instead, Ford shot around him, using the stuntman Chuck Hayward dressed in Martin Pauley's outfit.

The following day Ford shot sequences of the Indians chasing Ethan and Martin to a cave, a scene from much later in the story. Wayne and Hunter were doubled by Hayward and Chuck Roberson, who also did a series of spectacular falls dressed as Indians. Ford's stuntmen were always the most professional and among the highest paid, and both Hayward and Roberson had worked for Ford since the Cavalry Trilogy. "They had bodies like iron, their wrists and hands and forearms were like few other men," recalled Harry Carey Jr., himself an excellent rider. "When you shook hands with them, all you could feel was callous."

The stuntmen were Ford's personal favorites. He himself had started out doing stunts for his brother Francis's silent films, and he appreciated rugged men who followed orders and always got the job done. "I like the cowboys, I like the stuntmen," said Ford. ". . . They're a wonderful, kindly, gentle group of people. They're charitable, they're patriotic, and they're easy to work with."

The cowboys, in turn, took pride in being Ford's shock troops. Lee Bradley, a Navajo wrangler, had worked on fifty-seven films since 1925, eleven of them with Ford. Frank McGrath signed on to perform his patented fall and drag stunts off racing horses even though he was still recovering from breaking three vertebrae in a stunt eight months earlier. Jack Pennick, Pappy's personal aide-de-camp and a mournful-faced actor who seemed to have played bit parts in every Ford film since the early 1930s, came along to drill the men for the horse-riding scenes. "We were his personal soldiers, as dirty and stinking as any army that ever chased an Indian across the desert in the middle of July; probably dirtier," recalled Chuck Roberson. Ford liked to dress them up and use them in his trademark folk dance scenes, and they called themselves "Ford's chorus girls."

The fact that he had to tear up his original shooting plan for *The Searchers* didn't seem to bother Ford. He simply did what he had always done when commanding a film set: he plowed ahead. "He never shot in continuity, it didn't mean a damn thing to him," recalled Bill Clothier, a longtime colleague who served as director of photography on several of Ford's later films. "He could shoot a close-up here and put it in a scene that was shot three weeks later."

The Searchers was Ford's 115th film, and his daily routine was almost as immutable as the mesas themselves. It began each morning with Danny Borzage, his personal accordion player for more than thirty years, warming up the set with a selection of tunes. During the silent era, Borzage would play during the shooting itself, varying his tunes to the mood of each scene. Now Ford used him to establish an emotional climate on the set that might be called Early Americana: old folk tunes, dirges, and ditties. At around nine, Harry Goulding would pull up in his station wagon with Ford in the front passenger's seat. When Borzage spotted the car, he would break into "Bringing in the Sheaves" to announce Pappy's arrival.

The man who emerged from Harry's station wagon had aged considerably since his last journey to the valley. He was six feet tall, but he seemed shrunken, and his movements were hesitant and careworn. On the set he usually wore a flowing blue shirt and pleated khaki pants. Sometimes he held up his trousers with a leather belt with a silver buckle; other times he slipped a necktie through his belt loops and knotted it, recalled Harry Carey Jr. His socks often didn't match and his scuffed brown-and-white saddle shoes were usually unlaced. The black eye patch stuffed behind his black horn-rimmed glasses hid the left side of his face, and his battered canvas slouch hat cast a shadow over most of the rest. In the back he wore a lone Indian feather secured by his hat-band. No matter what the temperature, he usually wore a battered sport jacket or a windbreaker. On the set he would take out a huge white handkerchief and shove the corner in his mouth, chewing away when he was worried about a scene or an actor. The rest would hang in front of his chest, said Carey, "like a big windless sail."

He kept a soggy cigar clamped in a corner of his mouth as he went from actor to actor, lingering over their costumes and sprinkling a few last-minute words of encouragement. Even Wayne got the treatment: Ford carefully knotted and straightened Wayne's bandanna before he began shooting.

Everyone stood silently, awaiting his or her turn. "It was a feeling of reverence on every set," recalled Harry Carey Jr. ". . . You felt almost like you were in a church. It was something sacred, something beautiful going on."

AFTER ARRIVING ON THE SET, Ford usually headed straight to Winton Hoch, his Oscar-winning director of photography, to discuss where best to place the camera for the morning shot. The two men had been partners and antagonists for nearly a decade. Hoch was a bushy-browed man with a patrician nose and the bearing of a field general. Ford respected Hoch's impeccable skills but felt that Hoch was overly fussy and temperamental. He laid out his ground rules for Hoch in 1948 on their first day on location for *3 Godfathers*, after Hoch had had the temerity to suggest a camera angle to Ford. "Do you want to go home right now?" Ford demanded. "Who in the name of Christ do you think you are talking to? I mean, Jesus, you're going to lecture me about your pretty goddamned picture postcard shots? Well, we're not having those kinds of shots in this picture! And I tell you where the camera goes."

"Sorry, Jack," Hoch replied evenly. And according to Carey, who witnessed this scene, "they never crossed words again."

The most controversial moment of their tangled partnership was also one of their finest. It came on a late-afternoon during the shooting of a scene in *Yellow Ribbon* in which Captain Brittles leads a troop of cavalrymen through Indian Territory. Purple-black clouds were holding the sky hostage and a smattering of rain and lightning had begun. Ford ordered everyone back to Goulding's, then suddenly changed his mind.

John Ford surrounded by cast and crew—including John Wayne, Jeffrey Hunter, and Danny Borzage, who played accordion on Ford's film sets for four decades—on the set of *The Searchers*. A never-before-published photo by Allen Reed.

The darkening landscape was rich and disturbing, and Ford wanted to capture it on film.

"Winnie, what do you think?" he asked Hoch.

"It's awfully dark, Jack. But I'll shoot it. I just can't promise anything."

Ford decided to try. "Winnie, open her [the lens] up and let's go for it. If it doesn't come out, I'll take the rap."

The result was a brilliant Technicolor moment: blue-clad troopers leading their anxious mounts through a gathering storm under a black roof of sky as lightning flashed and snarled. Hoch went on to win an Academy Award for cinematography, but he and Ford squabbled for years over who deserved the credit.

By the time he worked on *The Searchers*, Hoch had won three Oscars, two of them with Ford. Still, *The Searchers* was a particularly trying project for Hoch, who was using for the first time a complex new technique known as VistaVision. It produced a film image of extra depth and clarity, and enabled Ford to capture Monument Valley's stunning beauty in long and medium shots while allowing for action to unfold within the frame. The result, wrote one observer, was "images that are so detailed that they seem to be painted on screen." But the technique required more cameras and a larger crew, and while Hoch was intrigued with its possibilities, he was also distracted and chagrined by the intricate and costly details.

For all their quarreling, Hoch and Ford shared a visual sensibility about Monument Valley. Hoch appreciated Ford's restraint. "In Monument Valley he avoided the temptation to shoot nothing but breathtakers," Hoch recalled. "He had only an occasional beauty shot. It's like diamonds. They are very valuable because they are rare. If the street was paved with then, then they would be worthless."

AFTER HE CHATTED WITH HOCH, Ford would prepare the actors. This was the moment when he would tear up parts of the script and present the fresh ideas he had worked through the night before. "Too many directors are too concerned with camera angles, and don't worry about anything else," recalled Ken Curtis. "Ford worried about his actors. He would get them together in the morning . . . [and] we'd run through the scene while they were lighting. He'd get it exactly the way it seemed to work best. He always knew what he wanted and when he got it he would print the take. He never shot more than he needed, he never shot less."

Ford believed that actors needed to be spontaneous. He didn't give the actors line readings, and he seldom verbalized what he wanted. He just gave clues, opening bits, a word or two, relying upon chemistry and intuition.

"He didn't want any rehearsing" until the morning that a scene was ready to be shot, Pippa Scott recalled. "I was new but it was fine for me. I just blithely stepped off the plank and went with whatever he wanted."

The last thing Ford wanted was for the actors to act like actors. He didn't mind mistakes, but he despised dramatic gestures and studied line readings.

"The actors get tired, they get jaded and lose their spontaneity—so that they're just mouthing words," he told Bogdanovich. "But if you get the first or second take, there's a sparkle, an uncertainty about it; they're not sure of their lines, and it gives you a sense of nervousness and suspense."

When Ford shot the emotionally powerful climactic scene of *The Grapes of Wrath* when Tom Joad, preparing to flee the police coming to arrest him for murder, says good-bye to his mother, Ford refused to allow Henry Fonda and Jane Darwell to rehearse. "He never let us get into the scene," Fonda recalled. "He knew, as well he should, that Jane and I knew our dialogue. He also somehow instinctively knew that he should get the first take, the first emotion."

Ford made the actors sit for two to three hours while the technicians set up and rehearsed the mechanics of the scene. "By this time [we] were like race horses at the wire," said Fonda. "We were ready . . . Finally we were allowed to. We began that scene and it went. We both went with the emotion. The emotion was there in the face, in the eyes, and in everything else. That was it."

LUNCH WOULD BE SERVED PROMPTLY at noon and Earl Grey tea at 4:00 p.m., usually marking the close of shooting, although sometimes Ford would shoot as late as 6:00. At dinner later in the evening no one was allowed to discuss work at the risk of banishment from the table. It was one of Pappy's many rules, enforceable according to Himself's whim. After dinner there would be poker, gin rummy, and a coin-toss game known as pitch. Ford would bring an old sock stuffed with silver dollars. People tried hard to let Ford win, a mark of deference he both expected and despised. "Oh God, how the man would cheat," recalled Ace Holmes, the property man. "But they would never call him."

Chuck Hayward, who had worked for Ford ever since *Yellow Ribbon*, said the Old Man was never more relaxed than on the *Searchers* set. "He had all his people there, they had no place to go except there," Hayward recalled. "Every night you played hearts, cards or whatever, and it was just like a little kingdom . . . He had his ship—Monument Valley—and he had a big crew and he was *it*—so he really enjoyed it."

The Searchers was indeed a family affair. Ford's son Pat served as associate producer, and his brother-in-law Wingate Smith was an assistant director, as was his brother Edward O'Fearna. He cast Ken Curtis, his son-in-law, as Charlie McCorry, and his daughter Barbara came along as an unofficial script girl. Ford gave John Wayne's fifteen-year-old son Patrick a part, as he did Natalie Wood's sister Lana, and he cast Merian Cooper's wife, Dorothy Jordan, as Martha Edwards (the Coopers donated her salary to charity), Olive Carey as Mrs. Jorgensen, and her son Harry Carey Jr. as Mrs. Jorgensen's son Brad.

Yet the spirit of generosity did not always overflow. While Ford insisted that Frank Nugent write parts for Harry Carey Jr. and Ken Curtis, he also told Nugent, according to the writer's widow, Jean, "Don't make them too good."

18.

The Valley, Part Two
(Monument Valley, June–July 1955)

John Ford had allotted himself just four weeks for the Monument
Valley film shoot, and he quickly fell behind due to high winds and
overcast skies. He knew he had to speed things up, and he started driving his crew hard, shooting anywhere between twelve and nineteen
scenes each day, including Sundays.

He took full advantage of Monument Valley's infinite facets. As
sprawling as it appears on film, the valley is actually fairly compact—just
144 square miles in total, with its most recognizable features stuffed
into an area less than half that size. Ford could pivot the camera and be
rewarded with a series of differentiated and breathtaking vistas. Within
a five-mile radius he was able to film scenes at the Jorgensen and Edwards ranch houses, the long "forty-mile" ride of the Texas Ranger
posse into Indian Territory, two dramatic horse chases in which the
searchers are pursued by Comanches, and the standoff in a cave between the searchers and Scar's men. Ford filmed the final attack on
Scar's village on a flat plain directly in front of the Jorgensen ranch
house.

He didn't bother writing down personal notes about how a scene
would look or what the characters would say. He kept it all in his head,
cutting bits of dialogue and scenes from the final shooting script as he
went. Early on, for example, he added a moment when Ethan, forced to
rest his weary horse, looks off anxiously in the distance, aware that forty
miles away his brother's family—including Martha, the woman he
loves—are the likely target of a Comanche murder raid and there's nothing he can do to stop it. The way Ford framed Wayne's reddish-brown
face against the mesa monument behind him makes it appear as if

Wayne, too, is carved from the same stone, and it makes his worried expression all the more powerful.

The average film director would do a master shot of a scene, then reshoot from various angles and trust the studio's film editor to cut and paste it together in a satisfying way. At minimum, there would be a master shot, two over-the-shoulder shots, and two individual close-ups, plus multiple takes of each setup. A simple two-page dialogue scene, which might run less than two minutes on the screen, could be the end product of three thousand feet of exposed film—slightly more than a half hour's worth of footage.

For many directors it was all about coverage: the more film you shot, the more choices your editor had in assembling the final cut. Overshooting was an insurance policy for the weak willed and supercautious.

Ford couldn't abide the process. Whenever possible, he shot only one take. Part of it was his artistic sensibility: unlike Hitchcock and a number of other visual storytellers, Ford never relied on storyboards to outline a scene before the actual shoot. Yet he knew exactly what he wanted on the first take. "John Ford shoots a picture in his mind before he ever turns on a camera," said Wingate Smith, the assistant director.

Part of it was about keeping the actors fresh and spontaneous. And part of it was about control. The less film he shot, Ford knew, the less material there would be for the studio bosses to cut or reshape. "If you give them a lot of film 'the committee' takes over," he told the author Tag Gallagher. "They start juggling scenes around and taking out this and putting in that. They can't do it with my pictures. I cut in the camera and that's it. There's not a lot of film left on the floor when I'm finished."

ON SUNDAY, JUNE 19, Ford and Harry Goulding, accompanied by Pat Ford and the stunt coordinator Cliff Lyons, drove along the valley floor selecting locations for the Indian encampment to be attacked near the end of the film. Then they headed up to Mexican Hat, twenty miles north, to choose spots along the San Juan River for the scene in which a small band of Texas Rangers is chased across the river by Comanches and makes a stand on the far side. The following day they filmed most of the battle in fifteen setups, working from 9:00 a.m. until 5:30 p.m. in temperatures that approached 120 degrees. On Tuesday they came back again, punching out seventeen additional setups and nine scenes in a day that lasted nearly nine hours. The work was sometimes ragged: Ward Bond fell off his horse during the chase across the river and dragged his horse to the other side while Ford kept filming. When the posse reaches the far side, a soaking-wet Sam Clayton, Bond's character, asks to borrow a pistol from Ethan and then flings his dusty top hat at Ethan in a comic gesture that caught an amused John Wayne by surprise. That moment remains in the final cut of the picture. At another point, as the Indians mass on the far side of the river, someone loses control of the camera, which jerks upward and then down again. No matter: this inadvertent movement is also in the final cut.

Wherever in the valley Ford and his actors roamed, an elaborate convoy of men and machines followed. Technicolor and VistaVision required massive setups and a far larger crew than Ford had used in previous Monument Valley film shoots. There were thirty-three drivers, five five-ton trucks, a three-ton truck, two horse trucks, one truck equipped with a camera crane, a large van specially designed to hold wardrobe, two medium-size trucks, a generator truck, a camera car, a sanitary truck, a radio jeep, three large tourist buses, three station wagons, three twelve-passenger vans, five jeeps, a water wagon, a hay truck, and a hot meals wagon. The traveling crew consisted of two 35mm cameramen, two camera operators, two technicians, three assistant cameramen, one mechanic, one 16mm cameraman, one assistant 16mm cameraman, one stills man, and a sound crew of one sound mixer, one recorder, one cable man, two boom men, and three radiomen.

On any given day, the shooting of action scenes needed a minimum of 65 horses. Lunch was served to 150 people.

Besides the huge logistical challenge and the blazing heat, Ford had another problem to contend with. On Sunday evening, Sonny Whitney and his third wife, Eleanor, arrived by Cessna to oversee his project and be entertained as Hollywood royalty. This was part of the devil's bargain Ford had struck. By relying upon Whitney's money, Ford had avoided being beholden to the studio system, with its extra layers of demands and constraints. But it meant he had to put up with Whitney's whims and suggestions, or at least carefully divert them. Whitney, after all, was paying most of the bills.

Alerted in advance by Cooper, Ford was prepared. As Sonny and Eleanor sat down at the head table for dinner that evening, a fistfight broke out between Chuck Roberson and another stuntman, Fred Kennedy. Eleanor was horrified. "Crockery flew, tables and benches overturned, men punched, tackled, rolled and shouted," she recalled. "Then abruptly the fracas stopped as suddenly as it had begun." It was all an act, staged by Ford for the benefit—and obvious embarrassment—of the Whitneys.

After fourteen years, Sonny and Eleanor's marriage was in trouble. While he liked to portray his film production venture as a patriotic enterprise designed to celebrate and promote the spirit of America to an ignorant and cynical world, Sonny was bored with his life and with Eleanor. Earlier, in the preproduction phase of *The Searchers*, he insisted to Cooper that Ford find a role for Virginia Copeland, a buxom twenty-five-year-old actress and singer who had caught Whitney's eye when he saw her working onstage in New York. There was a cantina scene in the second half of the picture when Ethan and Martin find a Mexican trader who is willing to take them to the Comanche encampment where Debbie may be living. Whitney pressed to give Copeland a feature moment in this scene. "I would surely like to give her this spot," he wrote to Cooper. "A very good song could be found or written for the occasion . . . I would ask you please to give this your urgent attention and discuss it with John Ford."

He enclosed a number of Copeland's photos and concluded, "If you don't like them, then I can only conclude that you have lost your eye for sex."

Copeland got neither the song nor the part. Still, Eleanor knew things had soured with Sonny and she was turning increasingly to her Christian faith for solace. With all the fervor of a new convert, she lamented the spiritual hollowness of their wealthy lives even while continuing to occupy her spousal seat on Sonny's private plane. The superrich, she wrote, "look upon everything in their lives as possessions and hope to find happiness or satisfaction from them, but emptiness, worthlessness, or inner loneliness is their constant reality." She clearly felt she was writing from personal experience.

With a wary Eleanor constantly by his side, Sonny had no opportunity to avail himself of the possibilities for female companionship on the film set. Still, Ford was taking no chances. He assigned his son Pat to entertain the Whitneys and keep them out of harm's way. Pat resented the duty but had no choice. He got Vera Miles to chaperone Eleanor, while he himself took Sonny on long horse rides through the stunningly picturesque valley.

"Whitney had been a polo player; well, I had been too," Pat recalled. "And Whitney would love to ride. He couldn't ride. I mean, how a man could be a polo player and not ride any better . . . ? But anyway, he loved to go on long rides with me."

Still, Whitney was restless. Ford had studiously ignored all of his suggestions for the film. But Sonny had paid $1 million for this movie and he wanted a piece of the action. "That was the worst thing about Whitney and his money," said Pat. "He had to be right in the middle of everything."

Ford gave Eleanor a small walk-on as a hymn-singing mourner by the grave site of the Edwards family. Sonny was not so easy to placate.

Ford devoted Wednesday and Thursday to filming the climactic raid on Scar's camp, set up on a flat plain at the entrance to the valley. It was a massive affair, with 130 Navajos as extras and 15 more dressed as Texas Rangers. Each work day started at 7:00 a.m. The stuntmen did numerous horse falls, and a camera truck raced back and forth past teepees and fleeing Indian men, women, and children, capturing two dozen Rangers riding at breakneck speed as they rampaged through the camp. Whitney, who despite Pat's disdainful critique fancied himself a fine horseman, asked Ford for permission to join the riders. The director issued an emphatic no. Much too dangerous, he told Whitney. It didn't matter. Sonny Whitney decided to ride anyway. The wranglers, who knew Sonny was ultimately responsible for their paychecks, abetted his stunt.

After the scene was shot, recalled Terry Wilson, one the wranglers, Sonny "came riding up and he was proud, and the Old Man looked at him and Jesus Christ he really blew his stack." Ford told Whitney, "God damn, don't ever do that again, you could get killed out there. I know you ride polo ponies and all that but this is a different ballgame."

Whitney acted suitably chastened, but in fact he was so proud of his escapade that he leaked the story to Cholly Knickerbocker's Smart Set column in the *New York Journal-American*, which was always happy to slobber over a wealthy patron. "That Sonny knows all there is to know about horses, plus the fact that he's backing the flicker for half a million, makes him the most important extra a movie ever had," the column dutifully reported.

Pat Ford, as usual, had a more cynical take. "We were scared to death he was going to break his check-writing arm."

JOHN FORD DID NOT LET Sonny Whitney's shenanigans divert his focus. Summer had come early to the valley: the gray-green sage and purple-spotted patches of grass and weeds had already been burned off, leaving no vegetation to hold down the sand once the thick red winds began to blow. Ford liked to use the wind and dust as tempestuous backdrops to add an extra layer of sweat and grit to the outdoor scenes. "Two things make Western pictures—horse manure and dust," Ford told Bill Clothier, who recalled how Ford almost fired a crew member who innocently sprayed water on the ground one day. He was only trying to tamp down the dust, the man explained. "Hell, that's why I came out here," Ford replied. "I *want* the dust."

Still, Ford struggled in the blazing sun to push himself and his crew through the long, arid days. Insect bites and sunstroke were common, and people were fainting in the heat. Two stuntmen went down on one fraught day, one with a seizure and the other with cracked vertebrae after falling off a horse, and both had to be flown out on a private plane. Ford himself began to falter physically.

"I don't think he was terribly well," recalled Pippa Scott. "His eye was running particularly badly out there in the desert heat and the wind that blew. We always had lunch covered in red sand. The wind would kick up by noon and it was hot as hell. But the evenings were gorgeous and cooled down quickly and the mornings were exquisite. We were up very early before the dawn and everything was beautiful. Earlier was better on the horses too."

The benign glow of Ford's first days back in the valley soon faded, and he reverted to the more familiar role of a demanding despot who could be as harsh as the noon sun. He found plenty of subjects for his wrath. Henry Brandon, who played Scar, became a favorite target. Ford forced Brandon to report to the set almost every day in full Comanche outfit and makeup, even though on most days there was nothing for Brandon to do. "He liked to push people to see how far they would go," Brandon recalled. Ford particularly liked to single out Ward Bond for ridicule. After Bond kept blowing his lines in one scene, Ford turned to Brandon, a native of Germany, and blurted out in German, "He isn't an actor, he's a pants shitter."

Even Ford's beloved stuntmen felt his wrath. Frank McGrath loyally reported to the set for work even though he had just spent eight months in a plaster cast after fracturing vertebrae while working on a previous film. McGrath was a heavy drinker who liked to stash gin bottles in various nooks and crannies of the tent he shared with five other wranglers and stuntmen. When Pappy heard that McGrath had broken the rule against drinking on the set, he entered the tent while McGrath wasn't there and asked the others which bunk belonged to McGrath. Ford pulled back the covers and urinated long and loud on the mattress—"as matter of fact as if he had been out for a stroll in his garden and had stopped to water the petunias," Roberson recalled—then made up the cot again. "If the man can drink it, he can lie in it," Ford told them.

NO ONE FIELDED and deflected more abuse from the Old Man than his star performer. The *Searchers* was Wayne and Ford's twelfth picture together, and by now the two men knew each other intimately. Yet Ford still took great pleasure in humiliating his star. During one scene when Wayne rode up awkwardly with his hand resting on his saddle horn, Ford screamed at him, "When will you learn to ride a horse?"

"Ah now, Pappy," was Wayne's embarrassed reply.

"Duke loved the Old Man," recalled Chuck Roberson, who witnessed the scene. "When the Old Man said 'Jump,' Duke found a trampoline."

Pippa Scott was surprised by Ford's habit of insulting Wayne in front of her and other cast members. "The whole relationship was something you wanted to stay away from. I have to say the other guys in the company were very supportive of Wayne. They felt very bad for him . . . It was mean, but it was daunting for everybody, it was scary. Everybody was walking on eggshells."

Still, Wayne took it without complaint. He lit one Camel after another all day long between takes and kept plugging away at his role. He saw Ethan Edwards as his most serious acting challenge, and he approached the part with a singular intensity. "My father would say that everything he had done on film to this time was building to this role," said Patrick Wayne.

In an early scene when the posse comes across the corpse of a prize bull killed by Comanches, Wayne demonstrated to Harry Carey Jr. that he meant business. "When I looked up at him in rehearsal, it was into the meanest, coldest eyes I had ever seen," Carey recalled. After the day's film shoot was finished, Wayne was Ethan at dinner time as well. "He didn't kid around on *The Searchers* as he had done on other shows. Ethan was always in his eyes."

An amiable man who knew his place as a role player, Carey was fond of both Ford and Wayne, but he had learned from hard experience to keep an emotional distance from both of them. Each was a complex character, he concluded, who could turn on a friend without warning. Carey spent only two weeks on location in the valley but his uncle Jack taunted him almost daily because he knew Carey was committed to finishing his role in time to get back to Hollywood for a part in "Spin and Marty," a new Disney serial. Still, on *The Searchers* he felt that both Ford and Wayne were at the top of their craft.

Carey's most memorable moment came in the scene—directly from LeMay's novel—where an excited Brad Jorgensen races back from scouting the Comanche raiding party's encampment to report he's spotted Lucy, his abducted fiancée. Ethan proceeds reluctantly to tell Brad that what he's seen is a Comanche wearing Lucy's dress: Ethan had found Lucy's naked corpse earlier in the day on a side trail in a canyon where she'd been taken by three warriors and killed, but had kept it from Brad.

"Was she . . . ? Did they . . . ?" a distraught Brad asks.

Ethan erupts. "What do you want me to do—draw you a picture? . . . Spell it out? . . . Don't ever ask me! . . . Long as you live don't ever ask me more!"

They did the scene in one take, only to discover the camera had not been turned on. Legend has it that the famously oblivious Ward Bond had pulled the plug from a socket while looking for a place to plug in his electric razor. They did the take again and did it perfectly. Carey, a veteran performer of more than ninety films, believed it was his finest scene as an actor, and one of Wayne's as well. A half century later, sitting in his living room in Santa Barbara, Carey at age eighty-seven could still recite from memory every line, both his and Wayne's.

After Ford turned off the camera, Wayne put his hand on Carey's shoulder. "He didn't say a word," Carey recalled. "He didn't have to. Those are the great moments for an actor."

WHILE FORD RAINED ABUSE on Wayne and the usual cast of characters, he worked gently and with great warmth with the younger actors, putting them at ease and building their confidence. Although her role was small, Pippa Scott found him charming, solicitous, and always in control. "He was very sweet with me," she recalled. ". . . If he played games I wasn't aware of it. He was very tender and praised us when we did what he approved of."

Patrick Wayne also enjoyed a close relationship with Ford on the set. "I was his godson. Plain and simple. But that was no guarantee that I wouldn't feel the barb at some point. So you always stay a little tense, waiting for the shoe to drop and hope it doesn't knock you down." At one point Ford caught Patrick purposely losing at gin rummy and banished him from the playing table. "From now on, you should just play with small children or Ward Bond!" Ford commanded.

Early on, Ford took Jeffrey Hunter aside to talk over the scene where Martin and Ethan race back to the burning remains of the Edwards ranch house after the Comanche raid. What Hunter recalled was the quiet and careful way Ford spoke to him. "He used no technical terms at all. He just discussed [it] in a very simple and touching way . . . I began to get the feel of a man who discovers that those he loves have been taken from him forever. Ford wasn't talking to Jeffrey Hunter, the actor, but to Henry H. McKinnies Jr., the man. He wanted emotion, not elocution."

By Sunday, July 3, Ford was ready to shoot the final scene of Debbie's homecoming. The script ended with Ethan and Martin riding home toward the Jorgensen ranch with Debbie nestled asleep in Ethan's arms, but Ford threw it away. Instead, he chose to end with Lars and Mrs. Jorgensen and their daughter Laurie standing in front of the house as the two searchers ride up with Debbie. Ethan dismounts, carries Debbie up to the porch, and hands her over to the Jorgensens. Then—echoing the opening shot in the film—Ford once again shoots from inside the house, looking out through the front door, as the Jorgensens escort a wary Debbie inside, followed by a reunited Martin and Laurie, who virtually race in together hand in hand. As Ethan watches from outside, he grasps his right arm with his left hand—a gesture that Wayne's idol, Harry Carey Sr., used in many Westerns. Then Ethan turns, pivots, and walks away alone.

"When I crossed my arm I did it the way Harry Carey used to do it, because his widow was on the other side of the door," Wayne later recalled. "And he was the man, Pappy said, who taught him his trade." Wayne, in other words, was honoring two men—Ford's mentor and Ford himself—and Olive Carey as well.

All of this was improvised on the set that afternoon. As Olive watched Wayne's gesture from off camera, she burst into tears. "Everybody thinks I'm crazy, but I think Duke has the grace of Nureyev," she said later. "He really is the most graceful man I've ever seen."

But Olive saved her most lavish praise for her old friend and nemesis John Ford. "He just moved you so that you could just turn it on," she recalled. ". . . Even if it was only a shot of opening the door and going through the door and shutting the door, he made you feel it was one of the high spots of the movie, and I think he did that with everybody. I think that's why he got such performances. You didn't do it for yourself, you did it for him. It was almost hypnotic, the thing that he had."

*   *   *

THE NEXT DAY, JULY FOURTH, they took a break. Frank and Lee Bradley, Ford's Navajo interpreters, came to Harry Goulding and said they wanted to make a Ford an honorary member of the tribe.

The film company staged a big rodeo-style celebration on the red-dirt airstrip below the lodge. Ford paid for three sides of beef and a truckload of watermelons. There were horse races in the morning, and then the Bradleys brought Ford down for the ceremony. They held the Old Man's Foot Race, featuring Pappy himself. "On your mark! Get set!" Ford jumped the gun, his cigar clamped tightly in his mouth. "Go!"

By the time the others started, Ford was already halfway to the finish line. He won easily.

Then they presented Ford with a sacred deerskin. They dedicated it to Natani Nez—"Tall Soldier" in Navajo—and inscribed it "as a token of appreciation for the generosity and friendship he has extended to us in his many activities in our valley," and added the following wish:

> *In your travels may there be*
> *Beauty behind you*
> *Beauty on both sides of you*
> *And beauty ahead of you.*

John Ford with Eleanor and C. V. "Sonny" Whitney, at the July 4, 1955, festivities near Goulding's Lodge in Monument Valley. Ford is wrapped in the Natani Nez deerskin presented to him by his Navajo crew members. A never-before-published photo by Allen Reed.

Carey, who was there, says his Uncle Jack was deeply moved by the presentation. So far as he was concerned, John Ford later said, the dedication was one of the fondest memories of his career. Ford liked being the Tall Soldier, just as he liked being the Great White Father. "More than having received the Oscars, what counts for me is having been made a blood brother of different Redskin nations," he later declared.

Better even than winning an Academy Award, said the man who had won four.

19.

The Studio
(Hollywood, July–August 1955)

The RKO-Pathé Studio in Culver City was as much a part of Holly-wood lore as the movies themselves. It was originally built in 1918 by Thomas Ince, an early pioneer of the Western. No stranger to the art of pretension, Ince had insisted on erecting a dignified two-story mansion with pillars, porticos, and a circular driveway as the administrative offices of the studio, which he tucked behind the stately façade. After his sudden and suspicious death aboard William Randolph Hearst's yacht in 1924, the studio went on the market. It was first bought by Cecil B. DeMille and later by Joseph P. Kennedy, who built a private bungalow on the site for his trysts with leading lady Gloria Swanson (who later discovered that the impecunious Kennedy had deducted money from her contract to pay for it). David O. Selznick occupied the studio for most of the 1930s, and its image can be seen at the beginning of *Gone With the Wind* as the symbol of David Selznick Film Productions. *King Kong* and *Citizen Kane* were also shot there—and, some forty years later, *E.T. The Extra-Terrestrial.*

By the time the *Searchers* crew arrived in July 1955, RKO and its various properties were in the process of being sold off by Howard Hughes, its latest owner, who ran the company into the ground but rented out the soundstages for cheap rates. Ford had shot here before and Merian C. Cooper, mindful of the need to economize, booked it again. For Ford it was a location as familiar in its way as Monument Valley.

Ford and his sunbaked crew returned to Los Angeles during the week of July 11 and reported for work on Stage 15 the following Monday. Here Ford went to work cutting and pasting bits of script, coaxing, cajoling, and bullying performances out of the actors. Ford was always more relaxed after a sojourn in Monument Valley. He cleaned himself up, put on fresh clothes, ate a few good meals, and got down to business. He summoned Frank Nugent, the screenwriter, for a bit of polish on some of the scenes. But mostly this was Ford himself, pushing his own vision, using the soundstage to fill in the gaps in the story he was telling. *The Searchers* is justly famous for the evocative landscape of Monument Valley, yet many of its most powerful moments were filmed on the RKO soundstage. What's more astonishing, virtually none of them were in the original screenplay.

Perhaps the most memorable is the breakfast scene that Ford shot on Wednesday, July 20. Ranger captain Samuel Clayton's posse of volunteers has ridden up to the Edwards farmhouse early in the morning (their thunderous approach on horseback having been filmed in Monument Valley several weeks earlier). Clayton, who is also a reverend, has come to deputize Aaron Edwards and his adopted son, Martin Pauley, to join the hunt for rustlers who have stolen cattle from the neighboring Jorgensen ranch the night before. The scene is a classic Ford tableau: the camera watches quietly from a stationary spot in the front of the dining room as the women of the Edwards family scurry to and fro, serving coffee and doughnuts to the Rangers, while Clayton swears in Aaron and Martin, and his men chat amiably with one another and the Edwardses. It's a domestic opera—lots of chatter and bustle. People are talking in clusters and moving around the room in a busy but balanced composition. Then from a back door Ethan Edwards enters the room and saunters forward. Ford's camera watches for a moment, then moves slowly toward him. Wayne almost swaggers as he makes his way toward the dining room table. Ethan and Clayton exchange wary greetings. They are both former Confederate soldiers, ex-comrades who haven't seen each other in the three years since the Civil War ended. Nugent's dialogue, spoken by Wayne and Bond, two old pros, is crisp and sardonic.

"Captain, the Reverend Samuel Johnson Clayton! . . . Mighty impressive," declares Ethan mockingly.

"Well, the prodigal brother," Clayton retorts in Ward Bond's trademark caustic, booming voice. "I haven't seen you since the surrender. Come to think of it, I didn't see you *at* the surrender."

"Don't believe in surrenderin'," Ethan responds. "I still got my saber, Reverend . . . didn't beat it into no plowshare either."

Ethan immediately takes charge, ordering his brother Aaron to remain at the ranch because those alleged cattle rustlers might turn out to be

Comanche raiders with more than thievery on their minds. Ethan says he'll take Aaron's place in the posse, although he refuses to be sworn in. "Wouldn't be legal anyway," he adds mysteriously.

Clayton wants to know why. "You wanted for a crime, Ethan?"

"You askin' as a Reverend or a Captain, Sam?"

"I'm askin' as a Ranger of the sovereign state of Texas."

"Got a warrant?" Ethan demands.

"You fit a lot of descriptions," Clayton replies.

It's one of the film's classic lines, capturing as it does the sense that Ethan is indeed many men—wrangler, scout, uncle, lover, outlaw, killer.

"I figure a man's only good for one oath at a time . . . I took mine to the Confederate States of America . . . So did you, Reverend." Ethan spits out the last line like an accusation.

An anxious Martha, worried that Ethan is pushing things too far, cuts through the escalating tension by offering more coffee and dough-nuts, and the posse and family members head out the door, leaving Clayton to drain his cup in the foreground, facing forward toward the camera while behind him we see Martha fetching Ethan's coat. She strokes it gently and hands it silently to Ethan, who kisses her chastely on the forehead and heads outside. The harpsichord music playing softly in the background is Martha's theme, a Civil War–era ballad called "Lo-rena," a tale of a thwarted, forbidden love affair. Clayton thoughtfully sips his coffee in the foreground, pretending not to see a thing. Then he slips out the door as well, passing close to Martha without a word. The posse rides off.

The dialogue is from the Nugent screenplay, each line faithfully ren-dered. But the silent grace notes—the coat, the gentle farewell, Clayton's noble discretion—were improvised on the set. The result is classic Ford—understated, ambiguous, bathed in silent emotion. We learn many things: about Ethan's disrespect for authority, his and Martha's enduring secret love, his sway over other men, Clayton's surprising sensitivity, Martha's hidden feelings. Most of it isn't expressed in words. "Show, don't tell" is the narrative writer's and filmmaker's first commandment. Ford, who was a natural storyteller, knew it by heart.

Later that same day, Ford filmed another classic moment, the scene in which Aaron, Martha, and their children realize they are about to come under attack by Comanches. This is the opening scene of Alan LeMay's novel, the starting point that Ford and Nugent decided to delay until later in the movie. They take LeMay's structure, setting, and intent, but add their own little cinematic twist. While Aaron is outside, checking to

The tender farewell between Ethan Edwards (John Wayne) and Martha Edwards (Dorothy Jordan), his sister-in-law and the forbidden love of his life, while the Rev. Samuel Clayton (Ward Bond) pretends not to notice.

see if anyone's hiding in the brush, his older daughter, Lucy, innocently lights an oil lamp inside. A panic-stricken Martha, knowing Comanches will see the light, snuffs it immediately and reprimands her. From the sharp, anxious tone in her mother's voice, Lucy suddenly realizes the mortal danger they are in. Ford's camera tracks in on Lucy's face as panic seizes her, too, and she screams. To silence her, Martha slaps her hard. Then mother and daughter collapse in each other's arms, an embrace of mutual terror and despair.

It is a devastating exchange. Martha, played by Dorothy Jordan, is a small, gentle woman who deeply loves her children. Just as in the novel, we know she is strong spiritually: Aaron has told Ethan in an earlier scene that she is the driving force that has kept them on the land despite many hardships. Now we see her steely core. Ford knew exactly what he wanted, and he carefully briefed Dorothy Jordan to make sure he got it.

"She slugged me," Pippa Scott recalled. "I swelled terribly the next day. I knew she was gonna sock me. We gently rehearsed it, but I think Pappy took her aside and said really let her have it, and she did."

The two actresses were so effective that nine-year-old Lana Wood, Natalie's younger sister, who was playing the young Debbie, was badly shaken. "I remember being very unnerved by it," she recalled five decades later. "There was a real sense of gut-wrenching terror to it that I know I reacted to very strongly."

Ford despised excessive camera movement—he felt it called attention to itself and was distracting to audiences. He once told Fred Zinnemann, the director of *High Noon* and a two-time Academy Award winner, that Zinnemann would be a hell of a filmmaker if he'd just stop moving the camera around. But Ford violates his own cardinal rule in the scream scene; he wants us to share the sense of fear that suddenly crashes down upon the Edwardses as they realize they are about to die.

The film company spent another month on the soundstage, shooting not only interior scenes but also a number of purportedly outdoor scenes that Ford had not been able to capture to his satisfaction in Monument Valley. Much of the outdoor stuff looks exceedingly phony; Bosley Crowther of the *New York Times* later wrote that some of the scenes "could have been shot in a sporting-goods store window."

Along the way Ford found a reason to move the camera again for another revealing close-up. It was Monday, August 8, and Ford was shooting a pivotal moment in the tangled psychology and morality of *The Searchers*. Journeying through a snow-laden stretch of Oklahoma in their search for Debbie, Ethan and Martin have come across the smoldering shell of an Indian village, where they find the bodies of men, women, and children slaughtered by Colonel George Armstrong Custer's Seventh Cavalry. Even Ethan is shocked by what he sees: it's clear that white soldiers are as capable of wanton brutality as Comanche warriors. He and Martin make their way to a military outpost where soldiers have forcibly hauled the surviving white female captives rounded up during the massacre. Like Cynthia Ann Parker, these woman have been twice brutalized—first by Indians during their original abduction, and now by the soldiers who have destroyed their village and killed most of those living there. Most of them seem crazed, either from living with Indians or from the horror they've just witnessed, or both. In a preproduction note, Ford makes clear that the women have been defiled by their Indian masters. Some of the captives, writes Ford, "have been enslaved so long, raped by so many bucks, that they no longer care and can only stare at the whites with dead eyes. They are too beaten to feel anything. Even their sense of shame has left them."

As Ethan and Martin look around the room to determine if one of the captives is Debbie, they must wade through the madness and grief. "It's hard to realize they're white," a soldier declares.

"They ain't white anymore," Ethan replies, slowly and deliberately, and Wayne renders every word like an oath. "They're Comanch."

In filming the scene, Ford mixes and matches bits of dialogue from the Nugent screenplay with his own improvised direction, but the key moment belongs to him and Wayne: as Ethan moves away from the living captives to examine the corpses of those who were massacred, one of the deranged women cries out. Ethan stops and turns his head toward her as Ford moves the camera in to capture his expression. Ethan looks toward the woman, lowers his eyes slightly, and turns away. His facial expression burns with distress, sadness, anger, pity, resignation, maybe even despair. As he walks away his shoulders seem to slump. Does he resolve here and now to kill Debbie when he finds her? Or is something more complicated churning in his psyche?

Ford never tells us. But Wayne understood that this was meant to be a morally ambiguous moment. "Helluva shot," he later told Peter Bogdanovich. "And everybody can put their own thoughts to it. You're not forced to think one way or the other."

The scene is the richest and most troubling in *The Searchers* and perhaps in all of American Westerns. Two civilizations, white and Indian, have collided murderously and the surviving captives are the legacy— the collateral damage, sexually abused to the point of madness. Like ambassadors without portfolio, Ethan and Martin have been traveling the dangerous no-man's-land between the two sides. They are representatives of the white world, yet have become untethered from it. They are on their own, each of them sticking to the quest for a different purpose. Ethan is searching for vengeance and retribution, while Martin is trying to restore the remaining pieces of his lost family. His search is for love and redemption. Most of all, Martin's mission is to prevent Ethan from wreaking vengeance on Debbie if and when they find her. At the burned village and the fort, they see the worst damage that each side can inflict on the other, and they struggle to understand what it means and to carry on with their search. Neither of them can turn back.

The fort scene is one of the few moments in *The Searchers* where the shadow of Cynthia Ann Parker plainly hovers. She and Prairie Flower, her baby girl, were ripped violently from the demolished Indian village by their white captors, then waited to be claimed by Cynthia Ann's uncle and returned to a home she had long forgotten. They could have easily been among the desperate, unhinged captives whom Ford depicts.

FOUR DAYS LATER, Ford took John Wayne, Natalie Wood, and a camera crew to Bronson Canyon to shoot the film's climactic scene in which Ethan finally hunts down Debbie. The canyon was one of Hollywood's classic outdoor locations, a former quarry carved into the southwest corner of Griffith Park just a few miles east of the Culver City studio. Brown and barren, it readily stood in for the rocky terrain of the West. From *Riders of the Purple Sage* (1925) to *I Am a Fugitive from a Chain Gang* (1932) to *Zorro Rides Again* (1937), anyone who needed a cheap natural location within a bus ride from a studio had resorted to Bronson Canyon over the years. Ford didn't go there to save money, however, but to solve a problem. As usual, he left no notes to explain. But it's likely Ford and his crew had filmed the climactic scene in Monument Valley in July according to the Nugent screenplay and that Ford had decided at the last minute to change it.

Nugent's original script spells out exactly what is supposed to happen and why:

Ethan dismounts with his gun drawn, pointing it at Debbie. "I'm sorry, girl," he tells her. "Shut your eyes."

The camera holds on Debbie's face—the eyes gaze fearlessly, innocently into Ethan's. After a moment, he lowers his gun and puts it away. "You sure do favor your mother," he tells her. Then he extends his hand, puts his arm protectively around her and a reconciled uncle and niece head for home.

Somewhere between the original filming of the scene and August 12, Ford decided to reach for a different ending. He clearly wanted something more visual and ambiguous—something the audience could see and feel and not have explained to them. "I wonder, did they box themselves into a corner and find themselves having to shoot this at the very end?" asked the Ford scholar James D'Arc. "Bronson Canyon's the obvious quickie solution."

As he did so many times, Ford threw away Nugent's dialogue and improvised. The fact that he would be jump-cutting from the flat parched floor of Monument Valley to the hilly rock-strewn path leading to Bronson Canyon did not seem to trouble him. In the filmed version, Ethan chases Debbie down, calling out her name—similar to the way he had called out Martha's name earlier in the film when he searched for her body among the flaming ruins of the ranch house. Desperate to escape him, Debbie reaches the mouth of a cave and then collapses. Ethan dismounts, stands over her, then lifts her over his head in one sweeping motion and takes her in his arms. "Let's go home, Debbie" is all he says.

For Ford and his crew, it was a quick visit. They started shooting at Bronson Canyon at 11:00 that morning and finished up at 12:45. They broke a half hour for lunch and then headed back to the studio, where Wayne and Hunter performed for a number of process shots with snow-covered fields in the background—looking about as realistic as the plastic flakes inside a glass snow globe. Then Wayne gave Ethan's "Turning of the Earth" speech, promising Martin that they would eventually find Debbie, taken word for word from LeMay's novel. The critic Andrew Sarris wrote that Wayne's reading is so powerful, it feels as if *he's* making the earth turn.

Ford wrapped up at 5:10 that afternoon after shooting a total of twelve setups for nine scenes. The next day at noon he completed principal photography.

The Searchers had taken fifty-six days to shoot, a week more than originally scheduled. Ford had shot 187,402 feet of film, only 80,540 of which was listed as wasted or discarded. His film editor, Jack Murray, who had done a dozen pictures for Ford, went to work, but as usual there was little for him to do. As with all his pictures, Ford had essentially edited *The Searchers* in the camera. Within weeks it was cut, recorded, and made ready for audiences. John Ford was done.

By early October they had a rough cut without music. Then Max Steiner took over. A Vienna-born Jew whose father and grandfather were theatrical producers, Maximilian Raoul Steiner had taken piano lessons from Brahms and had studied at a music conservatory under Mahler before emigrating at age seventeen, first to London and later to New York. To many he was the father of American film music, setting the standard with powerful, classical scores for Cooper's *King Kong*, Selznick's *Gone With the Wind*, and John Huston's *Treasure of the Sierra Madre*. He had done three scores for Ford films in the 1930s, including *The Informer*, for which he won an Academy Award. But by the 1950s, Steiner's lush melodramas were out of fashion. Cooper signed him for *The Searchers*, writes James D'Arc, "as a kind gesture from [an] old friend."

From preproduction days, Ford had insisted that Pat Ford and his staff come up with a search theme song "that is completely haunting . . . This should not be done lightly but research should be done exhaustively throughout the classics of the world, from which, after all, we derive our American folk music."

In the end Ford turned to Stan Jones, a former navy man, firefighter, and park ranger who sang in the Sons of the Pioneers and wrote the haunting Western classic "Ghost Riders in the Sky." Ford had first met Jones when the ranger had served as an informal adviser on the set of *3 Godfathers* in Death Valley in 1948, and Jones wrote songs for *Wagon Master* and *Rio Grande*, performed by the Sons of the Pioneers, one of whose members was the handsome baritone singer Ken Curtis. For *The Searchers*, Jones came up with an eight-verse search theme, which Ford cut down to two—one to launch the film and one to end it. But just as Ford had envisaged, Steiner wove the melody into the score throughout the film, most affectingly during the scenes of Ethan and Martin riding through the high, vast expanse of Monument Valley.

Still, neither Ford nor Steiner was happy with the results. Ford thought the musical score was too lush and classical. "You've got a guy alone in the desert and the London Philharmonic's playing," he complained to Peter Bogdanovich.

Steiner clearly did not care for the way Ford mutilated his score. There is no record that he ever put his complaints in writing, but there exists a letter from Whitney to Steiner praising the composer for his work on the film and noting, "I am sorry you are not altogether satisfied with the musical score as cut." It was clear that in musical choices, as in everything else about *The Searchers*, John Ford exercised ultimate control.

Sonny Whitney ran a pair of sneak previews in Los Angeles and San Francisco in early December, after which he told Ford that *The Searchers* "goes down as my favorite picture." Jack Warner sent Walter MacEwen, a studio lieutenant, who reported back that the picture was a success. "Wayne has never been better, in a rugged, sometimes cruel role—and the audience is with him all the way from his opening shots where he gets a good laugh from his weather-beaten appearance."

It's not hard to detect a few doubts creeping into MacEwen's glowing assessment. "The picture is brutal in spots to the point of being daring," he told Warner. He singled out as particularly gruesome the scene of the white captives at the fort and a scene near the end where Ethan scalps Scar's corpse, and he also called the pace "rather deliberate in spots, [although] it never seemed to lag."

Still, MacEwen added, "the whole picture has a real feeling of bigness and honesty, as if you were actually witnessing how the pioneers lived on the frontier."

Jack Warner's own doubts were apparent in the delays that followed. The studio had originally planned to release *The Searchers* in January 1956, but rescheduled for April 7. Then the film ran up against another John Wayne picture, *The Conqueror*, which RKO slated for general release on April 1. The *Searchers* contract specified that Warner's did not have to pay C. V. Whitney Productions its share of the production costs until the film was released. Whitney was eager to get paid: he told Jack Warner he needed the money to finance his next project. No matter. Warner's delayed its check until the release date, now reset for early June.

Whitney was unhappy with Warner's for other reasons as well. He feared his big investment was being bounced around the Warner's studio machine. He had Cooper write Warner a passionate five-page letter that was part plea, part threat, and part paean that clearly had been dictated by Whitney himself.

"Frankly, I have been very disappointed in the advertising copy and television advertising preparation that Warner Brothers has been doing, and when I explained exactly what it was to C.V., he was equally disgusted," Cooper begins. "We wanted to make a BIG picture which would show off the Whole West."

Cooper says he had sent over to the studio three scripts for movie trailers that captured "the scope and magnitude of the picture—the BIGGEST, ROUGHEST, TOUGHEST, and MOST BEAUTIFUL PICTURE ever made." But Warner's discarded all three and produced a trailer that "simply plays this as another John Wayne picture . . ." This was unacceptable to Whitney. "C.V. and I think *The Searchers* is bigger than any single star, no matter how big the star."

Cooper's discomfort in writing this letter is palpable. He swears his allegiance to Wayne ("I admire him tremendously") and pointedly notes to Warner that he's "writing at the request of C.V." Still, he closes with an ode to his boss: "When everyone else thought that over-ocean flying was folly, it was C.V. Whitney's brilliant idea that put over Pan American Airways. He understood how to advertise and exploit a new industry—flying—no one in America understood it as well . . . Indeed, I don't think anyone understands advertising and exploitation better than does our President—your friend and mine—C.V. Whitney. I hope you will consider well his suggestions—as expressed in this letter."

Jack Warner, like John Ford before him, ignored Sonny Whitney's unhelpful suggestions. The movie trailer focused on John Wayne from start to finish. *"From the thrilling pages of life rides a man you must fear and respect,"* proclaims the God-like narrator. *"It's John Wayne as Ethan Edwards, who has a rare kind of courage . . . Here is the story of a man hard and relentless, tender and passionate."*

The Searchers, according to Warner Brothers, was a John Wayne movie after all.

20.

The Movie (Hollywood, 1956)

After four months of delays, *The Searchers* finally opened on May 26, 1956. To the audience it looked like something very familiar: a John Wayne movie set in Monument Valley with cowboys, Indians, horses, and gunplay. It begins with a panel announcing the scene as "Texas 1868," then a door opens onto a Monument Valley vista—a subtle announcement that what follows is a fable. Ethan Edwards rides up slowly, tired, expressionless, but erect in the saddle. His sister-in-law, Martha, welcomes him with a shy, awkward gesture, stepping backward toward the house, drawing him in as if she were welcoming royalty—or the man she loves but cannot embrace. It is as beautiful, stylized, and ambiguous as the film that follows.

From its austere opening moment until its emotional climax, *The Searchers* is a mythic tale, only loosely connected to historical reality—"a myth based on other myths based themselves on still other myths," wrote the critic Tag Gallagher.

Its pioneers are eking out a hardscrabble existence in a setting as unyielding as the Sahara; its Comanches are mythic apparitions that Gallagher called "icons of savage violent beauty and dread . . . projections of white fantasy." It is a psychological drama, obsessed with race and sexual violation and fear of the other. The audience sees very little violence in *The Searchers*; what we witness instead are the devastating effects of violence on those who survive.

Ethan Edwards is the Man Who Knows Indians, a worthy successor to Daniel Boone and Natty Bumppo and to the image that Cynthia Ann Parker's uncle James had sought to project in his own troubled narrative more than a century earlier. Ethan is the person you'd most want by your side in a dangerous situation. "I wish Uncle Ethan was here, don't you?" Ben Edwards says to his mother, Martha, as Comanche raiders close in on the Edwards homestead. On this we all can agree. He is, after all, John Wayne—reliable, undefeatable, strangely menacing, as powerful and invulnerable as Monument Valley itself.

Wayne dominates. Ford usually films him from middle distance, so we can see his body as well as his face. He is controlled and heavy, yet somehow loose. When he twirls his pistol, it is with a knowing and flexible motion. When he swings his rifle into action, flinging its buckskin sheath to the ground, he is ready to kill. The only time he tenses up is in the winter scene when he goes crazy with bloodlust and kills as many bison as he can, and it's the one moment in the film when he's less than totally convincing. More often he's cold and deliberate—taking aim with his rifle at Scar from a distance, or smiling with icy pleasure as he shoots the eyes out of the Comanche corpse. It is a monumental performance, one that has slowly come to be recognized as one of the greatest in film history.

Then there is the psychological drama of Ethan and Scar, two blood enemies who are wounded warriors and effectively two sides of the same mirror. When they finally meet, they trade knowing insults. "You speak good American for a Comanch—someone teach you?" declares Ethan as he goes to enter Scar's teepee. Scar retorts with equal contempt: "You speak pretty good Comanch—someone teach you?" Ethan wants to do to Scar what Scar has done to him: destroy his family and steal and kill his women. Yet, just like Ethan, Scar has reasons for his brutality: he reveals that his own two sons were killed by whites. "For each son I take many scalps." Ethan can at least understand the grim equation.

Behind these rich, complicated men is John Ford, mythmaker and storyteller. With every choice Ford makes, he reduces the exposition of Nugent's final script, hacks away at dialogue and explanation, replaces literal certainty with subtle ambiguity. There is much about *The Searchers* that seems makeshift and haphazard. In the opening scene, a Navajo blanket sits atop a fence at one moment, then vanishes the next. There's no continuity in the chase scene: Comanche warriors are within a few feet of the Rangers one moment; then in the next the Rangers are halfway across the San Juan River with the pursuing Indians far behind. Later on in the winter Cavalry scene, a discerning eye can catch a station wagon in the distance lumbering incongruously down a road at the top edge of the shot. At the end of the film, Ethan races after Debbie on the flat plain outside the Indian village, then Ford cuts to a cave on a hill-side. There's an almost willful sloppiness at work that in later pictures—*Two Rode Together* and *Cheyenne Autumn*—becomes fatal to the films' meaning and ambitions. But in *The Searchers* none of it matters. If Ford is sloppy around the edges, sacrificing continuity and visual coherence, he is precise at the core.

One thing he has working for him is a tight, remorseless narrative that establishes its tension early and never relaxes its grip. The first third of the film is almost perfect in its power and pace. It introduces us to the Edwards family and then slaughters most of them, sending the survi-vors on an epic search to save the remaining members. We come away keen to know if Ethan and Martin will find Debbie and what will hap-pen when they do. The question, unresolved, keeps us riveted even when the story itself slows down for detours.

Ford hides in front of us the secret love between Ethan and Martha in virtually every early shot, yet no words are spoken and the casual viewer could miss it altogether. Ford also strips away several obvious references in Nugent's script, leaving us with a hint of doubt as to whether this love was ever expressed in words, let alone consummated.

The film's other intense relationship is between Ethan and Martin. It starts out with great abuse and contempt on Ethan's part, and abundant deference on Martin's, who recognizes Ethan's authority, superior knowledge, and skills when it comes to understanding and fighting Co-manches. Some have compared it to the relationship between Ford and Wayne—the demanding, abusive father figure and the talented, sensi-tive son. But over the course of the film the dynamic between the two subtly changes. Ford quietly records the growing admiration that Ethan develops for Martin's moral courage and conviction, while Martin be-gins to harbor deep doubts about Ethan's motives and sanity. Jeffrey Hunter's performance, while less commanding than Wayne's, is power-ful and compelling. Hunter has to shout and storm to match Wayne's quieter power, but he usually holds his own. It is Martin who in the end kills Scar and rescues Debbie, and Martin who gets to return home, re-build the remains of his shattered family, and resume a normal life with the woman he loves, while Ethan is banished to the desert itself, con-demned "to wander forever between the winds"—the same fate as the Comanches he has dispatched to eternity.

The Searchers is filled with stunning visual tableaux. There is the Ed-wards family funeral early in the film, set on a forlorn hill with a wagon at lower right, a cluster of mourners in the middle, and the graves at the top as the worshippers sing "Shall We Gather at the River" until Ethan loudly insists on cutting the ceremony short so that he and the Rangers can resume the search for Lucy and Debbie. And there is the search party in a valley as Comanche warriors suddenly appear on both sides of the screen as if rising out of the land itself, riding parallel and silhouetted against the sky. And there is Debbie plunging down the side of a distant sand dune to warn Ethan and Martin that Scar and his men are coming to kill them. And, of course, there are the opening and closing shots, framed in the eternal doorway, of Ethan arriving and leaving. "These shots," the critic Roger Ebert has written, "are among the treasures of the cinema."

The final shot of Ethan walking away, filmed from inside the doorway of the Jorgensen ranch, is one of American cinema's most eloquent. The mission is accomplished, but there is no place for the avenger in the new civilization he has helped forge. Ford cannot kill Ethan—John Wayne is simply too strong to die—but he can exclude him.

With so few written notes to go by, there is only one way to document the creative decisions John Ford made on the set: by comparing Nugent's final shooting script to what actually appears on the screen. Nugent's script is justifiably considered one of the great Hollywood screenplays. And yet an astonishing fact emerges: every time he has the opportunity, Ford chooses to reduce or eliminate altogether the dialogue and exposition, substituting lyrical ambiguity for the prosaic clarity of the script. Given the choice between more words and less, Ford opts every time for less—and every time, in retrospect, he makes the right choice. It is here, in the consistent discipline of Ford's narrative decisions, that *The Searchers* becomes more than just a good Western; it becomes a work of cinematic art.

As always, Ford steadfastly refused to acknowledge that *The Searchers* contained any intellectual content, yet the film overtracks the themes and claims of one of the most high-end discussions of the meaning of the Western: a 1954 essay titled "The Westerner." Its author, Robert Warshow, a tall, slim New Yorker who was an editor at *Commentary* magazine, was obsessed with movies, comic books, theater, and other forms of popular culture at a time when such matters were deemed less than legitimate subjects for intellectual discourse. Although there is no evidence to suggest that either Ford or Nugent ever read it, the essay reads like a blueprint for Ethan Edwards. It captures the moral and spiritual fragility of the Western.

Like Ethan, Warshow's classic Western hero suffers from a loneliness and isolation that are "organic, not imposed on him by his situation but belonging to him intimately and testifying to his completeness."

Similarly, Warshow focuses on the contradiction at the heart of Ethan's character—that his code of honor is both admirable and morally repugnant at the same time: "The truth is that the Westerner comes into the field of serious art only when his moral code, without ceasing to be compelling, is seen also to be imperfect . . . a moral ambiguity which darkens his image and saves him from absurdity; this ambiguity arises from the fact that, whatever his justification, he is a killer of men."

This is Ethan Edwards, his code of vengeance and justice tainted by his racism and bloodlust. In the end, as Warshow anticipates, Ethan's victory requires him to be exiled from others.

"The pictures . . . end with his death or with his departure for some more remote frontier," Warshow writes. ". . . What we finally respond to is not his victory but his defeat." Warshow died suddenly and prematurely in the spring of 1955 while *The Searchers* was still being planned. Yet no essay has ever captured more precisely the ethos of the film.

Warshow made no reference to the other moral dilemma at the heart of the film: its morally compromised treatment of Native Americans. The Western film critic Jon Tuska has called *The Searchers* "one of the most viciously anti-Indian films ever made . . . The entire film is in effect an argument in favor of killing Indians as the only solution to the 'Indian problem.'"

Ford's racial attitudes may have been concealed behind a façade of paternalism toward his Navajo wards and Indians in general, Tuska argues, but it is racism nonetheless, and Tuska has no time for those who defend Ford's films as mythical in their content and intent. "What these apologists forget . . . is that Native Americans are not mythical and that the lies told about them in Ford's Western films could scarcely be expected to engender any greater social and cultural understanding . . . ," Tuska writes. "What apologists really mean by a 'mythic' dimension to a Western film is that part of it which they know to be a lie but which, for whatever reason, they still wish to embrace."

Native Americans themselves tend to be less offended by *The Searchers*. JoEllen Shively, a graduate student in philosophy at Stanford University in the late 1980s, arranged for Indian and Anglo focus groups to watch the film for her Ph.D. dissertation. She reported that 60 percent of the Indians and 50 percent of the whites identified with John Wayne, and 40 percent of Indians and 45 percent of whites with Jeffrey Hunter. None of the Indians identified with Scar.

Equally curious, some of the Indians noted and appreciated the humor in *The Searchers*, while none of the Anglos did. But both Indians and whites rooted for the good guys and both viewed the Indians in the film as the bad guys. "John Wayne, he's always cool, yet tough and strong," said a Native American mechanic. "He doesn't take anything from anybody."

Tom Grayson Colonnese, a Sante Sioux and director of the American Indian Studies Program at the University of Washington, writes that "asking Indians to watch a John Wayne Western is like asking someone if they would like to go back and visit the schoolyard where they used to get beat up every day."

Colonnese praised the film for depicting "the terrible effects of hate and prejudice, and seems to say that life can only go on if one triumphs over these emotions." Scar cannot let go of his hatred and therefore he dies; Ethan is able to soften his at the last moment and is allowed to live, albeit in emotional exile. The film, Colonnese concludes, "goes further than any other Western of its day in the direction of truth and fairness; but finally *The Searchers* was frustrating to us because it stops well short of being truly fair."

Colonnese's critical reading is hard to dismiss. Indians in *The Searchers* for the most part are rapists and killers, and the only benign Indian we meet is made the butt of a cruel and painful joke. "Look" is a chubby young Comanche woman whom Martin encounters while he and Ethan are searching for Debbie among the many forts and trading posts of Indian Territory. Ford plays this sequence for laughs. After a particularly elaborate exchange of goods with a group of reservation Comanches, Martin finds himself trailed by the woman, who informs him that he has acquired her as his wife as part of the trade. To send her back to her people would be an insult. Ethan takes cruel pleasure in Martin's faux pas. "Come along, Mrs. Pauley, join our merry crew!" he proclaims.

As they camp for the night, Ethan continues to mock Martin and his new "wife." Martin recoils when Look spreads out her blanket and lies down beside him. He plants his foot in the small of her back and sends her sprawling down a hill. Ethan breaks out in laughter.

Martin's vicious kick is a despicable act and totally out of character for him. But Ford genuinely means for us to find it funny. After all, here is a man who kicked Harry Carey Jr. in the rear every day on the set of *3 Godfathers* and casually slapped and punched other actors throughout his career. He thought it was funny. In this regard, his instincts betray him on film just as they betrayed him in life.

Still, a few minutes later in the picture, Ford evokes a far different response. The two men question Look about Scar, and it's clear she's frightened by the name. Later during the night Look flees but leaves behind a sign for Ethan and Martin to follow. Perhaps she wants to help them find Debbie; as usual, Ford refuses to spell out the motives of his character, leaving it for us to decide. Not long after, Ethan and Martin come across the smoking ruins of the Indian village, where they find Look's body among the corpses: she is one of those who has been slaughtered by soldiers in the Washita River massacre.

Even Ethan, the proud Indian hater, is repulsed by the sight, and he places Look's hat gently over her corpse. Are we supposed to hate the racism with which Ethan and Martin treat Look, or approve of their moral indignation when they find her dead body?

Just as in LeMay's novel, the most brutal racist sentiments in the film are spoken by Laurie Jorgensen. But Ford intensifies the hatred by having her deliver them while dressed in her white gown after her wedding to Charlie McCorry has been aborted following Martin's unexpected return home. Laurie demands that Martin give up the search for Debbie and let Ethan finish the mission alone. And when Martin refuses to comply, she explodes.

"Do you know what Ethan will do if he has a chance? He'll put a bullet in her brain! And I tell you Martha would want him to!"

"Only if I'm dead!" Martin replies.

Laurie's outburst might be forgiven: she's desperate to keep Martin at home, protect him from harm, and preserve her one chance for happiness, and she is willing to resort to any argument to get what she wants. But Ford wants to make clear that Ethan's violent and racist obsession is not just his personal psychosis but the community norm; even our spunky Laurie—a young woman we are meant to admire and sympathize with throughout the film—is not immune. Still, we know Laurie is wrong: the Martha we meet in the first act of the film would never have wanted Ethan to kill her daughter. Martha, like Mrs. Jorgensen and ultimately Debbie herself, would have wanted the bloodshed to end. And Martin is their willing agent. *The Searchers* ultimately is the triumph of this feminized vision of civilization—loving, inclusive, conciliatory—over Ethan and Scar's macho war without end.

Are these Ford's attitudes or the attitudes of the characters in the film? And can Ford be excused for his distorted depiction of Indians by saying they are mythic, fictional forces rather than realistic depictions?

Even Ford biographer Joseph McBride, one of the greatest and most magnanimous students of Ford's work, says he cannot decide. "The film is not an aberration but a crystallization of all the fears, obsessions, and contradictions which had been boiling up under the surface of Ford's work since his return from World War Two," he told me. "Ford undercuts the morality of the noble quest for Debbie. Instead of rescuing the damsel in distress, he seeks to kill her. What the film does that is very daring and honest is it gets you into the whole racist mind-set in a way that makes us very uncomfortable."

We are, of course, a long way from the original tale of Cynthia Ann Parker. She is no longer the legend's principal focus nor its abiding concern. Ford has literally moved the camera from focusing on the external search and turned it instead on ourselves, our deepest fears, and our prejudices.

What ties the two tales together is the masculine-feminine dichotomy. Men have traditionally driven the narrative—from the young Comanche warriors who massacred the settlers and abducted Cynthia Ann Parker (and Debbie Edwards), to the alleged historians who wrote, rewrote, and made up the account that became the accepted history, to Alan LeMay and John Ford themselves. The theme they rang was the painful, bloody, but inevitable triumph of white civilization: How the West Was Won. The underlying psychosexual theme was the protection and preservation of white women from the forces of barbarism. Cynthia Ann's (and Debbie's) permanent stain was having sex, voluntarily or not, with Comanches. But while the men were the dominant storytellers, several enterprising women came along over the decades to undermine those themes or at least humanize them.

Martin Pauley (Jeffrey Hunter), Laurie Jorgensen (Vera Miles), and her mother (Olive Carey). Martin serves as willing agent of the strong women in *The Searchers*.

The same masculine-versus-feminine conflicts play out in *The Searchers*. Ethan and Scar drive the blood feud, seeking retribution, but the women undermine them. The gender divide isn't neat and clean: Laurie Jorgensen supports Ethan's bloodstained quest for vengeance, while Martin Pauley is the willing agent of the feminine counternarrative. And Ford exposes the underlying sexual tension of the original tale and makes it the driving force of his story. Feminine values ultimately triumph. The family is restored.

Love defeats hatred. Martha—from beyond the grave—tames Ethan.

John Wayne understood this exactly. He told biographer Michael Munn, "When Ethan picks up Debbie at the end, I had to think, what's going through his mind as he looks into her face? I guess he saw in her eyes the woman he'd loved. And that was enough to overcome his hatred."

THE REVIEWS WERE GENERALLY POSITIVE, and a few were glowing. "Undoubtedly one of the greatest Westerns ever made for sheer scope, guts, and beauty," opined the *Hollywood Reporter*. Jack Moffitt, the reviewer, praised the acting, photography, and script: "Ford and Nugent show fine dramatic craftsmanship."

Motion Picture Herald hailed it as "one of the greatest of the great pictures of the American West" and compared it favorably to *The Covered Wagon*, *Stagecoach*, and *Shane*. Bosley Crowther of the *New York Times* called it "a rip-snorting Western as brashly entertaining as they come . . . [It boasts] a wealth of Western action that has the toughness of leather and the sting of a whip . . . Mr. Ford's scenic stuff, shot in color and VistaVision, in the expanse of Monument Valley that he loves, has his customary beauty and grandeur."

Others were more critical. *Film Bulletin* called the film "strange but fascinating . . . The plot is interrupted by sub-plots without any apparent pattern, and the narrative is at times so suggestive and subtle as to be obscure . . . Yet for all this, the total effect is enormously rich, interesting, and exciting."

Variety said the film was "overlong and repetitious," and complained "there are subtleties in the basically simple story that are not adequately explained." *The Nation* called it "long on brutality and short on logic or responsible behavior." *Time* magazine lamented "the lapses in logic and the general air of incoherence," and opined that John Ford's stock company of actors and crew may have gotten "too practiced and familiar . . .

Even John Wayne seems to have done it once too often as he makes his standardized end-of-film departure into the sunset."

What none of the critics, positive or negative, grasped was that *The Searchers* was a different kind of Western, something much darker and more disturbing than the usual fare. No one seemed to see Ethan Edwards as anything less than a standard-issue John Wayne action hero. Ethan's racism, his mania, and his bloodlust all passed by without comment. "Racism was so endemic in our culture that people didn't even notice it," said Joseph McBride. "They treated Wayne as a conventional Western hero. Not one person got it."

Still, Ethan was a memorable character. Buddy Holly and his drummer, Jerry Allison, saw *The Searchers* when it first opened at the State Theater in Lubbock, Texas—the heart of what had once been Comancheria. They came out and wrote "That'll Be the Day"—a phrase Ethan Edwards utters four times during the film—which became a number one hit in the fall of 1957. It later became the first demo recorded by a Liverpool group known as the Quarrymen, who later renamed themselves the Beatles. Another first-rate Liverpool band called themselves the Searchers after the film.

The British film critic Lindsay Anderson, a longtime champion of Ford's work who was beginning to direct his own movies, disliked the film. Anderson felt Ford had abandoned his trademark optimistic celebration of the American spirit for something darker and more unsavory. Ethan Edwards was "an unmistakable neurotic," complained Anderson. "Now what is Ford, or all directors, to do with a hero like this?"

Others felt inspired. Jean-Luc Godard, the French New Wave critic and director, said he wept at the end of the film, overwhelmed by the "mystery and fascination of this American cinema." Although a committed leftist, Godard asked of himself almost plaintively, "How can I hate John Wayne upholding [Barry] Goldwater and yet love him tenderly when, abruptly, he takes Natalie Wood into his arms in the last reel of *The Searchers*?"

When the film failed to get any Academy Award nominations or other honors, Wayne pronounced himself mystified. "You know, I just don't understand why that film wasn't better received," he told one interviewer. Speaking of Ford, he added, "I think it is his best Western." Wayne was so impressed with the film, and with his character, that he named a son, born in 1962, John Ethan Wayne.

"Ethan Edwards," Wayne declared, "was probably the most fascinating character I ever played in a John Ford Western."

21.

The Legacy (Hollywood, 1956–2010)

The Searchers came and went, embraced lightly—just as Sonny Whitney and Merian C. Cooper had feared—as another John Wayne Western. It garnered positive reviews, made a reasonable profit, and then disappeared, exiled by the early 1960s to the relatively new medium of television, where it received an occasional showing, cut and pasted to coexist with commercials inside a two-hour frame. John Ford pronounced himself puzzled by the film's lack of success, John Wayne said he was surprised and disappointed, but both men quickly moved on. Wayne's career took a slight detour—he starred in several duds, including *Jet Pilot* (1957), Howard Hughes's bizarre Cold War romantic comedy, and John Huston's incoherent *The Barbarian and the Geisha* (1958)—before triumphing in *Rio Bravo* (1959), directed by Howard Hawks, Ford's foremost rival when it came to the proper use of the Wayne persona. Ford's career, meanwhile, resumed its slow arc of decline.

The Searchers was "a good picture," Ford told Joe McBride. "It made a lot of money, and that's the ultimate end." Spoken like an obituary.

Ford returned to the captivity theme in 1961 with the disappointing *Two Rode Together*, a tepid, uninspired effort. James Stewart and Richard Widmark play a marshal and an army officer dispatched to retrieve white captives from Comanches led by Quanah Parker. But the Quanah portrayed here is a cruel and avaricious warrior, not the conciliatory figure of real life. To add further insult, he is played by Henry Brandon, the same actor who played Scar in *The Searchers*. Tall and muscular, Brandon has the physicality to play Quanah, but Frank Nugent's script and Ford's direction give Brandon none of the depth.

Two Rode Together is a weird recapitulation of *The Searchers*—similar to the way Francis Ford Coppola's unfortunate *The Godfather Part III* inadvertently mocks the greatness of the first two *Godfather* films. Members of Ford's usual stock company of supporting players are on hand: John Qualen, Andy Devine, Anna Lee, Harry Carey Jr., Olive Carey, Mae Marsh, and Ken Curtis. But Nugent's script is crude and meandering, with none of the narrative tension that makes *The Searchers* so compelling. The acting is terrible: Stewart and Widmark play their roles for maximum humor and look uncomfortable and ridiculous throughout. Carey and Curtis painfully ham it up. Ford repeats older and better ideas from previous films. Stewart, playing the local marshal, is introduced balancing himself on a chair with his long legs up on a railing—just as Henry Fonda did much more charmingly fifteen years earlier as Wyatt Earp in *My Darling Clementine*. Carey and Curtis speak in the same inept dryland accents that Curtis used to play Charlie McCorry in *The Searchers*, and they stage a comic fight with Widmark's character that echoes the slapstick fistfight of Martin Pauley and Charlie McCorry in *The Searchers*. A blonde Shirley Jones in blue denims and pigtails generates the same tomboy energy and repressed sexuality of Vera Miles's Laurie, but it's all for a lost cause.

There is a kernel of an idea here—in effect picking up the story of Debbie after she is rescued from the Comanches, echoing the true story of Cynthia Ann Parker's miserable life with her white relatives after her purported liberation. But the racist sentiments of the main characters are endorsed rather than undermined, as they are in *The Searchers*.

"Would you like me to tell you what this little angel looks like now?" demands Jimmy Stewart's character, explaining to Shirley Jones's character how her younger brother, captured a decade earlier by Comanches, would have been raised. "That kid has braids down to here now, stiff stinkin' braids filled with buffalo grease, and he's got a scar there and scar there . . . just to prove he's a man. He forgot his English—he just grunts Comanche now, just grunts . . . and he's killed and he's taken scalps, white man's scalps, and given a chance, sister, he'd rape you . . . and when he's finished he'd trade you off to one of the other bucks for a good knife or bad rifle. Now is that what you want me to bring back to you?"

The speech is similar to the harsh outburst that Laurie Jorgensen makes to Martin Pauley, her fiancé, in *The Searchers*. The difference is that Ford, identifying with Martin, clearly repudiates these sentiments in *The Searchers*, whereas in *Two Rode Together* they are treated as unpleasant but undeniable truths.

As in *The Searchers*, there is a dance that serves as a pivotal moment in the life of the community, only in this case Ford uses the event—a military officers' ball—to illustrate the raging hypocrisy of white society toward former captives. Stewart gives yet another speech—for a director who hates exposition, Ford allows it to run amok in *Two Rode Together*—this time berating the white hypocrites who are polite to a newly freed captive to her face yet disdainful of her behind her back: "This afternoon she asked me to take her back because she was treated better by the Comanches than she was treated by some of you."

Ford took on *Two Rode Together* for the money and soon lost interest, according to his grandson Dan Ford. "The worst piece of crap I've directed in twenty years" was Ford's own definitive verdict.

He made one more great Western, *The Man Who Shot Liberty Valance* (1962), starring Stewart and Wayne. Stewart plays a lawyer-politician who is credited with confronting and shooting dead a murderous thug who is terrorizing a small town, thus bringing civilization and eventual statehood to the community, while Wayne is a rough-hewn rancher and man of action who actually did the killing. The Stewart character achieves fame and fortune and the hand in marriage of Vera Miles, while the Wayne character dies a lonely and forgotten alcoholic. Ford filmed it in black-and-white and shot most of it on a soundstage at Paramount, and it was a dark, somber, pessimistic picture. There was no Monument Valley, no Technicolor flourishes, and no Indians. Yet the film was Ford's final statement about the gap between fact and myth, and the role that legend played in the civilizing of the American West. It was also his final film with Wayne, whose character more than ever seemed to reflect Ford's own. It concludes with the famous moment when a newspaper editor rejects publishing Stewart's account of what really happened: "This is the West, sir. When the legend becomes fact, print the legend."

"*The Man Who Shot Liberty Valance* is a serious assault on everything," said Peter Bogdanovich. "It tells us our legends are false, that our history is wrong and that everything we believe in is a lie."

Ford made one more attempt to come to grips with the Native American experience. *Cheyenne Autumn* (1964) was his epic retelling of the attempt of a band of Cheyenne to escape captivity in Oklahoma and return to their native homeland in Wyoming and Colorado—the same story Alan LeMay had fictionalized in *Painted Ponies* in 1926. Ford, assisted once again by his son Pat, sought to tell the tale with great empathy and compassion, and he again employed Widmark and Stewart, along with stock company regulars like Ben Johnson, Harry Carey Jr., Patrick Wayne, George O'Brien, and John Carradine. He filmed for the seventh and final time in Monument Valley, using a large cast of Navajos to play the Cheyenne.

In *Cheyenne Autumn*, Ford reverses past roles, portraying the Indian leaders as reasonable, moral, and wise, and many of the whites as venal, brutal, and dishonest. Some of the scenes are stunning in their visual composition, but the narrative is flat and plodding and, at 156 minutes, the film is at least a half hour too long. It was a critical and commercial failure, although its reputation has improved over the years. The film's elegiac quality is only enhanced by the retrospective knowledge that it was Ford's final Western. His career was slowly deflating, his reputation for artistry buried under the perception that he was, indeed, what he had long claimed to be: a humble maker of Westerns at a time when the Western was in critical and popular decline. At the turn of the new millennium, noted the film scholar Gerald Peary, himself a rabid Ford fan, John Ford was largely forgotten by the public: "Young people, including film students, haven't seen Ford's movies, and seem uninterested in going back and catching up."

To an extent Peary blamed Ford himself for resolutely refusing to defend himself as an artist. "You say someone's called me the greatest poet of the Western saga," Ford told the author Walter Wagner in 1973 a few months before his death. "I am not a poet, and I don't know what a Western saga is. I would say that it is horseshit. I'm just a hardworking, run-of-the-mill director."

While much of Ford's work has drifted into obscurity, *The Searchers* is a notable exception. But its resurrection was a slow process. As was often true of mainstream Hollywood directors, the first fans to recognize Ford's artistic greatness were French film critics who were developing the auteur theory that despite the fact that filmmaking is a collective enterprise—and that each studio during Hollywood's golden era has its own distinct filmmaking personality—the director is its heart and soul, the one contributor whose personal sensibility is discernible and critical to the artistic process. While this might not be true for many directors, it surely is the case with Ford. Like Hitchcock, Hawks, William Wyler, Preston Sturges, and a handful of others, Ford's values, visual sense, and passions are readily apparent in all his films, even the bad ones. The French critic Jean-Luc Godard, soon to launch his own filmmaking career with *Breathless* (1960), compared the ending of *The Searchers* to "Ulysses being reunited with Telemachus." In the United States, the

Village Voice critic Andrew Sarris, Eugene Archer of the *New York Times*, and Peter Bogdanovich, another critic with filmmaking aspirations, championed Ford and Hawks. I recall Sarris showing *The Searchers* in the inaugural year of his introductory film course on Thursday evenings in the basement of Butler Library at Columbia University in 1970. He presented it as the apogee of great Hollywood filmmaking.

Like Sarris, film professors at scattered campuses revived and celebrated *The Searchers* in their classes and film festivals, spreading word of its greatness to a new generation of film buffs. A pivotal article was "Prisoner of the Desert," a 1971 essay by Joseph McBride and Michael Wilmington in *Sight and Sound* magazine. It praised in ringing terms Ford's artistry and power: "*The Searchers* has that clear yet intangible quality which characterizes an artist's masterpiece—the sense that he has gone beyond his customary limits, submitted his deepest tenets to the test, and dared to exceed even what we might have expected of him."

The essay explored the film's important themes, most especially Ethan's pathology and Ford's obsession with rape and miscegenation between whites and Indians. It traced the connection between Ethan and Scar as two warriors driven to madness and revenge by the murder of their families. Scar, it argued, "is not so much a character as a crazy mirror of Ethan's desires." The two men, "blood brothers in their commitment to primitive justice, have sacrificed themselves to make civilization possible. This is the meaning of the door opening and closing on the wilderness. It is the story of America." The article's conclusion eerily echoes the outsized original ambitions of C. V. Whitney, the man who bankrolled it.

The other cohort who loved and championed *The Searchers* was a younger generation of aspiring American filmmakers and screenwriters, including Martin Scorsese, Steven Spielberg, George Lucas, John Milius, Curtis Hanson, and Paul Schrader, all of whom grew up watching the film and were captured by its beauty, violence, and powerful storytelling. Each of them has testified to its abiding influence over their own filmmaking.

Scorsese was thirteen when he journeyed uptown from Little Italy in Manhattan with two friends to the landmark Criterion Theatre in Times Square to see *The Searchers*. They entered in the middle of the picture and were mesmerized by its stunning visuals and emotional resonance. Scorsese recalled the clarity of the VistaVision high resolution. Over the years, as he watched the film on television, the subtext of

Ethan Edwards's inner turmoil and slow psychological disintegration became more and more apparent to him. Curtis Hanson recalled being frightened by the violence and the emotions when he first saw it at the Sherman Theatre, a second-run movie house in the San Fernando Valley. John Milius first saw it four times in a row at a theater in Westwood Village in Los Angeles. "I wanted to be Scar," he recalled.

When he was about fifteen years old in the early 1960s, Spielberg met Ford at the director's office. Spielberg recalled being ushered into the empty office and stared at a series of Frederic Remington and Charles M. Russell paintings on the wall. Then Ford swept in, "dressed like a big game hunter" with his trademark floppy hat, eye patch, and half-chewed handkerchief. Spielberg recalled that Ford had smeared lipstick on his face.

"So you wanna be a picture maker," Ford declared. "What do you know about? You see these paintings around the office? Tell me what you see in that first painting."

Spielberg sputtered for a minute. "No, no, no, no," Ford broke in. "Where's the horizon? Can't you find the horizon? Don't point where it is. Look at the whole picture." When Spielberg pointed out that the horizon was at the very bottom, Ford replied, "Fine."

"When you can come to the conclusion that putting the horizon at the top of the frame or the bottom of the frame is a lot better than putting it in the middle of the frame, then you may someday make a good picture maker. Now get out of here."

By the late 1970s, when Spielberg, Scorsese, Lucas, and their fellow filmmakers were ascendant, they spoke fondly of the impact *The Searchers* had had on their work. Scorsese's first feature film, *Who's That Knocking at My Door* (1967), contains a six-minute sequence in which Harvey Keitel's character attempts to seduce Zina Bethune's while waiting for the Staten Island Ferry by telling her all about the film. There are unmistakable echoes of *The Searchers* in *Star Wars* (1977), *Close Encounters of the Third Kind* (1977), and *Hardcore* (1979).

"He was a great artist," said John Milius of Ford. "He could speak to your heart and it meant something . . . He could do it in two or three strokes where it would take other good directors seven or eight and they wouldn't get it as well. He's a storyteller like Homer. When Homer got through with a story, you had something you could read forever."

Spielberg still worships at Ford's altar. As executive producer of *Cowboys & Aliens* (2011), a mash-up of the Western and sci-fi genres, he screened a new print of *The Searchers* for director Jon Favreau and the screenplay writers to show them what a classic Western looks like. And *War Horse* (2011), Spielberg's World War One epic, echoes with Fordian themes and visual references. "Ford's in my mind when I make a lot of my pictures," Spielberg told the author Mark Harris. "I grew up with John Ford movies and I know a lot about his work and have studied him. I think the thing that might resemble a John Ford movie more than anything else is that Ford celebrated rituals and traditions and he celebrated the land. In *War Horse*, the land is a character."

Still, Scorsese's *Taxi Driver* (1976) probably comes the closest to reimagining *The Searchers* for the modern age. Travis Bickle (Robert De Niro), the crazed New York cabbie who decides to stage his own one-man guerrilla raid on the pimps who have turned a young girl into a prostitute, is Ethan Edwards transplanted a century later from the Texas frontier to the urban jungle. Travis's obsessions, his twisted personal code, his use of gun violence as a tool of purification—all of these mirror Ethan. So does the refusal of the object of the search—in this case Jodie Foster's child hooker—to acquiesce in her own rescue. Crashing through the boundaries of time and space, Jodie Foster played Cynthia Ann Parker.

In declaring the influence of *The Searchers* to be the cinematic equivalent of *Huckleberry Finn*, the film critic Stuart Byron attributed the film's cult status to "an unholy alliance of critics, buffs, and filmmakers." But *The Searchers* had not reached the same pinnacle of artistic acceptance as *Casablanca*, *Citizen Kane*, the films of Charlie Chaplin, or the Marx Brothers comedies, nor would it ever, Byron argued, because of John Wayne. The Duke's macho, right-wing politics prevented many cinephiles from embracing the film. It would take another generation to accept the artistry of his performance.

Still, the film gradually worked its way up the roster of great cinema. After failing to make the top 100 list in a 1962 poll of *Sight and Sound*, the magazine of the highly respected British Film Institute, ten years later it was ranked eighteenth best among American films. In 2008 it finished at the top of an American Film Institute poll as the greatest Western in film history. And in August 2012 the *Sight and Sound* poll ranked it the seventh-greatest film of all time.

Not every modern critic has embraced *The Searchers*. Richard Schickel blasted Ford as a drunk, tyrant, and bully. *The Searchers*, he wrote, was "a spoiled masterpiece," marred by Ford's "tasteless ridicule" of Look, the acquired Indian bride of Martin, and "a stupefying subplot" of the thwarted romance of Martin and Laurie. The *New Yorker* film critic

Pauline Kael called it "a peculiarly formal and stilted movie . . . You can read a lot into it, but it isn't very enjoyable. The lines are often awkward and the line readings worse, and the film is often static, despite economic, quick editing."

The aesthetic debate has been rekindled by a new generation of cultural critics. The novelist Jonathan Lethem, in his essay "Defending *The Searchers*," describes his lifelong love affair with the film, and his intense anger and humiliation when fellow students at Bennington College mocked it as stilted and old-fashioned. "The pressure of the film, its brazen ambiguity, was too much," writes Lethem. "It was easier to view it as a racist antique, a naïve and turgid artifact dredged out of our parents' bankrupt fifties culture."

The scene of Martin Pauley physically abusing Look, his Indian pseudo-bride, was "of such giddy misogyny, such willful racism, it seemed indefensible by design," writes Lethem.

Lethem's essay succumbs to his own obsessive ambivalence about America itself: "*The Searchers* strives on, maddened, obsessed, through ruined landscapes incapable of containing it . . . everywhere shrugging off categories, refusing the petitions of embarrassment and taste, defying explanation or defense as only great art or great abomination ever could."

Similarly, Lethem is obsessed by John Wayne. "His persona gathers in one place the allure of violence, the call away from the frontier, the tortured ambivalence toward women and the home, the dark pleasure of soured romanticism—all those things that reside unspoken at the center of our sense of what it means to be a man in America."

Others are less impressed. *The Searchers* "is preposterous in its plotting, spasmodic in its pacing, unfunny in its hijinks, bipolar in its politics, alternately sodden and convulsive in its acting, not to mention *boring*," writes Stephen Metcalf, in a piece titled "The Worst Best Movie" in the online magazine *Slate*. He attributes the film's enduring critical reputation to "two influential and mutually reinforcing constituencies: critics whose careers emerged out of the rise of 'film studies' as a discrete and self-respecting academic discipline; and the first generation of filmmakers—Scorcese and Schrader, but also Francis Ford Coppola, John Milius and George Lucas—whose careers began in film school.

"In Ford's Ethan the avatars of the New Hollywood found a very romantic allegory for the director as monomaniacal obsessive on a quest that others along the way may only find perverse," writes Metcalf. The film's ambiguity and intense focus on race and gender make it a feast for deconstructionists, he adds, with an audible sneer.

The one auteur who has almost always been missing from the discussion is the man who invented *The Searchers*, Alan LeMay. He went on to write two more Western novels, one of which, *The Unforgiven*, picked up the racial themes of *The Searchers* and took them another step. This time it was a white pioneer family that adopted a Kiowa baby who survived the massacre of her village. The members of the Zachary family never tell the girl her true origins until her Kiowa brother and his warriors return to claim her and lay siege to the family's sod dwelling. The prejudiced white community refuses to intervene, leaving the Zacharys to fend off the Kiowa attack alone. In the ensuing battle, Rachel must choose between her adopted white family and her Kiowa heritage. *The Unforgiven* was made into a movie in 1960 directed by John Huston and starring Burt Lancaster and Audrey Hepburn. If nothing else the film, which is awkward, stiff, and unconvincing, demonstrates that the kind of mastery of the Western that John Ford seemed to wield effortlessly is far from automatic; even a gifted filmmaker like Huston couldn't begin to get it right.

Alan LeMay died of a brain tumor in 1964 in relative obscurity; the few obituaries were brief. "Writers are forgotten people out here," Alan's widow, Arlene, told *Washington Post* film critic Gary Arnold in 1979.

Arnold was one of the few critics to have championed the novel version of *The Searchers* after the film's critical emergence; in fact, he regards the book as the indispensable element in the greatness of the movie. Arnold regrets that Ford sacrificed LeMay's original concluding scene for his own, more visual closure. "LeMay devised stunning climactic and concluding episodes," writes Arnold. "They leave emotional reverberations that the movie never quite equals."

Arnold admires Ford's ending, which left Wayne's character beyond the family threshold, proud and alone. "But there's also an unseen, forgotten man lingering out there in the cinematic ether," concludes Arnold, "the storyteller who imagined *The Searchers* in the first place."

Another debate has focused on gender issues. In 2007 the feminist social critic Susan Faludi invoked the film's purportedly macho themes as a prime example of how American society, whenever under sustained attack, falls back on familiar myths of male virtue and domination. This intuitive response holds true, argues Faludi, whether the enemy is Comanche warriors in nineteenth-century Texas or Islamic terrorists in twenty-first-century New York. Faludi reinterpreted the abduction tales of Cynthia Ann and Rachel Plummer from a feminist perspective, and she named her book *The Terror Dream* after a passage in LeMay's novel. But while she made a compelling point about the American response to the September 11 attacks, Faludi badly misread the meaning and message of *The Searchers*. Whatever stereotypes they may evoke, Ford's women are strong, fearless, determined, and in the end triumphant. Martha, Mrs. Jorgensen, Debbie, and their male surrogate, Martin Pauley, are the winners. The macho men—Ethan and Scar—are either killed or excluded.

And so *The Searchers* continues to ride the distant ridge in American cultural discourse, fated to be talked about and admired—and misunderstood—more than viewed.

Its fiftieth anniversary came and went in 2006 with little fanfare. James D'Arc of Brigham Young University worked with Brian Jamieson of Warner Brothers to put out a special DVD edition. "We worked together on a project that would include material from the collection, the original soundtrack and all of that, a booklet and everything," D'Arc recalled. But the executives at Warner Brothers killed the most ambitious parts of the project. The two-DVD set that was released was a shadow of what D'Arc and Jamieson had in mind. "It's a real shame," said D'Arc. "That struggle carried on for a good three years."

Several mysteries remain about the film. In a 1956 *Warner Brothers Presents* TV show promoting the movie, Jeffrey Hunter tells host Gig Young that John Ford shot seven reels of film about the making of the movie—"an unprecedented film about a film," says Hunter. The Warner Brothers program shows some scenes of bulldozers, crew workers, John Ford, and John Wayne. All of that footage seems to have disappeared.

Leith Adams, a Warner Brothers studio archivist, tried unsuccessfully to track it down. He spoke to the widow of Brick Marquard, one of Ford's favorite cameramen, who recalled that when her husband visited the set at Monument Valley during the filming, Ford handed him a camera and asked him to shoot the making of the movie. Mrs. Marquard said she and Brick later attended a private screening of an hour or two of the footage with Ford, his wife, and Merian Cooper. Then it vanished. "I've had people searching high and low for original color footage in the vaults and I'm pretty sure it isn't there," said Adams.

Adams also failed to locate most of Ford's outtakes from the film that might help explain the choices the director made and, most especially, the variations of the climactic scene when Ethan decides to spare Debbie's life. One likely explanation: Ford shot so economically that outtakes were rare, and he surely didn't want those that may have existed to fall into the hands of the studio executives he so richly despised. Perhaps he made them disappear.

Similarly, the notes and files that Alan LeMay compiled during of the writing of the novel have largely vanished. After her husband's death, Arlene LeMay donated twenty-three boxes of Alan's papers to the Charles E. Young Library at UCLA. The archives reveal Alan to have been a meticulous researcher of his historical novels and Westerns, but they contain virtually no *Searchers* material. Arlene died in 1993, and Alan's children have no idea where the *Searchers* files have gone.

By now *The Searchers* itself has become a legend and the mythmakers themselves have become mythic. Ford is an historic figure, revered by many. Wayne these days is more iconic than real. The purported macho meaning of his persona—captured in the still potent but sad and readily parodied figure of his later life and work—has outstripped his actual performances in his best films. And *The Searchers* is perhaps the greatest Hollywood film that few people have seen. It is hiding in plain sight, gaining in stature even as it lingers in a space between legend and obscurity. Like the generation that first dismissed it as just another Hollywood Western, we think we know what it is about, but its relentless ambiguity defeats us. We honor its ambition and its artistry. But we have no firm sense of what it means nor how truly great and disturbing it is.

Epilogue: (Quanah, Texas, June 2011)

The fierce Texas sun was incinerating its way toward another 101-degree day on a Saturday morning in early June as the procession began its solemn trek through the half-abandoned downtown of Quanah, Texas, population 2,437. A muscular young man named Ronnie McSwain led the way, dressed in a bright yellow vest and pants with white fringe and moccasins and a bristling array of eagle feathers, jingle-jangling up the broad, empty main street past a silent audience of boarded-up storefronts, artists' galleries, and preservation projects. He was followed by Don Parker, one of Quanah's great-grandsons, a dignified man of sixty-five riding erect on a handsome brown steed and gripping the red, blue, and yellow Comanche Nation flag in his left hand. Then came Don's older brother Ron, in a white-feathered ceremonial war bonnet similar to the one his great-grandfather wore more than a century ago. Then a handful of others, friends and relatives, including Sarah McReynolds, director of the Parker's Fort State Park, dressed in buckskins as a tribute to Quanah's long-lost mother, the tragic, iconic Cynthia Ann.

Even at a slow pace, it took them only ten minutes to reach the town square. They were met there by Baldwin Parker Jr., who at age ninety-three was Quanah's oldest surviving grandson, and a crowd of two hundred extended family members, local dignitaries, and onlookers. Baldwin, too, was wearing a bright red feathered chief's bonnet. His son Ron took his arm and helped him to the microphone, where Baldwin recited the gentle blessing that Quanah himself had once bestowed upon the town that bears his name:

"May the Great Spirit smile on your little town, may the rain fall in season, and in the warmth of the sunshine after the rain may the earth yield bountifully. May peace and contentment be with you and your children forever."

Baldwin was not a solemn man. When the mayor of Quanah handed him a key to the city, he asked if it opened any local bank vaults.

The story of Cynthia Ann Parker's abduction by Comanches in 1836, her recapture by U.S. cavalrymen and Texas Rangers in 1860, and the rise to prominence of Quanah Parker, her surviving child, was re-created and reimagined over many generations, each for its own needs and reasons. But the story did not end with *The Searchers*. Like the legend itself, the two sides of Cynthia Ann's family—Texan and Comanche—have endured. They hold separate annual family reunions each summer, send emissaries to each other's events, and get together to honor their ancestors, retell their stories, and bask in their myths.

There are Texas towns named after Quanah and his father, Peta Nocona, a Cynthia Ann Parker Elementary School in Houston and a Cynthia Ann Parker College of Liberal Arts at Hardin-Simmons University in Abilene, Texas. *Lone Star Trilogy*, a homespun ballet featuring Cynthia Ann, Charles Goodnight's wife, Molly, and Frenchy McCormick, a notorious saloon hall dancer, had its world premiere in Amarillo in April 2011. Country music star Larry Gatlin wrote the music, lyrics, and story for a musical called *Quanah* that had several public readings, including one at Pace University in Manhattan in January 2010. There are Cynthia Ann reenactors who tour Texas public schools, and a bay gelding named Quanah Parker who raced in the United Kingdom.

The year 2011 was the one hundredth anniversary of Quanah's death, and the emphasis was on peace and friendship between white people and red. The story had acquired an added layer of significance since the election three years earlier of Barack Obama. Like Quanah, the American president was the talented child of a union between a man and a woman of different races and different worlds. And, like Quanah's, his ascendancy was historic, holding out the possibility of reconciliation in a country founded on slavery, racial strife, and protracted warfare between whites and Indians on its limestone plains.

Ever since they first invited Quanah to the town's founding celebration in 1886, the town fathers have periodically welcomed his heirs. Like many North Texas towns, Quanah's downtown has suffered a steady economic decline, and city officials were hoping the family reunion might give their community a much-needed boost. There were storytelling sessions, a gourd dance, a chuck-wagon banquet in the local meeting hall, book talks, and field trips to places of significance in the saga of Cynthia Ann and Quanah, including the site of the Pease River massacre where she was recaptured by troopers in December 1860 and forced against her will to return to her white family after twenty-four years with the Comanches.

But there was one historic site seventy-one miles to the northeast in neighboring Oklahoma that was too far away to make the list. It was, however, the most significant and amazing place of all.

THERE IS NO ROAD SIGN for the Star House. Visitors knew to pull up at the Trading Post Restaurant and Indian Store on the main Cache road, just off State Highway 62—a four-lane designated as the Quanah Parker Trailway. You entered the coffee shop and asked for Wayne Gipson, a quiet man with curly blond hair, a rumpled T-shirt, and jeans. In the late afternoon, after the regulars had drained their final cups of coffee and cleared out, Wayne took visitors for a drive down a winding dirt road behind the trading post, past a collection of faded amusement rides and attractions. There was a rusted narrow-gauge railroad track, the sullen ruins of a wooden rodeo grandstand, an abandoned Ferris wheel and bumper cars, and a collection of old buildings: a church, a one-room schoolhouse, a newspaper office, a music hall, a drugstore, a livery stable, a ranger station, and a homesteader's cabin where the outlaw Frank James took up residence after retiring from a career in the family crime business. But the largest and most impressive site presided alone in the back of the property: Quanah Parker's aging two-story mansion.

After Herbert Woesner, Wayne's uncle, saved the Star House from destruction in 1958 by purchasing it and moving it to this site, he worked hard to preserve it. He replastered many of the interior walls and found matching wallpaper for Quanah's ground-floor bedroom and hallway. He nailed soda bottle caps to the soles of his shoes for traction and climbed the steep slanted roof to repair holes and replace missing shingles. He arranged for the return of some of the original furniture that had been sent to the Fort Sill Museum—including the long oak table on which Quanah had served dinner to Theodore Roosevelt—and found matching period pieces for the rest. When vandals threatened the property, he even slept on the premises. But Woesner was a fiercely independent man who followed his own code. He refused to accept government money for restoration or repair work, and he brooked no interference from outsiders. "I don't believe in restoring," he once said. "If you're going to restore, you might as well just build new. I believe in preserving."

Woesner loved history, and he made himself into the resident expert on Quanah Parker and the origins of the house. He also forged bonds of friendship and loyalty with the Parker family and encouraged Quanah's heirs to hold their annual reunion and powwow at the site. Baldwin Parker Jr. said he could feel his grandfather's spirit every time he visited there, and some of the Parkers reported seeing their illustrious ancestor on the porch at dusk. Herbert also considered it his personal obligation to give tours of the house to anyone who asked.

For a time Woesner saw the Star House as the centerpiece attraction for his grand vision of a family entertainment and historical center called Eagle Park, named in honor of Quanah. He purchased and installed the rides and the rodeo grandstands and a dance palace. And he began collecting orphaned historical buildings from around Oklahoma, jacking them up and hauling them to Eagle Park on the back of a long, low trailer truck just as he'd done the Star House. Woesner figured families would buy a day pass that included the historical sites as well as the rides. He believed they'd be as entranced as he was by the Star House and its neighbors. But few were interested. Eagle Park survived into the mid-1980s, when the combined forces of television, rising liability insurance rates, and demanding government safety inspectors finally shut it down. The buildings were now settling gently into irredeemable decay, all of them boarded up and seldom entered except for the Star House. Eagle Park was a ghost town.

As Herbert Woesner aged, he grew less able to maintain the Star House. The columns of the stately front porch began to sag, the porch skirt separated from its supports, and tree roots undermined its foundations. The roof dipped and leaked, and tree limbs punched holes in its skin, causing water damage to the second floor. Wind and rain loosened the shingles and peeled off the protective flashing. The ceiling of the dining room also leaked, staining the floor below.

When Herbert died of cancer in 2008 at age eighty-three, his funeral was held on the front porch. Ron Parker wept as he spoke of Woesner's warm deeds and friendship, and the following year's reunion was dedicated to his memory. Soon after the ceremony, the Parkers began to discuss how to save their famous ancestor's home from further deterioration. "For us it's a sacred place," said Ron. "The Woesners have always treated us wonderfully, and we know they want to do the best for the house, but we worry about its future."

Ron Parker in his great-grandfather's bedroom at the Star House, June 2008.

With his uncle gone, Wayne accepted the role of tour guide and cus-
todian. He proudly showed the dining room where Quanah entertained Teddy Roosevelt: on the wall is a photo of Quanah in a dignified
pose at the head of the table. In Quanah's bedroom was a photo of the
chief sitting stiffly next to the picture taken in Fort Worth in 1861 of his
mother and his sister, Cynthia Ann and Prairie Flower, that Texas governor Sul Ross sent to his former enemy. The woodstove in the room
next to Quanah's bedroom was original. So was some of the wallpaper.
The old wheelchair of Topay, Quanah's last surviving widow—she lived
until 1965—resided in a heap on the floor in the front foyer.

Ardith Parker Leming, one of Quanah's great-granddaughters, loved
to give tours of the house in her down-to-earth manner. She said Neda
Birdsong, one of her great-aunts, who lived there for nearly fifty years
after her father's death in 1911, used to keep a wig in the top drawer of
her dresser to show visitors when she got tired of people asking if there
was a scalp in the house.

Like lots of visitors over the years, Ardith couldn't help but bring up
Quanah's practice of polygamy. "They say there was no jealousy between
the wives," she told visitors. "Do you believe that? I don't believe it."

Inside, there were dark stains on the worn red carpet, and a family of bats had taken up residence in a downstairs hallway. The stairway lead-ing to the second floor had been sealed off: the leaky roof had made the floor too treacherous for visitors. There was no fire alarm system or in-ternal sprinklers, and it was clear that a mischievous juvenile delinquent with a box of matches could likely send the place to a fiery oblivion within minutes.

One contractor's report estimated that what it called "temporary stabi-lization measures" could be done for $20,000. It would likely cost hun-dreds of thousands more to restore and preserve the house. "In the event these temporary measures are not taken, we believe the structure will be-gin to accelerate and experience even greater damage," the undated report concluded. "At this time it is becoming unsafe to enter the structure."

The house has been on the National Register of Historic Places since 1972, and in recent years has been listed as one of Oklahoma's ten most endangered historic places. But there was no public funding attached to these designations.

"Lots of people had wanted to buy it," Kathy Gipson Treadwell, Her-bert's younger sister, told me in a 2009 interview. "They wanted to move it to the Fort Worth Stockyards, they wanted to move it to Quanah, Texas, they wanted to move it up here to the highway and make a visitors' center out of it. Herbert said the house is where it belongs and where it's going to stay. He just always wanted it to be left here, just as it was."

Kathy was devoted to her brother and to the trading post. She worked in the kitchen of the restaurant seven days a week and 365 days a year, including Christmas Day, when the trading post fed the needy for free. It was one of the few places in town where white folks and red folks mingled freely. But Kathy died in 2011, leaving Wayne and his sister Ginger to search for a solution that would preserve the house while maintaining the Parker family connection. It was a burdensome legacy. Officials of the Comanche Nation asked to take control of the house. Some proposed moving it yet again, back to the main road, restoring it, and perhaps even turning it into a casino. The Parker family was hor-rified at the prospect. A Texas businessman again proposed moving it to Fort Worth.

"There are people showing up all the time offering to help us, telling us we need to preserve this and that, but no one gives us any practical advice," said Wayne Gipson, who ruefully admitted he and his sister did not know what to do with the Star House.

* * *

SOME OF THE OTHER HISTORIC SITES connected to the Parker saga are far more secure. Isaac Parker's old log cabin in Birdville, west of Fort Worth, where he first brought his niece Cynthia Ann after she was recaptured from the Comanches, has survived for nearly 170 years. Like the Star House, it has been on the move. First built in the late 1840s, it was dismantled in 1920, restored to its original appearance, and moved to a ranch owned by Amon G. Carter, a wealthy Fort Worth newspaper publisher. After his death, it was dismantled once again—each log was numbered and photographed—and relocated to the Log Cabin Village, a city-owned living history museum, where it was painstakingly reconstructed.

Dorothy Poole, an eighty-eight-year-old widow, was working as a docent at the site in July 2008 when I paid a visit. A retired owner of a Baskin and Robbins franchise with her late husband, she recounted the story of Cynthia Ann and Prairie Flower twice a day to visitors, most frequently to elementary school children who come in vast regiments to the Log Cabin Village escorted by their teachers. With her long calico pioneer dress, carved wooden cane, old-fashioned rocking chair, and silver braids, Dorothy looked as if she had stepped out of a Texas history book.

She told me that she had heard many legends about the Parkers. One day, after she recited Cynthia Ann's story to a group of visitors, a woman approached who said her name was Elizabeth Runyon. She said Dorothy had gotten only one part of the tale wrong: Prairie Flower had not died of smallpox but had been packed off by her relatives for her own well-being and renamed Minnie Sneed. "The reason I know this is because I'm her great-granddaughter," the woman told Dorothy.

Dorothy said she did not know whether to believe such tales or not. "I know there are a lot of missing pieces in any of these stories," she said. Still, it's the emotions behind the stories that she found most genuine and readily understandable. Like the Star House, the modest little cabin is a testament to human aspirations and shortcomings. Uncle Isaac tried and failed to restore his niece to his family here and heal part of the terrible wound from the massacre of 1836. But Cynthia Ann saw the house as a prison keeping her from reuniting with her real family, her Comanche sons and her adopted community.

Keeping watch over the old cabin day after day, Dorothy often thought about Cynthia Ann's agony. "They said she'd sit out on this porch and pray to the Indian gods to take her back to her children, and I often wonder, what she was thinking when she was sitting here?" said Dorothy. "Who knows what she felt? It must have been a terrible trauma. I can see how terribly sad it would have been. It's a shame she never got to see her sons again."

HIDDEN AMID THE FLAT ANONYMITY of the plains, Palo Duro Canyon is virtually indiscernible until you're right on top of it. It is the Texas Panhandle's supreme geological surprise: the second-largest canyon in the United States, after its big brother, the Grand Canyon. Palo Duro (the name means "hard wood" in Spanish) is 120 miles long, 600 to 800 feet deep, and 6 to 20 miles wide. The canyon has three distinct layers: the flat plains on the rim, the floodplain and river valley at the bottom, and the sharp cliffs and rugged slopes of reddish-brown clay that connect the two. For a dry desert, it is full of grasses, trees, and wildflowers: star thistles, sunflowers, widow's tears, cockleburs, and prickly poppies; juniper, cottonwood, mesquite, saltbush, sumac, and willows. There is also a virtual aviary of vultures, mockingbirds, woodpeckers, meadowlarks, wild turkeys, and red-tailed hawks, not to mention rattlesnakes, turtles, horned lizards, bobcats, and antelopes. So many creatures, yet no buffalo, its former rulers, which were methodically eliminated from the canyon floor by Charles Goodnight and his men more than a century ago. Still, in the winter it's an ideal shelter for man and beast, and in summer a good jumping-off point for grazing on the adjacent plains.

The Comanches certainly thought so. Palo Duro was their winter stronghold, the place where they came to seek shelter and hide from their enemies. It's the place where Quanah Parker and his dwindling band took refuge after the failed Adobe Walls attack in 1874 and the staging ground for the dour Colonel Ranald Mackenzie's invasion later in the year that became the deathblow to the Comanches as a guerrilla force.

Palo Duro is now a state park, and near the entrance is the Pioneer Amphitheatre, with its stunning view of the red canyon walls, which blaze with rugged beauty when the sun begins to set. Each summer the nonprofit Texas Panhandle Heritage Foundation puts on a musical comedy-drama called *Texas!* It has run since 1966 and is sold out most evenings. The show celebrated the ranchers and homesteaders who settled here after the Indians were vanquished. The original songs were an exercise in shameless boosterism:

> *We expect you all to come to Texas!*
> *If you're willing to be bold,*
> *You can get it back tenfold—in Texas!*

This is popular history as written by the victors—a tale of hardship and triumph by courageous and enterprising pioneers. There is a brief scene in which an Indian chief in a war bonnet and white costume rides up on a white horse. Yes, it's the ghost of Quanah Parker, come to see what has happened to the land that used to be his domain and to ask whether whites and Indians can ever live together in peace. No problem, replies a glib young Texas homesteader: "Both sides have suffered for this land and we both have lost loved ones . . . Hate is not the way."

It only remains to Quanah to agree. "My young brother speaks with the sweet call of running water," he says, before he turns and rides away, concluding his role as a walk-on bit player in someone else's historical myth.

THE PILGRIM PREDESTINARIAN REGULAR BAPTIST CHURCH, organized in 1833 by the Reverend Daniel Parker as he prepared to move his family and his followers to East Texas, still occupies a one-room, whitewashed structure outside the town of Elkhart. The present building is the fourth in its long history. Nearby is a replica of the first, a tight one-room log cabin with a triangular roof and space for six small pews. Out back is the cemetery where Daniel and his tempestuous brother James were buried, along with succeeding generations of Parker sons and daughters. There is also a flagpole on the site that was erected in 2002 by John P. Parker, Daniel's great-great-great-great-grandson, as an Eagle Scout Service Project.

Pilgrim is part of a circuit of four small churches in the area; congregants have established a rotation for worshipping at each. They gathered here on the third Sunday of every month. On a scorching morning in mid-July, three open doors provided the only ventilation, a lazy hot breeze that licked the faces of the faithful. In the back of the room a Hotpoint refrigerator of uncertain vintage hummed fitfully alongside a small table with an old microwave oven and a well-traveled Mister Coffee machine.

A dozen congregants had gathered to listen to David Camp, a young preacher; most of them were members of his family. No Parkers were present, and Camp made no mention of Cynthia Ann or her family. But in its own emphatic way, Camp's sermon offered a religious explanation of what had happened to her, one that Daniel Parker would no doubt have endorsed.

"We are but lambs led to slaughter every day," Camp told the congregants. ". . . Satan is a roaring lion, but, people, we're prisoners of God's love. He made good and He made evil. He made peace and He made war. And it was perfect."

BACK IN QUANAH, TEXAS, on Saturday evening, people heaped their paper plates with barbecue brisket, potato salad, baked beans, white bread, and brownies, and balanced it all on their way to tables in the Three Rivers Ballroom on Main Street. The last formal event of the Quanah Parker Family Reunion featured Native American dancing; flute playing by Rebecca Parker, one of Quanah's great-great-grand-daughters, who has named one of her own daughters after Quanah; a long poem commemorating Quanah's life by Paul Davis, a Texas rancher who was part of the extended Parker community; and the ritual exchange of the silver bowl from Ron Parker of the Comanche side to Scott Nicholson, representing the Texas side of the family.

Nicholson was a lawyer who lived in Palestine, eleven miles north of Elkhart, one of the triangle of East Texas towns where the Parkers settled and still resided. He could trace his roots back seven generations to Daniel Parker via Daniel's son Dickinson, who fought with Sam Houston at the

The Comanche descendants of Quanah Parker at a pow-wow during their annual family reunion in Cache, Oklahoma, June 2008.

The Texan descendants of Cynthia Ann Parker at their annual family reunion in Ft. Parker State Park near Groesbeck, Texas, in July 2008.

Battle of San Jacinto; to "Virginia John" Parker, a Confederate soldier who surrendered at Appomattox and walked all the way home to Texas; to Ben J. Parker, the sheriff and part-time farmer who had met with Alan LeMay in 1952, and to Joe Bailey Parker, who was president of the Elkhart State Bank, and to Jo Nell Parker, Scott's mother, who was also in attendance.

"We're proud to have our Comanche cousins and we look forward every year to our Comanche cousins and to many years of reunions," Scott Nicholson told the crowd.

Next up was Sarah McReynolds in her Cynthia Ann Parker outfit of buckskins, fringe, moccasins, and long earrings. "I'll never forget May 19, 1836; the gates were open . . . ," she began, channeling Cynthia Ann as she retold the story of the original abduction and all that followed. It was a tale she had recited many times at gatherings over the years.

"It's horrible to be kidnapped; no one comes for you. I kept looking and looking but no one ever came . . .

"By the time I'm twelve years old white traders came and I made my mind up that day: I would not leave. By the time I was seventeen I was courted by a man named Peta Nocona . . . The man loved me. He never took another wife.

"They sent Sul Ross out to hunt down my husband and kill him. Quanah was twelve, Pecos nine. They were with their father. The same scenario happens again [as in 1836]. They took me away from my family.

"I sealed my fate that day when I said, 'I'm Cynthia Ann! I'm Cynthia Ann!'"

Sarah was close to tears as she finished. But she ended on a note of romantic optimism. "This is a tragic story," she concluded, "but it's a wonderful love story in many ways."

Paul Carlson told it very differently. A retired professor of history at Texas Tech in Lubbock, Carlson was coauthor of a scrupulously researched, myth-busting account of the Pease River massacre in December 1860, and he sought to deflate a few more myths in his keynote address. He told the audience that Cynthia Ann was only one of Peta Nocona's several wives—and "a chore wife, not a favored wife." That was why she was at the Pease River encampment, working the dreary winter buffalo meat detail, up to her elbows in greasy entrails, body parts, and blood.

This was not the version that most of the Comanche Parkers believe in, but no one seemed angry or tried to challenge Carlson's account. The legend of Cynthia Ann was so entrenched in their minds that no one could harm it. It had sustained them for generations, honored their name, and made them special through good times and bad. "We're not just Native Americans, we're a cross section of America because of Cynthia Ann Parker," Ron Parker had told me when I first met him in 2008. "I'm a Parker because my great-grandfather loved his mother. He never forgot her after they took her away, and he took his mother's name."

Baldwin Parker Jr., age ninety-three, at the family reunion in Quanah, Texas, marking the hundredth anniversary of his grandfather's death.

Paul Carlson continued. Sul Ross and his Texas Rangers didn't capture her at the Pease River battle, he insisted; U.S. Cavalry troopers did, but Ross took all the credit. The battle itself was a massacre that Ross and his supporters managed to repackage as a glorious military triumph. Carlson said he and his coauthor, Tom Crum, studied nineteen separate accounts from nine alleged participants, all of them partial and contradictory. Ross himself gave six different versions over the years, he added. Several of the most vivid accounts came from men who were not even at the site when the fight occurred. "But not having participated did not prevent them from reporting what they did not see," said an indignant Paul Carlson.

The argument could never end because it was not about specific facts so much as their larger meaning. Were the Comanches noble warriors or murderers and rapists? Were the bloody clashes between them and the Texans battles or massacres? Was Cynthia Ann Parker the ultimate Texas heroine or the ultimate victim? Were Comanches the victims or the perpetrators of their own demise? Was the Savage War of Peace and the Conquest of the American Frontier justified or immoral? Whose myth is real?

"We are shape shifters in the national consciousness, unwanted reminders of disagreeable events," writes Paul Chaat Smith, a Comanche who is associate curator of the National Museum of the American Indian in Washington. "Indians have to be explained and accounted for, and somehow fit into the creation myth of the most powerful, benevolent nation ever; the last best hope of man on earth . . . We're trapped in history. No escape."

THE NEXT MORNING, Don and Ron Parker and their cousin Bruce traveled out to the Pease River with a small entourage consisting of Lucia St. Clair Robson, author of a romantic historical novel called *Ride the Wind* about Cynthia Ann; Tom Crum, the retired Texas judge who cowrote the Pease River massacre book with Paul Carlson; and Tom's son Carl, a documentary filmmaker based in Fort Worth.

The caravan bounced down narrow dirt lanes, past the site of a Texas state marker located in the wrong place and inscribed with the wrong date for the battle, past salt cedar trees, bear grass, sagebrush, dove weed, prickly pear cactus, sand drop seed, and windmill grass, all of it going brown and brittle from the June heat invasion. Virtually none of this vegetation existed 150 years ago when waves of buffalo regularly swept through the area like Noah's flood, stomping or devouring every grow-ing thing in their path. "It would have been bare and flat as a billiard table," said Tom Crum, who led the way. "You could see everything."

The drought had sucked dry most of the wide bed of the Pease River, and Mule Creek was just a memory. Crum stood in the middle where a freshwater stream once flowed and told the story one more time: how Ross and Spangler in the early morning rain had observed the nine grass huts of the Comanche encampment from a ridge two hundred yards away; how Ross led his tired men forward while Spangler and his troopers flanked the camp from behind; how the Comanche women and children panicked and ran from the surprise attack; how Ross and his men ran down and shot the old warrior on horseback; how Cynthia Ann cried out *"Americano! Americano!"* as the trooper pointed his gun in her face.

Don Parker lit a small clump of sage and sent the smoke in four direc-tions. Then he reached into the cedar case he carried like a doctor's kit for rituals and solemn occasions and pulled out eagle feathers and a gourd. He gently shook the rattle as he sang the "Bull Eagle Song," about an eagle who flew so high it went into orbit around the earth. "This is holy ground to me," said Don when he had finished.

Then he put the items back in the case and snapped it shut. The par-ticipants climbed into their pickup trucks and cars and roared away. The Quanah Parker Family Reunion was over for another year.

NOTE ON SOURCES

This book uses a broad range of primary and secondary sources, including archives, interviews, newspaper articles, scholarly works, memoirs, Comanche oral tradition, and visits to historical sites. It covers events that span a century and three quarters and took place over a broad expanse of the southwestern United States, from Texas to Hollywood. Some of the research stops were to long-standing repositories of essential materials—for example, the Dolph Briscoe Center for American History at the University of Texas at Austin, which is home to the Joseph and Araminta Taulman Collection, the foremost archive of documents and photos for the Parker family. It includes many unpublished and unannotated documents, including the handwritten notebook and letters of Susan Parker St. John and similar treasures from Araminta Taulman. There is a web of museums, libraries, and archival collections in southwest Oklahoma and the Texas Panhandle that also house a host of treasures, many of them overlapping thanks to the miracle of modern photocopying: the Fort Sill Museum and Archives and the Museum of the Great Plains, both in Lawton, Oklahoma; the Panhandle-Plains Historical Museum in Canyon, Texas; the Oklahoma State Historical Society in Oklahoma City, and the University of Oklahoma Library in Norman. But virtually every public library in southwest Oklahoma and northern Texas, including the Panhandle, has a file of documents, letters, or photographs covering the years of Comanche-Texan wars and their aftermath. Bill Neeley's files, which he accumulated in researching his book *The Last Comanche Chief*, are an invaluable source of primary documents and are available at the Panhandle-Plains Historical Museum.

When it comes to Quanah Parker and the Comanches, the Kiowa Indian agency files, available on microfilm, are an invaluable source of official documents about life on the reservation. The National Archives—Southwest Region in Fort Worth is a repository for these files. The Works Progress Administration Indian-Pioneer Papers were an ambitious and systematic attempt in the 1930s to interview everyone of prominence or interest concerning the Indian agency and its residents. These, too, are available on microfilm in many locations, and the Western History Collection of the University of Oklahoma Library in Norman has a complete set. The Indian Archives of the Oklahoma Historical Society are also an excellent source of primary materials. *Chronicles of Oklahoma* is a tireless and thorough collection of articles, interviews, and memoirs of the state and its residents, all of it now available online.

Comanche oral tradition, as handed down from generation to generation by members of the extended Parker family, is neither more nor less accurate than many published accounts. It is a reliable gauge of the reverence for Cynthia Ann and Quanah Parker that is such an important part of the spiritual life and identity of the Parker clan. Another excellent source of oral lore is *Comanche Ethnology*, a collection of the field notes of a team of anthropologists who interviewed eighteen Comanche elders in the 1930s. These field notes also contributed to two valuable anthropological studies: *Comanches: Lords of the South Plains* by Ernest Wallace and E. Adamson Hoebel, and Thomas W. Kavanagh's *The Comanches: A History*.

Finally, two books that are required reading for anyone interested in Comanche history are *The Comanches: Destruction of a People*, T. R. Fehrenbach's magisterial and lyrical classic, now much criticized by modern historians for its imperial assumptions; and Pekka Hämäläinen's *The Comanche Empire*, a fresh interpretation of the meaning and the power of the Comanche nation, its allies and enemies.

Two writers who made essential contributions to *The Searchers* have been largely forgotten, but their lives and work can be traced in archives. The Alan LeMay Papers at UCLA contain twenty-three boxes of the novelist's research and letters, donated after his death by his widow, Arlene. His son Dan also has many important documents and letters, which he used for his own biography of his father's life, and the Harry Ransom Center at the University of Texas at Austin has a file of correspondence between LeMay and his book editor, Evan Thomas. Screenwriter Frank S. Nugent's widow, Jean, donated his papers to Boston University. There is no archive for Patrick Ford, John Ford's only son and a key architect of the film. The only interview with him that I am aware of was conducted by James D'Arc at Brigham Young University in April 1979, and it is an invaluable source for anyone seeking to understand this somewhat tragic figure.

The *Searchers* has no dedicated archive, and John Ford was famously averse to committing his thoughts to paper. But the John Ford Papers at the Lilly Library at Indiana University contain the film notes that John and Pat Ford prepared as they worked out the concepts and logistics of the movie. The notes are not comprehensive—for example, there no notes between John Ford and Frank Nugent—but they are the best account we have of John Ford's creative process going into the film shoot.

The other essential collection is the C. V. Whitney papers, which are the property of the Whitney family and which I was privileged to be the first researcher to examine. They offer a road map to Whitney's thinking and ambitions, and his constant interventions with Merian C. Cooper in an effort to achieve the film he keenly wanted.

Other useful archival materials can be found in the Ronald L. Davis Collection at Southern Methodist University, which contains transcripts of the interviews Davis conducted with Ford's and Wayne's friends and colleagues for his thoroughly researched biographies of the two men; and in the Ransom Center's John Wayne Papers, which contain the files of author Maurice Zolotow for a Wayne autobiography, *My Kingdom Is a Horse*, that the two men worked on but never completed. Zolotow went on to write *Shooting Star*, his own biography of Wayne, using the material. There are also intriguing shards of documents about *The Searchers* in the Warner Brothers Archive at the University of Southern California and at the Margaret Herrick Library of the Academy of Motion Picture Arts and Sciences.

For such an iconic film, *The Searchers* has been the subject of surprisingly few books. Edward Buscombe's *The Searchers*, part of the first-rate BFI Film Classics series, is an excellent introduction; while *The Searchers: Essays and Reflections on John Ford's Classic Western*, edited by Arthur M. Eckstein and Peter Lehman, is a fine collection of thoughtful academic articles. Michael F. Blake's *Code of Honor* gives a thorough account of the making of the film.

Fortunately, there are many fine books on Ford and Wayne to help fill the gap. The essential list includes *Searching for John Ford: A Life*, Joseph McBride's magisterial biography; *Print the Legend: The Life and Times of John Ford* by Scott Eyman; *Pappy: The Life of John Ford* by Dan Ford; and my sentimental favorite, *Company of Heroes*, Harry Carey Jr.'s candid but affectionate memoir of his life as a member of the John Ford Stock Company.

NOTES

Abbreviations

BYU Brigham Young University Library
CVW Cornelius Vanderbilt Whitney Papers
FSN Frank S. Nugent
JFP John Ford Papers, Lilly Library, Indiana University
JW John Wayne
JWP James W. Parker
KCA Kiowa-Comanche-Apache Indian Agency Files
MHL Margaret Herrick Library
NYT *New York Times*
OKU University of Oklahoma Library
OKHS Oklahoma Historical Society
PPHM Panhandle-Plains Historical Museum
QP Quanah Parker
SMU Southern Methodist University Library
TSL Texas State Library and Archives Commission
WB Warner Brothers Archive

Introduction: Pappy

1 *"It's so absolutely right"*: Fonda to JF, April 5, 1954 (Lilly).

2 *"Pappy, you know I love you"*: Henry Fonda, *Fonda: My Life*, pp. 233–4.

2 *Sometimes, when Ford was too wasted*: Joseph McBride, *Searching for John Ford: A Life*, p. 550.

2 *He had had cataract surgery*: Gerald Peary, *John Ford Interviews*, p. 32.

3 *"John Ford was going through changes"*: Maureen O'Hara, *'Tis Herself: A Memoir*, p. 193.

4 *"My name is John Ford"*: Robert Parrish, *Growing Up in Hollywood*, offers a detailed account of the meeting, pp. 207–210.

5 *Ford . . . had once commissioned*: See Larry Swindell, "Yes, John Ford Knew a Thing Or Two about Art," *John Ford Interviews*, pp. 146–7.

7 *"Wayne is plainly Ahab"*: Greil Marcus, "John Wayne Listening," p. 321.

7 *"It was a sacred feeling"*: Rachel Dodes, "IMAX Strikes Back," *Wall Street Journal*, April 19, 2012.

7 *"all modern American literature"*: Stuart Byron, "*The Searchers*: Cult Movie of the New Hollywood," *New York*, March 5, 1979, p. 45.

1. The Girl

11 *"Thus was the wilderness"*: James W. Parker, *Narrative of the Perilous Adventures*, p. 7.

12 *the Night the Stars Fell*: Joseph Taulman note, 2F 206 (Taulman Papers).

12 *"The remainder of the night"*: Carl Greenwood to Joseph Taulman, September 11, 1931 (Taulman); see also Jo Ella Powell Exley, *Frontier Blood*, pp. 36–7.For an extended family history of the Parkers in Illinois and Texas see Eugene G. O'Quinn, "Quanah—The Eagle: Half-White Comanche Chief," unpublished (Van Zandt).

13 *"not a good day for bee hunting"*: Charles E. Parker to Joseph Taulman, Feb. 8, 1928, 2F 205 (Taulman).

14 *"Farming was my only way"*: Joseph Taulman, "First Regularly Organized and Con-stituted Protestant or Non-Catholic Church in Texas" (Taulman).

14 *"He seemed full of his subject"*: Max Lee, "Daniel Parker," p. 2.

14 *"without education, uncouth in manners"*: Ibid., pp. 2–3.

15 *"awakened in me feelings"*: JWP, p. 5.

15 *"We now shot them down"*: Dyersbury (TN) *State Gazette*, May 29, 2002.

15 *"We believe that God created man"*: "Records of an Early Texas Baptist Church," p. 86.

16 *"The grass is more abundant"*: Stephen F. Austin, "Journal," p. 289.

16 *"vicious and wild men"*: *Texas by Terán: The Diary Kept by Manuel de Mier y Terán on His 1828 Inspection of Texas*, p. 79.

17 *"literally shot to pieces"*: JWP, p. 6.

17 *"an honest man"*: Character Certificate, July 20, 1833, 2F 192 (Taulman).

17 *"an Enemy to truth"*: Reverend Bing, undated handwritten note, Daniel Parker Papers 3G 479 (Briscoe).

17 *"the most fertile, most healthy"*: JWP, p. 63.

18 *"forests of cast iron"*: Washington Irving, *A Tour of the Prairies*, p. 113.

19 *They shot the two chiefs*: *Papers Concerning Robertson's Colony in Texas XIV*, p. 72. For description of tensions, see also Jack Selden, *Return*, pp. 22–4.

19 *"If this region was not infested"*: JWP, p. 70.

20 *"to destroy my reputation"*: "Defense of James W. Parker," p. 5 (Bancroft).

21 *The settlers had no nails*: See museum displays at Old Fort Parker, Groesbeck, Texas.

21 *"to secure the inhabitants"*: Telegraph and Texas Register, October 26, 1835.

21 *winter of 1836 was a desperate time*: Typescript ms. by Morris Swett, Fort Sill librarian who collected Comanche oral folklore (Fort Sill, Swett File Collection B1 F3).

21 *Daniel signed his name*: Bob Bullock Texas State History Museum, Austin.

22 *"To our minds this was a far more trying time"*: A. D. Gentry, "The Runaway Scrape," *Frontier Times*, p.9.

22 *"for the purpose of Killing the white people"*: Daniel Parker handwritten statement, June 18, 1836 (Taulman).

23 *"voices that seemed to reach the very skies"*: Rachel Plummer, *Narrative of the Capture and Subsequent Sufferings*, 1839, p. 6. The details of the massacre are from Plummer, pp. 5–8, and JWP, pp. 9–11.

2. The Captives

25 *"We were in the howling wilderness"*: JWP, pp. 12–13.

26 *"dressed in white with long, white hair"*: "The Charmed Life of Abram Anglin," *Groesbeck Journal*, May 15, 1936, p. 5.

26 *"We found the houses still standing"*: JWP, pp. 14–15.

27 *"feelings of the deepest mortification"*: Plummer, pp. 7–8.

29 *"abandon once more the habitations of civilized men"*: Richard Slotkin, *Regeneration Through Violence*, p. 430.

29 *clad in native garb*: Grant Foreman, *Pioneer Days in the Early Southwest*, p. 184.

29 *"jealous, envious, dissipated"*: Lawrence E. Honig, *John Henry Brown: Texas Journalist*, p. 11.

29 *"Your enemies and ours are the same"*: Thomas W. Kavanagh, *Comanches: A History*, p. 251.

30 *"All argument failed"*: JWP, p. 17.

30 *"with mingled feelings of joy"*: Ibid., pp. 18–9.

31 *"something inexpressibly lonely"*: Irving, p. 162.

31 *Comanches called themselves Nemernuh*: T. R. Fehrenbach, *Comanches: The History of a People*, p. 31; also Ernest Wallace and E. Adamson Hoebel, *The Comanches: Lords of the South Plains*, pp. 25–8.

32 *"most horrible attire"*: Gerald Betty, *Comanche Society*, p. 122.

32 *"the largest and most terrible nomadic nation"*: Jean-Louis Berlandier, *The Indians of Texas in 1830*, p. 114.

32 *"a vast hinterland of extractive raiding"*: Pekka Hämäläinen, *The Comanche Empire*, p. 182.

33 *Rachel Plummer never said*: This account of her captivity, including her baby son's murder, is from Plummer, pp. 9–18.

33 *"Its light turned the evening mist"*: Larry McMurtry, *Lonesome Dove*, p. 285.

34 *the country's first indigenous literary genre*: Gary L. Ebersole, *Captured by Texts*, p. 10.

34 *"the special demonic personification"*: Slotkin, *Regeneration*, p. 4.

34 *"Their glittering weapons so daunted my spirit"*: Mary White Rowlandson, *Narrative of the Captivity and Removes of Mrs. Mary Rowlandson*, p. 7.

35 *"the tresses of this lady were shining"*: James Fenimore Cooper, *The Last of the Mohicans*, pp. 16–17 and 109–10.

36 *"This intelligence kindled anew"*: JWP, pp. 22–3.

37 *She would soak the hides to soften*: Marcus Kiek, "Brain-Tanned Buffalo Hide."

37 *The dead bison provided food, hardware, clothing*: "Skinning and Butchering a Bison," PPHM video presentation.

38 *"It was the sweetest stuff"*: T. A. "Dot" Babb obituary, undated (PPHM).

38 *"The squaws did all the manual labor"*: T. A. Babb, *In the Bosom of the Comanches*, pp. 39–40.

38 *"if she attempted again to force me"*: Plummer, p. 17.

38 *"You are brave to fight"*: Ibid., p. 19.

39 *Humans became just one more commodity*: Michael Tate, "Comanche Captives," pp. 231–4.

40 *forced to scrape and clean her own dead mother's scalp:* J. W. Wilbarger, *Indian Depredations in Texas*, p. 401.

41 *"trained, from infancy to age, to deeds of cruelty:* Carl Coke Rister, *Border Captives*, p. 68.

41 *"all females were chattels":* Fehrenbach, p. 287. For a conflicting view, Joaquin Rivaya-Martínez, "Becoming Comanches."

42 *"The sweeping generalizations by Dodge and Fehrenbach":* Gregory and Susan Michino, *A Fate Worse Than Death*, p. 473.

43 *Bianca produced an unpublished memoir:* Her account finally appeared in print fifty-three years after her death: "'Every Day Seemed to Be a Holiday': The Captivity of Bianca Babb," Daniel J. Gelo and Scott Zesch, eds.

3. The Uncle

46 *"No man can regret":* Sam Houston, *The Writings of Sam Houston*, pp. 53–4.

46 *Still, James persisted:* The ambush is narrated in JWP, pp. 24–7.

47 *Houston was no city:* For details of the five capitals and the executive mansion, see Selden, *Return*, p. 106, and Exley, pp. 79–80.

47 *"Calling me a fool and a mad man":* Parker to Houston, June 6, 1837 (TSL).

48 *"flog those Indians":* Houston, p. 36.

48 *the truce did not last long:* Selden, p. 89.

48 *"As soon as the opportunity presented itself":* JWP, p. 30.

49 *"Had I the treasures of the universe":* Plummer, p. 28. For her account of her rescue and return to her family, see pp. 27–30.

50 *Her appearance was "most pitiable":* James W. Parker, p. 31.

50 *"The prejudice existing":* Petition, 1840, Star of the Republic Museum Archive.

51 *He went into hiding:* Exley, pp. 99–101.

51 *"My success engendered malice":* Parker, "Defense," p. 6.

51 *"feeling assured that before they are published":* Plummer, pp. 31–3.

51 *"This life had no charms":* JWP, p. 32.

51 *Wilson died two days later:* Exley, p. 104.

51 *"John Parker and Sinthy Ann":* Petition, November 22, 1840 (Star of the Republic).

51 *a wild scheme to raise an army:* Exley, p. 106.

52 *"If the wild cannibals of the woods":* Indian Relations in Texas (TSL).

52 *intimate enemies:* Rupert N. Richardson, *The Comanche Barrier to South Plains Settlement*, p. 101.

53 *the centrality of attacks on women and children:* see Slotkin, *Gunfighter Nation*, p. 48.

53 *The elderly Cherokee leader:* see Gary Anderson, *The Conquest of Texas*, p. 179.

54 *"Her head, arms, and face were full of bruises":* Mary A. Maverick, *Memoirs*, p. 44. This account of the Council House massacre is largely from her memoir, from Fehrenbach, pp. 322–9, and from "Hugh McLeod's Report on the Council House Fight," March, 20, 1840 (TSL).

56 *"These the Indians made free with":* Handbook of Texas Online.

57 *"The bodies of men, women, and children":* Fehrenbach, pp. 347–8.

57 *"The two cousins . . . exulted":* Foreman, p. 285.

58 *"He then asked if he had a father":* JWP, p. 36.

58 *"It evinces a degree of heartlessness"*: Houston, pp. 180–1.

58 *"holding correspondence with suspicious characters"*: Exley, p. 118.

58 *"My time is at hand"*: "Biography of Daniel Parker," 3G 749 (Daniel Parker Papers).

59 *"lamented that thear was many"*: Exley, pp. 123–5.

59 *"I wish to make this public"*: JWP letter, *Texas National Register*, June 26, 1845, p. 231.

59 *"we believe the church has bin . . . unjustly implicated"*: Records, p. 156.

4. The Rescue

61 *Williams sought to purchase her*: Hacker, p. 30.

61 *"she continued to weep incessantly"*: Exley, p. 134.

62 *"she is unwilling to leave the people"*: "Texas Indians—Report of Butler and Lewis," p. 8.

62 *The birth process was a communal event*: Wallace and Hoebel, pp. 142–4.

63 *"She shook her head in a sorrowful negative"*: James T. DeShields, *Cynthia Ann Parker*, p. 32.

64 *"She seemed to be separated"*: Rupert N. Richardson, "The Death of Nocona," p. 15.

64 *The cavalry, stretched thin*: Ranald S. MacKenzie's *Official Correspondence Relating to Texas, 1871–75*, p. 4.

64 *Ford joined forces with Shapley Prince Ross*: Exley, p. 139.

65 *"with both eyes shot out"*: Recollections of B. F. Gholson, p. 9, 2Q 519 (Briscoe).

65 *the worst moment came that November*: See account in Paul H. Carlson and Tom Crum, *Myth, Memory and Massacre*, pp. 22–3. Carlson and Crum offer the most painstaking and definitive account to date of the Pease River massacre and myth, and I rely on them for my own.

66 *"an Indian scalp thoroughly salted"*: J. Evetts Haley, *Charles Goodnight*, pp. 50–1.

66 *"a fine horseman and a good shot"*: This and other descriptions of Ross: Judith Ann Benner, *Sul Ross: Soldier, Statesman, Educator*, pp. 45–50.

68 *"killed every one of them"*: Haley, p. 55.

68 *"Sul ran up to him"*: Gholson, p. 29.

69 *"They had to force her away"*: Felix Williams interview with Frank Gholson, August 26, 1931, p. 20 2Q 519 (Briscoe).

69 *the woman "was so dirty you could hardly tell"*: Recollections of H. B. Rogers, p. 2, Ibid.

70 *"I'm greatly distressed about my boys"*: Gholson interview, p. 12 (Briscoe).

70 *"We rode right over her dead companions"*: Haley, p. 56.

70 *the volunteers found only four dead bodies*: *Dallas News*, November 28, 1937; see also Carlson and Crum, p. 5.

71 *killing a chief named Mohee*: Carlson and Crum offer the most thorough account on pp. 70–8.

72 *"this Pease River fight . . . made Sul Ross governor"*: Walter C. Cochran, *Reminiscences*, p. 11.

72 *"The fruits of this important victory"*: E. E. White, *Experiences of a Special Indian Agent*, p. 263; also pp. 271–2.

5. The Prisoner

73 *the child never cried:* Susan Parker St. John Notebook, p. 4, 2F 260 (Taulman).

73 *"would be a waste of the materials":* Selden p. 176.

74 *she looked and smelled like a savage:* Gholson, p. 40.

74 *"It was a race":* Gholson interview, p. 18.

74 *she was a wild Indian:* Marion T. Brown, Letters from Fort Sill, p. 78.

74 *Over the years he had honored the memory:* Selden, p. 117.

76 *"Make them plenty big, Nancy":* Ibid., p. 179.

76 *"After the lapse of a few moments":* Galveston Civilian, February 5, 1861, quoted in Hacker, p. 28.

77 *"Me Cynthia Ann":* Ibid.

77 *she pleaded with Horace Jones:* Brown, p. 78.

77 *They finally arrived in Birdville:* Selden, p. 182.

78 *Her "long night of suffering":* Hacker offers various press accounts on pp. 30, 33, and 40.

78 *"people came from near and far"* I. D. Parker to DeShields, ca. 1895 (SMU).

78 *"She looked like a squaw"* Exley, pp. 170–1.

78 *"I was told of the many futile efforts":* St. John, p. 5.

78 *"As savage-like and dark of complexion":* Taulman, Notebook No. 8, pp. 44–5, 2F 258 (Taulman)

79 *she often sacrificed herself:* Slotkin, *Gunfighter Nation,* pp. 14–5.

79 *"Theirs must have been a hard . . . life"* Taulman Notebook No. 8, p. 4.

79 *"When the fire was started":* Parker letter to DeShields.

80 *she bolted for the door:* DeShields, "Indian Wars of Texas," p. 42.

81 *A. F. Corning's photographic studio:* This account is from Araminta Taulman's interviews with Mrs. R. H. King, July 5 and September 13, 1926; and with Mrs. Turnbill, September 24, 1926 2F 263 (Taulman).

82 *"she took out the kidneys and liver":* I. D. Parker to DeShields.

83 *She interviewed William and Mattie:* Details of Susan Parker St. John's account are from her unpublished notebook, pp. 8–11, 2F 260 (Taulman).

84 *"My heart is crying all the time".* Coho Smith, *Cohographs,* p. 71.

85 *"She had a wild expression":* Exley, p. 178.

85 *As for James Parker . . . there is no record:* Selden, pp. 282–3.

86 *I. D. Parker . . . claimed that mother and daughter both died:* Parker to DeShields.

86 *Another legend:* "Mystery of Prairie Flower, Daughter of Chief, Solved," *Wichita Falls Times,* May 3, 1959; also Frank X. Tolbert, "More on Mystery of Topsannah," *Dallas News,* October 17, 1960.

86 *An 1870 census:* 1870 United States Federal Census in the County of Anderson, State of Texas, Page No. 212 (National Archives Fort Worth).

86 *"Cynthia Ann had united with the Methodist church":* St. John Notebook, pp. 19–20.

87 *"A Romance of the Border":* San Francisco Bulletin, October 26, 1885; also "A Border Romance," *St. Louis Globe-Democrat,* June 20, 1884; "Cynthia Ann Parker," *Dallas News,* March 4, 1928.

87 *"Strong as buffalo hide":* Jan Reid, "The Warrior's Bride," *Texas Monthly,* February 2003.

88 *"the most unhappy person [he] ever saw"*: Araminta Taulman interview with Mrs. J. J. Nunally, 1926, 2F 263 (Taulman).

6. The Warrior

92 *Tseeta . . . became Quanah . . . and Pecos became Pee-nah:* Aubrey Birdsong, "Reminiscences of Quanah Parker," 1965 (Fort Sill).

92 *his father became "very morose":* Quanah Parker to Charles Goodnight, n.d. (PPHM).

92 *Quanah was truly on his own:* See William T. Hagan, *Quanah Parker: Comanche Chief*, p. 11. Also Exley, p. 183.

92 *"so vast that I did not find their limit":* Francisco Coronado letter to the king of Spain, October 20, 1541.

93 *"The land is too much":* Timothy Egan, *The Worst Hard Time*, p. 1.

93 *A young Comanche male without standing:* James F. Brooks, *Captives & Cousins*, pp. 177–8.

94 Weckeah elopement tale: Parker family oral history; also White, *Experiences of a Special Indian Agent*, pp. 278–88.

95 *"stealing white women is . . . more lucrative":* Rister, *Border Captives*, p. 134.

95 *Sand Creek Massacre . . . sexual mutilation:* J. P. Dunn, *Massacres of the Mountains*, p. 152.

96 *"Sometimes a Comanche man dreams":* QP Interview with Hugh Scott (Fort Sill).

97 *Putting his skepticism aside:* QP to Scott, p. 23.

97 *The "Grand Council" met in a clearing:* Stanley Noyes and Daniel J. Gelo, *Comanches in the New West, 1895–1908*, p. 1.

97 *Behind them was Ten Bears:* This account of the Medicine Lodge Treaty comes largely from Henry M. Stanley, *My Early Travels and Adventures in America*, pp. 261–6.

98 *"The Comanches are not weak and blind":* from *Indian Oratory: Famous Speeches by Noted Indian Chieftains.* W. C. Vanderwerth, pp. 132–3.

98 *The Indian "must change the road":* Stanley, pp. 271–2.

99 *"I went and heard it":* QP to Scott, p. 23.

100 *the Civil War's ruthless apostle:* The description of Sherman's life and role is from John F. Marszalek, *Sherman: A Soldier's Passion for Order*, pp. 378–9, 390.

100 *"The only good Indian":* *New York Times*, January 29, 1887; *Southern Workman*, April 21, 1892, p. 63.

100 *"In the end they must be removed":* Sherman to David French Boyd, August 9, 1867, Marszalek, p. 390.

101 *In a two-and-one-half-year period:* The casualty toll is from Michino, *A Fate Worse than Death*, p. 471.

101 *Kiowas killed "several families":* Philip McCusker to General W. B. Hazen, December, 22, 1868, Sherman Papers, p. 478.

101 *Kiowas hauled out to the prairie:* W. S. Nye, *Carbine and Lance*, p. 114.

101 *Walkley recovered five white captives:* S. T. Walkley to Hazen, October 10, 1868, Sherman Papers, pp. 348–9 (OKU).

102 *"the mildest remedy":* Sherman Papers, p. 487.

102 *"If a white man commits murder"*: Hämäläinen, *Comanche Empire*, p. 328.

102 *"the aiders and abettors of savages"*: Sheridan's 1869 report, in *Report of the Secretary of War*, Vol. I, 1869, p. 48.

103 *"Let us have peace"*: Lawrie Tatum, *Our Red Brothers*, pp. 17–18. Tatum's experiences at Anadarko are detailed in his book on pp. ix, 25, 30–6, 42–3, 134, 152, and 182.

105 *Mamanti received a vision*: Bill Neeley, *The Last Comanche Chief*, p. 107.

105 *"The poor victims were stripped"*: Carter, *Tragedies of Cañon Blanco*, pp. 81–2.

105 *Sherman pushed on to Fort Sill*: Marzsalek, p. 395.

105 *The Kiowa chief quickly shifted into servile mode*: Nye, *Carbine and Lance*, pp. 195–6.

106 *"I answered . . . that it was a cowardly act"*: Stanley F. Hirshson, *The White Tecumseh*, p. 347.

106 *"Tell my people that I am dead"*: See Carter's account of Satank's death, pp. 188–91.

106 *His father had been a naval commander*: For Mackenzie's family tree, see Neeley, p. 105.

107 *"the most promising young officer"*: Michael D. Pierce, *The Most Promising Young Officer: A Life of Ranald Slidell Mackenzie*, pp. 46–7. See also pp. 52, 71–2, and 106.

107 *Mackenzie generously paid off the $500 debt*: Carter, p. 73.

107 *"They trembled and groaned"*: This account of the Cañón Blanco attack is Ibid., pp. 166–97. See also Exley, p. 214.

7. The Surrender

112 *buffalo hunters were a breed apart*: T. Lindsay Baker and Billy R. Harrison, *Adobe Walls: The History and Archaeology of the 1874 Trading Post*, p. 29. The gist of this account of the Battle of Adobe Walls is from Baker and Harrison.

112 *Born in West Virginia*: The description of Billy Dixon is from Olive K. Dixon, *Life of Billy Dixon*.

113 *destroying "the Indians' commissary"* T. R. Fehrenbach, *Lone Star*, p. 537.

113 *Buffalo were so plentiful*: G. Derek West, "The Battle of Adobe Walls 1874," p. 2.

113 *"I have seen their bodies so thick"*: The Recollections of W. S. Glenn, *Buffalo Hunter*, p. 6 (PPHM).

114 *"The whole country appeared one mass of buffalo"*: Richard Irving Dodge, *Our Wild Indians*, p. 284.

114 *"where there were myriads"*: Tatum, p. 295.

115 *The idea of attacking Adobe Walls*: Quanah's narrative is from "Chief Quanah Parker's Account of the Battle of Adobe Walls" as told to General Hugh L. Scott, 1897 (Fort Sill). I have blended his story with Dixon's firsthand story and with Baker and Harrison's history.

119 *"to act with vindictive earnestness"*: Marszalek, p. 397.

119 *A series of fourteen skirmishes*: Adrian N. Anderson, "The Last Phase of Colonel Ranald S. Mackenzie's 1874 Campaign Against the Comanches," pp. 72–4.

120 *Mackenzie trailed the Comanches*: Pierce, *The Most Promising Young Officer*, pp. 151–4.

120 *he set out from Fort Sill*: Sturm's journey is from "The Journal of Ranald S. Mackenzie's Messenger to the Kwahadi Comanches," Ernest Wallace, ed.

122 *one of them . . . took Jones aside:* Selden, pp. 1–3.

122 *"I shall let them down as easily":* Pierce, *The Most Promising Young Officer,* p. 168.

8. The Go-Between

123 *"They fed us like we were lions":* Nye, *Carbine and Lance,* p. 229.

124 *the Comanche population had been decimated:* James M. Haworth, *Reports of Agents in Indian Territory,* 1878, pp. 58–9 (KCA).

124 *Quanah volunteered:* Pierce, *Most Promising Officer,* p. 169.

125 *"I understand the heads are now preserved":* Haworth, *Reports,* p. 274.

125 *Quanah insisted that they not be shipped off:* William T. Hagan, *Quanah Parker,* pp. 24–5.

125 *"The plains were literally alive":* Hermann Lehmann, *9 Years Among the Indians,* pp. 167–8.

125 *a lone buffalo man named Marshall Sewell:* See Scott Zesch, *The Captured: A True Story of Abduction by Indians on the Texas Frontier,* pp. 215–6.

126 *He "told us that it was useless":* Lehmann, pp. 186–7.

126 *Quanah used a pair of army field glasses:* Zesch, p. 220.

127 *"the emergency is pressing":* Nye, p. 250.

127 *The letter was published: Dallas Weekly Herald,* June 5, 1875.

128 *"After an Indian custom":* Mackenzie to Isaac Parker, undated (Fort Sill).

128 *"I do not listen to any foolish talks":* Hagan, *QP,* p. 40.

128 *"all acts . . . had been considered void":* L. H. Miller to Philemon Hunt, June 4, 1881 (KCA).

129 *The buffalo would emerge again:* The Mount Scott buffalo legend is recounted in a display at the Fort Sill Museum.

130 *But the supplies came erratically:* Theft and profiteering on the reservation is from Hagan, *QP,* pp. 18–24.

130 *"The steers were penned in":* "Reminiscence of an Indian Trader," *Chronicles of Oklahoma* 14:2, June 1936.

130 *"The herd rushes out":* Dodge, *Our Wild Indians,* p. 536.

130 *"the place of putrid meat":* Noyes, p. 86.

132 *By the time Quanah and his hunting party arrived:* For QP's first meeting with Goodnight, see Haley, *Charles Goodnight,* pp. 306–12.

134 *"I got one good friend, Burk Burnett":* Neeley, *The Last Comanche Chief,* p. 231.

134 *cattlemen went to work cultivating . . . Indian leaders such as Quanah:* Hagan, *QP,* pp. 28–38.

9. The Chief

136 *"He was a fine specimen":* Susan Parker St. John Notebook.

136 *"Quanah Parker started the fight":* Neeley, p. 196.

137 *There were many conflicts of interest:* Hagan, *QP,* p. 39.

137 *"they will have a bully good time":* Burk Burnett to QP, October 24, 1908 (Fort Sill).

137 *a large, swarthy, well-dressed man: Fort Worth Gazette,* December 23, 1883.

137 *"He certainly was a wonderful friend":* Interview with Knox Beal, April 15, 1938, Neeley Archives (PPHM).

138 *Quanah first proposed the idea:* The building of the Star House is in Hagan, *QP*, pp. 43–4.

138 *"I did not deem it wise":* Thomas J. Morgan to Charles E. Adams, December 18, 1890, Parker Family File (Museum of the Great Plains).

139 *"Geronimo dipped in":* Neda Parker Birdsong as told to Gillett Griswold, Fort Sill Museum Librarian (Fort Sill).

139 *"Comanches on the War-Path":* St. Louis Globe Democrat, March 27, 1886.

140 *"Me and my people have quit fighting":* Quanah to James Hall, April 7, 1887 (OKHS).

141 *A woman . . . heard the shots:* Byron H. Price, "The Great Panhandle Indian Scare of 1891," pp. 128–29.

141 *Quanah and his moderate . . . ally, Apiatin:* James Mooney, *The Ghost-Dance Religion and the Sioux Outbreak of 1890*, pp. 171–73.

141 *The same kind of panic:* Author's interview with Towana Spivey, Fort Sill archivist, June 11, 2009.

141 *"a savage and filthy practice":* Thomas J. Morgan to U.S. Indian agents, July 21, 1890, Neeley Archive (PPHM).

142 *He even banned Indian participation:* See "Thomas Jefferson Morgan" in *The Commissioners of Indian Affairs, 1824–1977*, p. 200.

142 *"The Indians are destined to be absorbed":* Morgan to Indian agents, December 10, 1889, Neeley Archive.

142 *"kill the Indian and save the man":* Richard White, *It's Your Misfortune and None of My Own*, p. 113.

142 *"Me no like Indian school":* See "Chief Fought for Progress," undated (PPHM).

143 *"Like slaves on a plantation":* Hagan, *QP*, p. 53.

143 *Each wife had a specific set of household duties:* David La Vere, *Life Among the Texas Indians: The WPA Narratives*, pp. 223–24.

143 *"I cannot . . . ask you to turn him loose":* QP to S. M. McCowan, January 14, 1907, OKHS files.

143 *he met clandestinely:* For the fleeing-with-Tonarcy story, see *Comanche Ethnography*, p. 34. Also, Lena R. Banks Interview, May 5, 1938, WPA 10644, affirmed by Parker family and Towana Spivey in the author's interviews.

144 *"Now it's time to kill that white man":* Comanche Ethnography, p. 342.

145 *"one of the finest Indian women in America":* Daily Oklahoman, May 15, 1895, p. 3.

145 *The peyote plant is a small, spineless cactus:* Garrett Epps, *To an Unknown God: Religious Freedom on Trial*, p. 60.

145 *Peyote worship was a direct result:* See Epps and Omer Call Stewart, *Peyote Religion: A History.*

146 *"The white man goes into his church house":* Hagan, *QP*, p. 57.

147 *"It is a drug habit":* J. J. Methvin, *Reminiscences of Life Among the Indians*, p. 177.

147 *"My Indians use what they call pectus":* Hagan, *QP*, p. 75.

147 *The reporter was clearly fixated:* Daily Oklahoman, June 25, 1902, p. 5.

148 *"I am not a bad man":* Quanah Tribune, July 9, 1896 (Fort Sill).

148 *Brown . . . asked to introduce Isaac:* Selden, p. 210.

149 *Ross had killed a warrior named Mohee:* John Henry Brown, *Indian Wars and Pioneers of Texas*, p. 42.

150 *"narrative of plain, unvarnished facts"*: James T. DeShields, *Cynthia Ann Parker: The Story of Her Capture*, p. v. Other quotes in this section are from the book.

151 *DeShields's account became enshrined*: "Parker Fort Massacre," in J. W. Wilbarger, *Indian Depredations in Texas*, pp. 302–20.

151 *"maudlin, sentimental writers"*: Wilbarger, pp. 6–7.

151 *"a popular and trustworthy chief"*: Brown, p. 43.

152 *"I sent you plenty of paper"*: J. H. Brown to Marion Brown, undated, J. H. Brown Papers, 2 E5 (Briscoe).

152 *"I can scarcely understand anything he says"*: Marion T. Brown, *Letters from Fort Sill, 1886–1887*, p. 33.

152 *The two men sat out in the yard:* Ibid., p. 79.

152 *"What will Sul Ross say about Puttack Nocona?"*: Ibid., p. 65.

152 *Her father . . . made no attempt:* For discrepancies in J. H. Brown's book, see pp. 42 and 317.

153 *"No like to come this way"*: Marion Brown, p. 63–64.

153 *"Out of respect to the family of General Ross"*: See "Cynthia Ann Parker," an account by QP's daughter, Neda Birdsong, as told to Paul Wellman, in *Barb Wire Times*, October 1968.

10. Mother and Son

155 *"The Indian does not want to work"*: William T. Hagan, *Taking Indian Lands*, pp. 42–43.

155 *Commissioner Morgan designated February 8:* Hagan, *United States-Comanche Relations*, p. 166. My account of the Jerome Commission is largely from Hagan and QP's testimony, September 27, 1892 (KCA).

158 *He felt he had gotten the best deal: Indian Journal*, March 15, 1894, p. 4.

158 *"Quanah jumped up in a great rage"*: Hugh L. Scott, *Some Memories of a Soldier*, p. 200.

159 Lone Wolf v. Hitchcock: Kracht, Benjamin R., "Kiowa-Comanche-Apache Opening."

159 *Tent cities of 10,000 people each sprang up:* Details of the scene of the opening of Oklahoma Tribal lands are from Charles Moreau Harger, "The Government's Gift of Homes," *Outlook*, pp. 907–10.

160 *Theodore Roosevelt . . . ordered bison heads:* Douglas Brinkley, *The Wilderness Warrior: Theodore Roosevelt and the Crusade for America*, p. 630.

160 *a contest between a superior white race:* See "The Winning of the West" in Slotkin, *Gunfighter Nation*, pp. 29–62.

160 *"war was inevitable"*: Theodore Roosevelt, *The Winning of the West*, Vol. I, pp. 116–7 and 273–74.

160 *"a race of heroes"*: Slotkin, p. 54.

161 *the Comanche chief was "never forgetful"*: Hagan, *QP*, p. 113.

161 *"Roosevelt's own Buffalo Bill production"*: Brinkley, p. 583.

161 *"fully equipped with Indian clothing"*: W. A. Mercer to James F. Randlett, January 18, 1905 (KCA).

161 *"good Indians . . . most of whom had dipped their hands"*: Carter, *Tragedies of Cañón Blanco*, pp. 79–81.

162 *"Give the red man the same chance"*: Hagan, *QP*, p. 183.

162 *Quanah . . . wore his six-shooter*: Charles H. Sommer, "Quanah Parker: Last Chief of the Comanches," p. 10.

162 *serenaded by cardinals and mockingbirds*: Theodore Roosevelt, *Outdoor Pastimes of an American Hunter*, p. 113.

162 *"It was a thoroughly congenial company"*: Roosevelt, p. 114.

162 *Roosevelt mentioned the idea*: TR's buffalo repopulation plan is from Brinkley, p. 609; on the buffalo arrival, see p. 626.

162 *"My mother's job"*: Bill Neeley interview with Anna Birdsong Dean, March 27, 1985 (PPHM).

163 *"This is to certify that Quanah"*: W. A. Jones to QP, September 23, 1899 (Fort Sill).

163 *"I wish you to go over to Quanah's"*: Hagan, *QP*, pp. 107–109.

164 *an Interior Department bureaucrat rejected the request*: Acting Commissioner to Charles Adams, March 14, 1891, KCA Files; the files contain many similar examples.

164 *"My grandfather never trusted a white man"*: Baldwin Parker Jr., "Quanah Parker Lives," *Focus*, Autumn 1985, p. 13.

164 *"Painted, brandishing their bows"*: Hagan, *QP*, p. 102.

164 *he had sat down in a train coach*: Susan Parker St. John Notebook.

165 *"The real reason is because he is an Indian"*: *Oklahoman*, November 3, 1906.

165 *"You put me in little pen"*: Sommer, p. 10.

165 *Quanah was "a most interesting character"*: Adam Parker to Susan Parker St. John, undated, Box 2F 197 (Taulman).

166 *"Quanah is a man worth looking at"*: "Story by Ex.-Gov. J.P. St. John's Wife," *Indian School Journal*, October 1909, p. 37.

166 *"Is this the cousin?"*: Susan Parker St. John Notebook and quotes that follow.

167 *"Dear Sir, Congress has set aside money"*: QP to Governor Thomas Campbell, July 22, 1909 (Fort Sill).

167 *"I see your advertisement"*: J. R. O'Quinn to QP, June 19, 1908, Doc 997 (Fort Sill).

168 *"The relatives of Cynthia Ann . . . did not"*: Interview with Mrs. Ambrosia Miller July 5, 1926 (Taulman).

168 *Quanah dispatched . . . Aubrey C. Birdsong*: Aubrey Birdsong interview, February 23, 1959 (Fort Sill).

168 *Birdsong decided to put the bones*: Aubrey Birdsong affidavit, September 2, 1956, OKHS.

168 *"I felt that this meant so much to Quanah"*: Birdsong interview.

169 *"Are you sure this is my little white mother?"*: Birdsong interview in *Daily Oklahoman*, August 9, 1964.

169 *"I love my mother"*: "Cynthia Ann Parker Is Buried for Second Time," *Daily Oklahoman*, December 5, 1910, p. 1.

169 *"as you know there is considerable prejudice"*: Burk Burnett to QP, October 24, 1905 (Fort Sill).

170 *Quanah spoke to the crowd*: Sommer, p. 9, as well as description of the event and other quotes from QP's speech.

170 *"I run to one side and use this knife"*: Ibid. There remains a discrepancy with Carter's version, in which QP kills Gregg with a pistol.

171 *"I am going to bring some old Indians":* QP to Goodnight, January 7, 1911 (Neeley)

171 *Laura . . . believed the rheumatism:* Laura Birdsong's account is in an undated letter to Susan Parker St. John, 2F 203 (Taulman).

171 *"Father in heaven, this is our brother":* *Lawton Daily News*, February 23, 1911, p. 1.

171 *"Every automobile that could be rented":* *Cache Register*, March 3, 1911. It also gave a detailed account of the funeral day.

172 *"It just seemed as if my heart":* Birdsong letter.

11. The Legend

173 *Quanah's surviving relatives sat down:* S. Hilton to Ernest Stecker, May 29, 1911, KCA File 2246 (National Archives).

173 *"richest Indian in America":* See, for example, Carter, p. 80.

173 *"the Indian Who Made Good" Christian Herald*, July 26, 1911.

174 *"a beacon of light":* James C. Nance, unidentified news clipping, QP File (Fort Sill).

174 *"Fearless and Effective Foe":* Olive King Dixon, "Some Intimate Glimpses of Quanah Parker," *Fort Worth Star Telegram*, April 12, 1936.

174 *The opera, Cynthia Parker: Fanfare,* "40 Acres Arias" (Taulman).

175 *The world premiere was held:* *Dallas Times Herald*, February 17, 1939.

175 *the main architects of the . . . legend:* Details of Joseph and Araminta Taulman's lives are from *A Guide to Joseph E. Taulman Collection* (Briscoe).

176 *"So many wrong statements":* Joseph Taulman to Mrs. A. C. Birdsong, December 29, 1925, 2F 200 (Taulman).

176 *"I wonder if you are fortunate enough":* Mrs. Birdsong to Taulman, January 17, 1926.

176 *"The market for historical scenarios":* Adeline M. Alford to Araminta Taulman, October 10, 1936, 2F 201 (Taulman).

177 *"On one occasion the Redmen declared war":* The Rachel Plummer Narrative, 1926; the fantasy foreword is signed by "Mrs. Jane Kennedy, Granddaughter of J. W. Parker, Mrs. Rachel Lofton, great granddaughter, and Mrs. Susie Hendrix, granddaughter" (SMU).

178 *a primary school teacher in nearby Mexia:* Details of Elsie Hamill's efforts to learn about the Parker story are from "Mexia Teacher Brought Together White and Indian Descendants," *Mexia Daily News*, August 15, 1965 (Baylor).

178 *"Dear Mrs. Hamill,":* Wanada Parker Page to Mrs. Weldon Hamill, April 6, 1952 (Baylor).

179 *the army decided:* The story of the army's campaign to move QP and Cynthia Ann graves is from Angie Debo, "Two Graves in Oklahoma," *Harper's*, December 1956, p. 66; and Douglas C. Jones, "The Grave of Quanah Parker," *Public Relations Quarterly*, 1970.

181 *"To tell the truth, Captain":* *Houston Chronicle*, October 3, 1965, Sect. 3, p. 11.

181 *They left it there:* Saving the Star House is from Herbert Woesner speech at Parker Reunion, June 23, 2000; Edward Charles Ellenbrook, "Cache's Woesner Saves Historic Buildings," *Lawton Constitution*, December 9, 2003; author's interview with Kathy Treadwell Gipson, June 28, 2009.

181 *"It was one of the happiest moments":* Audrey Routh, "Chief Quanah's Star House and Its 4-Year Trek," *Daily Oklahoman*, October 13, 1963.

182 *Ben was born in 1868:* Details of Ben Parker's life are from author's interview with Jo Nell Parker and her son W. Scott Nicholson, June 9, 2011.

182 *Ben said later he was surprised:* Author's interview with Jim Bob Parker, July 4, 2009. Ben J. Parker told his own version of the Parker legend, "Early Times in Texas and History of the Parker Family" (Taulman).

12. The Author

185 *the orange-backed dime novels:* Henry Nash Smith, *Virgin Land: The American West as Symbol and Myth,* p. 91.

185 *One recurring character:* Ibid., p. 112.

186 *The first great cowboy novel:* Castle Freeman Jr., "Owen Wister: Brief Life of a Western Mythmaker, 1860–1938."

186 *He is not too fond of foreigners:* Owen Wister, *The Virginian,* pp. 14 and 39.

186 *"a slim young giant":* Ibid., p. 4.

186 *The land was a metaphor:* See Richard Slotkin, *Regeneration Through Violence,* p. 554.

187 *His ancestors were pioneers:* Dan LeMay, *Alan LeMay: A Biography of the Author of* The Searchers, pp. 6–13.

188 *Dan Brown, Alan's maternal grandfather:* Undated note, Box 11 (LeMay Papers).

189 *"in which I accomplished nothing":* Letter dated December 29, 1954, Box 23 (Le-May).

189 *"I've also tried several other things":* Ibid.

190 *It was, of course, a Western:* Dan LeMay, p. 20.

190 *"a face as friendly in expression":* Alan LeMay, *Painted Ponies,* p. 6. The plot description and quotations are from the novel.

192 *He broke into the high-end magazines:* Dan LeMay, p. 24.

192 *"a completely literate Western":* *New York Herald Tribune,* July 21, 1935.

193 *"I am now thirty-eight years old":* Dan LeMay, p. 37.

193 *"Dad said they tasted like a steam kettle":* Author's interview with Dan LeMay.

193 *"The deadline I believe would actually be a help":* Alan LeMay to Max Wilkinson, January 30, 1959, Box 23 (LeMay).

194 *he and Arlene got married:* Dan LeMay, p. 44.

194 *"a more primal tint of virility":* Jesse L. Lasky Jr., *Whatever Happened to Hollywood?* p. 195.

194 *He summoned Alan just days:* Dan LeMay, *Never Dull,* p. 59.

195 *"a hashed-over product":* Ibid., p. 57.

195 *"In social moments, as at dinner":* Ibid., p. 60.

195 *"the world's most bewildered inner tube":* Ibid., p. 65.

195 *Alan and Arlene's lifestyle:* Ibid., p. 51.

195 *The great Frank Sinatra rented a house:* James Kaplan, *Sinatra: The Voice,* p. 444.

196 *Gary Cooper intervened:* For Gary Cooper's purchase of *Useless Cowboy,* see *Never Dull,* p. 147.

197 *"All I want of this business":* Ibid., p. 226.

197 *an original screenplay treatment called* African Pitfall: For more on *African Pitfall,* see Box 1 (LeMay).

197 *It wasn't long before he found another, similar story:* There is an ongoing and perhaps irresolvable conflict among aficionados of *The Searchers* over the true origins of the novel. Some insist Alan LeMay was inspired by the story of Brit Johnson, a black teamster who ransomed his abducted wife and children from Comanches in 1865. Others point to the story of Millie Durgan, captured as a baby by Kiowas in 1864. LeMay's papers at UCLA are incomplete and inconclusive. But the parallels between the original story of Cynthia Ann Parker and the book—a nine-year-old girl captured by Comanches in a raid in which family members are slaughtered, her long sojourn as a Comanche, and the obsessive efforts of her uncle to find her—are undeniable. As is LeMay's journey to Elkhart, Texas, the heart of Parker country, and his visit with Ben Parker, the details of which have never been published before.

197 *He rented office space:* Author's interview with Dan LeMay, June 2008.

13. The Novel

198 *"holding the back door of Texas":* Alan LeMay, *The Searchers,* pp. 4–5. The plot summary and quotations are all from the novel.

199 *LeMay collected information on sixty-four Indian abductions:* LeMay Papers, Box 23, and LeMay letter to Mrs. Marcus McMillin, December 12, 1960.

199 *"a big burly figure on a strong but speedless horse":* LeMay, *The Searchers,* pp. 8–9.

199 *"a quiet boy, dark as an Indian":* Ibid., p. 4.

200 *"It was Martha who would not quit":* Ibid., p. 5.

200 *"This is a rough country":* Ibid., p. 53.

201 *"Did they—was she?":* Ibid., p. 58.

201 *"This don't change anything":* Ibid., p. 64.

201 *"That's what scares me, Laurie":* Ibid., pp. 82–83.

201 *"I see now why the Comanches murder":* Ibid., p. 247.

202 *"I believe you'd do it":* Ibid., p. 219.

202 *"That country seemed to have some kind of weird spell":* Ibid., pp. 173–74.

202 *"It tore at them, snatching their breaths":* Ibid., p. 122.

203 *"I have no place," she tells him:* Ibid., pp. 271–72.

204 *"I ain't larned but one thing about an Indian":* Ibid., p. 32.

204 *"The Comanches themselves seemed unable":* Ibid., p. 68.

204 *"A great deal has been written":* Alan LeMay letter, January 26, 1960, Box 23 (LeMay).

204 *Debbie has "had time to be with half the Comanche bucks":* The Searchers, pp. 203–205.

205 *"In all I wrote about 2,000 pages":* Alan LeMay letter, January 20, 1960 (LeMay).

205 *The Searchers . . . "represents about all I have":* Alan LeMay to Dolores Napoli, June 9, 1958 (Box 23).

205 *"Its simplicity is one of subtle art":* Orville Prescott, "Books of the Times," *NYT,* November 3, 1954.

206 *"One of the White House correspondents":* Evan Thomas to Alan LeMay, February 10, 1955 (Harper & Row Papers).

206 *"I am told (not too reliably)":* Alan LeMay to Evan Thomas, November 18, 1954 (Ibid.).

14. The Director

211 *"A running horse remains":* Frank Nugent, "Opening Scenes" in *TV and Screen Writing*, p. 22.

211 *a template for the Western film:* A. O. Scott, "How the Western Was Won," *NYT Magazine*, p. 56.

211 *The first moving pictures of Indians:* Paul Chaat Smith, *Everything You Know About Indians Is Wrong*, p. 44.

212 *One of the first was a short called* The Bank Robbery: "Sham Bank Robbery," *Clarion and Indiahoma News*, August 21, 1908.

213 *just as Indian characters helped shape movies:* Peter C. Rollins and John E. O'Connor, *Hollywood's Indian*, p. ix.

214 *"A director can put his whole heart and soul":* *Illustrated Daily News* (Los Angeles), February 22, 1925 (JFP).

215 *Francis acted in and helped direct:* Scott Eyman, *Print the Legend*, pp. 41–42.

215 *he played a Ku Klux Klansman:* Joseph McBride, *Searching for John Ford*, pp. 77–78.

215 *he teamed up with a dark-eyed actor:* Peter Bogdanovich, *John Ford*, p. 40.

216 *a strapping teenager named Marion Morrison:* For Marion Morrison's regard for Harry Carey, see Garry Wills, *John Wayne's America*, 114–15.

216 *The two men went on to make . . . twenty-three Westerns:* Dan Ford, *Pappy*, p. 18.

216 *"They weren't shoot-'em-ups":* Bogdanovich, p. 39.

216 *By 1923 he was making almost $45,000 per year:* Dan Ford, p. 27.

217 *"When he walked on the set":* Andrew McLaglen interview, *The Filmmaker and the Legend* (documentary).

217 *"bruised and battered":* Eyman, pp. 131–32.

218 *Born in Georgia of southern aristocrats:* For Merian C. Cooper's life story, see Mark Cotta Vaz, *Living Dangerously: The Adventures of Merian C. Cooper*.

218 *he would tear out enough pages:* "Man with Camera," *New Yorker*, May 30, 1931, p. 25.

218 *"That's too bad," said Cooper:* Merian Cooper to John Wayne, 1971 (BYU).

219 *Over time Cooper became the middleman:* Vaz, p. 250. See also Bea Benjamin interview, p. 1, Box 11, F17 (JFP).

220 *"There was an essence of fear":* Frank Baker interview, July 30, 1977, OH1 (MHL).

220 *"Daddy is what we called . . . a periodic":* Barbara Ford interview (JFP).

220 *"One drink—he's the type of person":* Mark Armistead interview (JFP).

220 *"They'd go on his yacht and drink":* McBride interview with author, November 14, 2008.

221 *His "thick eyeglasses protruded":* Maureen O'Hara, *'Tis, Herself: A Memoir*, pp. 65–68.

221 *"I looked at its enormity":* Ibid., p. 69.

221 *"I felt my head snap back":* Ibid., p. 104.

221 *Ford . . . "built walls of secrecy":* Ibid., p. 261.

221 *"one of the most famous leading men":* Ibid., p. 190.

221 *"I didn't really feel I could act":* Harry Carey Jr. interview with Dan Ford, B11 F18, Reels 3 and 4, p. 14 (JFP).

222 *"Ford was a bully":* Author's interview with Harry Carey Jr., March 25, 2009.

222 *"I remember Jack . . . put his head on my breast":* Olive Carey interview (JFP).

223 *"Read this," Pat told his father:* Pat Ford interview by James D'Arc (BYU).

223 *"I went into Dave's office":* Cooper to Wayne, March 15, 1971 (BYU).

15. The Actor

226 *With a wife and four children to support:* Randy Roberts and James S. Olson, *John Wayne American*, p. 117.

226 *"When I started, I knew I was no actor":* Dean Jennings, "John Wayne: The Woes of Box-Office King," *Saturday Evening Post*, October 27, 1962.

227 *Thus . . . "the beginning of the finest relationship":* John Wayne, *My Kingdom Is a Horse* ms., p. 9 (Zolotow).

227 *"I'd never seen a genius at work before":* Pilar Wayne, *John Wayne: My Life with the Duke*, p. 19.

227 *"I poured out my troubles to him":* *My Kingdom* ms., p. 6.

228 *"I walked out of the gate":* Ibid., p. 8.

228 *"I should have complained to Ford":* Ibid., pp. 1–2.

228 *Walsh was looking for a new talent:* Interview with Raoul Walsh, April 10, 1972, Box 12, F6 (Zolotow).

228 *"We looked high and low":* *Man and Superman* draft, "The Making of John Wayne," p. 204 Box 11, F1 (Zolotow).

228 *"He had a certain western hang":* Ibid., p. 209.

228 *"They came up with John Wayne":* *Playboy* interview, May 1971.

229 *"Instead of facing me with it":* John Wayne interview (JFP).

230 *John Ford "did not surround himself":* Dan Ford, *Pappy*, p. 118.

230 *The Gower Gulch cowboys:* Diana Serra Carey, daughter of cowhand Jack Montgomery, gives the most detailed and loving account of the horsemen and their work in *The Hollywood Posse*, dedicated to her parents and "the Gower Gulch men."

230 *"I studied him for many weeks":* "Lights! Camera! Action!" chapter of *My Kingdom* ms., p. 9.

231 *"Before I came along":* Ibid., p. 8.

231 *Paul "coached him, he taught him":* Author's interview with Carey.

231 *"Duke's basic problem":* Paul Fix, *Man and Superman* draft, p. 257, B11 (Zolotow).

231 *He believed the pause helped rivet the audience:* Joseph McBride note to the author, p. 5.

232 *no one expects Laurence Olivier:* Jeanine Basinger, *The Star Machine*, p. 75.

232 *"I've found the character":* "John Wayne—Arnold Michaelis Interview," *Saturday Evening Post*, 1962, p. 5.

232 *"We treated them as if they had the same moral code":* Joe McInerney, "John Wayne Talks Tough," *Film Comment*, p. 54.

233 *something that was true:* David Denby, "Clint Eastwood's Shifting Landscape," *New Yorker*, March 8, 2010, p. 55.

233 *"Christ, if you learned to act":* McBride, p. 280.

233 *"You idiot, couldn't you play it?":* Ibid., p. 281.

233 *"Can't you walk, for Chrissake":* Ibid., p. 298.

233 *"Ford took Duke by the chin":* Roberts and Olson, p. 155.

233 *"I was so fucking mad":* McBride, p. 297.

235 *Just like Humphrey Bogart:* Denby, p. 55.

235 *"One thing I can't understand":* Bogdanovich, p. 72.

236 *"Mr. Ford is not one of your subtle directors":* Frank Nugent, "Stagecoach," *NYT,* March 3, 1939.

236 *he got to Midway Island:* Account of JF's filming of the Battle of Midway is largely from McBride, pp. 335–7, and Robert Parrish, *Growing Up in Hollywood,* pp. 144–51.

237 *"Well Jesus, I'm forty years old":* JW interview, Tape 2, Side 4, pp. 4–5 in Box 12, F17 (JFP).

238 *"You represent the American serviceman":* Slotkin, *Gunfighter Nation,* pp. 514–15.

238 *"Duke, can't you manage a salute":* Lindsay Anderson, *About John Ford,* p. 226.

238 *"Don't ever talk to Duke":* Eyman, p. 279.

238 *Argosy, which was partly bankrolled:* Vaz, p. 335.

239 *"I never knew the big son of a bitch could act":* McBride, p. 459.

239 *"I don't think he ever really had any kind of respect":* Joseph McBride and Michael Wilmington, *John Ford,* p. 153.

240 *"It was an emotional reaction":* JW interview, Tape 80, 1 (JFP).

240 *the melancholy authority figure:* Wills, p. 13.

241 *"not the world's greatest actor":* "The Wages of Virtue," *Time,* March 3, 1952.

241 *"There is enough unacknowledged sorrow":* A. O. Scott, "How the Western Was Won," *NYT,* June 11, 2006.

242 *"His role . . . was to emerge after the battle":* Wills, p. 197.

242 *"My name is John Ford":* A detailed account of the meeting is in Parrish, pp. 207–10.

243 *three to six packs of cigarettes:* Pilar Wayne, p. 103; James Bacon, "John Wayne: The Last Cowboy," *Us,* June 27, 1978.

244 *"My dad had tremendous loyalty":* Author's email interview with Patrick Wayne, February 5, 2009.

16. The Production

245 *"No Western picture":* Frank Gruber, "The Western," in *TV and Screen Writing,* pp. 39–44.

246 *MGM offered a 50–50 split:* Merian Cooper telegram, December 14, 1954 (CVW)

246 *John Ford got a flat fee:* Whitney contract, Nov. 29, 1954, Box 12, F23 (JFP).

246 *"We are busy working on the script":* Ronald L. Davis, *John Ford: Hollywood's Old Master,* p. 271.

246 *Ford had intended to make a film:* Swindell, pp. 146–47.

247 *"I go out to Arizona, I breathe fresh air":* Ford undated audio interview (MHL).

247 *"a very strange man":* James D'Arc interview with Pat Ford, April 25, 1979 (BYU). Scott Eyman's *Print the Legend* has a detailed accounts of Pat's relationship with JF: see pp. 298–99, 307, 499–500, 507–508, and more.

248 *"Pat was an able guy":* Author's interview with Dan Ford, March 22, 2009.

248 *"that capon son of a bitch":* O'Hara, p. 179.

249 *"There is no communal life":* Inter-Office Memorandum, February 1, 1955; the account that follows is from Pat Ford's extensive notes (JFP).

249 *"We hope to portray . . . with as much barbarism"*: JF, "Notes on *The Searchers*," January 26, 1955 (JFP).

249 *"Their villages . . . are scenes of utter squalor"*: PF, Notes on *The Searchers*, January 26, 1955.

250 *"The Indians were to be treated fairly"*: Eleanor S. Whitney, *Invitation to Joy*, p. 5.

250 *"It is important that the costumes"*: JF, "Notes" (JFP).

251 *"rough . . . rugged . . . cold"*: JF memo, p. 3, January 26, 1955 (JFP).

251 *"in the style of Donald O'Connor"*: Kathleen Cliffton interview, Side 1, p. 7, Box 11, F20 (JFP). See also Joseph McBride, "The Pathological Hero's Conscience: Screenwriter Frank S. Nugent Was the Quiet Man Behind John Ford," *Written By*, May 2001.

252 *"The Grapes of Wrath . . . is just about as good as any picture"*: Nugent review, *NYT*, January 25, 1940.

252 *"a very exorbitant salary"*: Dave Jampel, "Films More Mature Today, Says Screenwriter Nugent," *Mainichi Daily News*, 1961 (FSN).

252 *"My opinion of this script"*: Nugent to Zanuck, May 20, 1942 (FSN).

252 *"Dear Frank"*: Zanuck to Nugent, May 17, 1944 (FSN).

252 *He even tried unsuccessfully:* Nugent to Lester Markel, March 14, 1944 (FSN).

253 *"to get the smell and feel of the land"*: Anderson, p. 242. British film critic Lindsay Anderson corresponded with Nugent, Dudley Nichols, and Nunnally Johnson in the early 1950s and published their accounts of screenplay writing for Ford.

253 *"groping like a musician"*: Anderson, p. 244.

253 *"He used to fight your grandfather"*: James W. Bellah interview, p. 5, Box 11, F16 (JFP).

254 *"just a little right of Attila"*: Ronald L. Davis, *John Ford*, p. 204.

254 *"I liked your script, boys"*: McBride, p. 497.

254 *"There's no such thing as a good script"*: Bogdanovich, p. 107.

254 *his favorite "body and fender man"*: JF interview, Tape 28 (JFP).

255 *"The difference between his Westerns"*: Kevin Nugent interview.

255 *"Character is not shown so much"*: Frank Nugent, "Notes on Screenwriting," January 30, 1947 (FSN).

255 *"Ford never has formally surrendered"*: Nugent, "Hollywood's Favorite Rebel," *Saturday Evening Post*, July 23, 1949.

255 *"There is a situation or a condition"*: Nugent, "Opening Scenes," pp. 20–21.

256 *"It is no accident"*: Ibid., p. 22. The quotes that follow are also from Nugent's explanation of how *The Searchers* begins.

257 *"I know John Wayne is a certain type of man"*: Jampel article.

257 *"the bedded-down meadow lark"*: LeMay, *The Searchers*, p. 7.

257 *"Yes . . . we got a chance"*: Ibid., p. 47.

257 *"A Texan is nothing but a human man"*: Ibid., p. 53.

257 *"a world of sadness and hopelessness"*: Nugent, "Revised Final Screenplay," p. 9.

258 *"Fella could mistake you for a half-breed"*: The actual film dialogue. In the screenplay: "Mistook you for a half-breed," ibid., p. 4.

258 *"She's your nothin'"*: Ibid., p. 49.

259 *Using a letter that Martin writes to Laurie:* Ibid, beginning on p. 59.

259 *"Frank worked awfully hard"*: Scott Eyman interview of Jean Nugent, p. 1.

259 *"He'd come home at night exhausted"*: Kevin Nugent interview.

260 *"What you did was simple"*: Harry Carey Jr., *In the Company of Heroes*, p. 7.

260 *"There was absolutely no chain of command"*: Ibid., p. 8.

260 *"I was dropped by the best studios"*: Vera Miles quote is repeated constantly, but never with attribution. See http://good-old-hollywood.buzzsugar.com/Vera-Miles.

260 *Natalie's mother consented:* Suzanne Finstad, *Natasha: The Biography of Natalie Wood*, p. 199.

261 *"They wanted you for that"*: "Fess Parker: An Interview with Michael Barrier," 2003–4, www.michaelbarrier.com/Parker/interview_fess_parker.html.

261 *"You'd like to play the part"*: Eyman, p. 444.

261 *another impossibly handsome young actor:* see Hunter's biographical information at www.jeffreyhuntermovies.com.

261 *"nowhere near the type"*: Hunter's account is from *Picturegoer*, September 29, 1956.

262 *Cornelius Vanderbilt Whitney was one of those improbable:* Eyman, pp. 442–43. For Whitney's authorized biography, see Jeffrey L. Rodengen, *The Legend of Cornelius Vanderbilt Whitney*.

263 *They formed a new film company:* Vaz, p. 355.

263 *"not for self-aggrandizement"*: Thomas M. Pryor, "Hollywood Newcomer," *NYT*, April 1, 1956.

264 *"Jack Ford is back and raring to go"*: Merian Cooper to C. V. Whitney, January 29, 1955 (CVW).

264 *"I wish to again emphasize to you"*: Whitney to Cooper, February 25, 1956 (CVW).

264 *"My husband admired Ford so much"*: Eyman interview with Marylou Whitney, p. 3.

264 *"HAVE BEEN WORKING INTENSIVELY"*: Whitney to JF, February 21, 1956, Box 12 (JFP).

265 *"It seems that the market is being flooded"*: Whitney to Ford, March 23, 1955 (JFP).

265 *Sonny Whitney "could afford to be a very nice man"*: Pat Ford interview (D'Arc).

266 *"A man with that many millions"*: Box 21, Tape 23 (JFP).

17. The Valley, Part One

268 *"My favorite location is Monument Valley"*: Peter Cowie, *John Ford and the American West*, p. 186. For the influence of Charles M. Russell, see also William Howze, "The Influence of Western Painting and Genre Painting on the Films of John Ford."

269 *Geologists don't know exactly:* Arthur Frankel e-mail to the author, August 5, 2010.

269 *Willa Cather wrote:* Willa Cather, *Death Comes for the Archbishop*, pp. 94–95.

269 *The Navajos loved canned tomatoes:* For this and other details of the Gouldings' early years in Monument Valley, see Sam Moon, *Tall Sheep: Harry Goulding, Monument Valley Trader*, pp. 46–48.

270 *"It was their lands"*: Ibid., p. 29.

270 *Harry "just wandered in"*: Pat Ford interview (BYU).

270 *Pat's father was entranced:* For the story of meeting JF, see Moon, p. 145–49.

271 *about ninety seconds of the footage:* James D'Arc, *When Hollywood Came to Town*, p. 208.

271 *It had a double bed:* Moon, p. 199.

271 *"It gives me a chance to get away"*: Burt Kennedy, "A Talk with John Ford," *Action!* September–October 1968, p. 6.

271 *bad weather in Arizona:* Daily Production Reports, June 13, 1955, Box 6, F. 22 (JFP).

271 *the Super Chief was the appropriate:* For a description of the Super Chief, see www .american-rails.com/super-chief.html.

272 *"A shooting schedule"*: Cooper to Whitney, June 15, 1955 (CVW).

272 *They carved roadways: Warner Brothers Presents*, March 12, 1956, TV show, narrated by Gig Young (see *Searchers* DVD).

273 *"The women were installed"*: *A Turning of the Earth* (documentary).

273 *"Wind was an enemy"*: Frank Perrett, C. V. Whitney Productions press release, undated, p. 4 (WB).

274 *"adobe, whitewashed but with the bricks showing"*: JF Notes, February 10, 1955 (JFP).

274 *Lana Wood recalled:* Finstad, p. 171.

274 *The men earned $15 a day:* "AGREEMENT between C.V. Whitney Pictures and District Tribal Council (MHL).

274 *"A lot of people came"*: Susie Yazzie interview with the author, March 24, 2008.

274 *"When we first went into the Indian reservations"*: Bill Libby, "The Old Wrangler Rides Again," 1964, in *JF Interviews*, p. 55.

274 *"People have said that on the screen"*: Ibid., p. 71.

275 *"We'll get it off"*: The Hosteen Tso story is from Moon, pp. 149 and 153–55.

275 *"the valley was buried"*: Eyman, p. 207.

275 *"At Monument Valley I have my own personal tribe"*: Ibid., p. 351.

276 *"They were a very dignified people"*: Bogdanovich, pp. 94–95.

276 *"My sympathy was always"*: Tag Gallagher, *John Ford: The Man and His Films*, p. 254.

276 *like a horror movie:* Slotkin, *Gunfighter Nation*, p. 361.

277 *"It was a job"*: McBride, p. 295.

277 *"The Indian children looked on him"*: Chuck Roberson, *The Fall Guy*, p. 169.

277 *a two-year-old Navajo girl:* CVW Productions press release, undated (WB).

277 *he filmed eleven setups:* Daily filing from Shooting Schedule and Daily Production Reports of CV Whitney Pictures (JFP).

277 *Ford also shot scenes:* Some of the few surviving outtakes contain this ride, which appears in *A Turning of the Earth*, Nick Redman's 1998 documentary.

278 *"They had bodies like iron"*: Carey, p. 159.

278 *"I like the cowboys"*: JF Interview, undated, audio file (MHL).

278 *Lee Bradley . . . Frank McGrath . . . Jack Pennick:* See *A Turning of the Earth*.

278 *"We were his personal soldiers"*: Roberson, p. 66.

278 *"He never shot in continuity"*: Clothier interview, p. 15, Box 11, F21 (JFP).

279 *The man who emerged:* For a physical description of JF, see Carey, p. 19.

279 *"It was a feeling of reverence"*: Carey interview, p. 13 (JFP).

279 *The two men had been partners:* See Carey's account of JF and Hoch, p. 18.

281 *"Winnie, what do you think?"*: Ibid., p. 67.

281 *"images that are so detailed"*: Ruthurd Dykstra, "The Search for Spectators," *Kino*, p. 1.

281 *"he avoided the temptation"*: Winton Hoch, p. 1, Box 12, F3 (JFP).

281 *"Too many directors"*: Ken Curtis, p. 4, Box 11, F22 (JFP).

282 *"He didn't want any rehearsing"*: Pippa Scott interview with author, March 24, 2009.

282 *"The actors get tired"*: Bogdanovich, p. 99.

282 *"He never let us get into the scene"*: Curtis Lee Hansen, "Henry Fonda: Reflections on 40 Years of Make-Believe," *Cinema*, p. 15.

282 *"Oh God, how the man would cheat"*: Ace Holmes, Box 12, F5, p. 20 (JFP).

283 *"He had all his people there"*: Chuck Hayward, Box 12, F1, p. 2 (JFP).

18. The Valley, Part Two

285 *The average film director:* For a discussion of master shots, over-the-shoulder shots and coverage, see *4Filmmaking* website: http://production.4filmmaking.com/cinematography1.html.

285 *"John Ford shoots a picture"*: Wingate Smith, Box 12, F15, p. 3 (JFP).

285 *"If you give them a lot of film"*: Gallagher.

286 *There were thirty-three drivers, five five-ton trucks:* Daily Production Report, June 13, 1955, Box 6, F22 (JFP).

286 *Sonny Whitney . . . arrived by Cessna:* Whitney telegram, June 14, 1955 (CVW).

286 *"Crockery flew"*: Eleanor Searle Whitney, p. 5.

287 *"I would surely like to give her"*: Whitney to Cooper, May 3, 1955 (CVW).

287 *The superrich . . . "look upon everything"*: E. S. Whitney, p. 122.

287 *"Whitney had been a polo player"*: Pat Ford interview by D'Arc.

288 *Sonny "came riding up and he was proud"*: Terry Wilson, Box 12, F19, p. 19 (JFP).

288 *Smart Set column in the* New York Journal-American: October 14, 1955.

288 *"We were scared to death"*: Pat Ford interview.

289 *"Two things make Western pictures"*: George Stevens, *Conversations with the Great Moviemakers*, p. 243.

289 *Two stuntmen went down:* Production Notes, June 22, 1955 (JFP).

289 *"I don't think he was terribly well"*: Pippa Scott interview.

289 *"he liked to push people"*: McBride, pp. 567–68.

289 *Even Ford's beloved stuntmen felt his wrath:* Roberson, p. 160.

290 *"When will you learn to ride"*: Ibid., p. 161.

290 *"The whole relationship was something"*: Scott interview.

290 *He lit one Camel after another:* Carey, p. 36.

290 *"My father would say"*: Patrick Wayne interview.

290 *"When I looked up at him in rehearsal"*: Carey, p. 170.

291 *"Was she . . . ? Did they . . . ?"*: Nugent, Revised Final Screenplay, p. 41.

291 *"He didn't say a word"*: Carey, p. 172.

291 *"He was very sweet with me"*: Scott interview.

291 *"I was his godson"*: Pat Wayne interview.

292 *"He used no technical terms"*: Louis Pollock, "Alone–but Not for Long," *Motion Picture* 46:550, November 1956.

292 *"When I crossed my arm"*: From *The American West of John Ford*, CBS documentary, December 5, 1971, p. 30 (JFP).

292 *"Everybody thinks I'm crazy"*: Olive Carey, pp. 21–3 (JFP).

293 *July Fourth, they took a break:* The description of the festivities is from the Carey interview and McBride, p. 555.

294 *"More than having received the Oscars":* JF Interviews, p. 71.

19. The Studio

295 *RKO-Pathé Studio in Culver City:* For a description of the studio's history, see www.seeing-stars.com/studios/culverstudios.shtml.

296 *"Captain, the Reverend Samuel Johnson Clayton!":* Revised Final Screenplay, pp. 12–14.

298 *"She slugged me":* Pippa Scott interview.

299 *"I remember being very unnerved":* A Turning of the Earth (documentary).

299 *He once told Fred Zinnemann:* McBride, p. 161.

299 *some of the scenes "could have been shot":* Bosley Crowther, NYT, May 31, 1956.

299 *Some of the captives . . . "have been enslaved":* JF Story Notes, February 15, 1955 (JFP).

300 *"It's hard to realize they're white":* Screenplay, p. 74.

300 *"Helluva shot":* Peter Bogdanovich, Who the Hell's in It, p. 289.

301 *"'I'm sorry, girl' he tells her":* Screenplay, p. 111.

301 *"I wonder, did they box themselves in a corner?":* Author's interview with James D'Arc.

302 *Ford had shot 187,402 feet of film:* Daily Production Report (JFP).

302 *Max Steiner took over:* Steiner's biography is from Thomas Kiefner, "Max Steiner," in *Film Music: The Neglected Art*, February 13, 2008.

302 *"as a kind gesture":* James D'Arc notes to The Searchers music CD.

303 *"that is completely haunting":* JF Story Notes, January 28, 1955, p. 2 (JFP).

303 *Ford turned to Stan Jones:* Jones's bio is from Carey, pp. 91–94, and Stan Jones, www.westernmusic.com/performers/hof-jones-stan.html.

303 *"You've got a guy alone":* Bogdanovich commentary on The Searchers DVD.

303 *"I am sorry you are not altogether satisfied":* Whitney to Steiner, December 9, 1955, (CVW).

303 The Searchers *"goes down as my favorite":* Whitney to JF, December 9, 1955 (CVW).

303 *"The picture is brutal in spots":* Walter MacEwen to Jack Warner, December 5, 1955 (WB).

304 *Whitney was eager to get paid:* See Warner to Whitney, October 25 and November 11, 1955; Whitney to Warner, November 2, 1955 (CVW).

304 *"Frankly I have been very disappointed":* Cooper to Warner, March 10, 1956 (BYU).

20. The Movie

306 *"a myth based on other myths":* Tag Gallagher, "Angels Gambol Where They Will," *The Western Reader*, p. 272.

306 *"icons of savage violent beauty":* Ibid.

307 *"I wish Uncle Ethan was here":* Searchers screenplay, p. 20.

307 *"You speak good American":* Ibid., p. 83. But in the screenplay Scar does not make his classic reply.

309 *"These shots . . . are among the treasures":* Roger Ebert, *"The Searchers,"* November 25, 2001.

310 *"organic, not imposed on him":* This and subsequent quotes are from Robert Warshow, "Movie Chronicle: The Westerner," in *The Western Reader*, p. 36.

310 *"The pictures . . . end with his death":* Ibid., p. 40.

310 *"What these apologists forget":* Jon Tuska, *The American West in Film*, pp. xix, 61, 58, and 237.

310 *Native Americans themselves:* JoEllen Shively's PhD thesis: *Cowboys & Indians: The Perception of Western Films Among American Indians and Anglo-Americans.*

311 *"asking Indians to watch a John Wayne Western":* Tom Grayson Colonnese, "Native American Reactions to *The Searchers*," in Eckstein and Lehmann, p. 335.

311 *Scar cannot let go:* Ibid., p. 342.

311 *"Come along, Mrs. Pauley":* Screenplay, p. 63. Martin's kick is in the script, p. 65.

312 *"Do you know what Ethan will do?":* Ibid., pp. 103–104.

313 *"The film is not an aberration":* McBride and Wilmington, p. 148.

314 *"When Ethan picks up Debbie":* Michael Munn, *John Wayne: The Man Behind the Myth*, p. 176.

314 *"Undoubtedly one of the greatest":* Hollywood Reporter, March 13, 1956.

314 *"one of the greatest":* Motion Picture Herald, March 17, 1956.

314 *"a rip-snorting Western":* NYT, May 31, 1956.

314 *"strange but fascinating":* Film Bulletin, March 19, 1956.

314 *"the lapses in logic"* Time, June 25, 1956, p. 60.

315 *"Racism was so endemic":* McBride interview.

315 *"an unmistakable neurotic":* Anderson, p. 156.

315 *"How can I hate John Wayne":* Lesley Stern, *The Scorsese Connection*, p. 38.

315 *"You know, I just don't understand":* McInerney, p. 55.

315 *"Ethan Edwards . . . was probably the most fascinating character":* JW voice-over in *The American West of John Ford* (documentary), 1971.

21. The Legacy

316 *"It made a lot of money":* McBride and Wilmington, p. 45.

318 *"The worst piece of crap":* Pappy, p. 290.

318 *"The Man Who Shot Liberty Valance is a serious assault":* Tara Brady, "In praise of an old Hollywood master," *Irish Times*, June 7, 2012.

319 *"Young people, including film students":* Peary, p. ix.

319 *"I am not a poet":* Ibid., p. xvi.

320 *A pivotal article:* Joseph McBride and Michael Wilmington, "Prisoner of the Desert," *Sight and Sound*, Autumn 1971.

321 *"I wanted to be Scar":* From *The Searchers: An Appreciation* (documentary).

321 *"So you wanna be a picture maker":* By John Ford (documentary).

321 *"He was a great artist":* A Turning of the Earth (documentary).

321 *As executive producer of* Cowboys & Aliens: Rick Marshall, *"Cowboys & Aliens'* Co-Writer Says Flick's 'Originality' Sets It Apart," April 27, 2011.

322 *"Ford's in my mind":* "War Horse and the Influence of John Ford on Steven Spielberg," November 27, 2011.

322 *"an unholy alliance of critics":* Byron, p. 45.

322 *"a spoiled masterpiece":* Richard Schickel, "The Man Who Shot the West," *NYT Book Review*, January 9, 2000.

323 *"a peculiarly formal and stilted movie":* Pauline Kael, *5,001 Nights at the Movies*, p. 662.

323 *"The pressure of the film":* Jonathan Lethem, "Defending *The Searchers*," *Tin House*, Winter 2001.

323 *"His persona gathers in one place":* Lethem, "The Darkest Side of John Wayne," *Salon*, July 1997.

323 *"preposterous in its plotting":* Stephen Metcalf, "The Worst Best Movie," *Slate*, July 6, 2006.

324 *"Writers are forgotten people":* Gary Arnold, "Hero's Welcome for *The Searchers*," *Washington Post*, September 23, 1979.

324 *feminist social critic Susan Faludi:* See *The Terror Dream*, 2007.

325 *"We worked together":* Author's interview with James D'Arc.

325 *"I've had people searching":* Author's interview with Leith Adams, June 23, 2009.

Epilogue: Quanah

327 *The fierce Texas sun was incinerating:* The author attended Quanah Parker Reunion on the one hundredth anniversary of QP's death.

327 *"May the Great Sprit smile":* Recorded on a monument outside Quanah's City Hall.

329 *Wayne took visitors for a drive:* Author's interview with Wayne Gipson, June 10, 2011.

330 *"I don't believe in restoring":* Herbert Woesner remarks, Parker Reunion, June 23, 2000.

330 *"For us it's a sacred place":* Author's interview with Ron Parker, June 13, 2008.

331 *"They say there was no jealousy":* Ardith Parker Leming tour, June 12, 2009.

332 *"In the event these temporary measures":* "Structural Stabilization Report: Star House," no author or date.

332 *"Lots of people had wanted to buy it":* Author's interview with Kathy Gipson Treadwell.

332 *"There are people showing up":* Gipson interview.

333 *"I know there are a lot of missing pieces":* Author's interview with Dorothy Poole, July 9, 2008.

339 *"We are shape shifters":* Paul Chaat Smith, *Everything You Know About Indians Is Wrong*, p. 58.

BIBLIOGRAPHY

Parts I and II (Cynthia Ann and Quanah Parker)

Archives and Collections
Bancroft Library, University of California at Berkeley
Baylor University, Waco, TX
  Sul Ross Family Papers
Copper Breaks State Park, Quanah, TX
Dolph Briscoe Center for American History
University of Texas at Austin
  B. F. Gholson Papers
  John Henry Brown Papers
  Daniel Parker Papers
  Joseph and Araminta Taulman Papers
Fort Sill Archives and Museum, Lawton, OK
Handbook of Texas Online. www.tshaonline.org/handbook/online/articles/
Hardeman County Historical Museum, Quanah, TX
Hutchinson County Historical Museum, Borger, TX
Log Cabin Village, Fort Worth, TX
Museum of the Great Plains, Lawton, OK
National Archives—Southwest Region, Fort Worth, TX
Oklahoma Historical Society, Oklahoma City (OKHS)
  Chronicles of Oklahoma: http://digital.library.okstate.edu/Chronicles/
  Kiowa Agency files
Old Fort Parker Historical Site, Groesbeck, TX
Palo Duro Canyon State Park Visitor's Center
Panhandle-Plains Historical Museum, Canyon, TX (PPHM)
  Bill Neeley Papers
Pilgrim Predestinarian Regular Baptist Church, Elkhart, TX
Southern Methodist University (SMU) DeGolyer Library, Dallas
  James T. DeShields Papers
Star of the Republic Museum Archive, Washington, TX
Texas State Library (online)
University of Oklahoma Library, Norman, OK (OKU)
  Western History Collection
  Works Progress Administration Files
Van Zandt County Library of Genealogy and Local History, Canton, TX

Books

Anderson, Gary. *The Conquest of Texas: Ethnic Cleansing in the Promised Land, 1820–1875.* Norman: University of Oklahoma Press, 2005.

Babb, T. A. *In the Bosom of the Comanches.* Dallas: Hargreaves Printing, 1912.

Baker, T. Lindsay, and Billy R. Harrison. *Adobe Walls, the History and Archaeology of the 1874 Trading Post.* College Station: Texas A&M University Press, 1986.

Benner, Judith Ann. *Sul Ross: Soldier, Statesman, Educator.* College Station: Texas A&M University, 1983.

Berlandier, Jean Louis. *The Indians of Texas in 1830.* Washington: Smithsonian Institution Press, 1969.

Betty, Gerald. *Comanche Society: Before the Reservation.* College Station: Texas A&M University Press, 2002.

Brashear, Charles. *Killing Cynthia Ann.* Fort Worth: Texas Christian University Press, 1999.

Brinkley, Douglas. *The Wilderness Warrior: Theodore Roosevelt and the Crusade for America.* New York: HarperCollins, 2009.

Brooks, James F. *Captives & Cousins: Slavery, Kinship and Community in the Southwest Borderlands.* Chapel Hill: University of North Carolina Press, 2001.

Brown, John Henry. *Indian Wars and Pioneers of Texas.* Austin: L.E. Daniell, 1890. Reprinted by Austin: State House Press, 1988 (originally published 1880).

Brown, Marion T. *Letters from Fort Sill, 1886–1887.* C. Richard King, ed. Austin: Encino Press, 1970.

Brownmiller, Susan. *Against Our Will: Men, Women, and Rape.* New York: Simon & Schuster, 1975.

Carter, Robert G. *On the Border with Mackenzie.* Austin: Texas State Historical Association, 2007 (originally published 1935).

———. *Tragedies of Cañón Blanco.* Hobson Brothers, 1919.

Comanche Ethnography: Field Notes of E. Adamson Hoebel, Waldo R. Wedel, Gustav G. Carlson, and Robert H. Lowie. Thomas W. Kavanagh, ed. Lincoln: University of Nebraska Press, 2008.

Commissioners of Indian Affairs, 1824–1977. Robert M. Kvasnicka and Herman J. Viola, eds. Lincoln: University of Nebraska Press, 1979.

Demos, John. *The Unredeemed Captive: A Family Story from Early America.* New York: Knopf, 1994.

DeShields, James T. *Border Wars of Texas.* Tioga, Texas: Herald, 1912.

———*Cynthia Ann Parker: The Story of Her Capture.* St. Louis: Printed for the Author, 1886.

Dixon, Olive K. *The Life of Billy Dixon.* Austin: State House Press, 1987.

Dodge, Richard Irving. *Our Wild Indians: Thirty-Three Years' Personal Experience Among the Red Men of the West.* Hartford: A. D. Worthington, 1882.

Dunn, J. P. *Massacres of the Mountains: A History of the Indian Wars of the Far West, 1815–1875.* New York: Archer House, 1958.

Ebersole, Gary L. *Captured by Texts: Puritan to Postmodern Images of Indian Captivity.* Charlottesville: University Press of Virginia, 1995.

Egan, Timothy. *The Worst Hard Time.* New York: Houghton Mifflin, 2006.

Epps, Garrett. *To an Unknown God: Religious Freedom on Trial*. New York: St. Martin's Press, 2001.

Exley, Jo Ella Powell. *Frontier Blood: The Saga of the Parker Family*. College Station: Texas A&M University Press, 2001.

Fehrenbach, T. R. *Comanches: The Destruction of a People*. New York: Knopf, 1974.

——*Lone Star: A History of Texas and the Texans*. Boulder, Colo.: Da Capo Press, 2000 (originally published 1968).

Foreman, Grant. *Pioneer Days in the Early Southwest*. Cleveland: Arthur H. Clark, 1926.

Gilles, Albert S., Sr. *Comanche Days*. Dallas: SMU Press, 1974.

Gwynne, S. C. *Empire of the Summer Moon: Quanah Parker and the Rise and Fall of the Comanches*. New York: Scribner, 2010.

Hacker, Margaret S. *Cynthia Ann Parker: The Life and the Legend*. El Paso: Texas Western Press, 1990.

Hagan, William T. *Charles Goodnight: Father of the Texas Panhandle*. Norman: University of Oklahoma Press, 2007.

——*Quanah Parker, Comanche Chief*. Norman: University of Oklahoma Press, 1993.

——*Taking Indian Lands: The Cherokee (Jerome) Commission, 1889–1893*. Norman: University of Oklahoma Press, 2003.

——*Theodore Roosevelt and Six Friends of the Indian*. Norman: University of Oklahoma Press, 1997.

——*United States–Comanche Relations*. New Haven: Yale University Press, 1976.

Haley, J. Evetts. *Charles Goodnight: Cowman & Plainsman*. Norman: University of Oklahoma Press, 1949.

Hämäläinen, Pekka. *The Comanche Empire*. New Haven: Yale University Press, 2008.

Hirshson, Stanley P. *The White Tecumseh: A Biography of General William T. Sherman*. New York: John Wiley and Sons, 1998.

Honig, Lawrence E. *John Henry Brown: Texas Journalist. Southwestern Studies* Monograph No. 36, El Paso: Texas Western Press, 1973.

Houston, Sam. *The Writings of Sam Houston, Vol. IV, 1821–1847*. Amelia W. Williams and Eugene C. Barker, eds. Austin: University of Texas, 1941.

Hunter, J. Marvin. *The Boy Captives*. Bandera, Texas: Frontier Times, 1927 (reprinted by New York: Garland, 1977).

The Indian Captivity Narrative: A Woman's View. Frances Roe Kessler, ed. New York: Garland Publishing, 1990.

Indian Oratory: Famous Speeches by Noted Indian Chieftains. W. C. Vanderwerth, ed. Norman: University of Oklahoma, 1971.

Irving, Washington. *A Tour on the Prairies*. Norman: University of Oklahoma, 1956.

Jackson, Grace. *Cynthia Ann Parker*. San Antonio: Naylor, 1959.

Jiles, Paulette. *The Color of Lightning*. New York: William Morrow, 2009.

Kavanagh, Thomas W. *Comanches: A History*. Lincoln: University of Nebraska Press, 1999.

La Vere, David. *Life Among the Texas Indians: The WPA Narratives*. College Station: Texas A&M University Press, 1998.

Lee, Nelson. *Three Years Among the Comanches: The Narrative of Nelson Lee The Texas Ranger*. Norman: University of Oklahoma Press, 1957.

Lehmann, Herman. *Nine Years Among the Indians, 1870–9*. Austin: Von Boeckmann-Jones, 1927.

Marcy, Randolph B. *Exploration of the Red River of Louisiana in the Year 1852*. Washington: A. O. P. Nicholson, 1854.

——*Thirty Years of Army Life on the Border*. New York: Harper & Brothers, 1866.

Marszalek, John F. *Sherman: A Soldier's Passion for Order*. New York: Free Press, 1993.

Maverick, Mary A. *Memoirs*. San Antonio: Alamo Printing, 1921.

Meyer, Marian. *Mary Donoho: New First Lady of the Santa Fe Trail*. Santa Fe: Ancient City Press, 1991.

Michino, Gregory and Susan. *A Fate Worse Than Death: Indian Captives in the West, 1830–1885*. Caldwell, Idaho: Caxton Press, 2007.

Mooney, James, *The Ghost-Dance Religion and the Sioux Outbreak of 1890*. Lincoln: University of Nebraska Press, 1991 (original edition 1896).

Namias, June. *White Captives: Gender and Equality on the American Frontier*. Chapel Hill: University of North Carolina Press, 1995.

Neeley, Bill. *The Last Comanche Chief: The Life and Times of Quanah Parker*. New York: John Wiley & Sons, 1995.

Noyes, Stanley and Daniel J. Gelo. *Comanches in the New West, 1895–1908*. Austin: University of Texas Press, 1999.

Nye, W. S. *Carbine and Lance*. Norman: University Oklahoma Press, 1937.

Papers Concerning Robertson's Colony in Texas XIV. Malcolm D. McLean, ed. Arlington: UTA Press, 1988.

Parker, James W. *Narrative of the Perilous Adventures, Miraculous Escapes and Sufferings of Rev. James W. Parker, to Which Is Appended a Narrative of the Capture and Subsequent Sufferings of Mrs. Rachel Plummer*. Louisville: Morning Courier Office, 1844.

Personal Civil War Letters of General Lawrence Sullivan Ross. Transcribed and compiled by Percy Wayne Shelton. Edited by Shelly Morrison. Austin: S and R Morrison, 1994.

Pierce, Michael D. *The Most Promising Young Officer:A Life of Ranald Slidell Mackenzie*. Norman: University of Oklahoma Press, 1993.

Plummer, Rachel. *Narrative of the Capture and Subsequent Sufferings of Mrs. Rachel Plummer*. Houston, 1839, 2nd edition.

Ranald S. MacKenzie's Official Correspondence Relating to Texas, 1871–75. Ernest Wallace, ed. Lubbock: West Texas Museum, Association, 1967.

Report of the Secretary of War, Vol. I. Washington: Government Printing Office, 1869.

Richardson, Rupert N. *The Comanche Barrier to South Plains Settlement: A Century and a Half of Savage Resistance to the Advancing White Frontier*. Glendale, CA: Arthur H. Clark Company, 1933.

Rister, Carl Coke. *Border Captives*. Norman: University of Oklahoma, 1940.

——*Border Command: General Phil Sheridan in the West*. Norman: University of Oklahoma Press, 1944.

——*Comanche Bondage*. Glendale: Arthur H. Clark Co., 1955. Includes annotated reprint of Sarah Ann Horn's Narrative.

Robson, Lucia St. Clair. *Ride the Wind*. New York: Random House, 1982.

Roosevelt, Theodore. *Outdoor Pastimes of an American Hunter*. New York: Charles Scribner's Sons, 1923.

——*The Winning of the West*. Seven volumes. New York: G. P. Putnam's Sons, 1907.

Rowlandson, Mary White. *Narrative of the Captivity and Removes of Mrs. Mary Rowlandson*. Lancaster: Carter, Andrews & Company, 1828. (William B. Cairns Collection of American Women Writers, 1650–1920.)

Scott, Hugh L. *Some Memories of a Soldier*. New York: The Century Co., 1928.

Sides, Hampton. *Blood and Thunder: An Epic of the American West*. New York: Doubleday, 2006.

Slotkin, Richard. *The Fatal Environment: The Myth of the Frontier in the Age of Industrialization, 1800–1890*. New York: Atheneum, 1985.

——. *Regeneration Through Violence: The Mythology of the American Frontier, 1600–1860*. Norman: University of Oklahoma Press, 1973.

Smith, Coho. *Cohographs*. Fort Worth: Branch-Smith, 1976.

Smith, Henry Nash. *Virgin Land: The American West as Symbol and Myth*. Cambridge: Harvard University Press, 1978.

Stanley, Henry M. *My Early Travels and Adventures in America*. London: 1895. Reprint, Lincoln: University of Nebraska Press, 1982.

Stewart, Omer Call. *Peyote Religion: A History*. Norman: University of Oklahoma Press, 1993.

Tatum, Lawrie. *Our Red Brothers and the Peace Policy of Ulysses S. Grant*. Philadelphia: John C. Winston, 1899.

Texas by Terán: The Diary Kept by Manuel de Mier y Terán on His 1828 Inspection of Texas. Jack Jackson, ed. Austin: University of Texas Press, 2000.

Tilghman, Zoe A. *Quanah: The Eagle of the Comanches*. Oklahoma City: Harlow Publishing, 1938.

Wallace, Ernest, and E. Adamson Hoebel. *The Comanches: Lords of the South Plains*. Norman: University of Oklahoma Press, 1952.

Webb, Walter Prescott. *The Texas Rangers: A Century of Frontier Defense*. Austin: University of Texas Press, 1965.

White, E. E. *Experiences of a Special Indian Agent*. Norman: University of Oklahoma Press, 1965.

White, Richard. *"It's Your Misfortune and None of My Own."* Norman: University of Oklahoma, 1991.

Wilbarger, J. W. *Indian Depredations in Texas*. Austin: Hutchings, 1889 (reprinted by Austin: Eakin Press, 1985).

Zesch, Scott. *The Captured: A True Story of Abduction by Indians on the Texas Frontier*. New York: St. Martin's Press, 2004.

Articles

Anderson, Adrian N., "The Last Phase of Colonel Ranald S. Mackenzie's 1874 Campaign Against the Comanches," *West Texas Historical Association Year Book*, 40 (1964), 74–81.

Austin, Stephen F., "Journal of Stephen F. Austin on His First Trip to Texas, 1821" *Quarterly of the Texas State Historical Association*, VII:4, April 1904, 286–307.

"'Every Day Seemed to be a Holiday': The Captivity of Bianca Babb," Daniel J. Gelo and Scott Zesch, eds. *Southwestern Historical Quarterly*, CVII, 1, July 2003.

Birdsong, Neda, "Cynthia Ann Parker" (as told to Paul Wellman), *Barb Wire Times*, Oct. 1968.

"Corona Helps Texas Opera in Premiere," *Dallas Times Herald*, Feb. 17, 1939.

"The Death of Nocona," Rupert N. Richardson, ed. *Southwestern Historical Quarterly*, 1992.

DeShields, James T., "Indian Wars in Texas III," *United Service, A Quarterly Review of Military and Naval Affairs (1879–1905)*; Oct. 1885, 13:4.

Detrick, C. H., "Quanah Parker, Gentleman," *Wichita Magazine*, April 23, 1930.

Dixon, Olive King, "Fearless and Effective Foe, He Spared Women and Children Always," *Fort Worth Star-Telegram*, April 12, 1936.

"The Frontier and Its Defense," *The White Man*, Weatherford, Texas, 1:18, Sept. 13, 1860.

Gelo, Daniel J., "'Comanche Land and Ever Has Been': A Native Geography of Nineteenth-Century Comancheria," *Southwestern Historical Quarterly* CIII:3, January 2000.

Gentry, A. D., "The Runaway Scrape," *Frontier Times* 4:6, August 1927, 9–12.

Harger, Charles Moreau, "The Government's Gift of Homes," *Outlook* 68:16, Aug. 17, 1901.

Harmon, George D., "The United States Indian Policy in Texas, 1845–1860," *Mississippi Valley Historical Review* 17:3, Dec. 1930.

Harris, Charles W., "The Red River War of 1874–75: The End of an Era on the Great Plains," *Red River Valley Historical Review* 3, Spring 1978.

Hodge, Kelly, "Forty Acres Arias: UT Opera Theatre Debuts Cynthia Parker," *Fanfare*, 3:2, Winter 1985.

"Hugh McLeod's Report on the Council House Fight," March 20, 1840, Texas State Library and Archives Commission, www.tsl.state.tx.us/exhibits/indian/war/mcleod-mar1840-1.html.

Jones, Douglas C., "The Grave of Quanah Parker: A Case Study in Persuasive Communication and Hostile Attitudes," *Public Relations Quarterly*, 14:4, 1970.

Jones, Lawrence T., "Cynthia Ann Parker and Pease Ross: The Forgotten Photographs," *Southwestern Historical Quarterly*, June 1990.

"Journal of the Permanent Council (Oct. 11–27, 1835)," *Texas Historical Association Quarterly*, VII:4, April 1904.

"The Journal of Ranald S. Mackenzie's Messenger to the Kwahadi Comanches," Ernest Wallace, ed. *Red River Valley Historical Review* 3, Spring 1978.

Kracht, Benjamin R., "Kiowa-Comanche-Apache Opening," digital.library-okstate.edu/encyclopedic/entries/k/kio20.html.

Lee, Max, "Daniel Parker: Politician, Baptist, and Anti-Mission Missionary," *Texas Baptist History* 6 (1986), 1–9.

Lutz, Ella Cox, "Quanah Parker: The Last Comanche Chief," *Daughters of the American Revolution Magazine*, n.d.

Mattinson, R. F., "A Story of Old Fort Parker," *Groesbeck Argus*, 1875, in *Frontier Times*, 13:8, June 1936.

McMurtry, Larry, "The Conquering Indians," *New York Review of Books*, 55:9, May 29, 2008.

——"Texas: The Death of the Natives," *NYRB*, 53:14, Sept. 21, 2006.

Miller, Edgar K., "A Visit to the Homes of Quanah Parker and Geronimo," *The Indian School Journal*, III:2, 1907.

"Mystery of Prairie Flower, Daughter of Chief, Solved," *Wichita Falls Times*, May 3, 1959.

Parker, Baldwin, "Life of Quanah Parker, Comanche Chief," August 29, 1930 (PPHM).

Parker, Baldwin, Jr., "Quanah Parker Lives," (as told to Bill Schardin) *Focus*, 3:4, Autumn 1985.

Parker, James W., "Defense of James W. Parker against Slanderous Accusations Preferred Against Him," 1839 (Bancroft).

Pearce, Roy Harvey, "The Significances of the Captivity Narrative," *American Literature* 19 (1947–8), 1–20.

Peattie, Donald Culross, "The Ballad of Cynthia Ann," *American Heritage*, 7:3, April 1956.

Pratt, R. H., "Indian Civilization: The Potency of Environment," *The Independent*, 43:2202, Feb. 2, 1891.

Price, Byron H., "The Great Panhandle Indian Scare of 1891," *Panhandle-Plains Historical Review*, LV, 1982.

"Quanah Lies Beside His Mother," *Cache Register*, March 3, 1911.

"Rachel Plummer Narrative," 1926, no publisher listed.

"Records of an Early Texas Baptist Church," *Quarterly of the Texas State Historical Association*, XI:2, Oct., 1907, pp. 85–156.

Reid, Jan, "The Warrior's Bride," *Texas Monthly*, Feb. 2003.

Smith, Burton M., "Anti-Catholicism, Indian Education and Thomas Jefferson Morgan, Commissioner of Indian Affairs," *Canadian Journal of History*, 23:2, Aug. 1988.

Sneed, R. A., "The Reminiscences of an Indian Trader," in *Chronicles of Oklahoma*, 14:2, June 1936.

"Story by Ex-Gov. J.P. St. John's Wife," *Indian School Journal*, IX:12, Oct. 1909.

Tate, Michael L., "Comanche Captives: People Between Two Worlds," *Chronicles of Oklahoma*, XXII:3, Fall 1994.

"A Texan of the Texans: Stories of Governor Ross as an Indian Fighter," *Galveston Daily News*, June 30, 1890.

"Texas Indians—Report of Messrs. Butler and Lewis," Letter from the Secretary of War, 29th Congress, 2d. Session, Doc. No. 76, Feb. 8, 1847.

"Triumph and Tragedy: Presidents of the Republic of Texas," Texas State Archives and Library Commission, www.tsl.state.tx.us/exhibits/presidents/houston1/jas_parker _jun6_1837_3.html.

West, Derek G., "The Battle of Adobe Walls," in *The Battles of Adobe Walls and Lyman's Wagon Train 1874*. Canyon: Panhandle-Plains Historical Society, 1964.

Unpublished Papers and Manuscripts

Birdsong, Aubrey, "Reminiscences of Quanah Parker," 1965 (Fort Sill).

Cochran, Walter C., *Reminiscences*, 1930 (Briscoe).

Gholson, B. F., *Recollections of B.F. Gholson, Told to J.A. Rickard, August 1928* (Briscoe).

Kiek, Marcus, "Brain-Tanned Buffalo Hide," www.primitiveways.com/buffalo_hide .html.

Linzee, E. H., "Development of Oklahoma Territory," self-published mimeograph, 1950 (Claude Hensley Collection, Western History Collection, University of Oklahoma).

O'Quinn, Eugene G., "Quanah—The Eagle: Half-White Comanche Chief," 1981 (Van Zandt County Library of Genealogy and Local History).

Parker, Ben J., "Early Times in Texas and History of the Parker Family," undated (Briscoe).

"Recollections of H.B. Rogers," told to J. A. Rickard (Briscoe).

Rivaya-Martínez, Joaquín, "Becoming Comanches: Patterns of Captive Incorporation into Comanche Kinship Networks, 1820–1875."

St. John, Susan Parker, "Notebook" (Briscoe).

Scott, Hugh, QP Interview with Captain Hugh Scott, 1897 (Fort Sill). Also available at Neeley Archive (PPHM).

"Skinning and Butchering a Bison," video presentation, Panhandle-Plains Museum Historical Society, 2001 (PPHM).

Sommer, Charles H., "Quanah Parker: Last Chief of the Comanches," mimeograph, Oklahoma Historical Society, August 1945 (OKHS).

Taulman, Araminta, Interviews with Mrs. R. H. King, July 5 and Sept. 13, 1926; and with Mrs. Turnbill, Sept. 24, 1926, handwritten notes (Briscoe).

——Interviews with Mrs. J. J. Nunally, 1926 (Ibid.).

Taulman, Joseph and Araminta, "First Regularly Organized and Constituted Protestant or Non-Catholic Church in Texas—Still in Existence," 1937, unpublished (Briscoe).

——Taulman Notebook No. 8 (Ibid).

Parts III and IV (Alan LeMay, John Ford, and John Wayne)

Archives and Collections

Ronald L. Davis Oral History Collection on the Performing Arts in America, De-Golyer Institute for American Studies, Southern Methodist University, Dallas, TX

Howard Gotlieb Archival Research Center, Boston University
    Frank S. Nugent Papers

Margaret Herrick Library, Academy of Motion Picture Arts and Sciences (MPAA), Beverly Hills
    Academy Oral History Program

Lilly Library, Indiana University, Bloomington
    John Ford Papers

L. Tom Perry Special Collections Library, Harold B. Lee Library, Brigham Young University, Provo, UT
    Argosy Pictures Corporation Archives
    Merian C. Cooper Collection

Harry Ransom Center, University of Texas at Austin
    Harper & Row Papers
    Maurice Zolotow Papers

University of Southern California, Los Angeles, Warner Brothers Archives

C. V. Whitney Papers (CVW) (family-held), Saratoga Springs, NY
Charles E. Young Research Library, UCLA, Los Angeles
   Alan LeMay Papers

Books
Aitchison, Stewart. *A Traveler's Guide to Monument Valley.* Stillwater, MN: Voyageur, 1993.
Anderson, Lindsay. *About John Ford.* London: Plexus, 1999.
Barden, Dan. *John Wayne: A Novel.* New York: Doubleday, 1997.
Blake, Michael F. *Code of Honor: The Making of Three Great American Westerns.* Lanham, MD.: Taylor Trade Publishing, 2003.
Bogdanovich, Peter. *John Ford.* Berkeley: University of California Press, 1978.
——*Who the Hell's in It: Portraits and Conversations.* New York: Knopf, 2004.
Buscombe, Edward. *Injuns! Native Americans in the Movies.* London: Reaktion Books, 2006.
——*The Searchers.* BFI Film Classics. London: British Film Institute, 2000.
——*Stagecoach.* BFI Film Classics. London: British Film Institute, 1992.
Canutt, Yakima. *Stunt Man.* New York: Walker and Company, 1979.
Carey, Harry, Jr. *Company of Heroes: My Life as an Actor in the John Ford Stock Company.* Lanham, MD: Madison Books, 1994.
Cary, Diana Serra. *The Hollywood Posse.* Boston: Houghton Mifflin, 1975.
Cather, Willa. *Death Comes for the Archbishop.* New York: Vintage Classic, 1990 (original edition Alfred A. Knopf, 1927).
Corliss, Richard. *Talking Pictures: Screenwriters in the American Cinema.* Woodstock, N.Y.: Overlook Press, 1974.
Cowie, Peter. *John Ford and the American West.* New York: Harry N. Abrams, 2004.
D'Arc, James. *When Hollywood Came to Town: A History of Moviemaking in Utah.* Layton, UT: Gibbs Smith, 2010.
Davis, Ronald L. *Duke: The Life and Image of John Wayne.* Norman: University of Oklahoma, 1998.
——*John Ford: Hollywood's Old Master.* Norman: University of Oklahoma, 1995.
Dyer, Richard. *Stars.* London: BFI Publishing, 1979.
Eyman, Scott. *John Ford: The Complete Films.* Paul Duncan, ed. Cologne: Taschen, 2004.
——*Print the Legend: The Life and Times of John Ford.* New York: Simon & Schuster, 1999.
Faludi, Susan. *The Terror Dream: Fear and Fantasy in Post-9/11 America.* New York: Metropolitan Books, 2007.
Finstad, Suzanne. *Natasha: The Biography of Natalie Wood.* New York: Three Rivers Press, 2001.
Fonda, Henry. *Fonda: My Life.* New York: New American Library, 1981.
Ford, Dan. *Pappy: The Life of John Ford.* New York: Da Capo Press, 1998.
Friar, Ralph E., and Natasha A. *The Only Good Indian . . . The Hollywood Gospel.* New York: Drama Book Specialists, 1972.
Gallagher, Tag. *John Ford: The Man and His Films.* Berkeley: University of California Press, 1986.

Hollywood's Indian. Peter C. Rollins and John E. O'Connor, eds. Lexington: University Press of Kentucky, 1998.

Howze, William. *The Influence of Western Painting and Genre Painting on the Films of John Ford.* Connexions, September 2, 2011. http://cnx.org/content/col11357/1.1/.

John Ford in Focus. Kevin L. Stoehr and Michael C. Connolly, eds. Jefferson, NC: McFarland, 2008.

John Ford Interviews. Gerald Peary, ed. Jackson: University Press of Mississippi, 2001.

John Ford Made Westerns. Gaylyn Studlar and Matthew Bernstein, eds. Bloomington: Indiana University Press, 2001.

Kalinak, Kathryn. *How the West Was Sung: Music in the Westerns of John Ford.* Berkeley: University of California Press, 2007.

Kaplan, James. *Sinatra: The Voice.* New York: Doubleday, 2010.

Lasky, Jesse L., Jr. *Whatever Happened to Hollywood?* New York: Funk & Wagnalls, 1975.

LeMay, Alan. *Painted Ponies.* New York: Popular Library (paperback edition), 1958 (originally published 1926).

——*The Searchers.* New York: Harper and Brothers, 1954.

——*The Unforgiven.* Harper and Brothers, 1957.

LeMay, Dan. *Alan LeMay: A Biography of the Author of The Searchers.* Jefferson, NC: McFarland & Co., 2012. Unpublished draft: *Never Dull: The Life of Alan LeMay* (Oct. 2007).

McBride, Joseph. *Searching for John Ford: A Life.* New York: St. Martin's Press, 2001.

—— and Michael Wilmington. *John Ford.* London: Secker & Warburg, 1974.

Moon, Samuel. *Tall Sheep: Harry Goulding, Monument Valley Trader.* Norman: University of Oklahoma Press, 1992.

Mortimer, Barbara. *Hollywood's Frontier Captives: Cultural Anxiety and the Captivity Plot in American Film.* New York: Garland Publishing, 2000.

Munn, Michael. *John Wayne: The Man Behind the Myth.* New York: New American Library, 2003.

O'Hara, Maureen. *'Tis Herself: A Memoir.* New York: Simon & Schuster, 2004.

The Old West in Fiction. Irwin R. Blacker, ed. New York: Ivan Obalensky, 1961.

Parrish, Robert. *Growing Up in Hollywood.* New York: Harcourt Brace Jovanovich, 1976.

Place, J. A. *The Western Films of John Ford.* Secaucus, NJ: Citadel Press, 1977.

Roberson, Chuck, with Bodie Thoene. *The Fall Guy: 30 Years as the Duke's Double.* North Vancouver, B.C., Canada: Hancock House, 1980.

Roberts, Randy, and James S. Olson. *John Wayne: American.* New York: Free Press, 1995.

Rodengen, Jeffrey L. *The Legend of Cornelius Vanderbilt Whitney.* Fort Lauderdale: Write Stuff Enterrpises, 2000.

Sarris, Andrew. *The John Ford Movie Mystery.* Bloomington: Indiana University Press, 1983.

Saunders, Frances Stonor. *Who Paid the Piper: The CIA and the Cultural Cold War.* London: Granta Books, 1999.

Schatz, Thomas. *The Genius of the System: Hollywood Filmmaking in the Studio Era.* New York: Pantheon, 1988.

——*Hollywood Genres: Formulas, Filmmaking, and the Studio System.* Philadelphia: Temple University Press, 1981.

The Searchers: Essays and Reflections on John Ford's Classic Western. Arthur M. Eckstein and Peter Lehman, eds. Detroit: Wayne State University Press, 2004.

Sinclair, Andrew. *John Ford.* New York: Dial Press/James Wade, 1979.

——*Gunfighter Nation: The Myth of the Frontier in Twentieth-Century America.* New York: Atheneum, 1992.

Smith, Paul Chaat. *Everything You Know about Indians Is Wrong.* Minneapolis: University of Minnesota Press, 2009.

Smith, Henry Nash. *Virgin Land: The American West as Symbol and Myth.* Cambridge, MA: Harvard University Press, 1978.

Stern, Lesley. *The Scorsese Connection.* Bloomington: Indiana University Press and BFI Publishing, 1995.

Stevens, George, Jr., *Conversations with the Great Moviemakers of Hollywood's Golden Age.* New York: Alfred Knopf, 2006.

Tuska, Jon. *The American West in Film: Critical Approaches to the Western.* Westport, CT: Greenwood Press, 1985.

TV and Screen Writing. Lola Goelet Yoakem, ed. Berkeley: University of California Press, 1958.

Vaz, Mark Cotta. *Living Dangerously: The Adventures of Merian C. Cooper.* New York: Villard, 2005.

Wagner, Robert J. *Pieces of My Heart.* New York: Harper Entertainment, 2008.

Wagner, Walter. *You Must Remember This.* New York: G. P. Putnam, 1975.

Warshow, Robert. *The Immediate Experience.* New York: Atheneum, 1979.

Wayne, Pilar. *John Wayne: My Life with the Duke.* New York: McGraw-Hill, 1987.

Whitney, Cornelius Vanderbilt. *High Peaks.* Lexington: University Press of Kentucky, 1977.

Whitney, Eleanor Searle. *Invitation to Joy.* New York: Harper & Row, 1971.

Wills, Garry. *John Wayne's America: The Politics of Celebrity.* New York: Simon & Schuster, 1997.

Wister, Owen. *The Virginian.* New York: Grosset & Dunlap, 1929 (original ed. Macmillan, 1902).

Zolotow, Maurice. *Shooting Star: A Biography of John Wayne.* New York: Simon & Schuster, 1974.

Articles and Periodicals

Arnold, Gary, "Hero's Welcome for *The Searchers.*" *Washington Post*, Sept. 23, 1979.

Bacon, James, "John Wayne: The Last Cowboy." *US*, June 27, 1978.

Barrier, Michael, "Fess Parker, An Interview by Michael Barrier," 2003–4, www.michaelbarrier.com/Interviews/Parker/interview_fess_parker.htm.

Bissinger, Buzz, "Inventing Ford Country." *Vanity Fair*, March 2009.

Byron, Stuart, "The Searchers: Cult Movie of the New Hollywood." *New York*, vol. 12, no. 10, March 5, 1979.

Card, James, "*The Searchers* by Alan LeMay and John Ford." *Literature/Film Quarterly*, 16:1 (1988).

Dykstra, Ruthurd, "The Search for Spectators: VistaVision and Technicolor in *The Searchers.*" *Kino*, I:1, 2010.

Ebert, Roger, "*The Searchers.*" Nov. 25, 2001, www.rogerebert.suntimes.com.

Eckstein, Arthur M., "Darkening Ethan." *Cinema Journal*, 38:1, Autumn 1998.

Freeman, Castle, Jr., "Owen Wister: Brief Life of a Western Mythmaker, 1860–1938." *Harvard Magazine*, July–Aug. 2002.

Hansen, Curtis Lee, "Henry Fonda: Reflections on 40 Years of Make-Believe." *Cinema*, 3:4, Dec. 1966.

Henderson, Brian, "*The Searchers*: An American Dilemma." *Film Quarterly*, 34:2, Winter 1980–1.

Hughes, Robert, "Art: How the West Was Spun." *Time*, May 13, 1991.

Jennings, Dean, "John Wayne: The Woes of Box-Office King." *Saturday Evening Post*, 235:38, Oct. 27, 1962.

Kennedy, Burt, "A Talk with John Ford." *Action!*, Sept.–Oct. 1968, p. 6.

Kiefner, Thomas, "Max Steiner," in *Film Music: The Neglected Art*. http://sdtom.word press.com/2008/02/13/max-steiner/.

Lethem, Jonathan, "The Darkest Side of John Wayne." *Salon*, July 1997.

———. "Defending *The Searchers*." *Tin House*, Winter 2001.

Marcus, Greil, "John Wayne Listening," in *Movies*. Gilbert Adair, ed. London: Penguin, 1999.

McBride, Joseph, "The Pathological Hero's Conscience: Screenwriter Frank S. Nugent Was the Quiet Man behind Director John Ford." *Written By*, May 2001.

McInerney, Joe, "John Wayne Talks Tough." *Film Comment*, September/October 1972, 8, 3.

Metcalf, Stephen, "The Worst Best Movie." *Slate*, July 6, 2006. www.slate.com/articles /arts/the_dilettante/2006/07/the_worst_best_movie.html.

Nugent, Frank, "Hollywood's Favorite Rebel." *Saturday Evening Post*, July 23, 1949.

McBride, Joseph, and Michael Wilmington, "Prisoner of the Desert." *Sight and Sound*, Autumn 1971.

Pippin, Robert B., "What Is a Western? Politics and Self-Knowledge in John Ford's *The Searchers*." *Critical Inquiry* 35, Winter 2009.

"*Playboy* Interview: John Wayne." *Playboy*, May 1971.

Pollock, Louis, "Alone—but Not for Long." *Motion Picture*, 46:550, Nov. 1956.

Scott, A. O., "How the Western Was Begun." *New York Times Magazine*, Nov. 11, 2007, pp. 55–58.

———, "*The Searchers*: How the Western Was Begun." *New York Times*, June 11, 2006.

Stone, Robert, "The Search Party." *New York Times Magazine*, Nov. 11, 2007, p. 58.

"Trip to Monument Valley." *Arizona Highways*, special issue, April 1956.

"*War Horse* and the Influence of John Ford on Steven Spielberg." www.directedbyjohn ford.com, accessed Nov. 27, 2011.

Warshow, Robert, "Movie Chronicle: The Westerner," in *The Western Reader*. Eds. Jim Kitses and Gregg Rickman. New York: Limelight, 1998.

"Welcome to Monument Valley." *Arizona Highways*, April 1956.

Unpublished Manuscripts

Dan LeMay. "Notes on Indian Raids," 2008.

Nugent, Frank. "Diaries." July 20 to Dec. 7, 1947.

———. "The Searchers: Revised Final Screenplay." www.aella.com/script/searchers.html.

Shively, JoEllen. *Cowboys & Indians: The Perception of Western Films Among American Indians and Anglo-Americans*. Stanford: PhD thesis, 1990.

Filmography

A select list of films referenced in this book. Except where noted, all were directed by John Ford.

The Battle of Elderbush Gulch (1913), D. W. Griffith

The Squaw Man (1914), Cecil B. DeMille

The Tornado (1917)

Straight Shooting (1917)

The Iron Horse (1924)

3 Bad Men (1926)

The Big Trail (1930), Raoul Walsh

Sagebrush Trail (1933), Armand Schaefer

Randy Rides Alone (1934), Henry Fraser

The Dawn Rider (1935), R. N. Bradbury

The Informer (1935)

Stagecoach (1939)

Young Mr. Lincoln (1939)

Drums Along the Mohawk (1939)

The Grapes of Wrath (1940)

The Long Voyage Home (1940)

North West Mounted Police (1940), Cecil B. DeMille

How Green Was My Valley (1941)

Reap the Wild Wind (1942), Cecil B. DeMille

The Battle of Midway (1942)

December 7th (1943)

The Fighting Seabees (1944), Edward Ludwig

Along Came Jones (1945), Stuart Heisler

They Were Expendable (1945)

My Darling Clementine (1946)

The Fugitive (1947)

Fort Apache (1948)

Red River (1948), Howard Hawks

3 Godfathers (1949)

She Wore a Yellow Ribbon (1949)

Sands of Iwo Jima (1949), Alan Dwan

The Sundowners (1950), George Templeton

Wagon Master (1950)

Rio Grande (1950)

High Lonesome (1950), Alan LeMay

The Quiet Man (1952)

Mogambo (1953)

The High and the Mighty (1954), William A. Wellman

Mister Roberts (1955)

Rookie of the Year (1955), NBC TV

The Searchers (1956)

Rio Bravo (1959), Howard Hawks

The Unforgiven (1960), John Huston

Two Rode Together (1961)

How the West Was Won (1962), JF, Henry Hathaway, George Marshall, and Richard Thorpe

The Man Who Shot Liberty Valance (1962)

Cheyenne Autumn (1964)

The Green Berets (1968), John Wayne

The Shootist (1976), Don Siegel

Documentaries on Ford and Wayne

American Masters: John Ford/John Wayne: The Filmmaker & the Legend

The American West of John Ford (1971), Denis Sanders

Directed by John Ford (1971), Peter Bogdanovich (revised 2009)

John Ford Goes to War (2005), Tom Thurman

The 50th Anniversary Two-Disc Special Edition DVD of *The Searchers* includes an introduction featuring Patrick Wayne; the theatrical trailer, and voice-over commentary by Peter Bogdanovich; as well as:

The Searchers: An Appreciation

A Turning of the Earth: John Ford, John Wayne and The Searchers (1998), Nick Redman.

Four clips from *Warner Brothers Presents: Meet Jeffrey Hunter, Monument Valley, Meet Natalie Wood, Setting Up Production*

Music

John Ford's Western Masterpiece The Searchers: Original Film Soundtrack Composed and Conducted by Max Steiner (CD). London: EL Records, 2007.

PHOTOGRAPH CREDITS

Frontispiece: Courtesy the Lilly Library, Indiana University, Bloomington, Indiana, and Warner Brothers.

Page 3: Allen Reed, courtesy Gregory Reed (originally appeared in *Arizona Highways*).

Page 20: Author's photograph.

Page 27: Author's photograph.

Page 40: William S. Soule Indian Photographs Collection, Dolph Briscoe Center for American History, the University of Texas at Austin, di_08011.

Page 49: William S. Soule Indian Photographs Collection, Dolph Briscoe Center for American History, the University of Texas at Austin, di_08010.

Page 67: A. Zeese & Co., Prints and Photographs Collection, Briscoe Center, di_08021.

Page 75: Briscoe Center, di_03693.

Page 76: Joseph E. Taulman Collection, Briscoe Center, di_08019.

Page 82: Research Division of the Oklahoma Historical Society.

Page 94: William S. Soule Indian Photographs Collection, Briscoe Center, di_05437.

Page 109: William S. Soule Indian Photographs Collection, Briscoe Center, di_08013.

Page 131: Betsyellen Yeager.

Page 139: Research Division of the Oklahoma Historical Society.

Page 140: Research Division of the Oklahoma Historical Society.

Page 149: Research Division of the Oklahoma Historical Society.

Page 166: Scotford, Kansas City, Joseph E. Taulman Collection, Briscoe Center, di_08018.

Page 172: Edward Bates, Joseph E. Taulman Collection, Briscoe Center, di_08020u.

Page 180: Betsyellen Yeager.

Page 189: Courtesy Dan LeMay.

Page 196: Courtesy Dan LeMay.

Page 206: Author's photograph.

Page 212: Courtesy the Lilly Library, Indiana University, Bloomington, Indiana.

Page 222: Lilly Library.

Page 234: Lilly Library.

Page 248: Lilly Library.

Page 268: Courtesy Peter McBride (originally appeared in the *Washington Post Magazine*, Sept. 14, 2008).

Page 280: Allen Reed, courtesy Gregory Reed.

Page 293: Allen Reed, courtesy Gregory Reed.

Page 298: Lilly Library and Warner Brothers.

Page 313: Lilly Library and Warner Brothers.

Page 331: Author's photograph.

Page 336: Author's photograph.

Page 337: Betsyellen Yeager.

Page 338: Betsyellen Yeager.

ACKNOWLEDGMENTS

Some book projects sneak up on you. When I first thought of writing about *The Searchers*, I had in mind a modest coffee table book for the film's fiftieth anniversary in 2006. That'll be the day. Six years, eleven states, and maybe 20,000 miles later, the result is far more ambitious, sweeping, and unwieldy, and boasts, as they used to say in Hollywood, a cast of hundreds, if not thousands. In researching this story, I covered vast amounts of ground ranging from the former Indian agencies of southwest Oklahoma to the high limestone plains of North Texas, to the stunning vistas of Monument Valley to the studios, archives and other man-made landmarks of Hollywood. Not to mention some wonderful side trips to Bloomington, Indiana, where the John Ford Papers reside; Provo, Utah, where James D'Arc has built an extraordinary archival film collection; Boston University, keeper of the Frank S. Nugent papers; Winterset, Iowa, birthplace of Marion Morrison, and Fallbrook, California, home of Dan LeMay, Alan's oldest son and keeper of his father's literary legacy.

The journey began at Stanford University, where I worked as a visiting professor of journalism between 2006 and 2010, with two essential courses. Richard White's "A History of No Place: The Creation of the North American West" lecture class was a powerful and lyrical introduction to the legends and reality of the settling of the West. Scott Bukatman's "Being John Wayne" seminar gave me the opportunity to study the actor and icon with an inspired teacher and a group of bright, engaging film students. Every paragraph about John Wayne in this book was informed by our discussions in this class and by Scott's deep insights and infectious enthusiasm.

I owe many more debts of gratitude. The proud members of Quanah Parker's extended family treated me with extraordinary warmth and hospitality over multiple trips to Cache, Oklahoma, and three annual family reunions, starting in 2008. My deepest thanks to Ron and Don Parker, Totsiyah Parker, Ardis Parker Leming and her husband Glen,

Baldwin and Marguerite Parker, Rebecca Parker, and Jacquetta J. McClung; plus their adopted kinfolk, including Anna Tahmahkera, Russell Neese, Chuck Waltrip, and Paul and Linda Davis; and W. Scott Nicholson and Jo Nell Parker, on the Texan side of the family. Thanks, too, to Donna Lindsay, my canny and well-informed guide to Cache, and to the Woesner clan: Wayne Gipson, Ginger Gipson-Seibold, and their wonderful mother, the late Kathy Treadwell.

Many fine experts in Texas and Comanche history helped guide me as well: Paul H. Carlson of Texas Tech in Lubbock, Tom Crum of Granbury, Texas, H. R. Fehrenbach of San Antonio, Margaret Hacker of the National Archives in Fort Worth, Pekka Hämäläinen of the University of California at Santa Barbara, Sarah McReynolds of Old Fort Parker, Joaquín Rivaya-Martínez of Texas State University in San Marcos, Garvin Tate of Rockwall, Texas, and David D. Turner of Copper Breaks State Park. A special thanks to many librarians and archivists along the way, including Deborah A. Baroff, of the Museum of the Great Plains in Lawton; Scarlett Daughery at the Hardeman County Historical Museum in Quanah, Texas; Towana Spivey of the Fort Sill Museum and Archive, who is a national treasure of Comanche history and lore and who loaned me Jo Ruffin, a volunteer worker, for a long day in the archive, and Warren Stricker, director of research at the Panhandle Plains Museum. Thanks, too, to Parker family geneaologist Doris Cozart, who ran her own small library out of a former coffee shop in Chillicothe, Texas; Dorothy Poole at the Log Cabin Village in Fort Worth; Joel Lowry, DDS, who showed my wife and me around the site of the Pease River battle located on his property; Bob Montrose and Herbert Riley, who helped us find Cynthia Ann's original gravesite and recounted their role as grade school boys in helping clean up and restore the cemetery for the Texas Centennial in 1936; and novelist Lucia St. Clair Robson for her hard-won insights and high spirits.

Dan Ford, grandson of the late director, granted me complete access to the John Ford Papers at Lilly Library at Indiana University and consented to interviews and countless email consultations. John Ford was a very private and difficult man, but he was so proud of his grandson's military service as an Army officer in Vietnam that he cooperated with Dan's book project, *Pappy*. The interviews Dan conducted in the 1970s with his grandfather, friends, and coworkers, along with the personal and professional papers Dan retrieved from his grandfather's attic, constitute the invaluable primary material for anyone researching John Ford's life and work.

Dan LeMay was generous in granting me an interview and access to his own research into his father's life and times, even accompanying me to review Alan LeMay's papers at the UCLA library. My thanks as well to Dan's wife Mary Ann and his younger sister Mollie. One of the highlights of my work was the day in June 2009 we spent journeying to the various LeMay homesteads in the Los Angeles area, culminating in a trip to the Toyopa Drive house in Pacific Palisades and the office where Alan LeMay wrote *The Searchers*.

The late Kevin Nugent, son of the screenplay writer Frank S. Nugent, shared memories of his father and devoted mother, including his father's unpublished diary, and lent me an obscure screenwriting book in which Frank Nugent discussed writing the opening to *The Searchers*. It has never been cited before.

Although we never met in person, I owe a great debt to Marylou Whitney and her husband, John Hendrickson, who granted me exclusive access to the papers of Marylou's late husband, C. V. Whitney. When I couldn't travel to Saratoga Springs, New York, Marylou and John arranged to have the papers shipped to me in Palo Alto. This was an extraordinary act of trust and generosity. Thanks, too, to Karrie Steuer of the Whitney staff and Barbara Lombardo, managing editor of the *Saratogian*.

Speaking of trust and generosity, Gregory E. Reed went through boxes of negatives of photos taken by his late father, Allen Reed, an extraordinarily talented freelance photographer who had complete access to the *Searchers* set in Monument Valley for a special issue of *Arizona Highways*. Allen's evocative photos dominated that issue, but Greg also discovered several wonderful shots that have never been published before.

Leith Adams, Harry Carey Jr. and his wife, Marilyn, Nick Redman, Pippa Scott, Charles Silver, and Patrick Wayne all shared their memories and insights. Ford biographer Scott Eyman generously shared his notes of interviews with Jean Nugent and Marylou Whitney; and Joseph McBride, author of the masterful *Searching for John Ford*, sat for two long interviews and corresponded with me over a three-year period. Kevin Stoehr at Boston University offered sources and encouragement.

The folks at Goulding's Lodge in Monument Valley maintain Ford's legacy there with great care and arranged for my travel around the Valley in 2008. Special thanks to the manager, Julie Viramontes, and her staff. David Rowell, deputy editor at the *Washington Post Magazine*, paid for the trip and introduced me to Peter McBride, whose fabulous photos also grace these pages.

Struggling authors need places to stay, and Karl Vick, Rick Levine and Janet Gold, Tom and Judy Wilson, and Donna Lindsay all provided guest beds. Fellow travelers Tom Frail, Bob Thompson, and Sharon Waxman offered good advice and moral support.

Margaret Edds, David Hoffman, Joseph McBride, and David Rowell read large parts of the manuscript and made many helpful suggestions. But I bear full responsibility for the accuracy of the material herein.

My thanks to my agent, Gail Ross, of the Yoon Ross Literary Agency, once again for her careful and conscientious stewardship. Howard Yoon and my friend Steve Luxenberg helped me craft the book proposal. At Bloomsbury, Anton Mueller, Rachel Mannheimer, Patti Ratchford, Laura Phillips, Lisa Silverman, and David Chesanow were thoughtful collaborators and good shepherds.

I have had the great fortune of teaching journalism at two fine institutions of higher learning, both of which provided me with funding and wonderful research facilities during the five years I worked on this project. At Stanford University, my thanks to Professor James Fishkin and Barbara Kataoka of the Department of Communication for their funding and logistical support; to Charlotte Lau, my research assistant; to Jim Kent and Ben Stone at Green Library, and to Joel Brinkley, Jim Campbell, Ted Glasser and Fred Turner for their friendship and moral support.

At the University of Texas at Austin, my thanks to Professor Roderick Hart, Dean of the College of Communication; to researchers Elissa Nelson and Tamir Kalifa, and to Janice Henderson, Sonia Krempin-Reyes, and Phillip Salazar on the staff at the School of Journalism. UT has many superb libraries and archives, and I relied on two: the Dolph Briscoe Center for American History, under the able leadership of Don Carlton; and the Harry Ransom Center under Tom Staley's inspired direction. My thanks to both of them and their dedicated staffs, especially Cynthia DuBois.

Finally, as always, to my family: my wonderful children, Abra and Paul Frankel and Margo Brush, and sons-in-law Matt Ipri and Danny Brush; my late father, Herbert Frankel, who encouraged my work even in the last months of his life; and most of all to my wife, Betsyellen Yeager, who accompanied me to Monument Valley, Hollywood, Texas and Oklahoma, watched more John Wayne movies than she ever thought possible, and gave me the moral and emotional support to see it through to a satisfying ending.

INDEX

A NOTE ON THE AUTHOR

Glenn Frankel worked for twenty-seven years for the *Washington Post*, as a reporter, foreign correspondent, and editor of the *Washington Post Magazine*. As Jerusalem bureau chief, he won the 1989 Pulitzer Prize for "sensitive and balanced reporting from Israel and the Middle East." His first book, *Beyond the Promised Land: Jews and Arabs on the Hard Road to a New Israel*, won the National Jewish Book Award. His second, *Rivonia's Children: Three Families and the Cost of Conscience in White South Africa* was a finalist for South Africa's prestigious Alan Paton Award. Frankel has been an Alicia Patterson Journalism Fellow and a visiting professor in the Department of Communication at Stanford University. He is currently the Director of the School of Journalism and holds the G. B. Dealey Regents Professorship at the University of Texas at Austin.